AMERICAS : AN ANTHOLOGY
F 1408 A62 1992

AMERICAS

AMERICAS
An Anthology

Edited by
Mark B. Rosenberg
A. Douglas Kincaid
Kathleen Logan

Americas is a coproduction of WGBH Boston
and Central Television Enterprises for Channel 4, U.K.,
in association with the School for International and
Public Affairs at Columbia University, the Latin American
and Caribbean Center at Florida International University, and
Tufts University.

Americas: An Anthology is part of a college credit course from

The Annenberg/CPB Collection

New York   Oxford
OXFORD UNIVERSITY PRESS
1992

Oxford University Press

Oxford   New York   Toronto
Delhi   Bombay   Calcutta   Madras   Karachi
Kuala Lumpur   Singapore   Hong Kong   Tokyo
Nairobi   Dar es Salaam   Cape Town
Melbourne   Auckland

and associated companies in
Berlin   Ibadan

Published by Oxford University Press, Inc.,
200 Madison Avenue, New York, New York 10016

Library of Congress Cataloging-in-Publication Data
Americas : an anthology /
edited by Mark B. Rosenberg, A. Douglas Kincaid, Kathleen Logan.
p. cm.   ISBN 0-19-507792-X
1. Latin America. I. Rosenberg, Mark B.
II. Kincaid, A. Douglas. III. Logan, Kathleen, 1948–
F1408.A62 1992 98—dc20 91-46298

Cover image: © Peter Menzel. Inset: "Hands at Work" by Tina Modotti, © Sotheby's.
Cover Design: WGBH Design

9 8 7 6 5 4 3 2 1

Printed in the United States of America
on acid-free paper

This book was developed as a general reader and for use by students enrolled in the *Americas* television course. This 13-unit television course consists of 10 one-hour public television programs, this anthology, the textbook *Modern Latin America*, a study guide, a faculty guide, and an optional book entitled *Americas: New Interpretive Essays*, all available from Oxford University Press.

Americas was produced for PBS by WGBH Boston and by Central Television Enterprises for Channel 4, U.K., in association with the School of International and Public Affairs at Columbia University, the Latin American and Caribbean Center at Florida International University, and Tufts University.

Major funding for *Americas* was provided by the Annenberg/CPB Project, with additional funding from the Carnegie Corporation of New York, the John D. and Catherine T. MacArthur Foundation, the Rockefeller Foundation, the Corporation for Public Broadcasting, and public television viewers.

Americas is closed captioned for the hearing-impaired.

For more information about the print components of the *Americas* television course, contact:

Oxford University Press
200 Madison Avenue
New York, NY 10016
1-800-451-7556

For more information about television course licenses and off-air taping, contact:

Americas
PBS Adult Learning Service
1320 Braddock Place
Alexandria, VA 22314–1698
1-800-257-2578
In Virginia: (703) 739-5363

For more information about *Americas* videocassettes and print materials, off-air taping and duplication licenses, and other video and audio series from the Annenberg/CPB Collection, contact:

Americas
The Annenberg/CPB Collection
P.O. Box 2345
South Burlington, VT
1-800-LEARNER

Foreword

For many of us who regularly teach or write about Latin America and the Caribbean, our interest has always been more than scholarly or professional. In traveling through the region, we have been absorbed by its sights and sounds. Who could forget the bleak, sweeping expanse of the Bolivian high plains, or the pounding tropical music in a Caribbean port city, or the exuberant colors and aromas of a Mexican marketplace?

We also often enjoy close friendships with people from the region. We have been moved by their spirit in facing the developmental challenges posed by the legacies of social injustice, economic inequality, and foreign intervention. And we have been impressed by the creativity of Latin American and Caribbean cultural expressions and political strategies.

The challenge for us in this context has been to communicate the sights and the sounds, as well as the complexity, the commitment, and the individual and collective action of the people of the region, to students and readers who have not had the opportunity of firsthand acquaintance. Until now, unfortunately, we have had few multimedia materials that were specifically designed to provide these types of insights.

Americas: An Anthology is part of a college-level television course on Latin America and the Caribbean that has been developed over the past 10 years to address this need by scholars, producers, and editors from public television. Designed as a comprehensive learning package and introductory course in Latin American and Caribbean studies, *Americas* consists of 10 hour-long video programs, as well as a textbook, faculty and study guides, this anthology, and an optional book of essays.

The project was originally conceived in late 1982 by a group of Miami-based journalists and professors at Florida International University as a television course on the Caribbean. We were motivated by dissatisfaction with the limited offerings and often polemical quality of film materials available on the region that could be used for educational purposes. At the outset, we could not have imagined that it would take more than a decade to bring the idea to fruition. Since then, however, the project has grown enormously in concept, scope, and involvement.

With early support from the Carnegie Corporation, the project got off the ground. The involvement of Columbia University and Tufts University as co-sponsors greatly expanded the team's scholarly expertise and organizational abilities. The decision in 1986 by public television station WGBH in Boston to produce the telecourse added the crucial elements of creative and technical capacity and fund-raising capabilities. This formative process culminated in the generous support provided by the Annenberg/CPB Project, the Carnegie Corporation of New York, the John D. and Catherine T. MacArthur Foundation, the Rockefeller Foundation, the Corporation for Public Broadcasting, and public television viewers.

The process of designing and producing the video programs and print materials has itself been an adventure. Throughout the latter part of the 1980s, Alfred C. Stepan of Columbia University, as chairman of the Academic Advisory Board, led a spirited scholarly debate over the core concepts and themes to be embodied in the various components of the telecourse. He assembled a highly influential group of academic advisors who were both area studies scholars and committed educators. In discussion among themselves, as well as with WGBH's production team, headed by executive producer Judith Vecchione, they have provided the framework for a television course that faithfully adheres to our original purpose of developing a new and innovative set of teaching tools on Latin America and the Caribbean.

Like the other print materials for the course, this anthology is designed to correspond to both the form and the content of the video programs. However, it can also be used independently of the videos and other course materials, either as supplementary reading for other courses on the region, or simply as a resource for the general reader who wishes to understand better our Latin American and Caribbean neighbors. The selection of readings is intended to be suggestive rather than exhaustive. Space limitations and the broad scope of the subjects simply did not allow the inclusion of many other important and exciting readings.

Our hope is that we have created a book that captures the complexity and uniqueness of the Americas while remaining consistent with the course's form and content. This book will be successful if it fosters knowledge about a region that is increasingly important to the United States, and if it encourages readers to seek out more information.

Mark B. Rosenberg
Latin American and Caribbean Center
Florida International University

Acknowledgments

In producing this volume, we have been assisted by a wide variety of scholars and experts who must be recognized. To begin with, we would like to thank the academic sponsors of the *Americas* telecourse: Columbia University, Florida International University, and Tufts University. The project would also not have been possible without the support of the Annenberg/CPB Project, the Carnegie Corporation of New York, the John D. and Catherine T. MacArthur Foundation, the Rockefeller Foundation, and the Corporation for Public Broadcasting, as well as co-production funding from Channel 4, U.K. The entire project has been coordinated by its executive producer, Judith Vecchione of the WGBH Educational Foundation.

The form and content of the telecourse have been shaped by members of the project's Academic Advisory Board—a multidisciplinary group of scholars, chaired by Alfred C. Stepan, who have periodically reviewed the materials for this anthology. They include Margaret Crahan, María Patricia Fernández Kelly, Albert Fishlow, Cornelia Butler Flora, Jean Franco, Franklin W. Knight, Anthony P. Maingot, Marysa Navarro-Aranguren, Rubén Rumbaut, Helen Safa, Thomas Skidmore, Peter H. Smith, and Kay Barbara Warren. One member of the board, Academic Director Peter Winn, read and commented on the entire manuscript at several stages in its development. The criticisms and suggestions of the board members have contributed greatly to both the essays and readings in each chapter of this anthology.

We have also benefited from the suggestions of Dennis Cudd, Ethel McClatchey, Joyce Nielson, Wayne Prophet, Kenneth Sharpe, and Pam Quinn, members of the project's Telecourse Advisory Board. Pam Benson, Adriana Bosch Lemus, Patricia Crotty, Ann Downer, Rachel Field, Orna Feldman, Beth Kirsch, Gaye Korbet, Juan Mandlebaum, Deborah Paddock, Margo Shearman, and Judith Vecchione of WGBH also made significant contributions to individual chapters and to the work as a whole.

Our colleagues here at Florida International University reviewed our efforts and provided useful suggestions for possible reading selections. Particularly helpful were Uva Clavijo, Bárbara Cruz, John French, Eduardo Gamarra, Tanya Saunders-Hamilton, Richard Tardanico, and Kevin Yelvington.

Ultimately, the telecourse and this book would not have been possible without the early vision and initiative of Carl and Kathy Hersh of Miami, and Steve Samuels and Avery Russell of New York.

While this book bears the imprint of many colleagues directly and indirectly involved with the *Americas* project, the editors alone bear responsibility for any errors or oversights.

Mark B. Rosenberg
A. Douglas Kincaid
Kathleen Logan
Latin American and Caribbean Center
Florida International University

The Americas Project

Academic Advisory Board

Dr. Alfred C. Stepan
Chair, Academic Advisory Board
Columbia University

Dr. Mark B. Rosenberg
Project Education Director
Florida International University

Dr. Peter Winn
Project Academic Director
Tufts University

Dr. Cynthia Arnson
Associate Director, Americas Watch

Dr. Margaret Crahan
Occidental College, Los Angeles

Dr. María Patricia Fernández
  Kelly
The Johns Hopkins University

Dr. Albert Fishlow
University of California, Berkeley

Dr. Cornelia Butler Flora
Virginia Polytechnic Institute and
  State University

Dr. Jean Franco
Columbia University

Dr. Franklin W. Knight
The Johns Hopkins University

Dr. Anthony P. Maingot
Florida International University

Dr. Marysa Navarro-Aranguren
Dartmouth College

Dr. Alejandro Portes
The Johns Hopkins University

Dr. Rubén Rumbaut
San Diego State University

Dr. Helen Safa
University of Florida, Gainesville

Dr. Peter H. Smith
University of California, San Diego

Dr. Kay Barbara Warren
Princeton University

Dr. John Womack
Harvard University

Utilization Advisory Board

Pam Quinn
Chief Utilization Advisor
Center for Telecommunications,
  Dallas Community College

Dennis Cudd
Central Piedmont Community College

Dr. Joyce Nielson
Western Illinois University

Wayne Prophet
University of Iowa

Dr. Kenneth Sharpe
Swarthmore College

WGBH Boston

Peter McGhee
Vice President for National Program
Productions

Brigid Sullivan
Vice President for Special
Telecommunications Services

Judith Vecchione
Executive Producer, Americas

Beth Kirsch
Director of Educational Print

Patricia Crotty
Project Director, Educational Print

Contents

AMERICAS

1

Introduction

The peoples and nations of Latin America and the Caribbean vary greatly, and have richly diverse histories, economic and political systems, cultures, and social structures. © Robert Frerck/Odyssey Productions

The countries of Latin America and the Caribbean form a vast and complex part of our hemisphere. Though they, along with Canada, are our closest neighbors, few of us in the United States know much about these countries—their geography, their cultures, their history and politics. Often what we think we know is based on unfair stereotypes and generalizations, the product of some dramatic event that once captured media attention, or the latest crisis preoccupying our government. Many Latin Americans, too, hold their own stereotypes about the United States, as the familiar references to gringos or "Yankees" attest.

As the twentieth century draws to a close, however, it is clear that our hemisphere would be well served by a greater degree of knowledge and understanding among its peoples. This is an era in which communications technology is bringing world news live into our living rooms; in which manufacturing industries are routinely locating various parts of their operations in different countries around the globe; and in which new patterns of migration across borders are turning yesterday's Hollywood caricature into today's next-door neighbor. It is also a period in which the cold war finally ended, giving rise to a wide array of efforts toward international economic integration and political cooperation, as well as new forms of competition, such as the creation of regional trading blocs linking Latin American countries and sometimes the United States.

The main objective of this book is to foster a greater appreciation of Latin American and Caribbean realities among readers in the United States, by giving voice to the region through a selection of writings and speeches by politicians and scholars, artists and activists, generals and labor leaders, women and men. We begin in this chapter with some broad observations about the region and its peoples, followed by a discussion of general themes that helps put the region's development into proper historical perspective. The last section offers an overview of topics covered in subsequent chapters.

The Region at a Glance

Striking contrasts are found in Latin America and the Caribbean. This is no surprise when one considers it encompasses nearly

9 million square miles, an area larger than that of the United States and Canada combined (see map). The contrasts begin with the land itself, most of which lies within tropical latitudes on both sides of the equator. At lower elevations, the tropics tend to be characterized by relatively constant high temperatures and high annual rainfall.

Much of the region is also mountainous. The chain of mountains beginning in Alaska and running south through the North American Rockies continues through Mexico and Central America and down the Pacific side of South America. In South America this chain forms the Andes, second highest mountain range in the world after the Himalayas, with numerous peaks towering above 20,000 feet. Other significant highland ranges can be found in southern Brazil and in the Caribbean.

Another notable physical feature is the presence of major river systems. The Amazon—the world's longest river—flows some 3,300 miles from its origin in the Peruvian Andes to northeastern Brazil, where it empties into the Atlantic Ocean. The Rio de la Plata system in Argentina, Uruguay, and Paraguay, the Orinoco in Venezuela, and the Magdalena in Colombia are the region's other major rivers. One consequence is that hydroelectric power plays a major role as an energy source in the region, apart from the handful of countries blessed with important oil reserves.

These factors have strongly influenced the geography of human settlement and development in Latin America and the Caribbean. The combination of rugged highlands and inhospitable tropical vegetation encouraged a concentration of population and industry in coastal lowland areas, one of two dominant demographic patterns in the region. Most of South America's great cities are located on or near the coast, where trade can be easily conducted with the European metropolis.

A second development pattern occurred where highland ranges are broken by plateaus and large valleys. A case in point is central Mexico, where metropolitan Mexico City, now the world's most populous metropolis with some 20 million inhabitants, was erected on the ruins of the old Aztec capital. Bolivia's capital city of La Paz is located in the *Altiplano*, a plateau about 11,000 feet above sea level. In Central America, Guatemala and Costa Rica also have their major cities and principal development concentrated in upland valleys.

Thirty-three independent countries compose Latin America and the Caribbean, along with a few relatively small Caribbean territories that remain dependents of Britain, France, the Nether-

U.S.A.
(241.0)

MEXICO

GULF OF MEXICO

BAHAMAS

ATLANTIC OCEAN

Havana

BELIZE

CUBA

HAITI

DOMINICAN REPUBLIC

Mexico City

JAMAICA

PUERTO RICO

GUATEMALA

CARIBBEAN SEA

BARBADOS

NICARAGUA

EL SALVADOR

Caracas

TRINIDAD & TOBAGO

GUYANA

HONDURAS

VENEZUELA

SURINAME

PANAMA

Bogotá

COSTA RICA

COLOMBIA

FRENCH GUIANA

ECUADOR

Quito

PERU

BRAZIL

Lima

LaPaz

BOLIVIA

PACIFIC OCEAN

Rio de Janeiro

PARAGUAY

ARGENTINA

Santiago

Buenos Aires

Montevideo

CHILE

URUGUAY

0   500   1000   1500 Miles

Strait of Magellan

FALKLAND ISLANDS
(ISLAS MALVINAS)

Cape Horn

lands, and the United States. The contrasts among the countries are easily appreciated by comparing almost any basic indicators. For instance, tremendous variations exist in size of territory, population, and national economy, as can be seen in Table I. Brazil, larger than the continental United States, has 23 times the population of neighboring Bolivia. Mexico's economy is nearly 18 times as large as that of its neighbor Guatemala. At the other extreme, a number of Caribbean island states, such as Barbados, are smaller than many counties in the United States. Such differences warn against hasty generalizations about these countries.

One regional trend of recent decades has been rapid population growth. At some point in the early 1960s, the population of Latin America and the Caribbean as a whole was equal to the population of the United States, somewhat in excess of 200 million people. Latin American growth rates, however, were the highest in the world at that time. By 1990 the population of Latin America and the Caribbean had more than doubled, reaching 440 million people. Meanwhile the U.S. census for that year, reflecting declining growth rates, totaled some 250 million inhabitants.

Latin American growth rates have also declined significantly since the 1960s, but the cumulative impact of growth continues to be felt as members of the "baby boom" generation reach childbearing age. Its most dramatic effect has been in the cities, where a combination of natural growth and migration from town and countryside has generated an extraordinary population expansion and accompanying demands on housing and urban services.

The problem of persistent poverty is felt throughout most of Latin America. For the region as a whole, the gross domestic product (GDP) per capita, which measures total economic output divided by total population, hovered around $2,000 during the late 1980s. This figure is higher than that of other Third World areas, but well below the standards of advanced industrialized countries in Europe, East Asia, and North America. Considerable variation in wealth is evident among the Latin American countries, as is seen in Table I. Very low levels of GDP per capita, a near certain indicator of widespread poverty, are apparent in Haiti, the Dominican Republic, Guyana, Bolivia, and several Central American countries. Significantly higher levels can be seen in the cases of some of the smaller, less populous, and/or oil producing countries of the region, such as the Bahamas, Barbados, Trinidad and Tobago, and Venezuela. However, a high GDP per

TABLE I.   Basic Characteristics of Latin America and the Caribbean, 1988

Country	Area (sq. mi.)	Population ('000)	GDP ($ millions)	GDP/capita ($)
Argentina	1,078,769	31,534	91,142	2,890
Bahamas	5,435	234	2,356	10,068
Barbados	166	254	1,541	6,067
Belize	8,848	192	247	1,284
Bolivia	416,060	6,918	5,321	769
Brazil	3,288,050	144,428	326,073	2,258
Chile	286,397	12,748	28,925	2,269
Colombia	439,520	30,568	43,250	1,415
Costa Rica	23,421	2,866	4,625	1,614
Cuba	44,206	10,413	NA*	NA
Dominican Republic	19,323	6,867	5,244	764
Ecuador	116,270	10,070	13,065	1,297
El Salvador	8,250	5,032	5,473	1,088
Guatemala	42,042	8,681	7,628	879
Guyana	85,000	755	460	609
Haiti	10,714	6,263	2,210	353
Honduras	43,227	4,829	4,457	923
Jamaica	4,232	2,427	3,185	1,312
Mexico	760,373	84,886	164,267	1,935
Nicaragua	57,145	3,622	2,659	734
Panama	28,576	2,322	4,518	1,946
Paraguay	157,000	4,039	5,856	1,450
Peru	514,059	21,256	33,694	1,585
Suriname	63,890	359	1,235	3,441
Trinidad and Tobago	1,980	1,157	5,077	4,388
Uruguay	72,172	3,060	8,827	2,885
Venezuela	352,150	18,757	63,752	3,399

*Cuba uses a different national accounting system based on the "gross social product" to measure economic performance.

Countries not shown: Antigua and Barbuda, Dominica, Grenada, St. Kitts and Nevis, St. Lucia, St. Vincent and the Grenadines

Sources: Inter-American Development Bank, Economic and Social Progress in Latin America, 1990 Report (Baltimore: The Johns Hopkins University Press, 1990), pp. 261, 265; Economic Commission for Latin America and the Caribbean, Economic Survey of Latin America and the Caribbean, 1988 (Santiago, Chile: United Nations, 1989) p. 259; Tom Barry, Belize: A Country Guide (Albuquerque, NM: The Inter-Hemispheric Education Resource Center, 1989), p. 69.

capita is not necessarily an indication of the population's standard of living—this depends entirely on how the country's wealth and income are distributed among its population. In this respect, most Latin American countries fare poorly, with major pockets of both urban and rural poverty testifying to the unequal distribution of resources. Brazil, one of the richest nations in the Americas, has some of the worst inequalities.

Instability and violence have long been associated with Latin American politics, at least in the minds of North American observers. Although such portraits may be overstated and unfair to particular countries, political turmoil clearly has been a recurrent and often debilitating feature of Latin American and Caribbean public life. During the 1960s, revolutionary movements emerged in many countries in the wake of the Cuban Revolution. In the late 1960s and 1970s, most of the region came under the control of authoritarian military governments seeking to impose stability and their own vision of development. By the 1980s, however, their economic failures and repressive political programs had generated such determined opposition, among elites and lower classes alike, that they were forced to restore power to civilian hands. Today, Cuba remains without a directly elected civilian government. The efforts to strengthen democratic institutions in the face of severe economic difficulties and long-standing social inequalities by contemporary Latin American and Caribbean governments and other political actors are at once among the region's most encouraging and vexing trends.

A final outstanding characteristic is the area's cultural diversity, encompassing language, religion, racial and ethnic identities, and numerous other dimensions. The main cultural strands derive from the interaction of European colonizers, indigenous peoples, and black Africans brought to the New World as slaves, with diverse consequences in various parts of the region. Immigrant groups from other parts of the world, including the Middle East, South Asia, and East Asia, have also contributed to the cultural blending.

While the dominant European languages of Spanish, Portuguese, English, French, and Dutch stand as the official tongues of Latin American and Caribbean countries, in accordance with their colonial past, numerous native American languages continue to be spoken among the region's Indian groups. Quechua is recognized as an official language, along with Spanish, in Peru, while in Guatemala, the various descendants of the Maya speak

at least 23 different languages. Meanwhile, in most of the Caribbean countries, African-based Creole dialects are commonly heard,
especially in rural areas and among the lower classes.

Another product of the colonial experience is Latin America's
strong association with Catholicism. Indeed, the region's history
and cultural profile have been influenced greatly by the Roman
Catholic Church, while the sheer size of Latin America's population has given it an increasingly important impact on the Church.
In recent decades, however, Protestantism has made important
inroads into the region, mostly among the poor. It is also important to note that the ethnic and linguistic diversity just described
is mirrored in the religious sphere. In many parts of Latin America
and the Caribbean, a variety of religions maintaining indigenous
or African beliefs and practices have flourished.

Unity amidst Diversity

While the many differences that separate Brazil from Guatemala
or Haiti from Chile, for example, should not be underestimated,
it is also important to realize that Latin America and the Caribbean have been shaped by historical forces that give the region
a certain unity. Four such patterns have guided the selection of
issues and sources for this volume:

1. *Latin America and the Caribbean have a unique historical relationship to the global order.* The region as a whole has been indeli-
bly marked by the nature of its integration into a global economic and political context, beginning with the first encounters
between European explorers and indigenous populations in the
fifteenth and early sixteenth centuries. The entire region was absorbed into the expanding empires of Spain, Portugal, England,
France, and Holland. Colonial societies took shape around the
organized subjugation and exploitation of indigenous or imported slave labor forces, and the imposition of European institutions.

The decline of Spain and Portugal as world powers, associated
with a growing desire for political autonomy among colonial elites,
led to the creation of independent Latin American republics
during the nineteenth century. But the thoroughness of the conquest and the length of the colonial period created European-

oriented elites in Latin America, with economic ties, language, religion, and cultural values that looked across the Atlantic to Europe. To maintain their positions and develop their countries, local elites sought new products that could be exchanged profitably in world markets. While Europe became increasingly urbanized and industrialized, Latin America continued to play the old colonial role of producer of raw materials and foodstuffs. In the Caribbean, the persistence of the British and French colonial systems into the twentieth century delayed independence but did not greatly change the area's status in the world economic order.

This economic dependency was reinforced by the rise of the United States as an industrial power in the late nineteenth century. Because of both physical proximity and a growing willingness on the part of the United States to flex its political and economic muscle in the area, Latin American and Caribbean economies turned increasingly toward U.S. markets and producers. The clear disparities of power and wealth between North America and Latin America, as well as a pattern of U.S. intervention in the region, made the United States the object of radically mixed emotions for many Latin Americans. They regarded the United States simultaneously as a model to be emulated and as an obstacle to their own development, as a benevolent benefactor and a fearsome bully.

In the twentieth century, efforts to create a more independent economic and industrial base have often ended in deepening the dependence of Latin American economies. More recently, the Latin American external debt has created new vulnerabilities.

2. *The region's relationship to the global order and key internal decisions have combined to create high levels of tension and instability.* As noted previously, the countries of Latin America and the Caribbean have a history of poverty, inequality, injustice, and political violence. These factors are closely related to the prevailing patterns of the region's involvement in the global economy and political order. The connection was clearly visible during the colonial period, when the indigenous populations and vast numbers of imported slaves were exploited by tiny elites closely attuned to the markets and tastes of their respective colonial powers.

Independence brought political autonomy, but did not alter the external constraints on the region's development. The incorporation of Latin America into the new industrial order, centered on Europe and the United States, required the imposition of political stability and social control by national elites. These measures were often resisted by workers and peasants, as well as by local leaders with other priorities. At times, this internal order was underwritten by external force. The United States, in particular, proved willing to intervene in Latin America and the Caribbean in order to support its economic and political interests and in opposition to movements threatening the established order. These interventions in turn have often produced nationalistic responses and renewed instability in the region.

It would nonetheless be a mistake to attribute Latin America's internal problems solely to the actions of external powers. The region's social tensions and unstable politics are also the result of local decisions and internal conflicts. The choices made by Latin American and Caribbean actors, within the constraints and in response to the opportunities defined by international forces and actors, have shaped the history of their nations. At the same time, the differences in the internal social relations and political processes of the various countries of the region help explain their differing degrees of success in capitalizing on international opportunities and meeting new domestic challenges.

Consequently, while much has changed in the region, sustained economic development has proved a difficult goal, and periodic efforts to break with the past have often been frustrated. Latin America is sometimes described as a "living museum" in which traditional social and political relationships persist alongside more contemporary forms and serve as a brake on positive changes, such as democratizing the political systems and redistributing economic resources to benefit the majority. It is not surprising that under these circumstances radical challenges to the established order can arise and enjoy substantial popular support.

3. *The region's tensions have provoked a search for new social, economic, political, cultural, and religious forms, resulting in innovations emphasizing the participation of formerly disenfranchised social groups.* If the prevailing forms of development in Latin America and the Caribbean have often led to serious problems of political exclusion, economic deprivation, and social inequality for the majority, these conditions have not been accepted with resignation. Rather, the history of the region is marked by continual efforts of poor or disadvantaged groups to adapt to or resist changes threatening their well-being. In so doing they have created novel

forms of organization or thinking that have subsequently altered their society's most basic institutions and relationships.

Examples of this inventiveness include the creation of new religious communities seeking to combine local development initiatives with resistance to repressive governments; the rise of new social movements among women, peasants, Indian communities, and other social groups long excluded from the political arena; and cultural expressions that have represented complex social identities through a blending of European, African, and Indian styles and traditions. These efforts have helped open some of the closed or hierarchical institutions that have long impeded a more democratic style of development in the region. Despite the economic and political problems that remain, popular innovations of this sort hold promise for a brighter future.

4. *Innovations created in Latin America and the Caribbean have in turn altered the region's relationship to the global order.* Just as the images of the Americas as a "New World" once roused the curiosity and passion of European thinkers, or the hopes of immigrants, so the societies of Latin America and the Caribbean continue to project their image beyond the region's boundaries. Many of the region's innovations have found receptive echoes in the international arena.

The contemporary fiction and poetry of Latin American and Caribbean writers, for example, have garnered international acclaim and are now routinely translated into many languages. The political and religious innovations of Catholic social activists have both affected the Roman Catholic Church as an institution and served as a model for popular movements pursuing social change in other parts of the world. Similarly, the multiclass coalitions formed by Latin American women, combining concerns for greater gender equality with a commitment to local or regional development, have also emerged as models to be emulated abroad.

Latin American and Caribbean countries are beginning to have a larger political and economic impact. Paradoxically, the mammoth foreign debt amassed in the region has given it new prominence and influence in the international financial community, even though the debt poses major development problems. With the world economy's increasing tendency to favor regional integration and trading blocs, Mexico has taken the lead in pressing for a free trade area in North America, while Argentina, Brazil, and Chile have begun to seek closer cooperation with their hemispheric neighbors. Finally, new migration patterns are binding the Americas ever closer together, socially, culturally, and economically.

Issues and Stories

The following chapters of this book focus on some of the most important issues of contemporary Latin America and the Caribbean. Each chapter consists of a brief introductory essay followed by a selection of readings. These have been chosen to provide an appreciation of the context and diversity of situations faced by the region's inhabitants, a sense of national and regional similarities and differences, and a close-up look at the people and ideas that make Latin America and the Caribbean such a compelling subject of study.

The next three chapters offer an overview of the region's historical development from colonial times to the present, along with a presentation of specific issues and countries. Chapter 2, "Legacies of Empire: From Conquest to Independence," examines the basic political, economic, and cultural features of the colonial order, paying particular attention to those features whose impact on the region has been enduring. It also considers the circumstances under which political independence was achieved during the nineteenth and twentieth centuries. Chapter 3, "The Garden of Forking Paths: Dilemmas of National Development," traces Latin America's development from the mid–nineteenth century, when newly independent countries experienced rapid growth based on new export products, to the 1930s and 1940s, when the impact of the Great Depression and World War II contributed to economic crisis and political change. Special attention is given to Argentina, an early development success story that turned sour after 1930, with the nation lapsing into cycles of instability and military dictatorship. Chapter 4, "Capital Sins: Authoritarianism and Democratization," explores the challenge of economic development and the rise of authoritarian military governments after 1960, with a focus on Brazil. It also discusses the weaknesses of these governments, which ultimately led to a transfer of power back to civilian hands in the 1980s.

The remainder of the book deals with specific contemporary

issues, though a historical perspective is frequently interwoven to make sense of the changing nature of problems and responses. Chapter 5, "Continent on the Move: Migration and Urbanization," examines migration. This is a topic of major importance for both the internal and external dynamics of Latin American and Caribbean societies, whose populations have shifted from predominantly rural to urban, and for external relations, where international migration is an increasing solution to economic hardship and political repression. The case of Mexico is given particular emphasis here. Chapter 6, "Mirrors of the Heart: Color, Class, and Identity," considers the region's prevailing patterns of race and ethnic relations. It focuses on the evolving social relationships and identities of Indians in the Andean highlands and on the complex question of color and identity in the Caribbean.

Chapter 7, "In Women's Hands: The Changing Roles of Women," describes how women in the hemisphere are assuming new roles that challenge many long-held stereotypes about gender and family relations. Special reference is made to Chile, where women of all social classes have had to confront violence and major political and economic dislocations since the early 1970s. Chapter 8, "Miracles Are Not Enough: Continuity and Change in Religion," examines one of the most important social institutions of the region, the Catholic Church, and the controversial ways in which it has responded to contemporary social and political changes. This chapter also takes a look at some of the area's other prominent religious traditions and innovations, including the persistence of indigenous and African religious forms and the growing presence of Protestant churches. Literary and artistic innovation is the focus in Chapter 9, "Builders of Images: Writers, Artists, and Popular Culture." Portrayed are a succession of influential artistic movements, the notable achievements of Latin American writers since 1940, and the diverse forms and influences on contemporary popular culture.

The final three units deal with issues having a wider international dimension. Chapter 10, "Get Up, Stand Up: The Problems of Sovereignty," examines the problems Latin American and Caribbean countries have experienced in maintaining national sovereignty. These difficulties include the traditional imbalances in the region's relations with Europe and the United States, as well as more recent challenges countries such as Colombia and Panama have faced with drug trafficking. Chapter 11, "Fire in

the Mind: Revolutions and Revolutionaries," considers the relatively infrequent but highly visible phenomenon of social revolution. The chapter examines the causes and consequences of
revolutionary transformations of power, along with the ways in
which revolutionary actors have had to confront external opposition, especially from the United States. The discussion is illustrated by the historic revolutions of Mexico, Cuba, and Nicaragua. Finally, Chapter 12, "The Americans: Latin American and
Caribbean Peoples in the United States," outlines the growing
significance and changing character of Latin American and
Caribbean communities in the United States. The result of greatly
increased immigration during the last quarter century, their
presence represents an important force in the evolution of North
American society, politics, and culture.

2

Legacies of Empire: From Conquest to Independence

The complex social structures of the Americas grew out of the existing native American cultures, and from those of the Spanish, Portuguese, English, Dutch, and French colonizers and the enslaved Africans they imported. © Abbas/Magnum

The origins of modern Latin America and the Caribbean begin with the expansion of European countries into the Western Hemisphere in 1492. European colonizers were driven by the search for wealth, power, and social status and by their desire to spread Christianity. By the mid-1600s, the Western Hemisphere had become the site of intense competition among the European imperial powers, including Spain, Portugal, England, France, and The Netherlands. These conflicts helped mold the histories of the Americas and created complex political, economic, social, and cultural legacies.

Early European competition in the Latin American continent was reflected in the Treaty of Tordesillas, signed in 1494 between Spain and Portugal. The agreement granted to Spain most of South America, except for a large section of what is now Brazil, which was granted to Portugal. During the early part of the 1600s, the English, French, and Dutch established colonies in the Caribbean islands and on the Guyana coast of northern South America, while the Dutch extended their presence to northeastern Brazil as well.

Early Impact on the Region's People

The early pattern of Europe's exploitation of the New World had a major impact on the region's development and on its people. When the Spanish arrived, a number of indigenous civilizations had achieved high levels of organizational and cultural complexity. Native inhabitants of Latin America and the Caribbean found themselves subjected to new political, religious, social, and economic structures that the Europeans brought with them (see readings 2.1 and 2.2).

Two historic confrontations occurred during the colonial period: the subjugation of the region's indigenous peoples, and the massive importation of Africans as slave labor for plantations, mines, and cities. The depopulation of the Caribbean islands and the overthrow of the Aztec empire (1521) and of the Incan empire (1537) marked the beginning of a catastrophic decline in the indigenous populations; mostly from epidemics of European diseases. African slaves assumed increasing importance as manual laborers, especially in the lowland areas in the Caribbean and northeastern Brazil (see reading 2.3). By the end of the seventeenth century, African slaves and their descendants were an important component of colonial society.

The initial racial dichotomy of Spanish colonizers and Indians was complicated by the rise of the mestizo population, primarily the result of Spanish men taking Indian women as their servants, concubines, and, more rarely, wives. Racial and ethnic divisions were reflected throughout the region in hierarchies of social class, with Native Americans and blacks generally at the bottom of the social pyramid, mestizos and impoverished whites in the middle, and a white elite at the top. Major commercial enterprises, high administrative posts, and senior Church positions were legally reserved for Spaniards and their descendants until well into the eighteenth century, although exceptions to the rule were occasionally permitted.

Economic Evolution

Throughout much of the colonial era, Latin America and the Caribbean were important suppliers of wealth and natural resources to the European nations, which imposed economic institutions on the Americas that have had lasting effects. Many postcolonial and even current dilemmas reflect the nature of production and commerce from earlier times.

Mining and agriculture were the backbone of the Spanish colonial economy. During the sixteenth century Indians were forcibly removed from their communities to labor in the silver mines of Bolivia and Peru (see reading 2.4) and in the gold and silver mines of central Mexico. As easily accessible ores were exhausted, however, the Spaniards turned increasingly to agriculture, and Indian communities found themselves under new pressures.

In some instances, the impact of export agriculture on native Indians was similar to that of mining. Many Indian workers were uprooted from distant communities and transported to haciendas on the Pacific coast of El Salvador, Guatemala, and southern Mexico to produce cacao and indigo for export to Europe. Elsewhere, Indian villagers found themselves sudden unhappy hosts to an influx of Spanish settlers intent on occupying the best lands and organizing profitable enterprises. In this way the hacienda took shape in Peru, Mexico, and other parts of Latin America (see reading 2.5).

Another major economic institution of the colonial period which has shaped today's Latin America and the Caribbean is the plantation (see reading 2.6), producing most importantly, sugar, but also tobacco, cotton, and coffee. Originally introduced into the Caribbean by Europeans seeking an efficient means to produce sugar for Europe, the plantations came to depend on imported slave labor. By the early 1600s northeastern Brazil had become Europe's single most important source of cane sugar, produced almost entirely with African slave labor. Large-scale commercial agriculture is still important in many parts of Latin America and the Caribbean.

The Spanish and Portuguese Crowns tried to impose a mercantilist system on the Americas. In theory, colonies were to trade exclusively with the mother country and internal commerce was to be controlled. In practice, alternative markets and production developed. Trade among the colonies and production were legally restricted until the late eighteenth century, but did develop to a degree. The poverty of a substantial proportion of the population limited the expansion of the internal market. The emphasis on production for export, along with restricted trade patterns and international market forces, reinforced monocultural production and dependence on foreign capital and technology.

As a result, the new republics that emerged after 1810 faced major impediments to economic development. Although substantial modernization occurred during this period, it was determined to a considerable extent by external factors.

Religion and Culture

When the Spanish arrived on the American mainland in the early sixteenth century, they encountered highly sophisticated and organized religious beliefs and practices. The Mayas, Aztecs, and Incas, as well as other groups, believed in an afterlife, a creator god, and mediating deities. These and other similarities with Christianity eased the task of conversion to Catholicism, which was promoted by an influx of Catholic religious orders.

The Catholic Church came to be an important factor in the Iberian colonists' efforts to pacify the Indians. As settlements spread throughout the Americas, the Church followed. Bishoprics were established as early as 1530 in Mexico City and 1539 in Lima. The first Brazilian dioceses were established in Bahia in 1551 and in Rio de Janeiro in 1577. In its mission to convert Indians to Christianity, the Church played an influential role in determining the Crown's policy concerning their treatment (see Chapter 8). Although the Church was at times in conflict with secular authorities, its overall impact was to reinforce Iberian control. In addition, its role as the principal educator and provider of social welfare, as well as a patron of the arts, gave the Church significant influence throughout colonial society until the mid-nineteenth century.

Africans also brought their religions to the Americas. The religious beliefs and rituals of Europeans and Africans were in time layered onto those of Indians, producing unique religious forms. Their richness and vitality are evident today in religious practices throughout Latin America and the Caribbean.

Colonial culture was complex, reflecting the variety of contributions from different racial, ethnic, and cultural groups. Among the elites, Spanish culture prevailed. But the culture of the majority was also heavily influenced by African and indigenous elements, which can be found in painting, music, language, social organization, and architecture.

Political Legacies

Another important legacy of colonial times was a tendency toward administrative centralism and regional or local autonomy. In theory, monarchical authority in Spain and Portugal at the time of their expansion into the Americas was absolute. In practice, royal officials had considerable autonomy in the colonies, partly because of local pressures and the distance from Spain and Portugal; the shortage, incompetence, and corruption of officials; and the frequent exemptions granted from, or local disregard of, royal decrees. Such a pattern of incomplete control and ad hoc local authority helped give rise to regionalism, strong-man rule, and ineffective government, each factor a threat to national unity after independence.

The struggle for Spanish American independence had its roots in the Enlightenment and in the Spanish effort to increase control over and profits from the colonies beginning around 1750. The French Revolution of 1789 had a powerful impact on Haiti, where a slave rebellion in 1791 led to the first independent state in Latin America and the Caribbean—the Haitian Republic of 1804 (see reading 2.7). A decade later, Simón Bolívar in northern South America (see reading 2.8) and José de San Martín in the south emerged as leaders of armies that would eventually liberate Latin America from Spanish control. By 1830 formal independence was virtually accomplished for all Spanish American countries, except the Dominican Republic under Haitian control, which gained its independence in 1864; and Cuba, which achieved independence in 1898; and Puerto Rico, which passed under U.S. control, also in 1898.

Brazil's attainment of independence from Portugal stood in marked contrast to Hispanic America's bloody struggle against Spain. More than three centuries of Portuguese rule in Brazil ended in 1822 when the Portuguese crown prince, Dom Pedro, declared political independence. The transition from colony to independent country was accomplished without civil war, though it took more than a year to drive the colonial garrisons out of the country. The monarchy was not replaced by a republic, however, until 1889.

Regionalism was strong in Brazil following Portugal's departure. Nearly every province rebelled against the central government during the turbulent postindependence years. This was also true in nineteenth-century Spanish America. The original eight Spanish American republics broke into twelve somewhat unstable polities, with more divisions to follow.

Among the region's elites, competition for power was intense, giving rise to armed conflicts, coups, new constitutions, and the rule of local bosses and regional caudillos. The wars for independence were not social revolutions and did not substantially change the lives of the majority, particularly Indians and blacks. In the turmoil, economies often suffered (see reading 2.9). Society continued to reflect the pattern of privilege and inequality of the preindependence period.

In the Caribbean, colonial control sustained itself in most countries into the twentieth century. Although it gained independence from Spain, Cuba was a virtual U.S. protectorate until 1933. West Indian nationalism stimulated a slow process of decolonization. Jamaica and Trinidad-Tobago became independent in 1962, followed by Barbados in 1966, and other Caribbean countries more recently, including some of the Dutch colonies. Guadeloupe and Martinique remain parts of France. Some of the smaller islands also remain in European hands, while Puerto Rico has a degree of internal self-government but is a possession of the United States. Though independence has redefined the region's legal status, it has not generally brought added social and economic well-being for most residents.

The length of the colonial period in the Caribbean and the small size of many of the countries contributed to difficulties in establishing and defining national sovereignty for many of the islands. The parliamentary tradition of the former British colonies has contributed to the emergence of competitive political systems and relative stability.

Colonial legacies thus include problematic economic development; a grafting of European social and religious institutions onto indigenous and African cultural forms; racial and ethnic mixing that has created new groups; and political structures that tend to be dominated by the elite. The historical evolution of Latin America and the Caribbean has transformed these legacies, producing new structures and institutions. These reflect both the past and the present and are unique in their response to the realities of the area today.

2.1 The Trauma of Conquest

Wherever the Spanish conquerors went in the New World, a major issue facing them was how to subjugate the natives and mold them into a productive labor force. Bartolomé de las Casas, a conquistador turned Dominican friar who subsequently became the bishop of Chiapas, was one of the earliest observers, chroniclers, and critics of the conquest. In the following reading, he provides a vivid account of the devastating effects of conquest on the Indian population in Cuba.

In the year 1511 the Spaniards passed over to the island of Cuba, which as I said, is as long as from Valladolid to Rome, and where there were great and populous provinces. They began and ended in the above manner, only with incomparably greater cruelty. Here many notable things occurred.

A very high prince and lord, named Hatuey, who had fled with many of his people from Hispaniola to Cuba, to escape the calamity and inhuman operations of the Christians, having received news from some Indians that the Christians were crossing over, assembled many or all of his people, and addressed them thus.

"You already know that the Christians are coming here; and you have experience of how they have treated the lords so and so and those people of Hayti (which is Hispaniola); they come to do the same here. Do you know perhaps why they do it?" The people answered no; except that they were by nature cruel and wicked. "They do it," said he, "not alone for this, but because they have a God whom they greatly adore and love; and to make us adore Him they strive to subjugate us and take our lives." He had near him a basket full of gold and jewels and he said: "Behold here is the God of the Christians, let us perform *Areytos* before him, if you will (these are dances in concert and singly); and perhaps we shall please Him, and He shall command that they do us no harm."

All exclaimed: it is well! it is well! They danced before it, till they were all tired, after which the lord Hatuey said: "Note well that in any event if we preserve the gold, they will finally have to kill us to take it from us: let us throw it into this river." They all agreed to this proposal, and they threw the gold into a great river in that place.

This prince and lord continued retreating before the Christians when

de las Casas, Bartolomé. "God's Angry Man." In *Latin American Civilization: History and Society, 1492 to the Present,* edited by Benjamin Keen, 66–68. Boulder, Colo.: Westview Press, 1986.

they arrived at the island of Cuba, because he knew them, but when he encountered them he defended himself; and at last they took him. And merely because he fled from such iniquitous and cruel people, and defended himself against those who wished to kill and oppress him, with all his people and offspring until death, they burnt him alive.

When he was tied to the stake, a Franciscan monk, a holy man, who was there, spoke as much as he could to him, in the little time that the executioner granted them, about God and some of the teachings of our faith, of which he had never before heard; he told him that if he would believe what was told him, he would go to heaven where there was glory and eternal rest; and if not, that he would go to hell, to suffer perpetual torments and punishment. After thinking a little, Hatuey asked the monk whether the Christians went to heaven; the monk answered that those who were good went there. The prince at once said, without anymore thought, that he did not wish to go there, but rather to hell so as not to be where Spaniards were, nor to see such cruel people. This is the renown and honour, that God and our faith have acquired by means of the Christians who have gone to the Indies.

On one occasion they came out ten leagues from a great settlement to meet us, bringing provisions and gifts, and when we met them, they gave us a great quantity of fish and bread and other victuals, with everything they could supply. All of a sudden the devil entered into the bodies of the Christians, and in my presence they put to the sword, without any motive or cause whatsoever, more than three thousand persons, men, women, and children, who were seated before us. Here I beheld such great cruelty as living man has never seen nor thought to see.

Once I sent messengers to all the lords of the province of Havana, assuring them that if they would not absent themselves but come to receive us, no harm should be done them; all the country was terrorized because of the past slaughter, and I did this by the captain's advice. When we arrived in the province, twenty-one princes and lords came to receive us; and at once the captain violated the safe conduct I had given them and took them prisoners. The following day he wished to burn them alive, saying it was better so because those lords would some time or other do us harm. I had the greatest difficulty to deliver them from the flames but finally I saved them.

After all the Indians of this island were reduced to servitude and misfortune like those of Hispaniola, and when they saw they were perishing inevitably, some began to flee to the mountains; others to hang themselves, together with their children, and through the cruelty of one very tyrannical Spaniard whom I knew, more than two hundred Indians hanged themselves. In this way numberless people perished.

There was an officer of the King in this island, to whose share three hundred Indians fell, and by the end of the three months he had, through labour in the mines, caused the death of two hundred and seventy; so that he had only thirty left, which was the tenth part. The authorities afterwards gave him as many again, and again he killed them: and they continued to give, and he to kill, until he came to die, and the devil carried away his soul.

In three or four months, I being present, more than seven thousand children died of hunger, their fathers and mothers having been taken to the mines. Other dreadful things did I see.

Afterwards the Spaniards resolved to go and hunt the Indians who were in the mountains, where they perpetrated marvelous massacres. Thus they ruined and depopulated all this island which we beheld not long ago; and it excites pity, and great anguish to see it deserted, and reduced to a solitude.

2.2 The Aztec Dirge

In 1519 the Spaniards invaded Mexico under the command of Hernán Cortés. Within two years the conqueror had subdued the Aztecs and destroyed their capital, Tenochtitlán. Through slaughter, plunder, and disease, the population of the ancient kingdom was decimated. A century after conquest, the Indian population of central Mexico had fallen from an estimated 18 million to less than 1 million. The Aztecs expressed the trauma of conquest in ritual laments. The first song below was written by an unknown Aztec poet in 1528. The second song was probably composed that same year by another unknown Aztec poet and was preserved in Cantares Mexicanos, *by Antonio Penafiel, in 1904.*

Broken Spears

Broken spears lie in the roads;
we have torn our hair in our grief.
The houses are roofless now, and their walls
are red with blood.

"Broken Spears" and "Flowers and Songs of Sorrow." In *The Broken Spears*, Miguel Leon-Portilla, 137–138, 149. Boston: Beacon Press, 1962.

Worms are swarming in the streets and plazas,
and the walls are splattered with gore.
The water has turned red, as if it were dyed,
and when we drink it,
it has the taste of brine.

We have pounded our hands in despair
against the adobe walls,
for our inheritance, our city, is lost and dead.
The shields of our warriors were its defense,
but they could not save it.

We have chewed dry twigs and salt grasses;
we have filled our mouth with dust and bits of
adobe;
we have eaten lizards, rats and worms. . . .

Flowers and Songs of Sorrow

Nothing but flowers and songs of sorrow
are left in Mexico and Tlaltelulco,
where once we saw warriors and wise men.

We know it is true
that we must perish,
for we are mortal men.
You, the Giver of Life,
you have ordained it.

We wander here and there
in our desolate poverty.
We are mortal men.
We have seen bloodshed and pain
where once we saw beauty and valor.

We are crushed to the ground;
we lie in ruins.
There is nothing but grief and suffering
in Mexico and Tlaltelulco,
where once we saw beauty and valor.

Have you grown weary of your servants?
Are you angry with your servants,
O Giver of Life?

2.3 African Slave Migration

As European demand for sugar grew, so too did the demand for labor. Lacking a large, tractable Indian labor force, Portuguese landowners turned to slaves from Africa. By the mid-1600s, sugar cultivation was booming in northeastern Brazil. During the century that followed, it spread throughout the Caribbean, thanks largely to massive numbers of slave laborers. The scope of slavery in Latin America and the Caribbean is outlined in the following selection.

From small beginnings in the 1440s until its demise in the second half of the nineteenth century, the Atlantic slave trade carried one of the greatest forced migrations of history: that of African peoples taken into slavery in the Americas. Estimates of the volume of the slave trade vary widely, but there is no doubt that it uprooted millions of people and involved a significant depopulation of the African continent. Of the slaves taken in Africa, an unknown number perished before embarkation for the Americas and many more died in the harsh conditions of the trans-Atlantic crossing. Probably about 9.5 to 10 million survived to become slaves who, with their descendants, came to constitute an important, sometimes preponderant element of the American regions in which they were settled.

The Atlantic slave trade was first developed by Portuguese traders during the second half of the fifteenth century, taking black captives up from sub-Saharan Africa as part of a trade in several commodities. Until the mid-sixteenth century the traffic in slaves—which soon came to dominate commerce with Africa—was primarily geared to meeting demands for unfree labour in the Old World. Between 1441 and 1550, more than half of the slaves extracted from the coasts of West Africa were destined for the labour market in Europe, particularly in the Iberian peninsula, or for use in the emergent plantation economies of the Atlantic islands. However, in quantitative terms, the slave trade to the Old World was to pale into insignificance compared to the formidable flows of human cargoes which swept across the Atlantic to the Americas after about 1550. Henceforth, the Atlantic slave trade assumed patterns of growth and distribution over time and space which responded to the rhythms of economic development in the areas of European settlement and dominion in the Americas. . . .

McFarlane, Anthony. "African Slave Migration." In *The Cambridge Encyclopedia of Latin America and the Caribbean*, edited by Simon Collier, Harold Blakemore, and Thomas E. Skidmore, 138–42. Cambridge: Cambridge University Press, 1985.

   In terms of distribution over time, the estimates given above suggest that slave immigration into the Americas passed through several distinct phases, in which changes in the scale of the slave trade were associated with variations in the distribution of slave imports between regions. The first broad phase of growth took place during the second half of the sixteenth century, when the number of slaves arriving in the Americas surpassed those who went to Old World destinations. At this stage, most of them went to the Spanish colonies which, between 1451 and 1600, took some 60 per cent of slaves landed in the Americas. Towards the end of the sixteenth century, the Portuguese settlements in Brazil gave a new impetus to African immigration and, by the early seventeenth century, Brazil emerged as the major market for black slaves. Over the century as a whole, Brazil absorbed about 42 per cent of all slaves brought to the Americas. In the latter half of the seventeenth century, the slave trade spread away from the Iberian powers' colonies into the possessions of North European nations in the Caribbean. The English West Indies, in particular, offered a new and important market in the latter half of the century when, in a burst of growth, they absorbed almost as many slaves as were taken into the Spanish colonies over the century as a whole. The emergence of new slave markets in the Caribbean presaged the great era of growth in the eighteenth century. Not only did Brazil continue to take in growing numbers of Africans, but demand in the Caribbean islands pushed the trade to unprecedented levels. The French and British islands alone accounted for about 45 per cent of total American slave imports during this period, while the additional demand of the Spanish, Dutch and Danish islands ensured that the Caribbean region received more than half of the six million slaves landed in the Americas during the period 1701–1810. Thus the major phase of African slave migration (in which about 60 per cent of all slaves carried to the western hemisphere were landed) was closely bound up with developments in the Caribbean and in Brazil. Not surprisingly, these were the areas in which African immigration had greatest impact on social and economic development, for between them they had absorbed about 80 per cent of all African migrants to the New World. Even when the trade entered into its final, declining phase in the nineteenth century, Brazil and the Spanish Caribbean islands continued to exert their baneful influence by keeping the institution of slavery and the currents of the slave trade alive long after they had been suppressed elsewhere.

   These developments in the scale and spatial spread of African slave immigrants corresponded with the changing requirements for manpower in the Americas. Already familiar with the use of African slaves, Spaniards took them as personal servants on their early expeditions of conquest and later extended the employment of slaves to meet a variety of special needs. By the end of the sixteenth century, African slaves and their half-caste offspring had become an important element in both

Spanish and Portuguese colonial societies, and were almost as numerous as the white settlers themselves. The settlement and occupational
patterns of nascent Afro-American society varied from region to region. African slaves were mainly located in areas where Amerindian
labour was inadequate for the needs of white colonists. In the highlands of Mesoamerica and South America, where the Spaniards encountered dense Amerindian peasant populations whose labour could
be used in agriculture and silver mining, black slaves were used chiefly
as skilled artisans and domestic servants, and formed a relatively small
part of the population. The main areas of African resettlement were in
the tropical lowland regions of the Caribbean islands and the mainland
coastal zones, where indigenous peoples were far fewer in number and
where Africans provided a substitute labour force in both rural and
urban areas. Here African slaves were used in a variety of occupations,
including gold mining, but the main source of demand arose from the
development of plantation agriculture, producing tropical crops for
overseas markets. . . .

As slaves, Africans were universally regarded as units of private
property, disposable chattels who were subject to the ownership rights
of their masters and deprived of the civil rights which the law bestowed
on free persons. Although the laws of slave societies expressed the interests of slaveowners, slaves could not logically be regarded merely as
inanimate objects devoid of recognized human needs for physical and
spiritual sustenance. Consequently, the absolute power of slaveholders
could be restrained, either by special legal codes laid down by governments, or by customs and conventions which emerged from local practices governing master-slave relations. In the Catholic cultures of Latin
America, slaves were theoretically afforded rights to marriage, to protection from cruelty, and, under special circumstances, to manumission
by self-purchase. In contrast, in the Protestant cultures of the West
Indies and British North America slaves were supposedly denied such
opportunities and treated with greater severity in more rigidly segregated societies. However, the recognition of the slave as a moral personality did not release him from a servile status, nor did it necessarily
influence the treatment that he received. . . .

The importance of African slave migrants for the development of
major regions in the Americas was not merely economic; Africans and
their descendants also contributed to the formation of distinctively
American cultures. Despite the deep trauma of capture, transportation
and enslavement, with the consequent severance of family and community ties, slaves did not lose all contact with the cultures of their past.
In Brazil and in the Caribbean islands, where the plantation was the
central social and economic institution, where there was a constant influx of Africans, and where blacks and mulattos formed the largest
element of the population, there appeared many of the most vigorous

Afro-American cultural forms. African influences manifested themselves in music, language, work techniques, and, perhaps most importantly, in religious beliefs and practices. Little is known of the history of African cultural survivals before the eighteenth century; however, from that time at least there were distinctive religious cults in Brazil and the West Indies, fusing with, and competing against the Christianity of dominant white society. Cults such as Obeah and Myalism in the Anglophone Caribbean, Vodùn in Haiti, and Candomblé, Xangó and Macumba in Brazil, all testified to the transmission of African patterns of worship.

The response of Africans and their offspring to slavery also took more tangible shape in various forms of open rejection of, and resistance to white society. Not only did individual slaves flee from servitude, but runaway slaves also formed their own communities, known as *maroons, palenques* and *quilombos,* which were *de facto* autonomous polities beyond the control of white-controlled governments. Organized rebellions by plantation slaves, seeking the redress of grievances suffered at the hands of their masters, were also common throughout Latin America and the Caribbean, though they rarely resulted in concerted movements for emancipation. Only in Haiti did slave rebellion form the basis for a revolutionary movement which overthrew slave society and, in 1804, replaced colonial government with an independent republic headed by an ex-slave.

2.4 Working the Mines in Peru

Under the system of forced labor known as the mita, *in the viceroyalty of Peru, one-seventh of all formally free, unskilled Indian males over eighteen years of age were required each year to provide labor services to the Crown and its delegates in the mines, on the ranches, on public works, and in the textile mills. The Indians were often forced to travel great distances, and the pay usually did not exceed the tribute dues they had to render. Conditions were particularly harsh in the highland areas, where*

Vasquez de Espinosa, Antonio. "Compendium and Description of the West Indies." In *Readings in Latin American Civilization: 1492 to the Present,* edited by Benjamin Keen, translated by C. U. Clark, 2d ed., 93–94. Washington: The Smithsonian Institution, 1942.

silver was mined at Potosí and mercury at Huancavelica. The following selections, written by Antonio Vasquez de Espinosa, a Carmelite friar who traveled throughout the Indies from 1612 to 1620, describe the mita.

According to His Majesty's warrant, the mine owners on this massive range have a right to the *mita* of 13,300 Indians in the working and exploitation of the mines, both those which have been discovered, those now discovered, and those which shall be discovered. It is the duty of the Corregidor of Potosí to have them rounded up and to see that they come in from all the provinces between Cuzco over the whole of El Collao and as far as the frontiers of Jarija and Tomina; this Potosí Corregidor has power and authority over all the Corregidors in those provinces mentioned; for if they do not fill the Indian *mita* allotment assigned each one of them in accordance with the capacity of their provinces as indicated to them, he can send them, and does, salaried inspectors to report upon it, and when the remissness is great or remarkable, he can suspend them, notifying the Viceroy of the fact.

These Indians are sent out every year under a captain whom they choose in each village or tribe, for him to take them and oversee them for the year each has to serve; every year they have a new election, for as some go out, others come in. This works out very badly, with great losses and gaps in the quotas of Indians, the villages being depopulated; and this gives rise to great extortions and abuses on the part of the inspectors towards the poor Indians, ruining them and thus depriving the caciques and chief Indians of their property and carrying them off in chains because they do not fill out the *mita* assignment, which they cannot do, for the reasons given and for others which I do not bring forward.

These 13,300 are divided up every 4 months into 3 *mitas*, each consisting of 4,433 Indians, to work in the mines on the range and in the 120 smelters in the Potosí and Tarapaya areas; it is a good league between the two. These *mita* Indians earn each day, or there is paid each one for his labor, 4 reals. Besides these there are others not under obligation, who are *mingados* or hire themselves out voluntarily: these each get from 12 to 16 reals, and some up to 24, according to their reputation of wielding the pick and knowing how to get the ore out. These *mingados* will be over 4,000 in number. They and the *mita* Indians go up every Monday morning to the locality of Guayna Potosí which is at the foot of the range; the Corregidor arrives with all the provincial captains or chiefs who have charge of the Indians assigned them, and he there checks off and reports to each mine and smelter owner the number of Indians assigned him for his mine or smelter; that keeps him busy till 1 P.M., by which time the Indians are already turned over to these mine and smelter owners.

After each has eaten his ration, they climb up the hill, each to his mine, and go in, staying there from that hour until Saturday evening without coming out of the mines; their wives bring them food, but they stay constantly underground, excavating and carrying out the ore from which they get the silver. They all have tallow candles, lighted day and night; that is the light they work with, for as they are underground, they have need of it all the time. The mere cost of these candles used in the mines on this range will amount every year to more than 3,000,000 pesos, even though tallow is cheap in that country, being abundant; but this is a very great expense, and it is almost incredible, how much is spent for candles in the operation of breaking down and getting out the ore.

These Indians have different functions in the handling of the silver ore; some break it up with bar or pick, and dig down in, following the vein in the mine; others bring it up; others up above keep separating the good and the poor in piles; others are occupied in taking it down from the range to the mills on herds of llamas: every day they bring up more than 8,000 of these native beasts of burden for this task. These teamsters who carry the metal do not belong to the *mita*, but are *mingados*—hired.

2.5 The Hacienda

The hacienda, or large landed estate, is one of colonialism's fundamental institutions in Latin America. More than just a form of land ownership, the hacienda was a complex social organization that was practically self-sufficient. While it provided the owner economic return, it also offered social prestige and political influence. In exchange for labor, the hacienda ostensibly offered workers a sense of security and place, even if the conditions were harsh. The reading below describes the nature and impact of haciendas in Latin America during the colonial period.

The great haciendas of Spanish America came into being through land grant, purchase, usurpation, accretion, merger, and economic competition. Lands originally granted in relatively small amounts were bought up by colonial speculators and often sold and resold a number of times

Gibson, Charles. *Spain in America*, 154–56. New York: Harper & Row, 1966.

before taking final form as segments of huge estates. Land values, like commodity prices, underwent progressive increase in the colonial period, and land represented an investment always available to those with money to spend and always disposable by those in need of liquid capital. Only rarely did viceroys or other land-granting authorities issue large tracts in the original instance. The title deeds of most haciendas were bulky files of records covering numerous small properties. Their legal status was often of great complexity, and the royal government periodically provided for legalization (*composición*) of defective titles through payment of fees—a procedure that encouraged additional usurpation of Indian lands and brought additional revenue to the crown.

The crown of course never openly advocated Spanish land seizures from Indians. The laws were explicit that haciendas should be located at a distance from Indian communities and that all grants should be "without injury" (*sin perjuicio*) to Indian livelihood.

But no such rules could be consistently enforced. Other laws, laws of *congregación*, or *denuncia*, and of *composición*, uniformly militated against them. Colonial lawyers were adept at exploiting legislation in their clients' favor and interest. It became physically impossible to separate haciendas from Indian towns. Haciendas employed the inhabitants of Indian towns as *peones* and controlled all their activities. The wealthiest and most powerful persons in the colony—viceroys, high-ranking officials, prosperous merchants, ecclesiastics—became *hacendados*. The process was irrevocable. Laws of entail assured the perpetuation of properties in Spanish hands. Very little land ever reverted to Indian control.

Haciendas repeatedly incorporated and absorbed native towns, and hacienda society emerged in the familiar form as a stratification of white owners and native laborers. The *peones* formed the proletariat of every hacienda. The *hacendado* was its absolute master, euphemized in the term *patrón*. The *hacendado*'s house was a magnificent dwelling, the residence of his large family of relatives and the scene of banquets and elaborate receptions. To the *peones* of the hacienda the *patrón* was an apotheosis of authority, immediate in a way that the viceroy and king never were. His ostentatious possessions—his horses and carriages, his elaborate attire, his silver and finery—were visible symbols of wealth. Disobedience to his will brought severe and exemplary punishment. A prudent servility was essential if the hacienda laborer were to adjust peacefully to his condition, and internal revolution was extremely rare in hacienda society. Thus the hacienda fitted the universal character of Spanish America.

Unlike conquest and encomienda[1], the hacienda did not, in the colonial period, receive criticism based on humanitarian sympathy for its

---

[1] A royal grant to a Spanish colonist of the rights to tribute and labor from specific Indian communities.

victims. Spanish self-criticism, and the tradition of the Black Legend[2] outside Spain, concentrated on the earlier institutions even while the hacienda developed and prospered. To Spaniards hacienda was a natural, precedented institution. The political power of landholding noble families in Castile had been broken by Ferdinand and Isabella, but the great landholdings themselves persisted. It remained for the twentieth century to identify and condemn the social inequalities of hacienda life, the forms of which were more subtle and far less overt than those of conquest and encomienda. The nature of hacienda society was such that its oligarchal features were often compromised or disguised, and it has accordingly been the subject of romantic interpretation, as encomienda never has.

From the point of view of its aristocratic proprietor, one can easily understand how hacienda society might be romanticized. But even from the point of view of the Indian worker, it could be argued that the hacienda brought benefits otherwise unobtainable in colonial society. The worker owed a financial debt to the hacienda, in the system of peonage. But this very indebtedness made him an object of economic importance to the *hacendado* and one that had to be cultivated if the *hacendado* were not to lose him through truancy. Thus haciendas ordinarily provided lands (lands, to be sure, that had been taken from the Indians) on which *peones* could live and raise crops. They provided local stores at which essential commodities could be obtained, and chapels for the satisfaction of spiritual needs. The laborers formed a community and were provided with a security that they could not have had outside the hacienda. All such benefits were of course limited, and they appear meliorative only in comparison with the practical alternatives. Exploitative and cruel the hacienda certainly was.

2.6 The Sugar Plantation

The sugar plantation, known as engenho *in Portuguese America, was a central feature of colonial life in Brazil and the Caribbean. The plantation was directly linked to the international economy and was dependent*

[2] Accusations against Spain of the slaughter and enslavement of Indians in the Americas. Lockhart, James, and Stuart B. Schwartz. *Early Latin America: A History of Spanish America and Brazil*, 204–7. New York: Cambridge University Press, 1983.

on world market conditions for its profitability. The nature of the crop and its processing, with its heavy technical component and high demand for labor, helped determine the complex social and economic basis of the engenho.

The central social institution of colonial Brazilian life in the seventeenth century was the engenho, that complex of land, coerced labor, technical skills, and capital that produced Brazil's primary export commodity, sugar. As we have seen, the way in which these elements could be combined effectively had already been worked out in the Mediterranean and on the Atlantic islands, but the rich soils of coastal Brazil seemed to offer opportunities for an increase in scale and hence of output unknown up to that time. It should be made clear that the term "plantation" was never employed to describe the unit of production in the sugar industry. Instead, Iberians used the word "engenho" (Sp. *ingenio*, related to Eng. "engine"), which strictly speaking meant only the mill itself but came to represent the whole operation, including houses, slaves, land, and animals. The term "engenho" evokes images of the rural seignur, of patriarchal dominance, of country estates, servants, and slaves, set among green cane fields and palms on the horizon. Although much of the image is true, there is also a heavy coating of romanticism that must be peeled away if we are to understand the nature of the engenho and its effects on the development of Brazilian society.

Let us begin with sugarcane itself, for the nature of the crop and its product, sugar, determined much of the engenho's structure. Although there were regional variations, the process described here was basically the same throughout the Americas. The first crop usually took some fifteen to eighteen months to mature, but thereafter for the next three or four years the same field would yield a new crop every nine months or so without replanting. The harvest, or *safra* (Sp. *zafra*), began at the end of July and continued for eight or nine months. During this period the engenho was alive with activity. Slaves cut the cane and loaded it onto oxcarts that were then driven to the mill. There another crew of slaves produced sugar from the cane under the direction of technicians and with the help of artisans who might be either slave or free. The process was difficult and complicated. First the cane was passed through vertical roller presses, which were usually powered on the big engenhos by waterwheels, and on the smaller ones by oxen. The syrup pressed from the cane was then passed through a series of kettles where it was boiled and clarified until finally it was sufficiently clean to make sugar. The liquid was poured into conical molds, which were then set on long rows of planks in a special drying shed. After further drainage, which required three weeks or a month, the molds could be opened, showing the crystallized sugar to have formed in its characteristic "sugar loaf." The best grade had the least impurities and was therefore white in color. Brown sugar (*muscavado*) sold for less, and the inferior grades were often used to make rum. The sugar was then dried, crated in large chests, and taken by boat or oxcart to Salvador, Recife, or some smaller port for shipment to Europe.

As one can see, sugar was a special crop in that it demanded not only agriculture but also highly technical processing. The need to process sugarcane at the point of origin meant that each engenho was a combination of agricultural and industrial enterprise, needing large amounts of capital and credit, the specialized skills of blacksmiths, carpenters, coopers, and masons, and the technical knowhow of men who understood the intricacies of the sugar-making process. Moreover, the labor demands of cane cultivation and sugar production were great and terrible. During the harvest, the engenho operated eighteen to twenty hours a day, and many observers remarked that the heat and fires of the cauldrons called up images of scenes of hell.

The average mill had some sixty to eighty slaves, but a few large ones had more than two hundred. Although conditions might vary from engenho to engenho according to the personalities of owners or overseers, sugar imposed its own realities. In general, no matter what the intentions of the planters, the arduous working conditions, climate, and problems of food, housing, and care produced very high rates of disease and mortality. In a single year an engenho expected to lose between 5 and 10 percent of its slaves. Father Cardim, a Jesuit observer, wrote simply in the 1580s that "the work is great and many die." But as contemporaries put it, from the bitter captivity of the slaves came the sweet sugar, and for the slave-owning sugar planters, profit and status were to be gained from the enterprise. To be called *senhor de engenho* (millowner) in colonial Brazil was to be respected and obeyed; it was a title that brought with it power and prestige. The Portuguese crown never created a Brazilian nobility of dukes and counts, but the title "senhor de engenho" often fulfilled the same function.

Given the nature of the economy, it is not surprising that the sugar planters came to exercise considerable political, social, and economic power. Their interests were favored by a royal policy which provided tax incentives and some protection from foreclosure on debts. Unlike Spanish America, where rural estates were not central to the international economy, Brazil depended overwhelmingly on agricultural export, and the senhores de engenho were continually favored.

It was not long before the senhores de engenho began to exhibit certain group characteristics and a distinctive life-style. First of all, the Brazilian planters were not an absentee class. The proximity of engenhos to the coastal towns and the long harvest season permitted and demanded their presence on the rural estates. Thus the planter families tended to live on the engenhos. The focus of life was the big house (*casa grande*), which was substantial in the sixteenth and seventeenth centuries but often not at all as magnificent as it was to become later on. Adjoining the planter's residence was usually a chapel, although most did not have resident chaplains. Gracious hospitality, rounds of visits, and conspicuous consumption became a way of life. "In Pernambuco one finds more vanity than in Lisbon," said Father Cardim. The engenhos he visited were so filled with food and luxury that the planters "appeared to be counts," which, of course, they were not. Often this style of life did not reflect the planters' real financial position, for one or two bad harvests could bring ruin. There were, in fact, a great many failures and a constant circulation of people into and out of the planter class, a fact often ignored because of the continued success of some families.

The planters set the tone of the society. For them and nearly everyone else the dominant social form continued to be the patriarchal family, a transplantation of the Iberian ideal. The engenho, or *fazenda* (like "hacienda" in Spanish, a term that was used for any large agricultural estate), provided the setting for this family-oriented social grouping so desired by the colonists. In Brazil, although the traditional distinctions between high- and lowborn were maintained, other criteria also emerged to mark status. Married men and heads of households held a privileged position and were often accorded rights of citizenship or local offices denied to others. This favoritism underlined the important role played by the family in the settlement of Brazil and its social formation. The "family," of course, included distant relatives, godchildren, and various dependents. Some slaves, especially house servants or children born in the big house, might also be included in the patriarchal grouping. Such arrangements did not mean that all were treated equally within the group or that class and color distinctions were ignored, but the extended family groupings did cut across class lines. The world of rural Brazil was dominated by these groups.

2.7 Latin America's First Revolution

In the late 1700s, Haiti had one of the most advanced systems of plantation agriculture in the world, although based on the intense exploitation of African slaves. Partly in response to the French Revolution of 1789,

Parry, J. H., Philip Sherlock, and Anthony Maingot. *A Short History of the West Indies,* 4th ed., 140–41. New York: St. Martin's Press, 1987.

planters in the colony of Saint-Domingue sought greater freedom from the mother country. They were also confronted by pressures on the island from the slaves for freedom. Although the Haitian Republic was not finally established until 1804, the critical event leading to the island's liberation from France was the uprising of 1791, described in the reading below.

In August 1791, in answer to signals conveyed by drumbeats or through nocturnal ritual gatherings, the slave population of the northern plain rose in revolt, systematically setting fire to cane fields and houses and murdering the white inhabitants. Within a few weeks the whole plain was a smoking ruin, given over to bands of rebels.

The northern rising was the first concerted slave revolt on a large scale in the history of the West Indies. It was a terrifying revelation of the explosive force of stifled savage hatred. Once it had begun, it clearly could not be suppressed by the few thousand white inhabitants and the handful of regular troops available, without help. The mulattoes feared the slaves as much as the whites did; but suspicion and prejudice amounting to hatred prevented any effective alliance. The almost incredible savagery with which the fighting was conducted on both sides was described by Bryan Edwards, who was in Cap Français at the time. Edwards estimated that in the first two months 2000 whites were killed, 180 sugar plantations and 900 coffee and indigo settlements were destroyed; and 10,000 slaves died, either fighting, or by famine, or at the executioner's hands. The total white population of the province cannot have been more than 10,000 as against at least twenty times that number of slaves. Cap Français and a string of fortified camps in the western mountains were soon the only places under white control in the north province. In the west there was as yet no slave revolt, but whites and mulattoes were at war with one another, and the mulattoes under their leader Rigaud were gaining the upper hand, except in Port-au-Prince, which was terrorized by a poor white mob under criminal leaders. In the south the white planters had armed their slaves—who had remained obedient—against the mulattoes. Everywhere, *grands blancs* and *petit blancs*, royalists and revolutionaries, mulattoes and blacks, *affranchis* and slaves, fought and plundered in shifting alliances and bloody confusion. The only hope of restoring order lay in the dispatch of troops from France. The Jacobin party in the National Assembly, however, resolutely opposed any move in support of slave-owning colonists and a royal governor; they found chaos in Saint-Domingue (with the consequent rise in the price of sugar and coffee) a useful stick to beat the government with; they made resounding speeches about the sufferings of the slaves and the oppressions practiced by the colonists, and effectually blocked all attempts to send troops to the colony. It was only in September 1792, after the Jacobins had gained control of the Assembly, that an army reached Saint-Domingue, and then it was a revolutionary army, under the orders of Jacobin "commissioners" sent out to enforce the rule of liberty, equality and fraternity. In this they were fanatically sincere; but the practical results of their efforts were immense bloodshed and complete disorganization. Their leader, Sonthonax, faced with royalist resistance, had no choice but to associate himself with the revolted slaves, who in June 1793, at his instigation, entered and sacked the town of Cap Français. In August he proclaimed a conditional emancipation. This decree, when subsequently confirmed by the republican government in France, had momentous consequences.

2.8 A Revolutionary's Look at Independent Spanish America

Simón Bolívar was born in Caracas, Venezuela, in 1783 into a Creole landowning family. Bolívar made his first trip to Europe in 1799 and while there was exposed to the ideas of the Enlightenment. He took an activist role in Venezuela's formal declaration of independence in 1811 and emerged as a major leader in the revolutionary effort during South America's long struggle for independence. To many, Bolívar was the "liberator" of the continent; to others he was the proverbial "man on horseback," a personalistic strong man not to be trusted. During a period of exile in the Caribbean, he wrote the following letter, which outlines his views on Spanish America and his hopes for its eventual unification.

More than anyone, I desire to see America fashioned into the greatest nation in the world, greatest not so much by virtue of her area and wealth as by her freedom and glory. Although I seek perfection for the government of my country, I cannot persuade myself that the New World can, at the moment, be organized as a great republic. Since it is impossible, I dare not desire it; yet much less do I desire to have all America a monarchy because this plan is not only impracticable but also impossible. Wrongs now existing could not be righted, and our emancipation would be fruitless. The American states need the care of paternal gov-

Bolívar, Simón. "Jamaica Letter." In *Selected Writings of Bolívar*, vol. 1, 1810–1822, 2d ed., edited by Harold Brieck, Jr. New York: Colonial Press, 1951.

ernments to heal the sores and wounds of despotism and war. The parent country, for example, might be Mexico, the only country fitted for the position by her intrinsic strength, and without such power there can be no parent country. Let us assume it were to be the Isthmus of Panamá, the most central point of this vast continent. Would not all parts continue in their lethargy and even in their present disorder? For a single government to infuse life into the New World; to put into use all the resources for public prosperity; to improve, educate, and perfect the New World, that government would have to possess the authority of a god, much less the knowledge and virtues of mankind.

The party spirit that today keeps our states in constant agitation would assume still greater proportions were a central power established, for that power—the only force capable of checking this agitation—would be elsewhere. Furthermore, the chief figures of the capitals would not tolerate the preponderance of leaders at the metropolis, for they would regard these leaders as so many tyrants. Their resentments would attain such heights that they would compare the latter to the hated Spaniards. Any such monarchy would be a misshapen colossus that would collapse of its own weight at the slightest disturbance. . . .

We know little about the opinions prevailing in Buenos Aires, Chile, and Perú. Judging by what seeps through and by conjecture, Buenos Aires will have a central government in which the military, as a result of its internal dissensions and external wars, will have the upper hand. Such a constitutional system will necessarily degenerate into an oligarchy or a monocracy, with a variety of restrictions the exact nature of which no one can now foresee. It would be unfortunate if this situation were to follow because the people there deserve a more glorious destiny.

The Kingdom of Chile is destined, by the nature of its location, by the simple and virtuous character of its people, and by the example of its neighbors the proud republicans of Arauco, to enjoy the blessings that flow from the just and gentle laws of a republic. If any American republic is to have a long life, I am inclined to believe it will be Chile. There the spirit of liberty has never been extinguished; the vices of Europe and Asia arrived too late or not at all to corrupt the customs of that distant corner of the world. Its area is limited; and, as it is remote from other peoples, it will always remain free from contamination. Chile will not alter her laws, ways, and practices. She will preserve her uniform political and religious views. In a word, it is possible for Chile to be free.

Perú, on the contrary, contains two factors that clash with every just liberal principle: gold and slaves. The former corrupts everything; the latter are themselves corrupt. The soul of a serf can seldom really appreciate true freedom. Either he loses his head in uprisings or his self-respect is in chains. Although these remarks would be applicable to all America, I believe that they apply with greater justice to Lima, for the reasons I have given and because of the coöperation she has rendered her masters against her own brothers, those illustrious sons of Quito, Chile, and Buenos Aires. It is plain that he who aspires to obtain liberty will at least attempt to secure it. I imagine that in Lima the rich will not tolerate democracy, nor will the freed slaves and *pardos* accept aristocracy. The former will prefer the tyranny of a single man, to avoid the tumult of rebellion and to provide, at least, a peaceful system. If Perú intends to recover her independence, she has much to do.

From the foregoing, we can draw these conclusions: The American provinces are fighting for their freedom, and they will ultimately succeed. Some provinces as a matter of course will form federal and some central republics; the larger areas will inevitably establish monarchies, some of which will fare so badly that they will disintegrate in either present or future revolutions. To consolidate a great monarchy will be no easy task, but it will be utterly impossible to consolidate a great republic.

It is a grandiose idea to think of consolidating the New World into a single nation, united by pacts into a single bond. It is reasoned that, as these parts have a common origin, language, customs, and religion, they ought to have a single government to permit the newly formed states to unite in a confederation. But this is not possible. Actually, America is separated by climatic differences, geographic diversity, conflicting interests, and dissimilar characteristics. How beautiful it would be if the Isthmus of Panamá could be for us what the Isthmus of Corinth was for the Greeks! Would to God that some day we may have the good fortune to convene there an august assembly of representatives of republics, kingdoms, and empires to deliberate upon the high interests of peace and war with the nations of the other three-quarters of the globe. This type of organization may come to pass in some happier period of our regeneration. But any other plan, such as that of Abbé St. Pierre, who in laudable delirium conceived the idea of assembling a European congress to decide the fate of those nations, would be meaningless.

Among the popular and representative systems, I do not favor the federal system. It is over-perfect, and it demands political virtues and talents far superior to our own. For the same reason I reject a monarchy that is part aristocracy and part democracy, although with such a government England has achieved much fortune and splendor. Since it is not possible for us to select the most perfect and complete form of government, let us avoid falling into demagogic anarchy or monocratic tyranny. These opposite extremes would only wreck us on similar reefs of misfortune and dishonor; hence, we must seek a mean between them. I say: Do not adopt the best system of government, but the one that is most likely to succeed.

By the nature of their geographic location, wealth, population and character, I expect that the Mexicans, at the outset, intend to establish a representative republic in which the executive will have great powers. These will be concentrated in one person, who, if he discharges his duties with wisdom and justice, should almost certainly maintain his authority for life. If through incompetence or violence he should excite a popular revolt and should it be successful, this same executive power would then, perhaps, be distributed among the members of an assembly. If the dominant party is military or aristocratic, it will probably demand a monarchy that would be limited and constitutional at the outset, and would later inevitably degenerate into an absolute monarchy; for it must be admitted that there is nothing more difficult in the political world than the maintenance of a limited monarchy. Moreover, it must also be agreed that only a people as patriotic as the English are capable of controlling the authority of a king and of sustaining the spirit of liberty under the rule of sceptre and crown.

The states of the Isthmus of Panamá, as far as Guatemala, will perhaps form a confederation. Because of their magnificent position between two mighty oceans, they may in time become the emporium of the world. Their canals will shorten distances throughout the world, strengthen commercial ties between Europe, America, and Asia, and bring to that happy area tribute from the four quarters of the globe. There some day, perhaps, the capital of the world may be located—reminiscent of the Emperor Constantine's claim that Byzantium was the capital of the ancient world.

New Granada will unite with Venezuela, if they can agree to the establishment of a central republic. Their capital may be Maracaibo or a new city to be named Las Casas (in honor of that humane hero) to be built on the borders of the two countries, in the excellent port area of Bahia-Honda. This location, though little known, is the most advantageous in all respects. It is readily accessible, and its situation is so strategic that it can be made impregnable. It has a fine, healthful climate, a soil as suitable for agriculture as for cattle raising, and a superabundance of good timber. The Indians living there can be civilized, and our territorial possessions could be increased with the acquisition of the Goajira Peninsula. This nation should be called Colombia as a just and grateful tribute to the discoverer of our hemisphere. Its government might follow the English pattern, except that in place of a king there will be an executive who will be elected, at most, for life, but his office will never be hereditary, if a republic is desired. There will be a hereditary legislative chamber or senate. This body can interpose itself between the violent demands of the people and the great powers of the government during periods of political unrest. The second representative body will be a legislature with restrictions no greater than those of the lower house in England. The Constitution will draw on all systems of government, but I do not want it to partake of all their vices. As Colombia is my country, I have an indisputable right to desire for her that form of government which, in my opinion, is best. It is very possible that New Granada may not care to recognize a central government, because she is greatly addicted to federalism; in such event, she will form a separate state which, if it endures, may prosper, because of its great and varied resources.

2.9 A Caudillo in Action

From 1820 until midcentury, the new Latin American states were wracked with political difficulties. Among the most serious was the emergence of strong-man rule—the dominance of political life by a caudillo, who often took power through force and charisma and attempted to dominate societal institutions. This problem was acute in Argentina, as educator and writer Domingo Fausto Sarmiento, in exile in Chile, makes clear in his portrait of the regional strong man Facundo Quiroga, of La Rioja province. Sarmiento later became president of Argentina, serving from 1868 to 1874.

Facundo, upon his triumphant entry into La Rioja, stopped the ringing of the bells, and after sending a message of condolence to the widow of the slain General, directed his ashes to be honored with a stately funeral. He appointed for governor one Blanco, a Spaniard of low rank, and with him began the new order of affairs which was to realize the best ideal of government as conceived by Facundo Quiroga; for, in his long career among the various cities which he conquered, he never took upon himself the charge of organizing governments; he always left that task to others.

The moment of the grasp of power over the destinies of a commonwealth by a vigorous hand is ever an important one and deserves attention. Old institutions are strengthened, or give place to others, newer and more productive of good results, or better adapted to prevailing ideas. From such a focus often diverge the threads which, as time weaves them together, change the web of history.

It is otherwise when the prevailing force is one foreign to civilization—when an Attila obtains possession of Rome or a Tamerlane traverses the plains of Asia; old forms remain, but the hand of philosophy

Sarmiento, Domingo F. "Facundo in Power." In *The Borzoi Reader in Latin American History,* vol. 2, edited by Helen Delpar, 38–42. New York: Knopf, 1972.

would afterwards vainly remove them with the view of finding beneath them plants which had gained vigor from the human blood given them for nourishment. Facundo, a man imbued with the genius of barbarism, gets control of his country; the traditions of government disappear, established forms deteriorate, the law is a plaything in vile hands; and nothing is maintained, nothing established, amid the destruction thus accomplished by the trampling feet of horses. Freedom from restraint, occupation, and care, is the supreme good of the gaucho. If La Rioja had contained statues, as it contained doctors, they would have had horses tied to them, but they would have served no other purpose.

Facundo wanted to have means at his command, and, as he was incapable of creating a revenue system, he resorted to the ordinary proceeding of dull or weak governments; but in this case the monopoly bears the stamp of South American pastoral life, spoliation, and violence. The tithes of La Rioja were at this time farmed out at ten thousand piastres a year; this was the average rate. Facundo made his appearance at the board, and his presence overawed the shepherds. "I offer two thousand piastres a year," said he, "and one more than the best bid." The committee repeated the proposal three times; no one made a bid; all present left, one by one, reading in Quiroga's sinister glance that it was the last one he would allow. The next year he contented himself with sending to the board the following note:—

"I give two thousand dollars and one more than the best bid."
"Facundo Quiroga"

The third year the ceremony of adjudication was omitted, and in 1831, Quiroga again sent to Rioja the sum of two thousand dollars, his estimates for the tithes. . . .

It was the immemorial custom in La Rioja that the *estrays,* or the animals that were not marked at a certain age, should become the lawful property of the treasury, which sent its agents to collect these gleanings, and derived no contemptible revenue from them, but the annoyance to the proprietors was intolerable. Facundo demanded the adjudication to himself of these animals, to meet the expenses he had incurred for the invasion of the city; expenses which were reducible to the summons of irregular forces, who assembled, mounted on horses of their own, and lived constantly on what came their way. Already the proprietor of herds which brought him six thousand bullocks a year, he sent his agents to supply the city markets, and woe to any competitor who should appear! This business of supplying meat for the markets was one he carried on wherever he ruled, in San Juan, Mendoza, or Tucumán; and he was always careful to secure the monopoly of it by proclamation or simple notification. It is with shame and disgust that I mention these disgraceful transactions, but the truth must be told.

The general's first order, after a bloody battle which had laid a city open to him, was that no one should supply the markets with meat! In

Tucumán he learned that a resident of the place was killing cattle in his house, in spite of this order. The general of the army of the Andes, the conqueror of the Citadel, thought the investigation of so dreadful a crime should be entrusted only to himself. He went in person, and knocked lustily at the door of the house, which refused to yield, and which the inmates, taken by surprise, did not open. A kick from the illustrious general broke it in, and exposed to his view a dead ox, whose hide was in the process of removal by the master of the house, who also fell dead in his turn at the terrible sight of the offended general.

I do not intentionally dwell upon these things. How many I omit! How many misdeeds I pass over in silence which are fully proved and known to all! But I am writing a history of government by barbarians, and I am forced to state its methods.

Mehmet Ali, who became master of Egypt by means identical with those of Facundo, delivers himself up to a rapacity unexampled even in Turkey; he establishes monopolies in every occupation and turns them to his own profit; but Mehmet Ali, though he springs from a barbarous nation, rises above his condition so far as to wish to acquire European civilization for himself and for the people he oppresses. Facundo, on the contrary, not only rejects all recognized civilization, but destroys and disorganizes. Facundo, who does not govern, because any government implies labour for others' good, gives himself up to the instincts of an immoderate and unscrupulous avarice. Selfishness is the foundation of almost all the great characters of history; selfishness is the chief spring of all great deeds. Quiroga had this political gift in an eminent degree and made everything around him contribute to his advantage; wealth, power, authority, all centered in him; whatever he could not acquire—polish, learning, true respectability,—he hated and persecuted in all those who possessed them.

His hostility to the respectable classes and to the refinement of the cities was every day more perceptible, and the governor of La Rioja, whom he himself appointed, finally was forced, by daily annoyances to resign his place. One day, Quiroga, feeling inclined to pleasantry, was amusing himself with a young man as a cat sports with a frightened mouse; he liked to play at killing; the terror of the victim was so ludicrous, that the executioner was highly diverted, and laughed immoderately, contrary to his habit. He must have sympathy in his mirth, and he at once ordered the *general** to be beat throughout the city of Rioja, which called out the citizens under arms. Facundo, who had given the summons for diversion's sake, drew up the inhabitants in the principal square at eleven o'clock at night, dismissed the populace and retained only the well-to-do householders and the young men who still had some appearance of culture. All night he kept them marching and countermarching, halting, forming line, marching by front or by flank. It was

*A certain call to arms.—Trans.

like a drill-sergeant teaching recruits, and the sergeant's stick travelled over the heads of the stupid, and the chests of those who were out of line; "What would you have? this is the way to teach!" Morning came, and the pallor, weariness and exhaustion of the recruits showed what a night they had passed. Their instructor finally sent them to rest, and extended his generosity to the purchase and distribution of pastry, each recipient made in haste to eat his share, for that was part of the sport.

Lessons of such a kind are not lost upon cities, and the skillful politician who has raised similar proceedings to a system in Buenos Ayres, has refined upon them and made them wonderfully effective. For example: during the periods between 1835 and 1840 almost the whole population of Buenos Ayres has passed through the prisons. Sometimes a hundred and fifty citizens would be imprisoned for two or three months, to be replaced by two hundred who would be kept, perhaps half the year. Wherefore? What had they done? What had they said? Idiots! Do you not see that this is good discipline for the city? Do you not remember the saying of Rosas to Quiroga, that no republic could be established because the people were not prepared for it! This is his way of teaching the city how to obey; he will finish his work, and in 1844, he will be able to show the world a people with but one thought, one opinion, one voice, and that a boundless enthusiasm for the person and will of Rosas! Then, indeed, they will be ready for a republic!

3

The Garden of Forking Paths: Dilemmas of National Development

Juan Domingo Perón promoted Argentina's industrialization and, with the help of his wife, Evita, mobilized urban workers into a powerful social and political force. AP/Wide World Photos

Latin America emerged from the political and economic instability of the early postindependence years searching for a new identity in the evolving international capitalist economy. By the latter part of the nineteenth century, Europe's booming industrialization was felt throughout the region, and this played a central role in molding the region's search for economic growth and social development.

Latin America's Outward-Oriented Strategy

During the late nineteenth century, Latin America began large-scale exports of mining and agricultural products to Europe in exchange for manufactured goods, capital, and technology. This outward-oriented economic strategy was widely supported throughout Latin America and brought significant economic transformation.

Countries in the region were able to capitalize on the growing demand in Western Europe for foodstuffs and other products. Argentina emerged as a leading producer of wool, wheat, and beef. Chile turned to mining nitrates and copper. Peru found keen interest in overseas markets in its rich deposits of fertilizer guano, as is illustrated in reading 3.1. Central America turned to coffee and then bananas as major export products. Cuban sugar dominated overseas markets.

The new flurry of commercial activity in Latin America and the Caribbean was accompanied by significant foreign investment in railroads, public utilities, and mining. Lacking capital to finance new projects, Latin American governments welcomed foreign investment flowing into the region from British, French, German, and North American entrepreneurs (see reading 3.2). In particular, the British invested in railroads, docks, packing houses, and public utilities—key sectors in the region's economy. A major U.S. investment in the Panama-based transit canal in the early 1900s symbolized a new era of interest in the region on the part of the United States.

During the early twentieth century, exports enabled Argentina to emerge as one of the world's wealthiest countries. Buenos Aires, the capital, became a major center of art and culture. The tango, popularized internationally during the 1920s, came to symbolize

Argentina's buoyant success. Reading 3.3 describes the tango's humble beginnings and its wide-ranging impact.

But problems associated with the export strategy soon surfaced. The wealth that exports generated was not invested in the creation of an industrial base. Leaders throughout the region began to realize they were highly dependent on foreign capital and external market demand for their national well-being. The export strategy further reinforced the power of land-holding elites and impaired income and wealth distribution. But it was the Great Depression of 1929, and the devastating consequences for the region's economy caused by the precipitous drop in demand and prices for export products, that brought home to Latin America the vulnerabilities of the export economy model.

As a result, the region's economists and leaders began to consider a new approach to economic growth: rapid industrialization was sponsored so that domestic consumption could take the place of exports as the engine of economic progress. The strategy eventually became known as "import substitution industrialization," because industries focused on the production of manufactured goods for the domestic market that previously had been imported.

New social and political forces arose with industrialization. A national entrepreneurial class and urban working class developed. Through labor union advocacy and state paternalism, many Latin American workers gained access for the first time to social welfare measures, such as workman's compensation and social security benefits.

The Emergence of Populism

These economic transformations were accompanied by the development of populism. State-promoted economic growth was achieved through the cooperation of nationalistic entrepreneurs and the urban working class. Older, more traditional forces were swept aside as the populist coalition assumed national leadership.

A group of forceful populist leaders emerged who used a variety of political and economic measures to achieve their nationalistic objectives. In Brazil, Getulio Vargas in 1931 led a triumphal march on Rio de Janeiro to take power, following contested presidential elections. During his tenure he took important initiatives to invigorate the government, establishing the "New State" (see reading 3.4). He ruled the country until 1945, when he stepped aside so democratic elections could proceed.

In Mexico, President Lázaro Cárdenas deepened his popularity with the working class by expropriating foreign oil companies during the 1930s, as described in reading 3.5. During the same period, Víctor Raúl Haya de la Torre used a populist theme to organize a new political party in Peru (see reading 3.6).

In the early 1940s, Juan Domingo Perón used populist appeals to mobilize the Argentine working class to support his new economic plans. His wife, Evita, played a major role in gaining working-class support for her husband and his program, as described in reading 3.7.

Under Perón, the government intensified its intervention in the nation's economic affairs and in the regulation of labor-management conflict. It took over exports and transferred earnings from the agricultural to the manufacturing sector. With the exception of wealthy landowners, who were excluded from the benefits of Perón's urban-oriented policies, all Argentina progressed at first. But soon the national treasury was exhausted because of Perón's efforts to expand social welfare and to nationalize many of the country's productive assets, including the railroad system, while maintaining a high level of military expenditures. When demand fell for Argentina's major export, beef, and world market prices fell, the country's economy went into a tailspin. With Evita's death in 1952, Perón lost a key asset, and when he tried to intervene in the military's internal affairs, the armed forces created an alliance with the rural oligarchs. A military coup in 1955 ended Perón's rule, and he fled the country.

Nationalism and Military Rule

Throughout the 1950s, import substitution industrialization continued apace, though it encountered increasing difficulties. Industrialization and modernization brought expanding expectations. Leaders throughout the region found it difficult to control political movements that articulated growing popular demands, particularly in times of economic difficulty. Military governments intervened to contain what they saw as a threat to order and stability from popular movements that were, in their view, under the control of leftist sympathizers, especially following the 1959 Cuban revolution.

In the aftermath of Perón's rule, Argentina alternated between civilian and military governments, each searching for an appropriate economic model to rekindle Argentina's economy and bring about national consensus. In 1973 Argentina turned once again to Perón, whose party had been outlawed for two decades. He was the only unifying force remaining and was elected with more than 60 percent of the vote. But his presidency, and later his death, pulled the country into deeper chaos. In 1976 the military took over the government again.

Tired of political violence, instability, and corruption, many Argentines pinned their hopes on the military's promises to bring about economic and political order. Jorge Luis Borges, Argentina's best-known writer, commented, "At last we have a government of gentlemen." Instead, the military further eroded national consensus through a campaign of repression, torture, disappearances, and widespread corruption. At least 10,000 Argentines—the *desaparecidos*—were taken from their homes and never seen or heard from again. And under military rule the Argentine economy worsened.

By 1980 political parties and Argentina's powerful labor unions began to call on the military to resign. The military, trying to regain popular support and institutional prestige by appealing to Argentine nationalism, took steps to assert Argentina's 150-year-old claim to sovereignty over the Malvinas/Falkland Islands from Great Britain, which still maintained control over the isolated and lightly populated islands 600 miles off the south Argentine coast. In April 1982 Argentine marines invaded the islands, rapidly subduing the small British garrison stationed at Port Stanley, the capital.

Most Argentines supported the military. The issue proved so powerful that even opponents of the discredited regime backed the military invasion (see reading 3.8). The British responded by sending their forces to the South Atlantic. War ensued. Superior organization, military intelligence, and logistics, including support from the United States, brought a quick and decisive British victory.

The Argentine military not only lost the war but further discredited itself. Civilian cries for a return to democracy could not be ignored. Shortly thereafter, the military was replaced by a democratically elected government.

3.1 Peru in the Guano Age

As the European economy diversified in the nineteenth century, Latin American products found new overseas market possibilities. Guano, deposits of manure left by birds attracted to Peru's offshore islands, was used by the pre-Inca and Inca civilizations as fertilizer for agricultural production. Between the 1840s and the late 1880s, guano was in high demand as a source of fertilizer for Western European and North American agriculture. However, as this article illustrates, the benefits of the guano "boom" were unevenly distributed throughout Peruvian society.

Peru's guano age had lasted forty years, from the first export contract to Chilean occupation of the islands in the War of the Pacific. During this period more than 10,800,000 tons of guano were exported, bringing over $600,000,000 on the retail market. Who received this money? What did they do with it and what effect did it have upon the Peruvian economy?

Because neither labor, nor capital, nor entrepreneurship was present in 1840 Peru in quantities sufficient to operate the guano industry, the industry was in large part operated by factors of production that came in from abroad. Part of the guano-trade proceeds went abroad to pay for these factors. The Chinese coolies [imported as laborers] probably did not remit any significant quantity of earnings to China but the $400 a head paid for the coolies at Callao dockside was distributed among ship captains and others engaged in the coolie trade between Macao and Callao. Foreign entrepreneurs and their capital were of great importance in the guano trade, as consignment contractors holding virtually all the exclusive country sales contracts before Peruvians were able to amass enough capital to take on contracts themselves in the 1850's and 1960's, and quite often as partners to Peruvians later on. The foreign consignment contractors' shares of guano-trade profit were the foundation of many a fortune in Europe, and particularly in Great Britain.

The desire of some Peruvians to share in this guano income going to foreign contractors led the Peruvian congress to grant preference to Peruvian contractors in 1849. Because capital and entrepreneurship were rather scarce in Peru in the 1850s—and because the Peruvian consignment contractors were able to perpetuate their hold on the guano trade

Levin, Jonathan V. "Peru in the Guano Age." In *The Borzoi Reader in Latin American History*, vol. 2: Nineteenth and Twentieth Centuries, edited by Helen Delpar, 45–52. New York: Knopf, 1972.

through a system which kept the government constantly in their debt and dependent upon their fresh credits—the guano contracts were in the hands of a relatively small group of Peruvians and an important share of the guano-contract profits, particularly in the late 1850's and 1860's, went to them.

The most important share of the guano-trade receipts—perhaps as much as half of the total—went to the government, which at the first sign of the profits ahead had sought to reserve the greatest possible portion for itself. A part of the guano proceeds the government lost to the contractors because of its inability to devise a guano sales system which would induce the contractors to work for the maximization of the government's guano earnings. Yet the government's guano income was vast and through its disbursement the government became the most important generator of income in the exchange sector of the Peruvian economy.

As might be expected, the government's disbursement of its guano income followed the political situation of the time. Some of the guano receipts were used to promote specific political objectives—to redeem the slaves, make the church more dependent on the state, wage several small wars, and pay off the Independence War debt to the foreign bondholders. Another portion of the guano revenues was used to wipe out the tax system and thus increase by the amount of the abolished taxes the retained income of most of the population. The greater part of its guano income before 1868, however, the government devoted to promoting the narrower interests of those in control. Political power in guano-age Peru rested not on a broad base of popular support, but on a small, mostly European-descended group, centered in Lima. Accordingly, it was to the benefit of this small group, rather than to the promotion of nation-wide welfare, that the government's guano-income expenditures before 1868 were dedicated. Through the consolidation operation,[1] corruption, and the maintenance of a huge military, civil and pensioned bureaucracy, the government guano funds were disbursed to the politically significant segment of the populace.

With seemingly unlimited guano funds pouring into the government's coffers, the bureaucratic traditions of Lima's Spanish colonial days came into full flower, and an "empleomania" [i.e., excessive hiring of employees] seemed to grip the city. The swollen army, bureaucracy and pension lists created a class whose continued financial support was of increasing importance for both the political stability of the government and the economic stability of the small exchange economy. Politically, the life of the government rested to a great extent on the continued welfare of this military and civilian group, as the Roman emperor's had rested on the praetorian guards. Economically, though Peruvian

---

[1] A consolidation of the internal debt during the administration of José Rufino Echenique (1851–1854), which permitted speculators to reap large profits.

guano contractors enjoyed an income from guano exports, and sugar exports had also risen to some significance, the government had become the most important generator of income in Peru's exchange economy. Stability of government expenditures, therefore, was of vital concern both to those holding political power and to the entire exchange economy.

This stability of government expenditures depended, of course, upon the maintenance of stability in the government's guano income. Yet, oddly enough, in all of the vast literature of controversy and debate over the merits of various guano-export systems, the problem of avoiding fluctuations in the government's guano proceeds found no place. This was not due to any absence of fluctuations in guano exports; a graph of annual guano export tonnage shows marked irregularity. The reason for this lack of a fluctuation problem lies rather in the fact that the government's guano receipts in any one year bore no relation to that year's guano exports or sales. By obtaining almost all of its guano revenues in loans and advances against future sales the government had divorced its guano income completely from the current level of sales. Though this stabilization through credit added considerably to the interest charges the government paid, it insulated the government effectively from any fluctuations in guano income so long as the government could borrow.

These then were the people who—before the government embarked on its railroad-building program in 1868[2]—shared the guano-export proceeds: the foreign contractors, the Peruvian contractors who succeeded many of them, the coolie traders supplying the laborers from China to Callao, the Chinese coolies on the islands and—through the government's treasury—the influential Peruvians relieved of their tax burden, the soldiers, the bureaucrats, and the pensioners. Among them in unequal portions the guano proceeds were divided.

How these guano-income receivers spent their money, and where, determined to a large extent what effect the guano trade was to have on the economic development of Peru.

---

[2] More than 750 miles of railroads were built with borrowed foreign funds and eventually transferred to the foreign bondholder's ownership when guano revenues ceased to cover the loan charges.

3.2 The Soto Keith Contract on Foreign Investment

A major impediment to the development of Latin America's export economy was the absence of capital. This was particularly felt in such areas as the construction of internal transportation systems. Although coffee could be produced in abundance in Costa Rica's central plateau, a poor road system prevented easy and efficient links to Europe. To promote greater access to the market, the Costa Rican government entered into a series of financial obligations in the late 1800s with London banks, which ended in disaster because the borrowed funds were not productively used. To extract itself from the financial bind, the Costa Rican government granted a U.S. citizen, Minor Cooper Keith, the authority to renegotiate the debts in exchange for a promise to extend the railroad into the country's coffee-growing region. The following excerpt is from Keith's contract with the Costa Rican government. In a fashion typical of many Latin American governments during the time, foreign investors were also given generous grants of land and natural resources.

XI

. . . The company will build a railroad that, beginning near the Reventazón River on the Atlantic railroad line, will cross the river's valley, and will end in the city of Cartago. The gradients of this railroad will not exceed 3 percent on the tangents, nor will the curves exceed twenty degrees, and the materials to be used will be as good as the best ones used in the construction of the railroad between Limón and the town of Carrillo (formerly called Río Sucio). . . .

XIX

. . . The Executive power is authorized to grant special faculties and powers to Mr. Keith, within the limits of the present agreement, for the settlement of the Republic's debt in Europe, to negotiate new con-

Facio, Rodrigo. "The Soto Keith Contract on Foreign Debt and the Railroad." In *The Costa Rica Reader,* edited by Marc Edelman and Joanne Kenen, translated by Leda Fernandez de Facio, 59–62. New York: Grove Weidenfeld, 1989.

ditions with holders of presently existing bonds, as well as for the conversion of such bonds and the issuance of new bonds to be guaranteed by revenues generated by the National Customs. . . . And, considering that the aforementioned Mr. Keith has agreed to return to Europe with these objectives, we agree for the present that the period established for beginning negotiations for the construction of the railroad will start from the date of the final agreement and conversion of the debt. That is to say, the construction will start six months after the debt's conversion, and will be concluded in a period of three years. If at the end of the three-year period, beginning on the date of approval of the present contract, the company has not obtained a settlement of the debt and capital for the construction of the railroad, this contract will be null and void without requiring anything of the parties.

To further guarantee that the railroad will be completed, it is agreed that if it is not finished within three years, the concessionary or the company created for this purpose will be subject to penalties mentioned in . . . this contract [a later clause specifies fines running from 5,000 to 20,000 pesos per month]. It is understood that the government in no instance will contribute to expenses incurred by Mr. Minor Cooper Keith, whatever they may be, because they will be paid out of his own resources. . . .

XXI

The government of Costa Rica cedes to the company, in full possession for ninety-nine years, the railroads built between Limón and Carrillo, between Cartago and Alajuela, and the one to be built between Cartago and the existing Reventazón bridge on the Atlantic railroad line. This includes telegraph lines, buildings and their land, as well as all the other rights and objects considered in the service of the railroad, or those built in the future for this purpose. From the moment the company begins work on the section it is required to build, the constructed lines and their facilities will be handed over to it. The ninety-nine years referred to in this clause will take effect when the railroad between Reventazón and Cartago is completed and put in service.

XXII

The government concedes to the company 800,000 acres of uncultivated state lands, along the railroad or at any other place in the national territory of the company's choice, including all natural resources within, in addition to the land necessary for the construction of the railroad and required buildings, as well as all kinds of materials needed for the construction work found inside the public lands all through the extension of the line, and two lots of the public land that was measured today in the Limón harbor, to build docks, warehouses, and stations, all without any cost. The surveys and all the preliminary work for the division and distribution of the 800,000 acres of land will be the company's responsibility, since the government's only responsibility is to extend free property titles when needed. The government will not be able to establish taxes on that land for twenty years from the beginning of the period of the present concession, it being understood that, after the end of the twenty years, lands that had not been cultivated or otherwise utilized will revert to the government's possession without compensation of any kind. . . .

3.3 Birth of the Tango

Europe's economic boom in the early 1900s generated an economic boom in some Latin American countries. Argentina was a major beneficiary of the robust economic growth, and became a flourishing and fashionable cultural center. The capital, Buenos Aires, came to be known as the "Paris of the South." In the midst of the country's economic expansion, Carlos Gardel, a popular composer, captured the exuberance of the period with his rendition of the tango, and he helped transform it into a highly popular song among Argentines and throughout the world. The reading below explains how the tango moved from the country's slums to the parlors of its most distinguished citizens.

The Argentine tango was born roughly a decade before Carlos Gardel. It has sometimes been called the second most famous dance in history, its only superior in world renown being the waltz. Like the waltz, the tango is associated above all with a particular city. Unlike the waltz, the tango actually originated in the city concerned, for, even though the waltz began its career of international fame in Vienna, it did not

Collier, Simon. *The Life, Music, and Times of Carlos Gardel*, 55–59. Pittsburgh: University of Pittsburgh Press, 1986.

originally spring from within the city itself. The tango's connection with
Buenos Aires, by contrast, started at birth.

Around its precise origins there nevertheless hangs a thick cloud of
uncertainty. Nobody can pinpoint an exact time or place where the first
tango was danced; an endless and somewhat profitless debate still rages
about the sources from which it came. All that can be said with reasonable confidence is that the tango first appeared in the *arrabales* [slums]
of Buenos Aires some time around the year 1880. It owed much to two
immediate ancestors: first, the native Argentine dance form called the
milonga, and second, the internationally well-known Spanish-Cuban *habanera,* whose lineage has sometimes been traced back through the
Spanish *contradanza* and the French *contredanse* to the English country-
dance of the seventeenth century [from which the French *contredanse*
took its name]. A less easily traceable but nonetheless vital influence
was the tradition of music and dance common in the inner-city districts
where the Buenos Aires black and mulatto communities lived.

All of these things went into the making of the tango: a dance in
2/4 time, played roughly half as fast again as the *habanera.* It was a
popular improvisation, a spontaneous fusion of raw elements into a
genuinely new creation. As a dance, it had a strongly sensual and even
lascivious figure, which became more formalized later on, when the
tango moved into polite society.

It certainly did not start there. Efforts to locate its precise birthplace
are doomed to failure. A strong tradition (but really no more than that)
associates its origins with the district then known as Corrales Viejos
(roughly the area of the modern barrio of Parque Patricios), in those
days an *arrabal* on the southern fringe of the city where until 1903 the
municipal slaughterhouse was sited. It is more probable that the tango
grew up across several such *arrabales,* in makeshift dance halls (some with
earth floors) and brothels. Its social background was poor, marginal, and
even semicriminal. For this reason it was long repudiated by Argentine
high society, although the pleasure-seeking young bloods of the upper
class played their part in spreading its influence through the city.

By the turn of the century the tango's musical tradition was beginning to develop fast. The bands of the period were still rather primitive
and unpolished. Trios and quartets predominated, the standard instruments being the guitar, the flute, the violin, the piano (sometimes), and
the bandoneon: this relative of the accordion was invented in Germany
in the mid-1830s and appeared in Argentina in the third quarter of
the nineteenth century. Whatever the reason (and despite the fact that
all bandoneons were made in Germany) it steadily became the quintes-
sential tango instrument. By the mid-1900s, tango bands were playing
in the cafés of La Boca, where people listened, rather than danced, to
the music; by now the first stars of the tradition were putting in their
appearance. Only a few years later, the dance and its music finally invaded the Center, where it entrenched itself in cafés and dance halls,

not least those along Calle Corrientes—a street of almost legendary significance for the tango tradition. . . . Cabarets such as the Armenonville and the Palais de Glace also became redoubts of the new dance.

By now the tango had spread its influence far from Buenos Aires and Montevideo (where it also took root at a very early date). In the early 1910s it was mounting its triumphant assault on the Old World. "Tangomania," an extraordinary social craze, reached its height in Europe just before World War I. Paris was rechristened Tangoville by the popular French caricaturist Sem. "Tango teas" (not to mention "tango vermouths" and "tango dinners") became the universal rage. "The year 1913," wrote an Englishwoman of the time, "might be called 'The Tango Year,' for the dance has provoked more conversation . . . than anything else." Bishops, cardinals, even Pope Pius X himself pronounced against the dance as lubricious and immoral; the emperors of Austria-Hungary and Germany prohibited their soldiers to dance it when in uniform. Like the waltz and the polka before it, and the Charleston a few years later, the tango triumphed over all such obstacles.

Fashionable society in Argentina had long regarded Europe as the source of all taste, intellect, and wisdom. Its original aversion to the tango—"that reptile from the brothel" as the writer Leopoldo Lugones put it—was bound to be tempered once high-society Europe had elevated the dance to the status of high fashion. "Will Paris, which imposes everything, end by winning acceptance for the Argentine tango in our best society?" Such was the question asked by a Buenos Aires magazine in 1911. In fact, the dance never lacked powerful local allies. The noted sportsman and socialite Baron Antonio Demarchi promoted it in various well-publicized ways. And in September 1913 a tango festival held at the Palace theater in Calle Corrientes . . . was presided over by a committee of ladies whose oligarchic credentials were impeccable. Snobbish disapproval may have lingered on for a while in certain circles, but the tango's triumph in its own homeland, so strangely delayed by stuffy prejudice, was now assured.

3.4 Getulio Vargas and the "New State"

As the economic depression of the 1930s closed Latin America's traditional export markets in Europe, a new generation of Latin American leaders sought to transform their economies and societies through nationalistic measures intended to stimulate domestic industrial production and to promote new urban entrepreneurial and worker interests. Getulio Vargas dominated Brazilian politics with his populist style from 1930 to 1945. Intent on unifying the country around a strong executive branch that would have political supremacy, Vargas attempted to transcend the traditional pattern of Brazilian politics, which was dominated by regional interests. The reading below outlines Vargas's political vision and refers to the Brazilian Constitution of 1937, issued by Vargas as the Statute of November 10. On that date, Vargas closed the country's congress, announced a new constitution, canceled presidential elections, and assumed dictatorial powers. His Estado Novo, *which formally emulated Portugal's fascist state of the same name, was basically a personalist instrument of* Getulismo, *as Vargas's brand of populism was known in Brazil.*

The new government is above all else the adaptation of the political system to the realities of Brazil. It integrates all the forces of the collective into a framework of order, social cohesion, and governmental authority. It assures the historical fundamentals of the nation, its essential elements for existence, and its claims to progress menaced, compromised, and sacrificed by the old order which was not only incapable of defending them but permitted and even stimulated factious disturbances, armed regionalism irreconcilable with national unity, and the formation of parties of an aggressive character, refractory by nature to the democratic processes, of the kind that aimed at territorial dismemberment and the subversion of society. . . .

Conserving the traditional lines of organic federation and what existed substantially in that system, such as the autonomy of the states, the democratic form, and the representative process; the Statute of November 10 created, nonetheless, a new legal structure. Among the profound changes brought about by the new regime are: the limitation of direct, universal suffrage, applicable only to specific questions of perti-

Vargas, Getulio. "Vargas and the Estado Novo." In *The Quest for Change in Latin America: Sources for a Twentieth-Century Analysis,* edited by W. Raymond Duncan and James Nelson Goodsell, 148–50. New York: Oxford University Press, 1970.

nence to all citizens thus making representation more valid; the municipality as the nuclear base of the political system; the substitution of the principle of the independence of powers by the supremacy of the Executive; the strengthening of the power of the Union; the effective and efficient participation of the economy, through its own organizations, in the constructive and integrating work of the government.

The new system consecrates a government of authority by instituting as law the legislative decree, by giving to the President of the Republic powers to expedite law decrees when Congress is not in session, by attributing to him the prerogative of dissolving it in special cases, and by taking from the Judiciary the privilege of supreme interpretation of the constitutionality or unconstitutionality of the laws which involve public interests of great importance. These new powers, placed under the guard of the government, always overcome private interests.

Profoundly nationalistic, the regime insures and consolidates national unity and formally restricts the autonomy of the states by suppressing regional symbols, extending interventions, establishing the supremacy of federal over local laws in the case of concurrent legislation by attributing to the central government the power to requisition the state militias at any time, etc.

The professions are represented in their own, independent chamber with consultative functions in all the projects concerning the national economy, and eventually it will have legislative functions. . . .

The movement of November 10th was, without doubt, brought about by the national will. We had need of order and security in order to carry on; conspiring against that was the critical state of political decomposition to which we had arrived. Slowly our public life had been transformed into an arena of sterile struggles where plots, clashing interests of the oligarchy, personal competitions, and differences in personal interests were decided. Men of character without ambition to govern drew away from it nauseated, leaving the field open to political professionals and to demagogic and audacious adventurers. It was thus that Communism succeeded in infiltrating and came to be at one time a national danger. Defeated in its violent attempt to seize power, it continued, nevertheless, its work of undermining authority by utilizing as its weapons the other evils that make the situation of the nation so unstable and chaotic: the weakness of political parties, regional jealousies, and dictatorial flights of fancy. Those three evils are in the final analysis simply the result of a single general cause, well-formed and known: the sterility and depletion of the sources from which the agents of stimulation and renovation of public life ought to come. The political parties had abdicated their social function. They survived at the cost of electoral exploitation and they proliferated often with a predominately local character using old political formulas, foreign to the modern contingencies throughout the world and to the national realities. Foresight of the danger in which we found ourselves and which was felt by all caused us decisively to favor the political unification of the nation, which is precisely why the regime was established on November 10th. The Estado Novo embodies, therefore, the will and ideas which oppose and work against all the factors tending to weaken and dissolve the fatherland—extremes, sabotage, and compromise. It is ready to fight against those evils. It will mobilize all the best that we possess in order to make our nation strong, dignified, and happy. . . .

3.5 The Expropriation of the Oil Industry in Mexico

The nationalistic policies effected by many Latin American leaders during the 1930s and 1940s were designed to foster greater national state control over natural resources. In Mexico, President Lázaro Cárdenas took office in 1934 and gradually implemented policies favoring the country's poor. Cárdenas accelerated the distribution of farmland and established collective enterprises, called ejidos, *throughout the country. Cárdenas also supported the creation of the Mexican Confederation of Workers, which he then mobilized to support his expropriation of the country's foreign-owned oil properties in 1938, as the following reading describes. This decision was justified as a means of consolidating Mexican control over the country and was an important symbolic statement to the country's poor about their ability to forge their own destiny.*

Our land, with valuable riches in its depths, was the object of penetration by companies that had been accustomed to regard the countries of Latin America as nothing more than colonies to be exploited, considering themselves as economic powers superior to the sovereign power of the state.

In the face of this problem the revolutionary government resorted to applying the provision [Article 27] of the 1917 Constitution that claimed the direct ownership of the subsoil as an inalienable right of the republic. Thus it was delivered from the tutelage of elements that

Cárdenas, Lázaro. "The Expropriation of the Oil Industry." In *Models of Political Change in Latin America*, edited by Paul E. Sigmund, 15–16. New York: Praeger, 1970.

were determined to make the rights of the nation a dead letter and to prevent the application of our fundamental laws through diplomatic pressure and mercenary revolts. This administration took it upon itself to apply the law to the oil companies after they rebelled against the express commands of the highest tribunal of justice. Faced with the attitude of the people, who gave solid support to the defense of our institutions by the expropriation decree, the companies resorted to violent attacks in the foreign press and tried to upset our domestic economy. Fortunately, the government prevented economic collapse and consolidated its position, with the result that the principles of the revolution became rooted still more firmly in the heart of the nation, establishing an important precedent that was finally recognized as legitimate by foreign tribunals.

The attitude of Mexico could not be interpreted as an attack on industrial capital; rather it was an unavoidable measure of legitimate defense against the rebellious actions of businessmen who disregarded the welfare of society in the interests of their own vast profits. Among the salutary effects of this situation, I should note that many investors have adopted an attitude that is more understanding of the needs of the workers and of our country, without endangering reasonable profits on their part.

The reincorporation of the rights over subsoil petroleum under national control is a contribution to the integration of the national patrimony that all Mexicans must cherish, particularly those who, since 1917, have devoted themselves loyally to the fulfillment of the principles and goals of the revolution, and especially all the young people of the country who now receive into their custody this national patrimony which has stirred up so many disturbances, domestic struggles, and insatiable appetites. . . .

A conscientious and disciplined attitude on the part of the oil workers and frank collaboration by the directors and technicians in the operation of the industry have followed the nationalization carried out by the government of the republic. For its part, the Ministry of Economics is concluding an evaluation of the expropriated property, which will be published in a few days. The conflict that arose with the oil companies over the expropriation of their interests is in the process of being resolved through a plan of cooperation that the companies themselves are offering to the government. The plan involved the expansion of the industry through the investment of the indemnity for the property expropriated as well as new investments offered by the companies under a plan of cooperation by which the government will maintain its control over the administration of the oil industry.

3.6 The Aprista Thesis

Within Latin America's growing populist movement, Víctor Raúl Haya de
la Torre emerged as one of Latin America's most dynamic political leaders
in the twentieth century. Born in Peru in 1895 of aristocratic parents,
Haya formed a political party, the American Popular Revolutionary Al-
liance (APRA), based on a coalition of working- and middle-class inter-
ests. Suppressed for much of the 1930s and 1940s, APRA advocated
antimilitarism and state capitalism to combat the country's entrenched oli-
garchic interests, which, Haya argued, had benefited from imperialistic
relations with other countries. After years of repression by the country's
ruling interests, many of APRA's policies were adapted by a reform-oriented
military after it assumed power in 1968. In this reading, Haya outlines
his famous program.

For the fulfillment of the *Aprista* [from APRA] doctrine, a party has
been created which, like the work it hopes to accomplish, is [Latin]
American in character. The base of the party is in the producers in
alliance with other middle classes, which are also involved in the struggle against imperialism. The party attempts to form an "anti-imperialist
consciousness" in the working classes—a consciousness that they are the
ones who produce for imperialism, and they alone are the ones who
can place conditions upon it and constitute a force of liberation—without hoping that the proletarians of Europe and the United States will
destroy the capitalist system, the origin of imperialism. The alliance
with the middle classes reinforces the action of the working classes,
especially those that are specifically laborers—new in their role as controlling forces in the state, just as the [economic] system in Latin America which determines their existence as a class is new.

Aprismo already has opened the doors to the future because, following the economic independence of Latin America—an independence
that will have to be based on equality in the exchange of raw materials
and finished products and the investment of capital according to the
principle of progressive nationalization of the sources of production
under the control of the state—it will bring about the industrialization
of our countries. As a result, a working class will be formed, and favorable conditions will be created for the rapid total direction of the economy and the abolition of the capitalist system. While this revolutionary
process is being carried out, *Aprismo* will utilize the anti-imperialistic

de la Torre, Victor Raúl Haya. "The Aprista Thesis." In *Models of Political Change in*
Latin America, edited by Paul E. Sigmund, 185–86. New York: Praeger, 1970.

forces of today, not excluding the middle classes, which are threatened with extinction by imperialism. It will seek to defend them through the anti-imperialist state which, by nationalization and progressive socialization of the sources of production, will be definitely oriented in the direction of state capitalism, preventing the middle classes from tending toward large private capitalism, which would mean a return to imperialism.

Aprismo thus presents a complete doctrine and a realistic method of realistic action—that is, an integral economic, social and political program to secure the economic independence of Latin America. . . .

3.7 Evita and the People

Juan Perón campaigned for the presidency of Argentina on a nationalist and populist platform in 1946. A key base of his political support was found in the urban workers attracted by his prolabor policies and promises to institute Argentine solutions to the country's problems. His mistress and second wife, Eva Duarte Perón, became one of the country's most formidable political figures as a result of her ability to identify with and capitalize on the interests of the country's working class. Eva Perón worked tirelessly to ensure worker support for her husband. In this selection from her autobiography, Eva explains her role as a conduit linking the common people to their "Leader," Juan Perón.

When Perón arrived at the presidency, he became convinced little by little that the responsibilities and tasks of his office were almost incompatible with his wish to maintain close contact with the people.

This contact, which was and continues to be absolutely necessary, must be permanently maintained.

Our people have lived under more than a century of oligarchical governments whose principal task was not to attend to the people but rather to the interests of a privileged minority, refined and cultured perhaps, but sordidly egoistic.

After that century, interrupted only by someone or other who tried

Perón, Eva Duarte. *Evita By Evita: Eva Duarte Perón Tells Her Own Story,* 53–56. New York: Lippincott & Crowell, 1980.

to establish a government for the people, or, rather, by some effort or other never converted into reality, Perón during three years of revolutionary fire reached the people as governor and as guide. And the people already knew how that contact had benefitted everyone.

For three consecutive years, men and women, labor, economic and political groups, the entire people, had come in procession with their old problems and their old hopes into the constructive presence of their Leader, and all their problems and all their hopes had been satisfactorily settled by him as far as was possible—and perhaps even a little further.

With Perón in the presidency with a fullness of power extraordinary in Argentina, how would not the hopes and illusions of people who had already known the taste of a "government of the people . . . for the people" be doubled?

But it was precisely the fullness of power which would prevent the Leader from having permanent contact with the people. While he was at the Secretariat of Labor and Welfare he had no other problems to settle but the old and urgent problems directly affecting the people. But in the presidency, the old and urgent problems were others whose solution was indispensable if all he had accomplished in the three years of social reform was not to fall to the ground. What would have been the use of three years of revolution if at the end of the war we had fallen anew into the arms of our traditional imperialistic exploiters?

All this Perón saw clearer than ever from the day he became President; and so that it should not happen, he had to devote himself entirely to achieving his main goal, which was nothing less than the economic independence of the nation.

In four months he elaborated his five-year plan of government.

In two years he had brought about economic independence. But I do not want to say just how much the General did as President, although I would gladly write an unending number of pages on this inexhaustible subject.

What is certain is that all this immense task, which had to commence with organizing the very government itself, and whose first stage culminated with the reform of the Constitution, could leave him only limited time for maintaining his contact with the people.

And if we had not searched together for a solution, and found it, the voice of the people—that of our *descamisados*—would have reached the seat of government with ever duller accent, and perhaps might have been hushed altogether.

On the other hand, it was necessary to keep the revolutionary fervor kindled in the people. The revolution was hardly under way, and Perón had to cover all its stages from the government itself. This could be done, but only if the people maintained their revolutionary fervor and were not won over by the teachings of "ordinary men" to whom all revolutionary action seems an unpardonable indiscretion.

Between the decree of the law of the revolution and its accomplishment, and between the government and the people, numerous barriers always exist which are not always seen from the government, but which are clearly visible to the people. Contact between Perón and the people was necessary also for this fundamental reason.

In addition, there were urgent though modest tasks to be done concerning the daily needs of the humble. Among the hopes of the *descamisados* were many little illusions which they brought to Perón just as children do to their parents.

The requests and wants of each family vary greatly. The grownups want important things, the children ask for toys. In the great family consisting of the nation, the requests presented to the President, who is the common father, are also infinite.

We were already aware of this when Perón was President-elect. The hopes of the people took the form of the most varied petitions, from a government undertaking of extraordinary and even fantastic nature urged by a whole town, to a football wanted by a "little monkey" from the north, or a doll which a little Indian girl desired.

And to attend to all this—big things and small—it was necessary that the people should not leave off looking to Perón as their guide.

I chose the humble task of attending to small petitions.

I chose my place among the people so as to see from there the barriers which might have hindered the progress of the revolution.

I chose to be "Evita" . . . so that through me the people, and above all the workers, should always find the way open to their Leader.

The solution could not have been better or more practicable.

Problems of government reach Perón every day through his ministers, from public officials or from those themselves concerned; but each one of them cannot take up more than a few minutes in the exhausting day of a President like Perón.

On the other hand, the people's problems reach the Leader every day during lunch or supper, on calm Saturday afternoons, on long, quiet Sundays, and they reach him through my voice, loyal and frank, under suitable circumstances, when the soul of the General is free from all pressing worries.

Thus the people may be sure that no separation is possible between them and their government. Because in the case of Argentina, in order to divorce himself from his people, the head of the government would have to begin by divorcing his own wife!

3.8 Labor Confederation Supports Falkland Recovery

Argentina claims the Malvinas/Falklands as part of its inheritance from the Spanish empire upon gaining independence in 1806. The British claim the islands were ceded to them by Spain in 1771, that the Argentine claim was never recognized, and that their removing the Argentines from the Falklands was only a continuation of the jurisdiction exercise of the eighteenth century. When the Argentines argued geographic proximity for their claim to sovereignty, the British countered with self-determination. Beset with economic and political problems, the Argentine military government of 1976–82 manipulated Argentine nationalism by provoking a conflict over the Malvinas/Falklands. As this reading illustrates, the country's most important labor confederation, frequently repressed by the military, put its partisan claims aside and rallied around the long-standing notions of sovereignty that justified the military's preemptive action.

BUENOS AIRES, 22 April 82—The General Labor Confederation [CGT] released a communique last night after the meeting of the governing council in which they jubilantly support the recovery of the Malvinas islands. The text of the communiqué reads as follows:

Hand in hand with the Argentine people, the CGT jubilantly supports the recovery of the Malvinas, South Georgia and South Sandwich Islands, because this is an action of legitimate justice which put an end to almost 150 years of usurpation and deprivation.

Moreover, in view of an integral concept of sovereignty, which because it is permanent transcends any circumstantial government, the CGT has designated delegations of union leaders to explain to the world on behalf of the Argentine workers the justice of our cause and the emphatic decision of our people that sovereignty is not negotiable.

The Argentines, owners now of a part of our own territory, hope that what has cost us blood to achieve will be preserved by diplomatic negotiations, an unavoidable responsibility of the national government, the results of which must be reported to the people.

In this regard, it is appropriate to point out that by territorial sovereignty we understand not only the presence of the national banner on a piece of land which legally belongs to us, but the integral exercise of the rights which may derive from it and that may include the free dis-

"CGT Communiqué Supports Falkland Recovery Action." In *Foreign Broadcast Information Service* (FBIS), B6, April 28, 1982.

posal of the riches of all nature which may exist there, within the framework of the historical, cultural and political values which define our national identity.

We also hope that this action which united all national sectors will be projected beyond the national sovereignty and will become the starting point for the integral exercise of the people's sovereignty which will only be achieved with the full implementation of the democratic institutions, the communique concludes.

4

Capital Sins: Authoritarianism and Democratization

The squalor of huge shantytowns contrasts sharply with the so-phistication of modern skyscrapers in Rio de Janeiro and many other Latin American cities. © Rick Reinhard/Impact Visuals

Along with economic growth, several political developments during the postwar period gave rise to optimism in much of Latin America. Conservative military dictators were ousted in Venezuela, Colombia, and Peru. Brazil experienced a period of rapid economic growth and electoral democracy. The Bolivian Revolution of 1952 displaced the traditional elite and brought to power a nationalist movement that carried out agrarian reforms and increased political participation. To many observers it appeared that Latin America at the outset of the 1960s was poised to combine capitalist development with modernization of its political and social structures.

The expansionary mood was perhaps best symbolized by the decision of the Brazilians to carve a new capital city out of the country's undeveloped interior. After three years of round-the-clock construction, the starkly modern glass and steel structures of Brasília were inaugurated in 1960 as the new site of the national government.

But the structures that upheld Brasília's facade were beginning to erode. The easy phase of import substitution had ended, and the overall demand for industrial goods was restricted by relatively small domestic markets, which reflected the high degree of concentration of wealth in Latin American societies. The majority of workers and peasants simply could not afford the kinds of products the new industries were turning out, so production was geared to the tastes and incomes of the wealthier classes. This orientation pushed Latin American industrial development in the direction of expensive imported technologies that were usually capital-intensive (that is, more likely to substitute machinery for human labor). Meanwhile, high tariffs and other protectionist policies reduced incentives for firms to keep their costs low, and exports suffered. As a consequence, the Latin American economies became increasingly troubled by trade deficits and inflation, prompting social unrest at home and forcing many governments to seek external assistance from the International Monetary Fund and other financial institutions.

In this context the Cuban Revolution of 1959 burst on the scene with a global impact. On the one hand, it proclaimed the viability of a socialist alternative to capitalist development, emphasizing redistribution and social welfare over private profits. On the other hand, it inspired (and in some cases directly supported) leftist movements throughout Latin America that sought to seize political power through armed stuggle. This period of revolutionary ferment is described in more detail in Chapter 11.

The Kennedy administration in the United States responded to the Cuban challenge with some innovations of its own. Under the label of "counter-insurgency doctrine," it tried to forestall any new revolutionary takeovers by training and supporting Latin American military institutions to combat guerrilla insurgencies. At the same time, recognizing the chronic nature of problems associated with long-standing inequalities and lack of development, Kennedy announced in 1961 an "alliance for progress," through which the United States would provide major economic support for democratic Latin American governments willing to undertake the necessary social and economic reforms. The text of this landmark speech is found in reading 4.1.

Growth First under Military Rule

The alliance, however, proved elusive. Reformist programs encountered stiff opposition from dominant classes in many countries, while Latin American military officials began to perceive a larger role for themselves than simply fighting guerrillas. For U.S. officials, reform also took a backseat to anti-Communism, especially as the war in Vietnam began to dominate the U.S. foreign policy agenda. Beset by economic difficulties, political instability, and U.S. indifference or opposition, Latin American democratic governments began to disappear and were supplanted by authoritarian military regimes. One of the earliest examples of this tendency was Brazil, where the military seized power in 1964 with the encouragement of business leaders and U.S. officials, as the events recounted in reading 4.2 illustrate.

In the latter half of the 1960s and through the 1970s, military regimes dominated the Latin American political scene. In addition to Brazil, they ruled in Argentina, Chile, and Uruguay (the "Southern Cone"); Peru, Bolivia, and Ecuador in the Andean region; and Guatemala, El Salvador, and Honduras in Central America. Though they varied widely in their ideology, politics, and repressiveness, none was favorably inclined toward democracy. The regimes of Brazil and the Southern Cone, however, gained particular notoriety as exponents of a stern authoritarian reordering of their societies (see reading 4.3).

In the political arena, the Brazilian and Southern Cone military governments pursued direct and often brutal repression. Not only did they annihilate left-wing guerrilla movements, they also cracked down on virtually all forms of political opposition. Political parties, labor unions, schools and universities, professional associations, the media, and other institutions all were subjected to military efforts to "discipline" society. Laws were suspended, rewritten, or ignored by authorities who carried out mass arrests, arbitrary imprisonment, and clandestine executions. Torture became chillingly commonplace, as reading 4.4 makes clear. Argentina, Chile, and Uruguay were the most notorious offenders; in Brazil, where the military perceived less of a threat from its opponents, the scale of repression was significantly less.

Although these regimes governed political activity with a heavy hand, they followed a variety of strategies to reactivate their economies. A succession of Brazilian generals pursued what has been called "managerial capitalism," in which the state actively intervened in the economic arena to expand basic industries and promote exports. The Argentine and Chilean military regimes of the 1970s, however, followed the advice of conservative U.S. economists and international bankers, seeking to free market forces by reducing state restrictions on foreign trade, foreign investment, currency exchange rates, and domestic prices.

At some points, military governments were successful in fostering economic growth, as in Brazil from 1968 to 1974, when the economy was expanding at more than 10 percent annually and admirers spoke of the "Brazilian Miracle." In Chile growth was slow during the late 1970s and more rapid in the late 1980s. In other cases, such as Argentina and Uruguay, military governments showed no more skill in promoting thriving economies than their civilian predecessors.

Even where economic growth was achieved, it usually came at a high price. In the Southern Cone, with labor movements suppressed, real wage levels fell, urban poverty increased markedly, and income distribution became sharply more unequal. In Brazil, indicators of social welfare such as life expectancy and literacy improved from 1970 to 1980, but poverty and inequality remained and popular discontent surfaced over what was perceived as an inequitable distribution of the benefits of growth. After the oil crisis of the mid-1970s sent import bills skyrocketing, Latin

American governments began to borrow heavily at low interest rates from foreign banks to finance their trade deficits and public spending. The shortsightedness of this strategy only became apparent by the end of the decade, as a second oil price hike made new loans necessary simply to meet the interest payments on earlier loans. In the global recession of the early 1980s, when foreign banks curtailed their lending to Latin America and interest rates on many existing loans rose sharply, the region's debt reached crisis proportions.

The Difficult Quest for Democracy

As economic performance declined, military governments gradually allowed more space for political and economic dissent. The timing of these opportunities differed among the countries. Brazil led the way with a gradual relaxation of political restrictions beginning in the mid-1970s, while the Chilean military under General Augusto Pinochet resisted making concessions for another decade. Labor unions were quick to raise their voices again when the opportunity arose; the Brazilian government, for example, was shaken by major industrial strikes in 1978 and 1979 (see reading 4.5).

Under growing pressure from churches, women's organizations, and human rights groups for their repressive records, and abandoned by some of their erstwhile business and middle-class supporters for mismanaging the economy, military officials sounded a retreat. Their decline was spurred by a new U.S. policy focus on human rights, beginning in the late 1970s under the Carter administration. The Argentine military, as noted in Chapter 3, withdrew in disgrace in 1983 after the defeat in the Malvinas/ Falklands War with Britain. In Brazil and Uruguay civilian presidents assumed office in 1985, and in 1989 open elections were held in Brazil for the first time since the 1960s. By 1990, as Pinochet stepped down in Chile, Latin American military governments had everywhere ceded the presidency back to civilian hands.

The general exuberance over the departure of unpopular regimes was tempered, however, by recognition of the enormous difficulties facing these countries. The problem of foreign debt loomed like an insatiable mortgage on future economic development, necessitating difficult and often painful renegotiations with international financial institutions. No less daunting was the "social debt"—the legacy of years of neglect in key areas such as housing, health care, and education. Rather than undertake expensive new initiatives, however, the new civilian governments found themselves compelled by the debt crisis and the 1980s global recession to sell off state enterprises and curtail public spending.

On the other hand, democratization also required more than just a change of faces in leadership positions. Two decades of authoritarian military rule had left behind an edifice of centralized executive power, weakened representative institutions such as legislatures and parties, and many repressive laws and decrees, all of which could not be demolished quickly. Human rights movements have demanded that military officials be held accountable for their past repressive actions. Faced with a host of conflicting political and economic demands, the majority of the new civilian regimes have seen their popularity quickly plummet.

New problems were presenting themselves as well. Dramatic changes in global political and economic realities—the end of the Cold War, the approaching economic unification of Europe, and the burgeoning East Asian economic power, among others—have demanded innovative Latin American responses. Meanwhile, public awareness has gradually increased regarding environmental concerns, including pollution, natural resource conservation, and sustainable food, water, and energy production. Deforestation and the rights of indigenous peoples in the Brazilian Amazon, for example, have captured worldwide attention (see reading 4.6). In very real ways, the price of growth in post–World War II Latin America weighs heavily on the challenges of the 1990s.

4.1 The Alliance for Progress

As a response to Castro's 1959 takeover of Cuba and the revolutionary
movements it inspired, John F. Kennedy called Latin American diplomats
to the White House in March 1961 for his first speech on Latin American
affairs since his electoral victory over Richard Nixon the previous Novem-
ber. The surprised gathering heard a U.S. president call for sweeping
changes in the hemisphere, with respect to both reducing poverty and in-
equality in Latin America, and increasing U.S. support for the region's
reformist movements in pursuit of those goals. Excerpts from Kennedy's
speech follow.

One hundred and thirty-nine years ago this week the United States, stirred by the heroic struggles of its fellow Americans, urged the independence and recognition of the new Latin American Republics. It was then, at the dawn of freedom throughout this hemisphere, that Bolivar spoke of his desire to see the Americas fashioned into the greatest region in the world, "greatest," he said, "not so much by virtue of her area and her wealth, as by her freedom and her glory."

Never, in the long history of our hemisphere, has this dream been nearer to fulfillment, and never has it been in greater danger.

The genius of our scientists has given us the tools to bring abundance to our land, strength to our industry, and knowledge to our people. For the first time we have the capacity to strike off the remaining bonds of poverty and ignorance—to free our people for the spiritual and intellectual fulfillment which has always been the goal of our civilization.

Yet at this very moment of maximum opportunity, we confront the same forces which have imperiled America throughout its history—the alien forces which once again seek to impose the despotisms of the Old World on the people of the New. . . .

We meet together as firm and ancient friends, united by history and experience and by our determination to advance the values of American civilization. For this new world of ours is not merely an accident of geography. Our continents are bound together by a common history—the endless exploration of new frontiers. Our nations are the product of a common struggle—the revolt from colonial rule. And our people share a common heritage—the quest for dignity and the freedom of man. . . .

Kennedy, John F. "The Alliance for Progress," In *The Central American Crisis Reader*, edited by Robert S. Leiken and Barry Rubin, 119–23. New York: Summit Books, 1987.

. . . We North Americans have not always grasped the significance of this common mission, just as it is also true that many in your own countries have not fully understood the urgency of the need to lift people from poverty and ignorance and despair. But we must turn from these mistakes—from the failures and the misunderstandings of the past—to a future full of peril but bright with hope.

Throughout Latin America—a continent rich in resources and in the spiritual and cultural achievements of its people—millions of men and women suffer the daily degradations of hunger and poverty. They lack decent shelter or protection from disease. Their children are deprived of the education or the jobs which are the gateway to a better life. And each day the problems grow more urgent. Population growth is outpacing economic growth, low living standards are even further endangered, and discontent—the discontent of a people who know that abundance and the tools of progress are at last within their reach—that discontent is growing. In the words of José Figueres, "once dormant peoples are struggling upwards toward the sun, toward a better life."

If we are to meet a problem so staggering in its dimensions, our approach must be equally bold, an approach consistent with the majestic concept of Operation Pan America. Therefore I have called on all the people of the hemisphere to join in a new Alliance for Progress— *Alianza para el Progreso*—a vast cooperative effort, unparalleled in magnitude and nobility of purpose, to satisfy the basic needs of the American people for homes, work and land, health and schools—*techo, trabajo y tierra, salud y escuela.*

Ten-Year Plan for the Americas

First, I propose that the American Republics begin on a vast new 10-year plan for the Americas, a plan to transform the 1960s into an historic decade of democratic progress. These 10 years will be the years of maximum progress, maximum effort—the years when the greatest obstacles must be overcome, the years when the need for assistance will be the greatest.

And . . . if our effort is bold enough and determined enough, then the close of this decade will mark the beginning of a new era in the American experience. The living standards of every American family will be on the rise, basic education will be available to all, hunger will be a forgotten experience, the need for massive outside help will have passed, most nations will have entered a period of self-sustaining growth, and, although there will be still much to do, every American Republic will be the master of its own revolution and its own hope and progress.

Let me stress that only the most determined efforts of the American nations themselves can bring success to this effort. They, and they alone, can mobilize their resources, enlist the energies of their people, and modify their social patterns so that all, and not just the privileged few, share in the fruits of growth. If this effort is made, then outside assistance will give a vital impetus to progress; without it, no amount of help will advance the welfare of the people.

Thus if the countries of Latin America are ready to do their part . . . then I believe the United States . . . should help provide resources of a scope and magnitude sufficient to make this bold development plan a success, just as we helped to provide . . . the resources adequate to help rebuild the economies of Western Europe. . . .

Secondly, I will shortly request a ministerial meeting of the Inter-American Economic and Social Council, . . . [to] begin the massive planning effort which will be at the heart of the Alliance for Progress. . . .

A greatly strengthened IA-ECOSOC, working with the Economic Commission for Latin American and the Inter-American Development Bank, can assemble the leading economists and experts of the hemisphere to help each country develop its own development plan, and provide a continuing review of economic progress in this hemisphere.

Third, I have this evening signed a request to the Congress for $500 million as a first step in fulfilling the Act of Bogotá. This is the first large-scale inter-American effort—instituted by my predecessor President Eisenhower—to attack the social barriers which block economic progress. The money will be used to combat illiteracy, improve the productivity and use of their land, wipe out disease, attack archaic tax and land-tenure structures, provide educational opportunities, and offer a broad range of projects designed to make the benefits of increasing abundance available to all. . . .

Fourth, we must support all economic integration which is a genuine step toward larger markets and greater competitive opportunity. The fragmentation of Latin American economies is a serious barrier to industrial growth. Projects such as the Central American Common Market and free-trade areas in South America can help to remove these obstacles.

Fifth, the United States is ready to cooperate in serious, case-by-case examinations of commodity market problems. Frequent violent changes in commodity prices seriously injure the economies of many Latin American countries, draining their resources and stultifying their growth. . . .

Sixth, we will immediately step up our food-for-peace emergency program, help to establish food reserves in areas of recurrent drought, and help provide school lunches for children and offer feed grains for use in rural development. . . .

Seventh, . . . I invite Latin American scientists to work with us in new projects in fields such as medicine and agriculture, physics and astronomy, and desalinization, and to help plan for regional research laboratories in these and other fields, and to strengthen cooperation between American universities and laboratories.

Eighth, we must rapidly expand the training of those needed to man the economies of rapidly developing companies. This means expanded technical training programs, for which the Peace Corps, for example, will be available when needed. It also means assistance to Latin American universities, graduate schools, and research institutes. . . .

Ninth, we reaffirm our pledge to come to the defense of any American nation whose independence is endangered. As its confidence in the collective security system of the OAS [Organization of American States] spreads, it will be possible to devote to constructive use a major share of those resources now spent on the instruments of war. . . . Armies can not only defend their countries—they can, as we have learned through our own Corps of Engineers, help to build them.

Tenth, we invite our friends in Latin America to contribute to the enrichment of life and culture in the United States. We need teachers of your literature and history and tradition, opportunities for our young people to study in your universities, access to your music, your art, and the thought of your great philosophers. For we know we have much to learn. . . .

To achieve this goal political freedom must accompany material progress. Our Alliance for Progress is an alliance of free governments, and it must work to eliminate tyranny from a hemisphere in which it has no rightful place. Therefore let us express our special friendship to the people of Cuba and the Dominican Republic—and the hope they will soon rejoin the society of free men, uniting with us in our common effort.

This political freedom must be accompanied by social change. For unless necessary social reforms, including land and tax reform, are freely made, unless we broaden the opportunity of all of our people, unless the great mass of Americans share in increasing prosperity, then our alliance, our revolution, our dream, and our freedom will fail. But we call for social change by free men—change in the spirit of Washington and Jefferson, Bolívar and San Martín and Martí—not change which seeks to impose on men tyrannies which we cast out a century and a half ago. Our motto is what it has always been—progress yes, tyranny no—*progreso si, tiranía no!* . . . .

Let us again transform the American Continent into a vast crucible of revolutionary ideas and efforts, a tribute to the power of the creative energies of free men and women, an example to all the world that liberty and progress walk hand in hand. Let us once again awaken our American Revolution until it guides the struggles of people everywhere—not with an imperialism of force or fear but the rule of courage and freedom and hope for the future of man.

4.2 When Executives Turned Revolutionaries

On March 31, 1964, João Goulart was deposed as president of Brazil in a coup that inaugurated 21 years of military rule. The coup followed a period of increasing political polarization and social unrest, after Goulart in 1963 abandoned efforts to reconcile his government with foreign creditors and instead embraced a radical nationalist alternative based on restricting foreign capital and initiating far-reaching domestic reforms. This reading, originally published in a U.S. business magazine a few months after the coup, reveals how conservative businessmen, publishers, and other members of the Brazilian elite became so hostile to the Goulart regime that they were willing to sacrifice democracy to restore economic and political stability. In the Latin America of the 1960s and 1970s, many of the upper and middle classes were willing to make this trade.

. . . In typically sardonic fashion, one Brazilian remarked about the March coup, "Now that it has turned out so beautiful, everybody wants to be father of the child." The army generals provided the critical show of force that provoked the showdown. But this was not just another Latin-American military take-over. Significantly, much of the inspiration and planning was provided by business executives and professional men, aroused by Brazil's leftward drift. Not only were they aroused,

Siekman, Philip. "When Executives Turned Revolutionaries." *Fortune* 70:3 (September 1964): 147–49, 210–21.

they organized to do something about it. Most of these leaders were from the state of São Paulo, and the March 31 uprising can justly be called "the Paulistas' revolt." . . .

Fiercely individualistic and proud of a tradition of self-reliance and hard work, the Paulistas have always looked on any Brazilian central government with suspicion—including those they controlled in the early days of the republic. At one time their attitude toward public issues was rooted in the single idea that what was good for the coffee market was good for Brazil. But the businessmen and professionals who have come up since World War II are far more concerned than their predecessors about the social tensions and individual injustices rampant in a society where perhaps a third of the 77 million people are condemned at birth to a life of poverty and ignorance. They believe that Brazil needs sweeping change—through the operations of limited government, private enterprise, and individual freedom.

Among these Paulistas is a soft-spoken pharmaceutical-company executive, Paulo Ayres Filho. Now forty-five, Ayres succeeded his father in 1956 as president of Instituto Pinheiros, an ethical-drug firm named after the outlying district of the city of São Paulo in which it is located. . . .

A Drug Maker's Antidote

In the early Fifties, Ayres was becoming increasingly concerned about the demagoguery and left-wing activity that were infecting Brazilian politics. At this point he became aware of the work of the Foundation for Economic Education in Irvington-on-Hudson, New York. Mostly through booklets and pamphlets, the U.S. foundation proselytizes in the cause of limited government and free enterprise, as an antidote for what it calls the "something for nothing" philosophy. Ayres read a number of the foundation's publications (e.g., Henry Hazlitt's *Economics in One Lesson*) and began to circulate its pamphlets as well as translated excerpts from other works among scores of his friends.

Looking back on those early years of activity, Ayres recalls: "We were losing the fight." In 1955, Juscelino Kubitschek was elected President of Brazil as the candidate of the Social Democratic party, and with the backing of the leftist-dominated Labor Party. Kubitschek pushed Brazil into a frenzy of development and government spending. Whole new industries were built, São Paulo boomed, and Brasilia, the new capital, appeared like a concrete mirage cast in the wilderness. Millions upon millions of *cruzeiros* were spent, wasted, and stolen. Brazil's chronic inflation was inflamed. And, at least as Ayres and others saw it, "Communists began showing up in student groups, labor unions, and even

professional and managerial associations and chambers of commerce." . . .

A few days before Kubitschek's term ran out in January, 1961, Ayres
received a long-distance telephone call from a stranger who shared his
fears. The caller was Gilbert Huber Jr., a young Rio businessman who
had built a thriving postwar business, Listas Telefonicas Brasileiras,
publisher of Brazil's telephone-directory "yellow pages." . . .The two
men began to meet regularly, often in Rio where Ayres was beginning
a short term as a director of the Bank of Brazil.

The head of the bank was another São Paulo businessman, João Bap-
tista Figueiredo. He and a handful of other friends of Ayres and Huber
were drawn into the discussion of how to counter the statist and leftist
propaganda echoing through Brazil. The outcome was a decision to set
up the Instituto de Pesquisas e Estudos Socials (Institute of Social Research and Studies)—IPES, for short. Some of the group contended
that IPES should be a clandestine movement. But the founders finally
agreed that they would operate in the public view—publishing booklets
and pamphlets, underwriting lectures, financing trips by students to
the U.S., and helping to support democratic student and labor associations.

"The Destruction of Our Hopes"

Just before IPES got started, Jânio Quadros was inaugurated as President of Brazil. He showed an encouraging determination to come to
grips with inflation and government corruption and halt the drift that
so alarmed São Paulo's businessmen. But after only seven months in
office Quadros suddenly resigned and was replaced by the Vice President, João Goulart.

For Ayres, João Goulart's ascendancy meant "the destruction of all
our hopes." A protégé of onetime dictator Getulio Vargas, Goulart had
built the Labor party into a powerful political machine by carefully fertilizing friendships with government patronage and by promising workers
higher and higher wages. Under his benevolent eye, Communist-
influenced labor leaders took control of the majority of the nation's
labor unions.

Frightened by the thought of what Goulart might do now that he
had presidential power, IPES quickened its efforts to influence public
opinion. . . .

With limited funds and no real idea of just how to go about the task
it had set for itself, IPES attempted too much. "We tried to save the
country," said Ayres. "And we failed to think in proper depth. But the
seeds we threw helped many isolated initiatives." The organization turned
out a stream of pamphlets and booklets that it gave away to anybody

who would make use of them. (Its publications include "Inflation, Its Causes and Consequences," "The Truth About the Industrial Revolution," a series on "Economics for Everybody.") It helped finance a democratic leadership-training program for businessmen, students, and laborers, which has educated 2,600 people. And it encouraged women's groups and student and other organizations by contributions of funds, literature, cheap office space, free office equipment, and subsidized clerical help.

Toward the end of 1962 the attitude of many IPES members began to undergo a change. "At first," says Ayres, "the whole idea was to resist, not to attack. We all wanted João to end his term. We knew everyone in other parts of the world would be against us if we threw him out." But as Goulart's government got more and more reckless, it became apparent that intellectual resistance was not going to work fast enough. While IPES continued its propaganda and educational work, individual members of the organization began to look for more direct ways of asserting their opposition.

An alphabet soup of anti-Communist organizations sprang up on the Brazilian scene. Some held rallies; others painted signs on walls; one attempted to buy politicians. A São Paulo industrialist, who belongs to IPES, decided the time had come to adopt "their methods." He organized vigilante cells to counter left-wing hecklers at anti-Communist meetings with "intellectual methods—like a kick in the head." Later, the vigilantes armed themselves with light weapons, set up a clandestine hand-grenade factory, and picked out a site from which to carry out guerrilla operations in the civil war they considered unavoidable and imminent.

What was to become the important activist movement against Goulart began with three members of IPES who are all São Paulo lawyers: Flavio Galvão, Luiz Werneck, and João-Adelino Prado Neto. . . .

Before long they were meeting with a growing number of other São Paulo professional and businessmen in and outside the ranks of IPES. One of the most prominent recruits was Júlio de Mesquita Filho, who became the nominal head of the group. (The Mesquita family owns *O Estado de São Paulo*.) Another was Adhemar de Barros, Governor of the state of São Paulo. His adherence to the group of businessmen revolutionaries was especially important because he had a well-trained and well-armed state militia of some 40,000 men. . . .

"It Is No Longer Possible to Endure"

By the latter part of 1963, Brazil appeared to be dangerously close to coming apart at the seams. Continued inflation was not only sapping the country's productive strength, but further depressing the living standards of most Brazilians (on a per capita basis, the real gross national product actually declined last year). In the destitute northeast, illiterate peasants were being organized with money from Red China and arms smuggled in from Cuba. In the south, Leonel Brizola, a fanatic congressman who is Goulart's brother-in-law, was stepping up his attacks on foreign and national business.

By this time, men who were openly sympathetic to Communism and Castro had taken over key posts in the government and its agencies. And a Communist-dominated top labor command was openly using strikes as a political weapon. In October some thirty major strikes were in progress or threatened.

Goulart shuffled Cabinet ministers (he had fifty-five different ones in two and a half years), set up an economic stabilization plan, and then abandoned it, talked of reforms and did nothing. On the face of it, he appeared simply unable to govern, but the Paulistas' interpretation was more sinister. They believed Goulart was contriving crises in order to demand more power. . . .

In São Paulo, Adhemar de Barros talked of impeaching Goulart and openly threatened revolt: "São Paulo is ready to fight. . . . It is no longer possible to endure this crisis of authority, this lack of discipline." But open revolt would require help from the Brazilian Army.

Informally, IPES members had long cultivated friendships in the military services, had invited officers to São Paulo ostensibly to visit factories, and over coffee and dinner had told them of their fears. But the most consequential meeting took place in early 1963, when Werneck, Galvão, and others became acquainted with a young lieutenant colonel, Rubens Resstel, then stationed in the São Paulo headquarters of Brazil's Second Army.

A Paulist by birth and a military-academy graduate, Resstel saw action (and won the U.S. Silver Star) with the Brazilian Expeditionary Force, which fought as part of the U.S. Fifth Army in Italy in World War II. As IPES became the mother cell of the civilian resistance to Goulart, so the veterans of the B.E.F. became the moving force in the military. Since the war, explains Resstel, "we have had a horror for any regime like the one we fought, whether it is Fascist or Communist." Encouraged by the Mesquita group, Resstel and some of his fellow officers began to circulate through Brazil sounding out other military men. A number of young officers agreed that the time had come to act; but many in the highest ranks did not. . . .

In early 1964 the young military men in the Mesquita group began to piece together bits of evidence which indicated that the Communists around Goulart were planning a coup of their own—with or without Goulart's help. . . . The Paulistas feared an overnight attempt to create a totalitarian state, with a wave of violence and murder, guerrilla actions, strikes in key industries, and an uprising of enlisted military men.

As some civilians saw it, the choice now was to die in defense of their freedom or be imprisoned and shot later because they had failed to defend it. They began to arm themselves. In time the Mesquita group alone spent about $10,000 on weapons, including a handful of machine guns. Groups in residential sections of São Paulo obtained weapons, ammunition and supplies, and carefully plotted out defense plans for their blocks.

Resstel and the other military officers reckoned that with some elements of the regular Army, the state militias, and the civilians they could hang on for ninety days. Before that time ran out the Mesquita group hoped for outside help. They sent an emissary to ask U.S. Ambassador Lincoln Gordon what the U.S. position would be if civil war broke out, who reported back that Gordon was cautious and diplomatic, but he left the impression that if the Paulistas could hold out for forty-eight hours they would get U.S. recognition and help. . . .

4.3 The Military's Role in Politics

General Aurelio de Lyra Tavares was minister of war under General Arthur da Costa e Silva, who occupied the Brazilian presidency between 1967 and 1969. The following reading, written by Tavares, shows how military leaders defined their political mission as defending national security against Communism, while professing a commitment to democracy. Shortly after this statement was published in 1968, the Costa e Silva government proclaimed Institutional Act No. 5, which gave the president the power to dismiss the national legislature and local governments, to take away the individual political rights of any citizen, and to suspend the right of habeas corpus for individuals accused of political crimes.

As a national institution in a democratic state, the Army cannot be an organization apart, autonomous, and immune from changes in the government, particularly since the government has the power to select, promote, and assign military leaders as serves the interests of those in

de Lyra Tavares, Aurelio. "The Army and the Ideological Struggle." In *Models of Political Change in Latin America*, edited by Paul E. Sigmund, 153–56. New York: Praeger, 1970.

power. This means that, both in the past and at present, the Army is less political and more professionalized where the democratic structure of the state is the most stable and developed.

Two forces which sometimes converge are capable of weakening the cohesion and discipline of the Army, compromising its role as a supporter of democracy: an external one, directed by international Communism, and an internal one, resulting from distortions and fluctuations in the policy of the government. The first of these forces, which possesses vast means and resources, is directed from abroad but also makes use of domestic agents. It exploits the discontent of the poorer sections of the civilian population and incites the worker in the city and the countryside against the Army; it tells him that one of the principal causes of his low standard of living is the large unproductive expenditure for the maintenance of the armed forces, which are depicted as an instrument of oppression in the service of the privileged classes. At the same time, it lends the Communist name to the worldwide movement for peace through the brotherhood of the workingmen of all nations.

This ideological effort is directed at the minds of men without civic education, and it attempts to persuade them to become revolutionaries and potential instruments of subversion. It is important to be aware of this fact and to consider it in military recruiting, so that the Army is not infiltrated by elements capable of compromising its unity of spirit and action.

To neutralize the effects of this propaganda, it is necessary to demonstrate the popular character of the democratic army by explaining to the man of the less favored classes the meaning of free government and the dignity that it assures him, in contrast to life under a Communist regime. This effort is most convincing when it points to the participation of the army in constructive civic-action and aid programs, especially in areas that are vulnerable to Communist propaganda.

In the case of Brazil, this kind of orientation has proved to be beneficial. I could see this as Commander of the Fourth Army. The area of jurisdiction of the Fourth Army stretched from Maranhão to Bahia; it included the nine states most influenced by Communist propaganda before the democratic revolution of March 31, 1964, and the areas that were most vulnerable in the defense of the continent, because of the strategic location of the Northeast and the shocking contrast between the wealth of a small minority and the poverty of the general population. Under the influence of a government that was involved in subverting the social order, the country was rapidly moving toward Communism through the organization of the peasants and the progressive weakening of the cohesion and discipline of the Army.

At that time, I could see for myself the firm commitment to democracy of our military officers, including the noncommissioned officers, who were the particular objects of subversive teachings. Because of its hierarchical structure, the Army could therefore resist this effort and at the appropriate time rise up to preserve our traditional institutions.

In this effort, the Brazilian military had the support and confidence of the people of the Northeast. These feelings, resulted from the great influence of the Army, in civic education, in aid and training programs, and, especially, from the substantial support that the Corps of Engineers enjoys in the interior of the Northeast because of the essential public works it undertakes for the improvement of the living conditions of the people. The Army's involvement in this and other types of civic action is a longtime tradition in Brazil.

This does not mean that the Army is immune to Communist propaganda, especially when the political and administrative structure of the government is open to the infiltration and activities of Communist elements, as was the case in Brazil prior to the revolution of March 31, 1964. Against the possibility that this second force may develop because of the internal weakness of the governmental structure, it is important to preserve the morale of the armed forces. In extreme cases of action, or inaction, by the government, which may compromise the security of our democratic institutions, the armed forces face a grave dilemma, caught between violating what appears to be the legal structure and betraying the country of which they are supposed to be the ultimate guardian. . . .

We have a horror of militarism. Dictatorship? Never. Much less a military dictatorship. History proves what I am saying. You may recall that the only dictator this country ever had was not a military man. The Brazilian Army's tradition of respect for civil power has been uninterrupted throughout our national history. This demonstrates the unalterably civilian orientation of the military in Brazil and illustrates the role it has played in guaranteeing and strengthening our democratic structure. In Brazil, we have never had the figure of the military strong man [caudillo], nor has the military power usurped the functions of the civilian power in order to assume direction of the nation.

In exceptional circumstances, on the rare occasions in which the continuity of the democratic process was threatened in Brazil and the very survival of its institutions and sovereignty was in peril, the strictly legalistic spirit of the Army had to give way; the Army then rose up to intervene among the parties and to take power, for the sole purpose of re-establishing the democratic order. It has been led to that extreme by its inalienable and lofty duty. This is a mission that it has exercised at various points in the democratic development of the nation, in order that Brazil might advance with determination and security. This is the great desire of all true democrats, both military and civilian. As I said during Army Week in Recife, the Army has tried to remain invulnerable to the repeated appeals and attempts of groups that invoke the prestige of the uniform as a magic solution to the problem of strengthening political power in Brazil. But that prestige derives precisely from the aversion of the Brazilian military man to any kind of dictatorship. . . .

[The movement of March 31] once again demonstrated the Army's fidelity to democracy. It was a proof of its vitality and represented a general and forceful reaction by the democratic spirit of the Brazilian people. And the Army, as well as the other branches of the armed forces, had to demonstrate its solidarity with the people. It does not have an attitude different from that of the people. The Revolutionary Command took power into its hands for the minimum period necessary before transferring it to the President of the Republic. When the nation invests the presidency in a military man, it is clear that his role as a citizen overshadows his role as a soldier, for that is what the term "civil power" means to him. No one is more of a civilian than the Brazilian military man invested with civil office. No force in Brazil is more vigorously opposed to military dictatorship, a well as to the dictatorship of any class, than the civic conscience of the soldier. . . .

[The opponents of the restoration of Brazilian democracy], because they do not find the climate suitable for subversion and corruption, seek to present the revolution of March 31 as a military movement to establish a military dictatorship. The very liberties that they use and abuse constitute a convincing public refutation of their position, the proof that invalidates the basis of the argument to which they appeal. The Brazilian Army never was and never will be a militaristic army, or one subject to any party that arrogates to itself the right to select its membership, to prescribe the attitudes and even the thinking of its men, as is the case in politicized armies. Our Army does not take part in politics because it is not a party but a national institution. Power is for it a temporary responsibility, which cannot be refused in moments of national crisis or prolonged beyond that period, for the Army is aware that power is justified only when it is exercised in order to overcome a crisis, and for no other purpose. . . .

We are individuals and interested citizens who favor development. We were the forerunners in this field, for Brazil was born when the Army Engineers marked off and guaranteed our frontiers. The Army is a force for the dynamic development of the interior, particularly through the construction battalions, which are building highways and opening up distant regions. How can they help but rush to the defense of our petroleum and other subsoil resources? . . .

Is there a "hard line" faction [within the armed forces]? I realize that it exists in the newspaper columns, but it does not exist within the military family. There is simply a pyramidal hierarchy, a homogeneous structure in spirit and action, under the direction of the President of the Republic. Everything else is pure speculation. . . .

4.4 Torture in Brazil

Under the authoritarian military regimes of the late 1960s and 1970s, it became extremely dangerous to voice any sort of political dissent. During this period the Church was one of the few institutions able to speak out against the systematic violation of human rights carried out by the government. The following statement by Cardinal Arns, the archbishop of São Paulo and the highest-ranking Catholic official in Brazil, bears witness to the scars such abusive practices inflicted both on individuals and on society as a whole.

I

. . . During the period when the so-called subversives were being most intensively hunted down, I received in the archdiocesan offices twenty to fifty people every week, all trying to discover the whereabouts of their relatives.

One day two women came to me, a young one and and an older one. The young one, as soon as she sat down in front of me, put a wedding ring on the table and said, "It's my husband's wedding ring. He disappeared ten days ago. This morning I found it on my doorstep. Father, what does its being returned to me mean? Is it a sign that he is dead or is it a sign that I should continue my search for him?"

To this day, neither of us has found the answer to that harrowing question.

The older woman repeated the question she had been asking me for months: "Do you have any news about the whereabouts of my son?" Immediately after he was abducted she would come every week. Later she came every month. For more than five years I followed the search for her son, through our Justice and Peace Committee and even through the president's personal assistant for civilian affairs. The body of that mother seemed to shrink from visit to visit. One day she also disappeared, but her imploring look will never be erased from my mind's eye.

No one on earth can describe the hurt of those who saw their dear ones disappear behind prison bars, without being able even to guess

Evaristo Arns, Paulo, "A Testimony and an Appeal." In *Torture in Brazil*, edited by Joan Dassin, xxv–xxviii. New York: Vintage Books, 1986.

what had happened to them. The darkness deepens and the last glimmer of hope that the disappeared person is still alive flickers and dies.

For that mother and that wife, deep darkness covers the earth, as it did when Jesus died.

II

One unusual evening, a military judge came to my residence. He had studied in a Catholic school and showed understanding about the Church's work in São Paulo in defense of political prisoners.

At a certain point the conversation changed direction. The magistrate, apparently cool and objective, was overcome with emotion. He told me he had just received two documents from different sources signed by different persons. Two political prisoners each stated they had assassinated the *same* person, at an unlikely time and in altogether improbable circumstances. The judge concluded: "Imagine the psychological and maybe even physical condition of someone who reaches the point of declaring himself an assassin, even though he isn't!"

Interrogation under torture or the threat of torture, however, reaches even greater heights of absurdity and futility.

III

Before testifying to our Justice and Peace Committee, an engineer told me his tragic experience. He believed he had nothing to fear when he was detained. But since he had heard that torture was applied to those who did not confess at least something, he prepared to tell in detail everything about himself that could be interpreted in any way as opposition to the military regime. He would even tell more than he might in sacramental confession.

Yet, after taking down his personal data, the interrogators made him sit down—immediately—in the "dragon's chair." From that moment, he said, "everything got mixed up. I no longer knew what I had done, nor what I had wanted to tell or even elaborate upon, in order to achieve credibility. I confused names, persons and dates, for it was no longer I who was speaking but rather the inquisitors who dominated and possessed me in the most total and absolute meaning of the word."

After such degradation, how and when is such an innocent man to become a whole person again?

IV

What impressed me most during the years of vigil against torture, however, was how torturers themselves are degraded. . . . That is why I give this testimony.

Toward the end of January 1974, when the leaders of Catholic Workers' Action were detained, I spent four afternoons inside the Political and Social Police Department in the hope of seeing them. I had been called from the southern Brazilian city of Curitibia for this purpose, where I had been with all my brothers and sisters comforting our mother in the last days of her life.

During the long wait in the prison corridors, I was able to talk with police officers who conducted interrogations. . . . Five of them told me about their studies in Catholic schools. One of them had attended the Catholic University of São Paulo. They were all having problems with their families and in their private lives, problems which they themselves saw as a divine judgement on them. When I urged them to give up their horrific work, they answered, "It's impossible. You know why!"

Finally, late on Friday afternoon, in the presence of those police officers to whom I had spoken so bluntly, I was able to see two of our pastoral workers. They were in terrible shape. Months later, one of those same police officers was waiting alone to see me after mass in the church at Aclimação in São Paulo. With a cry of desperation he asked me, "Is there any hope that I will be forgiven?" . . .

I then remembered a warning given by a general, who was in fact against all torture: "Whoever tortures once, becomes changed as a result of the demoralization he has inflicted upon others. Whoever repeats torture four or more times becomes a beast. The torturer feels such physical and emotional pleasure that he is capable of torturing even the frailest members of his own family!" . . .

4.5 Interview: "Lula," Brazilian Labor Leader

The Brazilian automobile industry was one of the leading success stories in the Brazilian economic boom of the early 1970s. As the Brazilian military government cautiously began to relax its control, however, the working class made its pent-up demands known. A major strike of metalworkers in 1978 was followed by an even larger walkout the following year. In this period, the energetic young president of the union representing São Paulo autoworkers, Luis Inacio da Silva (better known as "Lula"), attracted much public attention as a spokesperson for the revived Brazilian labor movement. Ten years later, running on the most radically left-wing platform of any major candidate in Brazilian history, Lula would finish a close second to Fernando Collor de Mello in the country's 1989 presidential election. It was a clear symbol of the country's efforts to return to democratic politics, and of the political polarization that had outlasted military rule. The following interview was published in the Brazilian journal Cara a Cara *after the automotive industry strikes of May 1978.*

What comparison can be established between the present workers' movement and that of a few years ago?
Today's worker movement is not too different from that of a few years ago. What has changed some are the basic ideas of some union leaders who believe that the unions should become independent once and for all and who have tried to apply this with the rank and file in their sectors. This was not the case before 1964, when we knew that many movements were started for partisan reasons, many times for the benefit of those in power or for those who were not in power but who desired to be.

Some unions began to insist on the necessity of our fighting our own battles, since we didn't need the interference of outsiders. The workers, they said, ought to learn to win on their own and should judge their own strength and learn how important they are in the process of the development of their country. And I think it has really happened. It is not that we are going to stand back and clap and celebrate the laurels of victory. However, we understand that the strikes which took place since May 12 [1978] have shown that there is a greater class consciousness on the part of the workers. Workers have ceased to believe in many things that deceived them for a long time. They had believed,

Inácio da Silva, Luis. "Interview." *Latin American Perspectives* 6:4 (Fall 1979): 90–100.

for example, that the governments could do many things for the working class. . . .

Today the worker does not believe in that anymore. Today he believes more in his own strength. Maybe it is just that we believe in our own strength to solve our immediate problems. But I think that this is the basic difference between the workers before 1978 (not to speak of going back to 1964) and those of today. The worker started to see that the people talking about freedom and using the term "working class," were in fact far removed from him. After having been massacred for a long time, workers started to believe that they could resolve their own problems.

Lula, there are those who say that the strikes over "wage recovery" took on a spontaneous character . . .
Many people think that the strike occurred for this or that reason. The strike had only one thing which was its father: the stomach of the working class. I don't feel put down when it's said that the strike was spontaneous. I put forth the thesis of spontaneity, and I would die to defend it. It was a spontaneous movement of the working class which felt its salaries were more devalued than ever. The worker would arrive home and would find his woman asking for money to buy food, and he did not have it. That's when the workers decided to strike. . . .

What impressed me deeply about the strike was the workers' confidence in the union. And I think that this was for a good reason: this was the result of the concerted work over five, six, and seven years. For the first time I started to believe in words. I think that if you start to throw many ideas at the head of the worker, eventually he will accept them. And I think that this was the reason the strikes developed with great spontaneity. . . .

Do these strikes indicate, in some way, the collapse of the present union structure?
I think that these strikes already started the collapse of the current union structure as well as the present strike law. We always said, here in the union, that the legality of the movement would come from the movement itself. If it was victorious, it would be legal; if it wasn't, it would not be legal because we wouldn't have won anything. Almost everybody recognizes the archaic nature of the current labor-union structure. It was constructed when there were hardly any workers in Brazil. . . . It was made around 1939 and it couldn't last. Today's Brazil is not the Brazil of 1939: it's a developed Brazil, with a city like São Bernardo, for example, which can be compared with the great industrial centers of the world, and it cannot be submitted to a legislation which attracts the interests of the multinationals to the extent that labor is cheap and that the union structure is tied to the government. The only thing we want is the freedom to fight with capital without making

any distinction between national and multinational capital, because the
national companies are in no way better than the multinationals. But,
if we can't get the right to fight on an equal footing, it will always happen that a few make a lot but that most earn very little.

The union leaders should not assume the responsibility of resolving
the problems of the working class; they must have the guts to say that
the union is bound and castrated and that it's the worker who will resolve the problems.

*. . . Given the limitations that distort the Brazilian system, isn't it important,
at least in certain cases, for the workers in many companies to have coordination
outside the union?*
No, I think that position is not valid. Now, if there is a legally constituted union to represent the workers, what must be done? We must
bring into the unions the best elements that are in the factory. I think
that the union can orient the working-class struggle without the union
leadership going out and preaching. Imagine that you are fighting to
have a free student organization. Imagine that you set up the free student directorate and that each class then set up a student commission
parallel to the student organization which did not follow the policy of
the official organization. So then what was the student directorate established for?

I think we must show the worker what the Brazilian union structure
is, so he can start fighting against it. He must know that it must change
because it is no good. But the union must orient the worker. . . .

What happened with the Brazilian worker is that for a long time he
was conditioned to look to someone at the top to do everything for him
because he felt he was impotent, weak, poor, miserable and, that up
there, the people with power were capable of doing something for him.
The politicians always said that they had the solution for problems, that
the workers should trust them, and that everything would be resolved
inside congress, etc. The truth is that the politicians say they cannot do
anything because of the special laws that weaken the legislature. But
before 1964, there was no special legislation and they also did nothing.
What did these people give the working class? What was changed in
the union structure? What did the working class gain during Juscelino
Kubitschek's period—and he was considered the great Brazilian states-
man? Nothing. It did not change because it was never in the interests
of those in power to change. And Mr. João Goulart? He also did nothing to change the union structure. . . .

*How does the working class look at the fight for amnesty, for a constituent as-
sembly, and for democratic liberties? What do you think today really mobilizes
the working class?*
Let's start with the democratic liberties. I think that this demand is

important not only to one or other group of Brazilian society, but to all groups. I expressed some reservations about the demand for a constituent assembly because I was afraid it might repeat the experiences of 1946 and that we workers would be subordinated to an assembly controlled by the elites. I think the constituent assembly could be valid if all sectors of Brazilian society participated.

As for amnesty [for people accused of political crimes, or stripped of their rights], I believe that in good conscience, no citizen could be against it. And I go further than amnesty for just the politicians thrown out of office and deprived of their political rights. I support the amnesty that the working class needs: the right to live with dignity, because the working class is the eternal prisoner, the eternal thrown-out-of-office; it doesn't participate in anything in this land except in the process of production. So I defend more emphatically a broader amnesty which would give the working class what belongs to it. This is why people are frequently confused, because it's not just a question of amnesty for political prisoners and people deprived of their political rights. I think it is legal to cancel a person's political rights if it is done by the courts in a legally constituted regime with civil rights, where it is determined that a person acted wrongly and must pay for it. But I'm against depriving people of their rights arbitrarily. In conclusion, I am in favor of these demands as long as they involve the proportional participation of the working class. . . .

Should the labor movement work by itself, or should it try to establish relations with the other sectors of the Brazilian opposition like the student movement, the medical interns' movement, the bank workers, etc.? If it should establish these relations, how can they be made concretely?
I have maintained the following: to participate in a movement that is outside of labor before participating in our own movement would be to do the impossible; it would be putting the cart before the horse. The type of freedom that we workers want, if it is the same type of freedom that the students want, that the middle class wants, that all groups want, then I think it will be impossible to refuse the common aspirations after each specific struggle has developed. The biggest problem for the workers today, what motivates them today, is wages. Obviously we must start by fighting for wages. Once this problem is partially solved, we must move to other types of struggle. What cannot happen, for example, is for me to stop fighting for salaries, which is what interests the working class, and go and demonstrate in the Largo de São Francisco [a large square in São Paulo where human rights demonstrations are held]. Then I would be running away from reality. I cannot stop fighting for wages in order to join the interns' struggle.

I feel everyone can contribute to restoring normality to the country. What cannot happen is that the SBPC [Sociedad Brasileira para o Progresso da Ciencia—the Brazilian Society for the Progress of Science] starts to give contributions at the factory gate; nor should the worker contribute at the SBPC office. I think each one should keep to his or her own struggle.

Today people are already talking about reconstructing parties, including the establishment of a workers' party. What do you think about this?
I think that the participation of workers in politics can be independent of political parties. But it depends on the worker having someone elected to defend his rights and his principles. I believe that we have arrived at the moment of forming a party of the working class which does not need to have only workers. What we cannot do is put the owner of a company in the workers' party, because he will never support legislation in our interests; he will do what interests him. But there are many people who are not workers—liberals, professionals, intellectuals, etc.— who identify greatly with the working class and who could participate in a workers' party. What should be important in this party is that workers should be the majority, the coordinators and the determinants in the party.

I feel that we are not too far from having this party. There is a gradual evolution of the working class. Today, at least in São Bernardo do Campo, there is a group of new workers who will not be as submissive as in the past. And these people, more than ever, ask for freedom for political participation.

4.6 Deforestation and the Rights of Indigenous Peoples

The disappearance of Latin America's authoritarian military regimes in the 1980s left the new civilian governments facing a multitude of difficulties. One of the most pressing issues concerns the need to reverse the seemingly inexorable trend toward a degraded natural environment. In many rural areas, the problem is compounded by issues of respect for the Indians' cultural and economic traditions. In Brazil, for example, the

Greenbaum, Linda. "Plundering the Timber on Brazilian Indian Reservations." *Cultural Survival Quarterly* 13:1 (1989): 23–26.

> *question of deforestation in the Amazon basin is bound up with that of the livelihood of dozens of indigenous groups. The final reading in this chapter sheds light on this complex problem, and on the need for innovative political thinking.*

Because of the obvious bad consequences, lumbering has traditionally been prohibited, at least in principle, on Indian reserves in Brazil. Recently, however, this protective stance has been reversed: the National Indian Foundation (FUNAI) itself has encouraged the greedy and wasteful destruction of Indian forests, with severe consequences for the Indians involved. This article presents a brief overview of this grave and growing menace, focusing on two states in Brazil—Rondônia and Pará. The problem is not confined to these areas alone, however, and threatens to become universal. . . .

The Situation

In Rondônia, most but not all of the Indian posts that have access by road were involved in some sort of lumbering activity in 1987. In some cases—always with FUNAI involvement—lumbering has been going on for as long as three years.

In southern Rondônia much of the lumber from the Macurap-Sacurap reservation is already gone. On the A.I. (Indigenous Area) Rio Branco previous lumbering expanded greatly in 1987. Lumber contracts now exist for the reserve of the Tubarão-Latundê, the A.I. Rio Mekens and the Guaporé Valley of the Uru-Eu-Wau-Wau, previously invaded, undergoes extensive lumbering.

In eastern Rondônia lumbering began on the P.I. (Indigenous Post) Roosevelt about three years ago; it continues today, both with contracts made by Cinta Larga Indians and contracts made by FUNAI. The idea has spread rapidly throughout the region. The Cinta Larga of P.I. Sierra Morena are selling wood from an area to be inundated, and their fellow tribesmen on the P.I. Capitão Cardoso and P.I. Rio Preto are trying to get roads built in order to sell lumber. The most serious threat is a project to open a road from the city of Vilena to the P.I. Tenente Marques in return for 40,000 cubic meters of mahogany (export value: an astronomical $20,000,000). This project would expose the entire center of the Aripuanã Park to further invasion and exploitation. The project was initiated in 1987 but has since been dropped, at least temporarily.

On the Suruí reservation the rate of lumbering increased greatly in 1987; each "native leader" made an oral contract with a lumber company. Lumbering began on the reservation of the Gavião and Arara

Indians for the first time (except for previous removal by squatters) in the dry season of 1987, at first clandestinely and on a modest scale, then with a large contract, which, however, was not accepted by FUNAI because of all the scandals surrounding wood deals. The Zoró reserve has been invaded massively for several years by settlers, who at one point had three sawmills in operations.

The situation appears to be more controlled in Pará, but at least five Kayapó posts—Gorotire, Kikrêtum, Kubekrãken, A-ukre and Korai-môrô—are selling mahogany very actively. Lumbering was stopped on the Cateté reservation. Some other Kayapó villages, however, are eager to begin lumbering.

How the System Works

Lumbering can be instigated by lumbermen, Indians or FUNAI officials. They all live in a certain proximity and can easily find each other. Sometimes lumbermen steal wood outright, quickly taking a few logs and disappearing before they can be apprehended. This has been going on for some time, for example, in the Guaporé Valley, which has relatively easy road access. At times lumber is felled but immediately seized before it can be transported. If this lumber is then sold by FUNAI, the action sets a precedent; Indians grow more interested in further transactions, while the lumber company contracted to remove the fallen wood is given the chance to persuade the Indians to sell more.

The lumbermen are extremely adept at bribing influential Indians; they ask around to find out who the local "chief" is and then make promises and give presents to him. In the case of the Gavião and Arara Indians, for example, lumbermen gave about $300 worth of goods—most of it food—to each of the groups to induce them to sign lumber contracts. Lumbermen offer to pay travel expenses for Indians to go to the regional FUNAI office and demand to sell wood. If necessary, lumbermen take Indians to Brasília to sign contracts with the approval of the FUNAI president. . . .

Under traditional circumstances Amazonian Indians have no arithmetic skills, market economy or long-range economic planning. If a piece of land was despoiled, they could always pick up and move to another place. As a result, Indians are quite unprepared for the dangers of extractive activities such as lumbering. Furthermore, if one man does not want to sell wood, he is powerless to prevent someone else from selling his share. . . .

Certainly the unnecessary lack of economic alternatives for Indians propels them in the direction of the simple, known option of selling wood. Indians have abundant opportunities for making money from their wood in a sustainable manner (through cutting rubber, collecting Brazil nuts, and cultivating coffee, cacao and other tree crops). Unfortunately the present FUNAI administration lacks the will and the competence to implement such projects.

The Damaging Effects of Lumbering

According to Article 46 of the Statute of the Indian in Brazil's constitution, lumbering on Indian land is illegal because it is not "conditioned to the existence of programs or projects for developing the respective land by crop and stock farming, industry or reforestation." It is also illegal under the Forestry Code because timber removal is completely unsupervised and uncontrolled and there is no reforestation nor the slightest concern for forest ecology. Aside from these legal matters (which the mining and lumbering interests are trying to remove from the forthcoming new constitution) there are many reasons why lumbering on Indian lands has proven to be a disaster.

1. The payment for lumber is seldom divided in a just and equal manner. This unequal access to the money or goods creates an undesirable system in which some Indians control money, power and goods, leaving others more powerless and often poorer than before.

In one Kayapó village, the money from wood sales (and mining) goes directly to the "chief" in defiance of FUNAI regulations, which state that such funds must be used for the good of the community. The chief's sons receive a much larger share than others. A similar situation exists among the Suruí Indians of Rondônia, who speak of *caciques* ("chiefs") as opposed to "peons," who don't get to have lumber contracts. . . .

2. Indians receive very little money for the wood in relation to its value. The money they do receive is not being invested for the future, but is spent instead on consumer items, especially those of prestige value, and on "improvements" in Indian reservations that are of no real benefit to the Indians.

Consider the terms of a 1984 contract to sell Kayapó wood to the firm Azzayp-Industria e Comercio de Madeiras: 70 km of road in return for 10,000 mahogany trees. Estimating at least 5 cubic meters of wood per tree, at the current mahogany price of $500 per cubic meter at the port of export, the final value of the wood should be $25,000,000. Granting that the value of the standing wood is less than it is in the city, the value received is still ridiculously less than the value of the wood given.

A contract dated 28 September 1987 for 5,000 cubic meters of mahogany from the A.I. Rio Branco stipulates a payment of only about

$25 per cubic meter of mahogany, to be paid for in the form of a 15-km road, a Toyota, various hardware and consumer items, a pharmacy building plus supplies and some livestock. Certainly within three years very little will be left of these things. In general, nobody on Indian reserves is trained to fix such items.

Most of the Suruí men who had lumber contracts in 1987 were living in hotels in the nearby city. Those who were more prosperous had cars with chauffeurs and maintained steady relationships with white prostitutes. Exactly the same pattern occurs with the Kayapó chief Pombo and some of his sons: alcohol, white women, hotels and automobiles for the elite prevail. . . .

3. The money from wood sales, rather than resolving any local problems on the reserves, instead serves to create more difficulties. For example, the mortality rate of the Arara and Gavião Indians in Rondônia increased with greater access to the city. None of the Suruí wood money is being used for health care, in spite of a massive tuberculosis problem. Even areas in which pharmacy buildings are being built see no improvement due to the limitations of poor training or lack of medical attendants. Many of the Uru-Eu-Wau-Wau, a group first contacted only about five years ago, are dying from disease; the presence of loggers simply increases the contagion. . . .

None of the wood proceeds are spent on education. The Cinta Larga are not literate, and the profits from selling wood are not changing that at all. The native groups' economies are adversely affected by lumbering since other, nondestructive economic activities are discouraged. Many Suruí planted less in 1987 because they expected they would eat in restaurants.

Settlers can use the lumber roads for land invasions. As these roads multiply, land defense becomes more difficult.

4. Violence and disorder increase with lumbering. In 1987 a Suruí, frustrated at seeing nearby trees cut while he could not share the profits, shot a lumber worker. Three lumber workers were shot by the Kayapó in a dispute over lumber between two Indian groups. The Guajajara took prisoners in order to force permission to sell lumber. Because Indians are not subject to the usual legal penalties, this violence is very difficult to control.

5. Measuring the amount of lumber removed is difficult and the large amount of money involved makes corruption inevitable. One noteworthy case of corruption involved the president of FUNAI, the regional superintendent in Cuiabá and an assistant to the superintendent—all accused of attempted extortion of funds in signed statements by two lumber companies.

6. The ecological destruction from lumbering is serious, especially since Indians traditionally depend so much on the forest.

7. In spite of the illusion of economic development, the selling of natural resources on Indian lands destroys self-sufficiency, creating a

population without the will to work and without a subsistence base. Traditionally, Indians have displayed excellent general competency (apply themselves well, learn, execute) and excellent specific competency (knowledge of nature, techniques). When they become dependent on selling resources, however, they lose their traditional competency without gaining new, Western competency. Their general competency also diminishes as alcoholism and idleness increase.

8. The extraction of lumber and other natural resources from indigenous areas does not favor the economic development of Brazil, as some will imagine. Rather, extracting natural resources simply intensifies the country's dependency on low-skill, low-technology industries extracting non-renewable resources, when just the opposite focus is needed.

Pretending It's a Good Thing

In a recent interview the FUNAI president declared, "The Brazilian Indian is potentially rich. He has rich land, has minerals, has lumber. And he knows that these riches can be used in favor of his entire community. What right do we have to prohibit this?"

As has been proved by the facts above, this statement completely distorts the issue. The end result of the resource exploitation will not be rich Indians (in the sense that non-Indians are rich: educated, healthy, secure masters of the system). Rather, the end result will be marginalized, degraded, dependent Indians, some of whom, for a few years, had a lot of cash slipping through their fingers or stared out at unnecessary airstrips, roads and buildings of putative community benefit. . . .

5

Continent on the Move: Migration and Urbanization

The majority of Latin American and Caribbean migrants move within their own countries, from rural to urban areas, in search of better opportunities. © Robert Frerck/Odyssey Productions

Patterns of migration in Latin America and the Caribbean changed dramatically during the twentieth century. Long a focus of immigration from Europe and Africa, the region has become an area of major internal migrations and significant emigration.

The growing number of Latin American and Caribbean migrants who have moved from the countryside to the city has led to an intensified process of urbanization since 1950. Rates of expansion in urban areas have exceeded those of the total population in almost every Latin American country. Four Latin American metropolitan areas—Mexico City, São Paulo, Rio de Janeiro, and Buenos Aires—are among the most populous in the world. In some countries of the region, the capital city accounts for upwards of 30–40 percent of the country's entire population. At present rates of urban growth, it is estimated that 80 percent of the population in Latin America and the Caribbean will live in cities by the year 2000.

Patterns and Types of Migration

Latin American and Caribbean migration includes two forms: people who move from rural areas to towns and cities in the same country; and those who move from one country to another Latin American and Caribbean country or to the United States.

Individuals who move from rural areas to towns and cities in the same country have a variety of motives, but generally they are seeking better economic opportunities, as reading 5.1 illustrates. They are usually less literate and have few marketable skills, so they pursue employment at lower levels of the occupational structure—as day laborers, maids, car washers, or fruit or lottery ticket sellers on the street. The difficulties of this kind of life for migrants working in Mexico City's garbage dumps are described in reading 5.2.

The movement of migrants from rural areas to cities has placed new demands on urban centers. Established city dwellers often regard migrants with disdain and concern, perceiving them to be associated with crime, poverty, and misery. The lack of housing for new arrivals has led to the growth and proliferation of slums and shantytowns known by different names in different countries: *favelas, pueblos jovenes, solares,* or *villas miserias.* Usually the land on which these settlements are constructed is illegally occupied.

The emergence of these alternative forms of urban communities has increased stress on public services, such as water, electricity, transportation, education, and police. These services have become practically nonexistent for large segments of the population. But contrary to popular belief, these squatter settlements are not "hotbeds" of unemployment. Rather, the proportion of unemployed there tends to be no higher than for the total urban labor force. The problem is that wages paid to workers from these settlements tend to fall below basic consumption needs—including the need for adequate shelter, if it could be found.

The second form of migration involves people who move to other Latin American and Caribbean countries or to the United States. Some of these individuals are refugees forced to leave their own country because of political abuses, as is illustrated by the problems of Guatemalan Indians in Mexico, described in reading 5.3. Other migrants seek better economic opportunities for themselves and their families, as is shown in reading 5.4, which traces the course of West Indian laborers who helped to build the Panama Canal in the early 1900s, and then migrated to work on sugar plantations throughout the Caribbean.

Migrants come from every social class and move for a variety of reasons. Professionals such as doctors, nurses, and engineers leave their native countries in search of better employment opportunities. Political refugees and exiles leave their countries in fear for their lives. Most migrants leave their homes in search of new work opportunities. They may cross borders, often in perilous circumstances, without the necessary visas or work permits, as described in reading 5.5.

The Larger Migration Pattern

The movement of Latin American and Caribbean peoples is part of the changing pattern of global migration. A number of explanations of migration help in understanding the broader phenomenon.

First, government policies toward exchange rate management, taxation, land ownership and redistribution, and social services, including housing, health care, and education, directly influence migration. The Mexican government's decision to locate its most important offices in Mexico City, for example, has been a major cause of rural migration to the capital.

Second, Latin American and Caribbean migration tends to be related to the larger processes of economic and social change within the hemisphere. Introducing new farming methods in one region can have a dramatic impact on working conditions and opportunities there. Changing consumer preferences can also affect migration since market desires can determine which local products are produced.

Third, the development of social networks has promoted and enhanced the possibilities of and prospects for migration. Composed of friends and relatives, these networks can provide a steady source of information and assist in facilitating a new arrival's efforts to adapt to new surroundings. Social networks also have a very practical end: they identify employment opportunities. Most employers hire new workers from the references of trusted employees. Similarly, migrants rely on their networks to identify prospective employment opportunities. One of the best illustrations of such a phenomenon can be found in Tijuana, Mexico, where whole communities of rural Mexicans from Zacatecas have relocated as the result of the initiative and connections of one respected migrant.

Finally, migration tends to be linked to global patterns of capital accumulation and development. The large-scale transfer of wealth from rural to urban areas and from one nation to another has encouraged and promoted labor migration—the most common form of population movement in the world. This explanation points to structural rather than individual or personal motivations for migration.

Migration and the Economy

However one interprets the causes, Latin American and Caribbean migration patterns have had an obvious impact on the region's economy. The emergence of the *maquiladora* plant in tax-free export manufacturing zones has also had an impact on patterns of migration. A relatively new phenomenon, the *maquila-*

dora industry is designed to take advantage of low-wage workers who assemble electronic equipment and other consumer goods, the components of which are produced elsewhere, usually in the United States. The assembled product is then shipped back to the United States duty-free.

The emergence of *maquiladoras* in northern Mexico and other parts of Latin America has had a significant effect on these regions. The labor force for *maquiladora* work is highly selective—especially in terms of gender, age, and workers' marital status. *Maquiladoras* in Mexico tend to employ three times as many women as men. Most of these women are between the ages of 16 and 25 and unmarried. Reading 5.6 offers a graphic example of the relationship between migration and *maquiladora* employment.

Recent research suggests that the emergence of *maquiladora* production in Mexico creates an alternative for would-be migrants to the United States. *Maquiladoras* tend to attract young, single, and relatively well-educated workers from neighboring areas or adjacent states. Those who work in *maquiladoras* generally prefer the labor there to the uncertainties and hardships of illegal migration to the United States. The *maquiladora* trend steadily accelerated in the late 1980s as Mexico's economic crisis deepened. By the late 1980s *maquiladoras* accounted for close to 15 percent of Mexico's manufacturing jobs and earned about $3 billion in foreign exchange.

In recent years the migration of individuals from one country to another has brought with it a financial transfer—migrants send earnings back to family and friends in their country of origin. These remittances are now as important as traditional commodity exports and tourism as primary sources of foreign exchange in such countries as Mexico, the Dominican Republic, El Salvador, and the Anglophone Caribbean.

The income tends to be used to pay for basic necessities of family members left behind, and little is devoted to productive investment that could generate further employment. The absence of such productive investments is notable given that this form of income often exceeds or matches large foreign assistance programs, such as U.S. development aid.

Remittances to Latin America and the Caribbean will likely grow in importance during the 1990s. Governments and private institutions during this period may need to find innovative ways to channel these reverse flows of income into more productive activities with a larger national impact.

5.1 Urban Poverty and Politics in Rio de Janiero

The decision to migrate is a complex one, involving a mix of "push" and "pull" factors. In Brazil an accelerating process of rural-to-urban migration has taken place since the 1930s. A concentration of land ownership has barred many rural families from access to land, and the mechanization of commercial agriculture has reduced the need for farm labor. But even peasants who own a small farm have found that their growing families (due to declining infant mortality) can no longer subsist on subdivided plots whose soils have been exhausted by constant use. These "push" factors have spurred migrants to leave rural areas. At the same time, government centralization and import substitution policies, as well as the expansion of services, have made urban life more attractive. Attempting to explain why people migrate, the author of the following reading offers four case studies illustrating various reasons for moving to the city.

We found most migrants unable to describe their decision to migrate with any precision. It was clear that specific decisions involved complex factors, many of them not even conscious. Often a mixture of motives, involving pushes and pulls, works differently for persons in different life circumstances, as the following four vignettes demonstrate.

Adult men with rural backgrounds and families tend to leave their homes only when it seems impossible to stay. For example, Sebastião left a small town in Pernambuco's interior at the age of 54. He came to Rio with his wife and three of 16 children, some of whom were already in the city, because, as he put it, "I couldn't make it there anymore. . . . There weren't any more jobs to be found and the land wasn't supporting us." To make the trip he sold his only possession, one cow, and walked two days to arrive at Recife, where he bought a ticket to Rio for the equivalent of about U.S. $50.00.

Contrasted with this is the case of Amaro, a younger man who came to Rio from Minas Gerais at the age of 19 to search for "better opportunities." At 17 Amaro had already left his birthplace, a *fazenda* (Brazilian-style plantation) and moved to the nearest municipal seat because "the situation was lousy and I wanted a better life." He had a brother in Rio who came to visit him and described "all the advantages in Rio, includ-

Perlman, Janice. *The Myth of Marginality: Urban Poverty and Politics in Rio de Janeiro*, 68–69. Berkeley: University of California Press, 1976. Copyright © 1976 by The Regents of the University of California.

ing better salaries and more *movimento*." Shortly afterward, Amaro borrowed money from his mother for the trip and convinced a cousin to go along. Amaro lived in three other favelas before settling on Catacumba as his home. The prominent factor in his decision, and that of many like him, was the desire to "be where the action is." In his mind the countryside was a dead-end where the years plodded on in dull predictability while the city represented the unknown, exciting, and unforeseeable future.

A third example is Dona Juliana, who came to Rio from Paraiba do Norte when she was 20. She was single and worried about becoming "an old maid." Relatives arranged for her to go directly to the home of a wealthy family in Copacabana as a domestic, a common pattern among the 24 percent of migrants in this age-sex bracket. Soon after arriving, she found a boyfriend and became pregnant. The family she worked for expelled her, and she moved in with her boyfriend in Catacumba. Three children later, he abandoned her. Now Dona Juliana takes in washing so she can earn some money without leaving her children for long periods of time; she lives in the worst part of the favela—an open sewer runs by her front door—and she longs for the opportunity to buy some land and have a house of her own. (Others like her, however, who also came as maids, still work, with fairly good pay, high job security, and lots of "fringe benefits" in the homes to which they were originally sent.)

Older women tend to come for family-related reasons, often to join husbands who had gone ahead to look for a job and a place to live. Dona Cecilia, the Nova Brasilia schoolmistress, originally came to Rio seeking medical help for an ailing child who had swallowed some caustic soda and desperately needed help. The trip took two days of walking and three days on the train. When she arrived, she looked up her husband's brother who lived in Nova Brasilia, but he refused to take her in. Finally, she found a doctor who would operate on her son and who saved his life. Since then, Dona Cecilia has become one of the most active community leaders in Nova Brasilia, not only setting up the school, but also organizing many of the campaigns with city officials over land titles and city services. Although barely literate herself, she has dictated a number of powerful, scathing letters to public officials and agencies, having them typed on behalf of the Residents' Association and signed like petitions.

Each of these four people, in different life circumstances, came to the city for a mixture of reasons, hardship weighing more heavily for some, the attraction of urban opportunity more compelling for others.

5.2 Mexico City's Garbage Society

Mexico City is the world's largest metropolitan area. Rapid population growth, coupled with rising expectations and the emergence of a consumer-oriented economy, has placed enormous strain on the city's services including its waste disposal system. The following article illustrates the problems of rapid urban growth and the necessity for the urban poor—usually immigrants from rural areas—to adapt to new, often appalling conditions in order to survive. It also shows the pervasive spread of the "informal economy," which exists even in a garbage dump.

Garbage has become an obsession for the inhabitants of Mexico City, spawning any number of fantastic stories, all of them true. There is, for example, the story of the open-air garbage dumps that spontaneously ignited one day in July, spreading fire and toxic fumes over acres of refuse stacked twenty yards high. There is the story of the cacique who controlled more than half the city's seventeen thousand-odd *pepenadores,* or garbage pickers, demanded sexual favors from the garbage pickers' daughters, and also took all his workers off to Acapulco on vacation once a year. There is the story of a sixty-square-mile garbage dump that the city government decided to turn into a park, complete with picnic tables—tables that have since been sinking gently into the settling layers of trash and loam.

   Then, there are the rats. One of the most memorable stories dates from the beginning of the decade, when an evening paper announced above the fold that a "giant mutant rat" had been discovered floating dead in a sewage canal. The article said that the rat was the size of a Volkswagen, and in the accompanying photo one could verify the caption's claim that the beast had "the face of a bear, the hands of a man, and the tail of a rat." Two days later, a morning paper explained that the corpse belonged to a lion owned by a three-flea travelling circus. The old thing had finally died, but before throwing the corpse into the sewage canal the owners had decided to skin it, in case the pelt proved salable. Purists among those who collect accounts of Mexican trash dismiss this story on the ground that it turned out to be false, but the point is not that the mutant rat was a figment but that in the general state of decay and disrepair of one of the world's most chaotic cities, many of us who read the story assumed at the time that it was true. The fact is that once started on the subject, most city residents can

Guillermoprieto, Alma. "Letter from Mexico City." *The New Yorker,* September 17, 1990, 93–96. Reprinted by permission; 1990, Alma Guillermoprieto.

come up with giant-rat stories of their own, and few are more thoroughly documented than the one told by Iván Restrepo, a genial scholar of garbage who directs a government-financed institute for ecological research called the Centro de Ecodesarrollo. Five years ago, in Chapultepec, the city's most popular public park, Restrepo and his center mounted an exhibit on the subject of garbage. A tent, designed by an artist, had a long, dark entrance, filled with giant illustrations of microbes and garbage-related pests, from which the public emerged into "the world of garbage." One of the exhibits, Restrepo said, was "the most gigantic rat we could find."

Dr. Restrepo was telling his story in one of Mexico City's best restaurants, and he interrupted himself briefly to order roast kid, guacamole, and a millefeuille of poblano chilies and cream. "It was huge!" he went on, gesturing descriptively. The rat, one gathered, must have been about the size of a large cat. "It weighed almost eight pounds. But we had a problem. We began to realize that the rat was dying on us. It wasn't used to the nice, healthy pet food, or whatever it was, that we were feeding it. So we went out and collected fresh garbage for it every evening. Kept it happy. And that was important, because thousands and thousands of people came to see the garbage exhibit, and the rat was the absolute star of the show."

If *capitalinos*—the residents of Mexico City—flock to an exhibit on garbage featuring a giant rat, it is because the subject is never very far from their minds. The problem of waste disposal may be only one of the critical aspects of the city's ongoing public-services emergency, but it is certainly among the most visible. One of the world's three largest urban conglomerates, the city never had a proper service infrastructure to begin with and has been growing too much too fast for too many years. Figures from the 1990 national census show that although the Federal District, or capital proper, has a relatively stable population of 8.2 million, the surrounding sprawl in the neighboring state (also called Mexico) brings the total urban population to sixteen million. This is triple the 1965 estimated total, and the rate is not slowing. By the year 2000, if current trends persist, the urban area will be home to twenty million souls, all clamoring for services that are already strained to the breaking point in some areas and nonexistent in others.

Not only are services dangerously insufficient but there is almost no way to expand them. Water is now piped in from as far as fifty-five miles away. Ringed by mountains, the urban area is also gasping for fresh air. At least fourteen tons of waste, including lead, carbon monoxide, and what is known euphemistically as the products of "open-air fecalization," now floats in what the city breathes every day. Visibility has improved markedly since late last year, when the government passed a law restricting circulation of a fifth of the city's 2.5 million vehicles each weekday, but, because public transport is also in an awful state, car owners are now buying spare vehicles to use on the day their regular cars aren't allowed out. The poor, who can't afford any car at all, can spend as much as four hours a day travelling between the outlying shantytowns and their urban workplaces: the metro system, which has seventy miles of track and provides more than four million rides a day, serves only a small part of the Federal District, which covers some five hundred and seventy-nine square miles, and the same is true of the crowded, aging buses that spew their fumes along the city's uncharming streets. Twelve million more rides are provided by a network of *colectivos*—privately operated minivans and small buses—which clog traffic and gouge working-class salaries. And the deep-drainage system—nine miles of cavernous tunnels and thousands of miles of pipes, hailed as an engineering marvel when it was inaugurated, barely fifteen years ago—is now hopelessly overloaded, as anyone knows who saw the sewers backing up during each of this summer's downpours.

Bad as the city's public-service difficulties are, most of them appear to have fairly straightforward solutions: build more subways, install more phones. Not trash. The question is not how to put more of anything in but how to reduce the sheer bulk of what exists. The poor, who constitute the vast majority of Mexico's population, have lately produced almost as much waste as the rich; eager initiates into the world of junk consumerism, they find some consolation for their fate in the First World's plastic-encased gewgaws. And although the city has so far heroically managed to keep more or less abreast of the growing tonnage of waste, cleanup-service problems merely have their beginning in the dumps. Here Mexico's First and Third Worlds meet and fester. Rats are the least of it. There is pollution and, above all, the tangle of human misery and political intrigue represented by a peculiar sector of Mexico's body politic—the thousands of *pepenadores,* and their leaders, who stand in the way of neat solutions.

Contemplating the lovely city of Tenochtitlán, rising from the now vanished waters of Lake Texcoco, the conquistadores marvelled not only at the personal cleanliness of the inhabitants but at the immaculate streets that fanned out in an orderly grid from the great plaza, now occupied by the National Palace and the Cathedral. The Aztec people could hardly conceive of waste: they used cornhusks to wrap food in and inedible seeds to manufacture percussion instruments. All organic waste went into the compost-filled rafts with which the Aztecs compensated for their lack of agricultural land. Each street was swept clean every morning, and the day's cargo of excrement was deposited in a special raft tied at the street's end.

By contrast, colonial Mexico was a filthy place, but the long-term accumulation of waste did not really become a problem until after the 1910 revolution, which yanked the Indian population out of self-sufficient subsistence economies and into the world of buying, selling, and discarding. In the nineteen-forties, when the economy finally stabilized after the long devastation of civil war, consumerism made its first in-roads. Waste multiplied. Each month, thousands of peasants abandoned their land and came to the capital looking for a better life. By the nineteen-sixties, urban prosperity had proved to be a mirage, but the situation in the countryside was infinitely worse, and the mass urban migration continued. The newcomers settled in shacks along the roads leading into the city, stole their electricity from the highway power lines, and made do without running water, drainage, or garbage-collection systems. The communities grew at such a rate that one of them, Ciudad Nezahualcóyotl, is the country's fourth-largest city. Thoroughly integrated by now into the consumer economy, its million-plus inhabitants carry their groceries home in plastic bags, use their spare change to buy hair spray, splurge at United States-based fast-food chains on soda pop served in plastic-foam cups, and pour milk for their children from plastic-coated-cardboard cartons. The intractable accumulation of mixed waste—rotting, toxic, and non-biodegradable—generated by this fraction of the Third World's urban poor can be contemplated at the Bordo de Xochiaca municipal dump, on the southern edge of what was once Lake Texcoco, and a few blocks away from Nezahualcóyotl's city hall. Not many who pass by it linger; the stench causes motorists to accelerate way past the speed limit, and in their haste they may fail to notice what is most striking about this vast expanse of putrefaction. Scarecrowlike figures can be seen moving slowly over the dusty mounds, poking methodically. The garbage is inhabited.

The best view of Bordo de Xochiaca is from the driver's seat of a tractor that is used all day long to flatten out the incoming loads. From this vantage point one can look north across the clay-colored lake bed to the volcano-ringed horizon. In the opposite direction, the garbage dunes recede for half a mile to Ciudad Nezahualcóyotl. A few people work the edges of the dump, and a few others live in plastic-and-cardboard shanties there, but most of the dump's activity takes place in a clearing in the center—where people try to sift through a newly deposited truckload of garbage before the tractor runs over it—and in an expanse just to the west of this clearing, where Celestino Fernández Reyes, the dump boss, weighs and purchases the scavengers' daily take of glass, rags, tin, cardboard, wood, plastic containers, animal bones, and other recyclable materials. Behind the scales and Celestino's headquarters, a row of shacks marks the beginning of the living quarters—scores of lopsided houses, some of them quite large, that are built of and on rubbish, along reeking alleys and paths with names like Virgin of Guadalupe Lane.

It proved a little difficult to get into Bordo. At a sentry gate set between two small hills of garbage, a stocky man in dark glasses, jeans, and cowboy boots waved in a procession of trucks and quite a few mule-drawn carts—the latter belonging to the Nezahualcóyotl municipal service and decorated with the red-white-and-green logo of the nation's ruling party, the Partido Revolucionario Institucional, or PRI. The sentry said there was no access to the public. As I argued with him, loaded trucks continued to file by, and the drivers of trucks not belonging to Nezahualcóyotl's municipal fleet stopped to press the sentry's hand, which then flew to a pocket in his quilted vest. During the seconds required for these transactions, children climbed up on the trucks' back wheels and then onto the loads of refuse, and as each truck moved past the gate the children scrabbled frantically through the load, throwing things overboard; they would return to collect them as soon as the truck reached the dumping site, which is invisible from the gate, being hidden by hills of piled-up trash. Eventually, the sentry agreed to let me in for a brief visit.

After a week of rain, the pickers were working ankle-deep in a thick slush; it was tinted blue or bright red in patches, and these exhaled a mist of choking chemical fumes. Oblivious of the smell, a cluster of children crouched in a blue puddle, poring over a small pile of plastic comic-book figures—the Joker, Superman, and the like. The children did not want to talk to a stranger (indeed, they avoided even looking at me), but after I made a couple of tries the tallest boy answered a question, saying that he and his friends wanted the toys not to play with but to sell. Nevertheless, as they salvaged the few dolls that had no arms or legs missing they deployed them in a brief, soundless mock battle before tossing them into a scavenging sack.

One of Celestino's overseers waved each arriving truck to a spot on the edge of the clearing, where a family or a team of friends was waiting, each member equipped with only a long-handled pitchfork, and no boots, masks, or other protective gear. The team began sifting through the waste even before the truck's shower of refuse ended, expertly plucking out the salvageable bits with their bare hands. The fork was designed to help the pickers separate the mounds of trash on the ground, but an elderly man in faded blue overalls said that since the tractor had been brought in there was hardly any time for the garbage to pile up, so a lot of salable material was left unsalvaged. (The tractor was somebody's idea of a landfill operation, but since the garbage wasn't covered with anything after being flattened out it seemed to serve no practical purpose.)

The garbage pickers proved to be a closemouthed lot, especially when I asked their names or put questions about Celestino, but the man in overalls was willing to explain the various stages of trash-picking. "You have to know what to select," he said, working with precision and delicacy as he talked. "For example, this pair of trousers is good, because the buttons and zipper can be removed and sold. If they were made of natural fibre, like cotton, you could sell the cloth as a rag. There are a lot of tennis shoes in this pile, but they're not good enough to sell to the secondhand-clothes dealers." He was picking through a revolting pile of what seemed to be the refuse of a very large family, but by the time the things he had chosen to keep reached his sack they looked almost clean. He waved toward a point in the rubbish heap which I found indistinguishable from its surroundings. "That's my spot," he said. "When I'm through for the day, I take my sack over there and sort it. It's not enough just to pick the garbage. We have to put work into it afterward to make it salable."

A truck unloaded a pile of refuse from what someone said was an open-air market—a cascade of burst tomatoes, crushed bananas, empty egg crates, clear plastic bags, and wadded-up vegetable peelings. None of it was rotting yet, but, according to a group of women and children investigating the pile, there was nothing of any use other than a score of orange halves that had had most of their pulp pressed out of them, and that one woman picked up and immediately began eating.

I struck up a conversation with another member of the team, a woman with long gray braids who was wearing a clean checked apron over a faded dress. She told me that in general market waste was virtually worthless, except for an occasional pile of butchershop bones, which gelatin and bouillon-cube manufacturers would buy. Other pickers were saving the organic waste for pigs they kept along the edges of the dump, but she said she didn't own any. While quite a few of the garbage pickers looked filthy, her clothes, I noticed, were not only clean but crisply ironed. "I used to wash clothes for a living," she explained. "But now my arms can't take being in the water so long." The sun was directly overhead, and hitting hard, so the smells around us—acetone, vegetable rot, used disposable diapers—ripened and concentrated in the heat. . . .

5.3 Guatemalan Indians Escape to Mexico

Racial discrimination and political abuse have been staple features in the lives of Guatemalan indigenous peoples (Indians) for centuries. During the 1970s, with the aid of the Catholic Church, indigenous communities

Simons, Marlise. "Guatemalan Indians Crowd into Mexico to Escape Widening War." *Washington Post*, February 19, 1982, p. A-23. Reprinted by permission of Marlise Simons, *began to organize to improve their lot. When the military governments of the era responded to their cooperatives and requests for reform with violent repression, some Indians took up arms and joined the leftist Guerrilla Army of the Poor (E.G.P.). During the early 1980s, the Guatemalan military took steps to eliminate all revolutionary opposition. The armed forces targeted entire indigenous communities in the northern part of the country for military attack. Villages were bombarded and burned, and atrocities were common. Military brutality sent tens of thousands of Indians fleeing across the border to seek refuge in Mexico, where they found little aid or comfort from overtaxed authorities.*

CUIDAD CUAUHTEMOC, Mexico—The insistent whir of a Guatemalan Army helicopter broke the silence of the hot afternoon. The helicopter circled just short of the Mexican border, then swooped down and fired into the trees below.

"Guatemalan families came running out of nowhere, screaming," recalled Carlos Gomez, a Mexican farmhand who witnessed the scene. "There was terrible panic. When they got to our side, some of the people gave away their children to the Mexicans."

No one was hurt that afternoon of Jan. 14, but by the time the chopper rumbled off, nearly 300 men, women and children had sought refuge in Mexico. They said they had traveled on foot much of the night, fleeing from an Army raid that they said had left 18 dead in the village of Santa Cataria and 16 dead in the village of El Limonar. The chopper's crew had spotted their group as they approached the border and, apparently under the impression that they were guerrillas or sympathizers, had opened fire.

The group was another trickle in the flood of about 2,000 refugees each week that is pouring into Mexico as the Guatemalan Army wages the fiercest antiguerrilla campaign in its history. Over the past six months, the Army has stepped up its hunt for a tough, often invisible guerrilla force, and the refugees say it has inflicted a scorched-earth policy on Guatemala's western highlands. As a result, entire villages and hamlets have fled, often into Mexico.

In this rugged, unpatrolled land, there are few documented statistics. The State Department in its latest annual report on international human rights estimated that nearly 100 peasants a month were killed in Guatemala's escalating guerrilla war. It estimated that an additional 250 to 300 persons were murdered each month for what appeared to be political reasons.

"Increasingly, noncombatants are the principal victims of the violence from both sides," the report said.

who worked as a correspondent for the *Washington Post* and the *New York Times* in Latin America from 1971 to 1989.

A Western diplomat in Guatemala recently put last year's death toll at 5,000, most of them civilians, while the newly formed Guatemalan Unity Committee, an opposition group, put the figure at 13,500.

In interviews last month with *Washington Post* correspondent Christopher Dickey, Guatemalan military officers in the field readily conceded that civilians caught between them and the guerrillas were considered expendable.

"These people [the guerrillas] are difficult to distinguish from most of the rest of the local population," Gen. Benedicto Lucas Garcia, chief of staff of Guatemala's armed forces, told Dickey. ". . . Because of that, well, the population suffers."

The guerrillas have stated publicly that they at times also have killed civilians suspected of being government informants.

Guatemala's ambassador to Mexico, Jorge Palmieri, conceded in a recent interview that "there are military actions, and people who have nothing to do with it are afraid to be caught up in it, [so] they travel." He contended that there is evidence that the guerrillas "have manipulated people and led them to Mexico to cause upheavals."

Whatever the reason, there is no dispute that the refugees are coming here in record numbers. The Mexican Interior Ministry estimates that there are 120,000 Guatemalan refugees in this country now, more than double the figure of a year ago.

The winding, 565-mile-long dividing line between North and Central America has always been porous. Marked only by an occasional border post, like here at Ciudad Cuauhtemoc, it climbs across the peaks of the Sierra Madre, becomes the Usumacinta River, then loses itself in the dense tropical jungle farther north.

For as long as anyone remembers, merchants and migrant workers have crossed the border freely. But never has the flow been so large. Thousands of terrified, impoverished and often illiterate Indians have come to see the distance between their old homes and the Mexican border—often only a few hundred yards—as the difference between life and death.

Although it is quiet on the Mexican side of the mountains, the war has deeply strained the modest resources of the string of border towns where refugees have arrived. It has also unsettled officials of the Mexican government, who disclosed earlier this week that Mexico has authorized the training of a 4,000-man-quick-reaction military force in part to cope with any possible spillover of the conflict.

Mexico has refused to allow the formation of refugee camps near the frontier for fear that the camps would quickly turn into armed guerrilla bases and worsen the country's already poor relations with Guatemala. Instead, the refugees are scattered all over southern Mexico, working in cities or on farms or relying on the good will of religious charity groups.

Pressure has been building on the government from conservatives who argue that Mexico already has enough social problems of its own and should put a stop to the new flood of penniless foreigners.

But when the government ordered the deportation of 1,800 Guatemalans last summer, it drew sharp criticism from the left as well as from Guy Prim, then the representative of the Office of the United Nations High Commissioner for Refugees, who said there was strong evidence that some deportees were being murdered on their return to Guatemala.

Most of the refugees, like much of Guatemala's highland Indian peasantry, seem conservative, devout and xenophobic. The stories they tell in broken Spanish of half-empty or deserted villages, burned homes and dismembered bodies present a picture far removed from the tight social order that for centuries has ruled one of the oldest cultures in the Americas.

Their accounts offer glimpses of a bitter, often bloody conflict that has gone largely unreported to the outside world. Few outsiders travel to the remote villages in the provinces of Huehuetenango, Quiche and San Marcos, where most of the fighting has occurred, and suspicious locals seldom confide in those who do.

The Guatemalan government insists that the guerrillas bear much of the responsibility for any atrocities that have occurred. Earlier this week, the Army blamed guerrillas for the massacre of 53 Quiche Indians in the village of Chumac.

But in a week of interviews, more than two dozen refugees offered repeated accounts of brutality by the Army and none by the guerrillas.

Near Motozintla, a village tucked against a barren mountainside, Jacinto Pascual, 60, explained why he, his wife, their children and grandchildren had abandoned their home in the Guatemalan village of Tacana last December. He said the *pintos,* a Guatemalan pejorative for soldiers, had killed 40 villagers in Tacana, including "whole families."

Pascual, whose possessions were reduced to what he could carry across the border in a plastic shopping bag, apologized for crying "right here in front of my wife. I'm not afraid of death. I've lived my time. But I'm afraid of the way the *pintos* kill. They first cut off the ears, then the nose, with a machete. They cut out the eyes and the tongue. I heard them say they don't want to waste their bullets."

On the flight to Mexico, he said, his family had found four bodies in a forest. "Two had their hands and feet cut off," he recalled. "Two had no more tongue."

Women express the same fears: being raped by the soldiers and being burned alive in their huts. Religious workers said that many frontier families tend their land and animals in Guatemala in the daytime and sleep in Mexico at night.

One widow who lives in Guatemala, but sleeps in Mexico, said she could no longer sleep when at home. "I've seen the fires at night. The soldiers bar the doors [of the huts], throw gasoline and burn everyone inside."

Candido, a wounded Catholic lay preacher from Neton, said he had been dumped from an Army truck a few days earlier after faking death. Soldiers had tied his brother behind the truck, "pulling him at great speed until he died," he said. Efrain Moreno, a former government employee just arrived from Neton, said the village had been completely abandoned.

A Mexican nurse, who said she has extracted "many a bullet" from the refugees, angrily recalled an incident two months ago when a woman from Neton brought her badly burned 9-month-old granddaughter for treatment.

Government soldiers had come to the woman's house seeking her son. When she told them she did not know his whereabouts, she said, they held the baby's feet over burning coals in the fireplace.

"Its feet were burned to the bone," said the nurse. "I saw it with my own eyes." The nurse, who asked not to be identified because she feared that Mexican authorities disapproved of her work with the refugees, said the baby survived and subsequently was taken to a hospital for a series of skin grafts.

Sometimes the impact on Mexicans of the Guatemalan conflict is a subtle one. In the Mexican village of Niquivil, built in a high pass often covered in clouds, the villagers do not go out at night. The mountains are haunted, they say, by the souls of the scattered, unburied dead across the border.

For the past six months, peasants have pulled bodies out of the Cuileo and Selegua rivers that run from Guatemala into Mexico. "The people here have been very shocked," said a local Catholic priest. "Many of them will not eat fish from the rivers any more."

5.4 West Indians on the Move

For the people of the Caribbean, migration is deeply embedded in their social and economic traditions. Their predisposition to migrate in search of economic opportunities was a powerful factor in the key role West In-

Richardson, Bonham D. "Caribbean Migration, 1835–1985." In *The Modern Caribbean*, edited by Franklin W. Knight and Colin A. Palmer, 209–12. Chapel Hill: University of

dians played in constructing the Panama Canal in the early 1900s. As
this reading illustrates, many West Indian workers continued to migrate
after the construction of the canal, seeking new labor opportunities in
other parts of the Caribbean, and they continue to migrate today, with the
United States often their preferred destination.

Construction of the Panama Canal (1904–14) by the United States uprooted and dislocated tens of thousands of West Indian men and women
who traveled to Panama for jobs. The failed French attempt two decades earlier also had attracted perhaps 50,000 West Indians, mainly
from Jamaica. Jamaicans had traveled to Panama even before that, many
working on the isthmian railroad in the 1850s. So when officials of the
Isthmian Canal Commission (the U.S. governmental agency responsible
for canal construction) sought labor for the blasting and earth-moving,
it is not surprising that they turned to Jamaica. To their disappoint-
ment, however, Jamaica denied the commission a labor recruiting ter-
minal in Kingston, claiming that too many Jamaicans already had died
and suffered working for the French.

The Americans eventually established their principal labor-recruiting
station for canal workers in Barbados. From 1905 to 1913, U.S. officials
shipped 20,000 Barbadian male contract laborers—as well as hundreds
of others from nearby islands—from Bridgetown to Panama. But men
and women traveling informally from their home islands to the Canal
Zone far outnumbered contract workers during the construction decade. Barbadian historian Velma Newton estimates that as many as
40,000 Barbadians (besides the 20,000 contract workers) traveled informally to the Panamanian isthmus before the canal was completed, and
that between 80,000 and 90,000 Jamaicans did so as well. British West
Indians were not the only Caribbean peoples traveling to the Canal
Zone. Men and women from Danish, Dutch, and French islands went
too. Between 1905 and 1907, U.S. labor recruiters shipped 7,600 contract laborers from Guadeloupe and Martinique to Panama before the
continental French government ended the recruiting.

Whatever the total number (insular demographic data were still no-
toriously vague and unreliable), the West Indians who traveled from
their home islands to Panama—and often back again—set in motion
demographic trends that reverberated throughout the region. Thousands of West Indians perished on the isthmus from exhaustion, disease, and landslides; nearly 6,000 Barbadians alone died of all causes
from 1906 to 1920 in Panama. Probably over 15,000 British West Indians altogether died in Panama before 1920. Others never returned
home but drifted west to new destinations such as the new American

banana plantations in Honduras and the Limón district of eastern Costa Rica. Hundreds joined the British West Indies regiment of World War I and fought against the Turks in Palestine. Thousands stayed in Panama and became the black "Zonians" whose presence would become a treaty issue between the United States and Panama decades later.

The flow of British West Indian laborers to the Panama Canal Zone in the first two decades of the twentieth century was paralleled by a countercurrent of money that workers sent home to their families and friends. The "Panama money" softened the effects of a severe economic depression in the British Caribbean that could be traced to competition with European beet sugar for the London market. Wives and mothers on the home islands used the wages sent from Panama to purchase foodstuffs, clothing, and membership in local burial societies. In thousands of cases, money from Panama also purchased land plots, fishing sloops, and shops throughout the islands, thereby affording working-class blacks a measure of independence from local plantocracies. This was not the first time small-island West Indians had prospered from money sent and brought home from a wage destination, but Panama money intensified the search for wages abroad by migrants from small Caribbean islands because it represented a volume and continuity of remittances that had never been known before.

When it became obvious to American officials that the canal project would soon be finished, they began to repatriate many of the West Indians to their home islands. Thousands of the labor migrants, now accustomed to receiving American wages, traveled on to Cuba and the Dominican Republic where U.S. capital had helped expand sugarcane acreage in both countries after the beginning of the century. The further "development" of the sugarcane industries of the Greater Antilles represented, in a broad sense, the same sort of challenge to American engineers that the Panamanian isthmus had; any economic problem, it was thought, could be solved with a lavish application of modern North American technology. Cuban sugar-processing techniques and field methods were thereby modernized by the turn of the century. Similarly, the "idle" lands of the southeastern quadrant of Hispaniola were rapidly converted from tropical forests and scrublands into enormous fields of sugarcane intersected by cog rails and commanded by the towering smokestacks of newly constructed grinding factories, built mainly with U.S. money.

The attraction of wage jobs in modernizing and constructing new agricultural facilities, and eventually harvesting the sugarcane, in Cuba and the Dominican Republic drew thousands of migrating black "Antillanos." Some were veterans from Panama. Many came directly from the English-speaking islands. Thousands of Haitians came too, mainly as seasonal cane cutters. Sailing schooners, and later steamers, had taken men from the English-speaking islands of the Leeward Caribbean to

San Pedro de Macoris—in the heart of the Dominican Republic's sugarcane belt—since before the turn of the century. And Jamaican workers traveled to Cuba, mainly on steamships, in ever larger numbers as the Panama Canal construction wound down. In 1919 and 1920, the peak years for Jamaican migration to Cuba, nearly 50,000 Jamaicans sought work on the larger island. As a linguistically alien, dark-skinned, Protestant, and mostly male labor force, black West Indians were not always welcome in the large Roman Catholic, Spanish-speaking island. In Santo Domingo they were derided as *cocolos* by native Dominicans. Authorities in both countries insisted that these migrants—many of whom arrived for the annual cane harvest in January and departed after the crop was in in July—were holding jobs that should be performed by locals.

The application and withdrawal of U.S. capital at various locations throughout the circum-Caribbean region thus pulled and pushed labor migrants here and there. Accordingly, insular demographic patterns continued to reflect the familiar characteristics that migration societies have been known for before and since. Females, children, and old people had tended to predominate in the small Caribbean islands ever since principally male laborers had traveled away after slavery. But by the early twentieth century, insular populations had become even more mobile and fluid from season to season and from year to year as external job opportunities appeared, disappeared, and reappeared. For instance, the massive exodus of men from Saint Kitts, Nevis, Anguilla, and Antigua to Santo Domingo at the beginning of each year in the first decades of the twentieth century began a six-month period in which mothers, wives, and children back home waited, hoping for remittances through the mail. Colonial officials in the same islands dreaded the men's return in the late summer because, for the next few months, unemployment always became a problem on the local sugarcane plantations, incipient labor protests and disturbances surfaced, and burglary rates rose. The population characteristics, economic opportunities, and even cultural attributes of these small Leeward Islands in the early twentieth century were influenced not so much by local events as by the rhythms of the sugarcane harvests in the Greater Antilles.

Although migration-induced demographic patterns had become intensified, Caribbean migration in the early twentieth century had changed in at least two ways from what it had been like in the decades immediately following emancipation. First, the number of people moving about became much larger as U.S. capital investment was concentrated in selected places, creating thousands of ephemeral work opportunities for multi-skilled laborers and their families. Second, migration was no longer simply a matter of traveling from one neighboring island to the next. Rather, it often involved journeys to the far edges of the circum-Caribbean zone.

5.5 The Perilous Journey of Nicaraguan Migrants

Migration is ultimately a human drama fraught with excitement and danger. As civil war and uncertainty gripped Central America in the 1980s, many individuals chose to leave their home countries in search of new opportunities. Though some privileged migrants could amass the documents and financial resources to fly out of their countries, the more common form of departure involved difficult and often dangerous overland travel. This reading illustrates the perils of undocumented migration by Nicaraguan pilgrims to the United States through Central America. As described by U.S. journalist Guy Gugliotta, who traveled undercover with photographer Antonio (Tony) Olmos, the group encountered a range of obstacles as they illegally crossed the border between Guatemala and Mexico on their difficult journey to the United States.

CIUDAD HIDALGO, Mexico—The bus headed northwest in the pre-dawn darkness, winding downward from the Guatemalan plateau to tropical lowlands on the Mexican border. The passengers sat in silence, practically holding their breath, hoping that at this point, when it had finally begun, nothing would go wrong. . . .

It was a crisp, clear, gorgeous Guatemala night bathed in light from a waxing moon, and the travelers were optimistic. By the end of the day, things would be different, for Wednesday would be the first of six days of little or no sleep, of thirst and of fear. By the end of Wednesday we would all understand what our coyote guide had meant when he warned that this trip would be the worst experience of our lives.

Our route this morning lead south from Guatemala City to Escuintla, then northwest through the town of Mazatenango to Tecun-Uman on the Guatemalan border across the Suchiate river from Ciudad Hidalgo, Mexico. In all we were traveling 130 miles. With luck we would be locked inside a Tecun-Uman safehouse by daybreak. At dusk we would cross the river into Mexico.

Our guides included three Nicaraguan coyotes, specialists in the art of human contraband. Manuel, the leader, was 24, a former accountant who handled money and planning for the trip. His assistants were Jorge and Rolando, both in their late 30s. Jorge specialized in bribes and logistics; Rolando handled personal relations with the passengers.

Gugliotta, Guy. "From Nicaragua to Texas: A Desperate Journey." *Miami Herald*, February 26–29, March 1, 1990. Reprinted with permission of the *Miami Herald*.

All three had warned us that the Guatemala-Mexico border would be the most difficult part of the trip. We had traveled legally from Nicaragua to Guatemala on tourist visas, but once in Mexico we would be illegal—*mojado*, or "wet," in coyote slang. The Mexicans, the coyotes assured us, would be certain to take advantage.

"Mexicans Are Thieves"

"Mexicans are thieves," Jorge had said before we left Guatemala. "They can't help it; it's in their blood."

At the river we would be exposed and alone, just 42 others among thousands of lemming-like Latin American pilgrims flowing northward each year toward the United States. The cost of travel depended on how many times the Mexicans caught us, how greedy they were and how skillfully our coyotes negotiated. Ideally the coyotes would handle everything, but in case they didn't, Manuel had briefed us in detail:

"Never try to bribe the Guatemalan army or the Mexican army," he had said. "They don't take money and it makes them mad. We see them, we avoid them.

"Same thing with the Americans," he added. "None of them take money—not the border patrol, not immigration, not the police—don't even bother. One thing, though: you don't have to be afraid of the gringos. They're well-trained and educated, and they won't mess with you.

"The Mexicans are different. The Mexicans will beat on you, and if they start, you have to take it. You're Mr. Humility. On our last trip, the federal police handcuffed me, knocked me down, pushed my face into the ground and kicked me. Understand that this can happen and be prepared for it."

We drove into Tecun-Uman at 5:30 a.m. It was the heart of the dry season, and the dust was so deep and omnipresent we couldn't tell which streets were paved. Tecun was shabby and bustling, a rough grid filled with clapboard houses and small, brightly colored stores whose contents were described in garish letters written on the walls. It was a typical border town, crammed with teamsters, drummers, businessmen and, one imagined, with transients like ourselves and the smugglers who moved them.

Our bus stopped next to a set of rusty railroad tracks in front of Pension La Frontera, a rustic hotel whose gate opened as we drew to a halt. We grabbed our few belongings, hustled off the bus and scooted inside the hotel compound. The door clanged shut.

Manuel's warnings of discomforts to come had prepared us for the worst, but an uneventful trip aboard a comfortable bus had dulled our anxiety. Pension La Frontera also had a calming effect. Rooms were simple but spacious, arranged in a square around a central courtyard. Toilets, washbasins and showers were communal, but there was plenty of warm water and a certain degree of privacy. For our group, accustomed to a Guatemalan safehouse with a single toilet and sometime running water, Pension La Frontera was paradise.

"Maybe they were just trying to scare us with all that earlier talk," Merevia suggested, as we rearranged our belongings and settled down for a nap.

"Maybe," I replied. . . .

As the day progressed, it became obvious that we had an additional hardship to overcome. In the Central American lowlands, even in February, midday temperatures climb into the 90s. Most of us had jackets we had needed in Guatemala City and planned to use in the Mexican mountains. For the crossing we were either going to have to wear them or carry them. Neither prospect was attractive.

Our departure came at 5 p.m. sharp, and was fully as sudden as our arrival. We gathered our belongings and massed in the pension's doorway, ready to tumble aboard the three vans that stopped next to the railroad tracks. Then we were gone, lurching down a pitted dirt road through choking clouds of dust, heading, we imagined, toward the Rio Suchiate and Mexico.

We rode for about 15 minutes, through a crowded Tecun street market, then down a country lane through sections of fenced-in pasture burned yellow by the sun. Finally we turned off the track at a campesino cottage where about a dozen people—men, women and children—awaited us.

Rolando dickered with Guatemalan coyotes assigned to get us safely across the river. We were sweating now and complaining, the great adventure starting to look a lot tougher than it had at Pension La Frontera. . . .

"Get down!" commanded Rolando suddenly, and we stopped in our tracks. Seconds later a Guatemalan on horseback rode up and stopped.

"You'll have to stay here for a while," the outrider said. "There are Mexican Federales all over the place."

Crouched in the Dust

We crouched in the dust for a half-hour, coughing, sweating and drinking frequently from canteens and water bottles. Many of the men, including myself, took off their trousers and folded them into suitcases, following the coyotes' lead.

At 6:15 p.m. we moved out, this time divided into three groups, each group traveling with a different coyote. . . .

The crossing looked easy—knee-deep water, perhaps 50 yards wide. We slid down a five-foot embankment and began a final traverse across a stone riverbed leading toward the water.

Suddenly we heard gunshots and shouting. We crouched behind a pile of stones and ducked. Within seconds Rolando appeared on the opposite bank, flushed like a pheasant from a hedgerow. He knelt, waved his arm, then ran into the water. A moment later more heads popped into sight. Spurred on by Rolando, groups one and two came back across the river toward us.

"No way, not now," gasped Rolando, when we had withdrawn to a ribbon of thin hardwoods standing along the river bank. "The Federales chased us back. They're everywhere."

We retreated finally in pitch darkness, lurching blindly into a dusty lane and collapsing for another impromptu bivouac. We drank more water, ate some cookies and threw away more baggage. Tony and I discarded two blankets we had bought as a hedge against the mountain cold. Merevia relinquished the cosmetics she purchased in Guatemala. It occurred to me that the Guatemalan coyotes and local campesinos probably mined a fortune in salvaged goods after each river crossing.

At 8 p.m. we decided to try again. We were all in a bunch now, with Rolando leading. Again we plunged into the hardwoods and stumbled downriver for about 200 yards, urged on by whispers of "Vamos, Vamos!" from the Guatemalan coyotes. And again we slid down the river bank and skittered across the dry riverbed, scrambling and tripping in the dark.

And then, finally, we were in the river. I walked slowly, holding the hand of Merevia's 10-year-old son. He was a quiet boy, something of a brooder, but as we approached the far bank he suddenly looked up at me and smiled. What a blast!

A Helping Hand

Indeed, it was another beautiful, quiet evening, with comfortable temperatures and a bright moon. The other side of the river looked like a sheer six-foot escarpment, seemingly impossible to climb. But one of our number, Enrique, a former member of the Nicaraguan national basketball team, was stationed below to offer a helping hand. He grabbed Merevia's son in his ham-like grasp and virtually tossed him up the hill. I found a foothold, grabbed Enrique's hand and followed quickly.

"We're not through yet," a woman's voice told me as I crouched in the brush above the river. "This is only an island." Daniela, 28, had come across the river with her two children and was rearranging her belongings for the next ordeal. Tough, resourceful and uncomplaining most of the time, she had begun to look a little frantic: "I've lost my shoes."

"I have another pair," I said. "Wait until we get across."

About four hours had elapsed since we left Pension La Frontera. We were tired and desperately thirsty, but there were no complaints from anyone. Merevia, forced to concentrate on the business at hand, had proved to be surprisingly strong and in excellent shape, keeping up easily while others lagged behind. I was warm in a T-shirt but not sweating as before.

The final crossing came in about 20 minutes. Moving six at a time behind Guatemalan coyotes, we crept to the top of a high bluff, then slid down to the water. Here the river was deep and narrow, no more than 15 yards wide. We would cross on makeshift rafts made from the huge inner tubes of tractor tires. Each raft had a single board strapped across it and would be towed across the channel by two Guatemalan swimmers.

It was pitch dark. One of the swimmers pointed to a spot on the tire and I sat down, but the tube sank as I tried to adjust my position. Suddenly we were whirling into the river.

"Listen, whatever happens, I want you to know it's been great." It was Tony, sitting next to me and speaking in English. I hadn't seen him for about two hours.

"Yeah, well you better grab hold of me or I'll fall in."

And then we were ashore. We ran across a short stretch of open riverbed and into a stand of brush and trees where Rolando told us to change clothes. I took off my shorts, put on my trousers and rummaged around in my bag looking for my extra shoes. Then I found Daniela and handed them to her.

"They're size 10s," I warned.

Mexican Guides

Shortly we moved off, walking quickly but without urgency. Our guides were Mexicans now, two or three of them carrying machetes. They led us out of the riverbed, up a short rise and into what felt like the back yard of a farmhouse. I could smell chickens and see a back door with a light above it. We sat down beneath a large tree and waited in the darkness.

"Get your feet wet?"

It was Edwin, an easygoing, high school math teacher from the Nicaraguan town of Diriamba.

"I'm afraid I did, professor," I said. "And you?"

"Hah, you bet, and my underwear, too."

At 9:30 p.m. two taxis pulled into the yard. The procedure now, as Manuel had explained, was for us to drive to the city of Tapachula 22 miles away and hide out there in a hotel until we left for Mexico City on a bus. Arranging the layover at the farm, the drive to Tapachula and the dead time in the hotel was, Manuel had said, the most difficult part of the trip.

We had divided ourselves into three groups for the ride to Tapachula. I was in the second segment. With 17 people it was the biggest, but we had most of the kids. Tony was in group three.

After the first group left in the two taxis, we settled back to wait some more. We were exhausted now, and most of our water was gone. The farmer who sheltered us, as if reading our minds, suddenly appeared with fresh slivers of cantaloupe and watermelon. He was, he explained, a melon farmer. Help yourselves.

The second pair of cabs arrived at 10:30 p.m. I rode in the back seat with Merevia's oldest boy and sat next to Daniela and her two kids. The cabdriver was a dashing young fellow with a mustache who drove at 90 miles per hour with his radio blasting. After 15 minutes we passed a highway sign with an arrow pointing left toward Tapachula. Our driver turned and stepped on the gas. With luck we would be taking a shower in the Rochester Hotel in about 10 minutes.

Then our luck ran out. An unmarked red sedan pulled up alongside us and an arm extended from the front seat passenger window and motioned the driver to pull over.

The red sedan stopped, the doors opened and three men carrying guns and wearing khaki uniforms stepped to the pavement. It was the Mexican immigration police. . . .

Ed. note: The group eventually made it safely to Texas, only to miss the deadline for political asylum, as described in the following.

An Epilogue

Tony and I said goodbye to our companions an hour later, then left the Colonial Motel to catch a cab to Harlingen and a flight home to Miami. Around 7 a.m., we checked into a small motel near the airport to get a shower and a shave.

We turned on the television news. The biggest story of the day concerned hundreds of Nicaraguans lined up outside INS Headquarters in nearby Laguna Vista, Texas, to beat the deadline and file for asylum under the existing lenient guidelines. After today, the report said, it would be infinitely more difficult, if not impossible, for Nicaraguans to obtain political asylum.

We telephoned the Colonial Motel to urge members of the group to get to Laguna Vista as rapidly as possible. No one picked up the phone. We waited 20 minutes and called again. We tried a third time from the Harlingen Airport. Still no answer.

Finally, without talking to anyone, we flew home. Surely the coyotes would know what to do.

On the morning of Feb. 22, Tony received a call at his Miami Beach home from Jonathan, 31, a former Managua mapmaker and traveling companion. Our group had spent most of Feb. 20 filling out immigration forms, Jonathan said, and in the afternoon had driven by bus to Laguna Vista to request asylum.

They arrived at 5 p.m., 45 minutes after INS closed its doors. The next day all 40 of the travelers were arrested, and one week later the INS was holding them at different camps in Texas, threatening to deport them to Nicaragua within eight days.

"At 4:15 p.m. (Feb. 20) we went outside and took everybody inside who was there at that time, " said INS spokeswoman Virginia Kice.

She acknowledged the lenient guidelines had said only that they would expire on Feb. 20; they had said nothing about the INS ceasing to take asylum requests after 4:15 p.m.

5.6 Portrait of a Maquiladora Worker

The maquiladora *industry, which assembles goods using Mexican labor and U.S. materials, has emerged as an important new source of employment in Mexico. Taking advantage of the proximity to the U.S. market and special laws facilitating the cross-border movement of materials, the* maquiladora *was one of the few sources of dynamism in the Mexican economy during the 1970s and 1980s.* Maquiladora *production has been an important source of employment, and it has had a major impact on the*

Fernández Kelly, Mária Patricia. "Francisca: A Profile of a Maquiladora Worker." In *For We Are Sold, I and My People: Women and Industry in Mexico's Frontier*, 177–83. Albany: State University of New York Press, 1983. Reprinted by permission of the State University of New York Press.

*country's occupational structure and migration patterns. This reading il-
lustrates the opportunities and dilemmas posed by* maquiladora *employment for one Mexican woman.*

Francisca Lucero is nineteen years old and has worked for three years
at the largest electronic assembly plant in Ciudad Juárez, a subsidiary
of a U.S. multinational corporation. Born in Santa Barbara, a town in
the interior of the state of Chihuahua, Kika (as she is known to friends
and family) was brought to Juárez at the age of three. With her came
two brothers and her parents to swell the ranks of the hopeful that
constantly migrate to the Mexican-American border.

Earlier, her father, who once had owned a small parcel of promising
farm land, was forced to sell it and join other displaced agricultural
workers who had been driven out by large agribusiness. It is not that
Kika's father wanted to move from the Santa Barbara area or that he
was lured by the mirage of urban opportunity and progress, as some
migration students believe. Rather he knew, even then, that suffering
was to be expected in a big city, for cities are often cruel to newcomers.
He had heard that life was expensive. But he had no choice. It was
either further impoverishment in a small town or the gamble for a
better life in Ciudad Juárez. At that time he placed his faith in two
somewhat encouraging signs. First, Ciudad Juárez was growing. There
had to be work in a big city like that for a man willing to do virtually
anything to earn a living. Besides, Valente, his uncle, had migrated to
Juárez five years earlier and was willing to help him for as long as it
took to find a house and settle down. Second, Juárez was very close to
the United States, only a few minutes away from El Paso, Texas. If
things became too difficult he could cross into U.S. territory. Many were
doing so in spite of the ever-present danger of *la migra,* and he might
also try. He was not afraid.

Kika can still remember those early days in Juárez. The city turned
her father from an impoverished migrant into an unskilled general
worker with no stable or regular income. In time he did have to cross
the border and toiled in the fields of Arizona as an "illegal alien." The
gringos treated him well, but the ordeal was trying. Eventually, he came
back to Juárez, a more silent and older man. It was fortunate that he
returned. Many men don't; they find ways to remain in the United
States while their families are left behind to fend for themselves.

Francisca can vividly describe, amidst sighs of regret and nervous
laughter, the hardships of living with seven other persons of various
ages in a one-room adobe house in Las Lomas, an area on the outskirts
of the city with no paved streets, no electricity and no piped water.
Three younger brothers and two sisters were born there. For ten-odd
years her mother worked as a maid in order to help support the family.
But the most she ever earned was one hundred pesos a week (about

$8). Occasionally, she would wake up earlier than usual, brush away from her face the signs of discouragement and cook *burritos, empanadas* or *gorditas,* which she later sold at the local stadiums. There were only a few assembly plants or *maquiladoras* in Juárez at that time, although people hoped their presence would change the city; they were seen as a sign of progress. Kika's mother tried to get a job at one of the new factories, as it soon became clear that they hired mostly women. However, they required a primary school diploma. Having attended school irregularly for only four years, she didn't have one.

Their situation improved, however, when Kika's oldest brother turned sixteen and was able to supplement their father's income by becoming an unskilled construction worker. Kika too had to help but not before completing six years of schooling. By then her parents knew that without a primary school certificate her chances of finding work at a maquiladora would be poor. And the consensus is that assembly plants, which operate as subsidiaries of multinational corporations, offer the best employment alternative in Ciudad Juárez. Maquiladora workers regularly earn the minimum wage stipulated by Mexican law and, more significantly from the perspective of the workers, they insure medical care through the participation of their personnel in the Instituto Mexicano del Seguro Social (the Social Security System). These are benefits which unfortunately cannot always be obtained by working in other sectors of the economy.

Kika had been a good student. She would have liked to attend secondary school and to become a nurse. But familial duties dissipated her hopes. Although she doesn't remember any sort of direct parental pressure, she felt partly responsible for the well-being of her family. The needs were many and the earnings scant. When her father ruefully encouraged her to continue studying, she refused by arguing that school was boring. At fourteen she went to work as a clerk in a grocery store. Hours were long, the wage small and she was excluded from the benefits that the Mexican Labor Law requires, but nothing could be done. She knew it would be impossible to get a better-paying job until after her sixteenth birthday. Patiently, she waited.

At fifteen, however, she started looking for employment at the largest industrial park in Ciudad Juárez. She had learned about young women who lie about their ages and alter birth certificates in order to qualify for work in the plants. She was willing to do whatever was necessary to become an *operadora* (line worker). As time passed, the industrial park acquired formidable dimensions in Kika's mind. She began to admire the geometric profiles of factories aligned by the side of carefully manicured lawns and the design of multi-national emblems. In particular she learned to contemplate, in awe, the sharp contrast between the industrial park—a symbol of modern opportunity—and the drab neglect visible throughout Ciudad Juárez.

In 1975 Kika and one of her best friends would regularly arrive at the industrial park at six-thirty in the morning. Wearing their best clothes, hungry, expectant and shy, the two would walk from plant to plant in search of precious job applications. It wasn't easy to get one. Signs reading *No hay solicitudes* (no job applications) or *No hay vacantes* (not hiring) hung on the doors of many maquiladoras. At one of them a young and smartly dressed secretary looked them over and told them to come back next week. At another a guard with an air of solemnity about him asked if they had letters of recommendation and, after receiving a negative response, triumphantly stated that a personal recommendation was indispensable to apply for a job at an assembly plant.

After two months of similar experiences, Kika was confused. She felt belittled and impotent; incapable of gaining control over a situation that deeply affected her life and that of her family. If, as common knowledge has it, there are so many opportunities for women in Juárez, why was she having difficulty finding a job? She did not know that for every production operator working along the assembly lines, behind the sewing machines, or attached to welders and wire cutters, three other women with similar economic need and similar abilities constantly search for employment. Those who are older, who support children or who have not completed primary school find it particularly difficult to get a job. Many are driven across the border and work illegally as domestics in El Paso. Women, single or married, of different levels of education and age who roam the streets and industrial parks in need of jobs, have become a distinctive feature of Ciudad Juárez. It is part of the irony of their quest that until the maquiladora program appeared, the majority were not members of the labor force. Fourteen years later these women have become urban proletarians.

Kika may have despaired at her difficulty to find a job in an environment where the only viable employment opportunities were geared to women almost exclusively. But the apparent paradox in which she found herself obscured many of the advantages of relocation from the point of view of multinational corporations. Women who are forced to compete against one another for a limited number of jobs turn out to be efficient and docile workers when competition occurs in a social milieu devoid of occupational opportunities for men.

"We hire mostly women because they are more reliable than men; they have finer fingers, smaller muscles and unsurpassed manual dexterity. Also, women don't get tired of repeating the same operations nine hundred times a day." Such was the explanation offered by Kika's personnel manager when asked why 90% of the plant's workers are women. His was a lucid articulation of the ideology that justifies the employment of women (particularly young women) in low-paying assembly operations by referring to presumed biological and emotional differences between the sexes.

By distorting and over-simplifying complex phenomena, ideology obviates the need to center attention upon economic and political realities. To the social scientist, statements like the one recorded above may appear as trivial, irritating or quaint manifestations of "false consciousness," but they should not be taken lightly; they make social events understandable to members of the managerial sectors as well as most workers. Kika certainly agrees that women tend to be more responsible, patient and dexterous than males. But she doubts that men would be willing to perform the sort of exhausting and repetitive work that she does for the kind of wage that she earns. Also, Kika feels women are more shy and submissive, more used to following orders. They can be easily intimidated and forced to obey. Here lies the economic and political crux of the matter. As Kika herself explains, "I would prefer to stay home and not do factory work. But my family needs my earnings. My father cannot support us, my brothers and sisters are young. I *have* to be efficient and patient at my job."

Until recently, when her seventeen-year-old sister was able to get a similar position at another plant, Kika provided the only source of stable income for her family. Earlier her older brother had left to become one of the countless wetbacks, or *mojados*, sporadically working on the ranches of the U.S. Southwest. With three younger brothers and one sister still in school, Kika feels obliged to give at least five hundred pesos ($22), that is, half of her weekly wage, to her mother who uses it to buy food and pay other household expenses. Thanks to her and her sister's contribution a younger brother will be able to attend secondary school.

Of the half wage she keeps for herself, about 17% is spent in transportation and meals at the factory. With what is left she attends to personal needs. She would like to furnish a room for herself. She is tired of sharing her bed with other members of her family. Also, she is fond of fashionable clothes, cosmetics and, much to the dismay of the city's moralists, she enjoys disco dancing. True, she sometimes has to treat a male companion unable or unwilling to pay the entrance fee at the Malibú, one of the many popular dancing halls in Ciudad Juárez. But more often she may be seen sitting alone or in the company of other female friends waiting to be approached by a young man. Her relative affluence has been a mixed blessing in a context in which men are expected to take the initiative in most areas of social life. The dancing and the euphoria of discotheques provide Kika with the only means of release in an uninterrupted cycle of monotonous work and domestic problems which remain unresolved day after day.

After four years of tedious labor at the plant, Kika admits she is exhausted. More discouraging than monotony is the realization that promotions are hard to come by and wages are forever shrinking. Since she began work, she has put in at least forty-eight hours each week for an average of 58 cents an hour. She has worked from 6:30 a.m. to 3:15 p.m. on weekdays and from 6:30 a.m. to 11:30 a.m. on Saturdays. From

Monday to Friday she, like the rest, is allowed ten minutes in the morning to have breakfast and thirty minutes in the afternoon to eat lunch.

The rest of her time is filled by attempts to fulfill production goals set up by Mexican industrial engineers who have been recruited by U.S. management. Quotas are high to the point that the loss of a few minutes at the beginning of the day may create confusion and delays along the assembly line throughout the rest of the shift. The conveyor belt never ceases to move at the same exasperating speed, and operations are minute and complex. They demand undivided attention. Even basic needs like going to the bathroom require special permission from the supervisor.

Transportation is also a problem. Although 90% of Ciudad Juárez is covered by public transport, the quality is inadequate at best. During the rush periods which precede the entrance of workers at the factories, it is possible to see hundreds of women crowded like cattle inside rundown ruteras and buses. To arrive punctually at the plant, Kika must take two ruteras every morning (one from her house to the downtown area and another one to the industrial park), because she lives in one of the colonias in the periphery of the city, where the majority of working people are concentrated. The neighborhood where she lives still has no paved streets, although electricity and sewerage were recently provided. Usually it takes Kika between forty-five minutes and one hour to get from her home to the plant.

In this respect, as in many others, hers is a situation markedly different from that of managers who, almost without exception, live in the U.S. El Paso suburbs. Every morning, shortly after the ruteras have delivered the women to the plants, the managers may be seen commuting from the United States to Ciudad Juárez (a thirty-minute ride, at the most). The proximity of the industrial parks to El Paso enables management and their families to enjoy the advantages of the "American way of life." What better example may be found to illustrate the convergence of two different styles of life in an international setting which lays bare the contradictions of a gender differentiated labor division?

The personnel manager at the plant where Kika works often reflects that "maquiladoras have brought about an industrial revolution to the Mexican border. They have taught an otherwise inexperienced work force about the merits of punctuality and industrial discipline." Maybe! But Kika has experienced another aspect of this story. In the last three years she has learned what it is like to work as an appendage of a machine. She knows about the boredom bred in dark surroundings filled by lead vapors due to defective ventilation. She has often felt the nerve-racking effects of continuous high levels of noise and the nausea induced by glues and solder.

Kika must go on working because she has no choice. She longs for the day when she will be able to get married, leave the work force and have a home of her own. Being a member of a generation of female factory workers that is barely a decade old, Kika does not see herself as a member of the proletariat, but as a potential wife and mother. Novels and soap operas have instilled and reflect romance in her mind. But marriage is a hazardous prospect in a context characterized by economic constraints that keep men in her circle from performing their traditional role as providers.

To promoters of the In-Bond Manufacturing Program, maquiladoras may represent a success, but Kika knows she lives in a painful bind. And is that not what the terms underdevelopment and dependency mean in a most precise manner? Cut from their abstract embellishments, they describe a social reality in which persons like Kika and the members of her family must always move perilously between destitution and mere subsistence, even while surrounded by the glitter of "progress." Kika agrees with her personnel manager that *maquiladoras* are the best thing that ever happened to Ciudad Juárez. That, indeed, describes the real paradox.

6

Mirrors of the Heart: Color, Class, and Identity

These Bolivian women, dressed in the traditional Andean *polleras,* sell high-tech audio equipment at an urban market. © 1989 Vera Lentz/Black Star

The profile of the Americas—North, South, and Middle—is being continually reshaped by immigration from many parts of the world, as we saw in the preceding chapter. By far the most enduring and dramatic stories of racial and ethnic relations, however, stem from two historic processes: the subjugation of major indigenous civilizations by Spanish conquerors, and the massive importation of African slaves to labor on New World plantations. This chapter describes some of the complex ways in which these relationships have shaped Latin American and Caribbean societies, often interacting with disparities of wealth and power among social classes.

Indian Identity in Latin America

The term *Indian* represents an identity imposed on the peoples of the Americas by European conquerors and settlers, as if all of them could be lumped together by virtue of the continents they inhabited and a presumed racial commonality. From the indigenous perspective, social identity was more a matter of civilizations and cultures, which were widely diverse. In the wake of conquest and the destruction of larger indigenous political structures, these identities were greatly reduced in scope.

In the Andean countries, where most of Spanish settlement took place in the Pacific coastal lowlands, indigenous identities tended to regroup around particular highland regions. These distinctions reflected natural divisions imposed by the rugged terrain of the Andes, as well as shared languages and other cultural features. In Mesoamerica, on the other hand, indigenous identities were more fragmented by the colonizers' closer proximity and intrusiveness. There the new focus tended to become the community or village.

Although the Spanish colonial regime featured an elaborate code based on particular combinations of racial ancestry, in practice the distinctiveness of individual groups became more and more a matter of ethnicity—that is, distinctions based on language, religion, dress, and other cultural elements. Despite the persistence of prejudicial views toward Indians (as if they composed an inferior race), the true cultural character of this division is demonstrated by the fact that Indians have long been able to "pass" into Hispanic society by abandoning their local cultural practices and taking up those of the dominant groups in their vicinity. Many have chosen not to do this, however, and their efforts to maintain various aspects of their cultures, while confronted with greater or lesser pressure and hostility from white and mestizo groups, constitute one of the enduring sources of conflict in Latin America.

The ethnic divisions among Indians, mestizos, and whites have been continually reinforced throughout Latin American history by divisions of social class, with Indians confined to the lowest rungs of the social ladder. During the colonial period, Indians were forcibly removed from their communities to labor in the mines of Bolivia, Peru, and northern Mexico; the textile workshops of Ecuador and central Mexico; and the cacao and indigo plantations established along the Pacific coast of El Salvador, Guatemala, and the southern Mexican region of Chiapas. Elsewhere, Indian villagers found themselves converted into a peasant labor force for white and mestizo owners of haciendas.

The advent of independence and the rise of new export economies in the nineteenth century did little to alter the subordinate status of Indians, and in many cases these changes reinforced it. The coffee plantations of El Salvador and Guatemala and the henequen (hemp) plantations of Mexico's Yucatán Peninsula were carved out of Indian community properties, with peasants either incorporated into the estates as resident laborers or displaced to more distant, less fertile lands. Meanwhile, around the turn of the century, new cotton and sugar plantations along the Peruvian coast were reaching into Indian highland communities to meet their seasonal need for workers.

Not surprisingly, the Indians did what they could to resist these continual depredations (see reading 6.1). The historical record is full of revolts and lesser acts of protest on the part of Indian communities seeking to defend their lands, local institutions, and way of life. Occasionally these protests would coalesce into larger regional rebellions, such as those led by Tupac Amaru II in Peru in 1780, Tupac Katari in Bolivia in 1781, or Miguel Hidalgo in Mexico in 1810. In the face of concerted opposition by all non-Indian sectors of society, such movements were inevitably defeated.

In the twentieth century, rural Indian communities began to suffer other effects of their subordinate status. Caught between a declining land base and a growing population, they found it increasingly difficult to support themselves. As a result, growing numbers of Indians began to migrate out from their traditional homelands. Some sought new land in remote frontier regions, while others eked out a meager existence through seasonal labor on lowland plantations. Many, however, joined the migratory currents of the rural poor swelling the population of the cities, where they again occupied low-status and poorly paid positions.

Ethnic identities continue to link urban migrants with their rural communities of origin, but in much altered form, as traditional social relationships and life-styles have undergone substantial modification in the cities. These changes include the adoption of new occupations and gender roles, the disruption of traditional family structures, and alterations of religious beliefs. Such changes have also diffused back to the countryside as family members and friends journey back and forth, as described in reading 6.2.

Persistent poverty and discrimination have made rural Indian populations a natural target for contemporary revolutionary movements, albeit with mixed success. The Bolivian Revolution of 1952, carried out by urban middle-class reformers who succeeded in mobilizing support among Indian peasants, brought about the nationalization of the country's mines and an agrarian reform that destroyed the old hacienda system. Highland Indian peasant villages in southern Peru provided an important base of support for the Sendero Luminoso ("Shining Path") guerrillas during the early 1980s, but later many withdrew their support as Sendero expanded its violence against nonsupporters, including peasants. In Guatemala, rural Indian villages generally ignored left-wing guerrilla movements during the 1960s, but responded to government repression during the 1970s by forming their own clandestine networks and aligning themselves with the revolutionary left (see reading 6.3; also reading 11.7).

Five centuries after conquest, the Indian question remains a vexing one for these societies. Government policies vacillate between protecting the vestiges of pre-Colombian cultures and promoting the assimilation of rural Indians into national society (see reading 6.4). Such efforts contribute to the continual reshaping of racial and ethnic identities in the region, as do the efforts of Indian populations themselves to cope with or resist prejudicial treatment. In the Amazon rain forest, as was shown in Chapter 4's final reading, once-remote communities are struggling to preserve their way of life against developers who exploit natural resources with little regard for social or environmental consequences. Similarly in Bolivia, militant peasant movements have linked the defense of their traditional coca plant cultivation to the reassertion of larger-scale ethnic identities.

Color and Class in the Caribbean

Issues of race and ethnicity in the Caribbean and Brazil have a history quite different from that of the Andes and Mesoamerica. The general legacy in the Caribbean and coastal Brazil is one in which the indigenous populations were largely exterminated by European conquerors, leading to the massive importation of African slaves to labor on sugar plantations after about 1650.

The easy dichotomy between white European owners and black African slaves was soon complicated by the mulatto offspring of owners and slave women. Though their official status varied from one colony to another, mulattoes were rarely enslaved and came to constitute an important intermediate group in colonial societies. Major differences also existed among the islands, reflecting both their natural contours and the variations among British, French, Dutch, Spanish, and Portuguese colonial regimes, as reading 6.5 describes.

Through the eighteenth century, New World sugar plantations generated immense wealth for their owners and the empires they represented. Saint Domingue was widely regarded as the world's richest colony when, in 1791, the initial upheavals of the Haitian Revolution signaled the end of an era. The days of slavery were numbered. By 1850 slavery had been abolished throughout the Caribbean, except in the remaining colonial possessions of Spain, notably Cuba and Puerto Rico. On these two islands, the Haitian Revolution and the gradual decline of British plantations were experienced as an opportunity to develop their own sugar plantations, and so the early nineteenth century saw the peak period of slave-based agriculture in the Spanish Caribbean. By the century's end, however, the slave trade had disappeared and the institution was suffering from both political attack and economic decline. In many of the British and Dutch possessions, indentured East Indians were introduced to replace African slaves. Formal abolition in Cuba in 1886 marked the disappearance of slavery from the Caribbean, and with abolition in Brazil two years later it was gone from the Americas.

Notwithstanding the islands' small size and proximity, the varying colonial experiences and subsequent migration patterns of the Caribbean island nations have given the region an extraordinarily diverse profile of racial and ethnic relations. Although distinctions based on color tend to be much more complex in the Caribbean islands than the black-or-white division in the United States, lighter skin is generally associated with social positions of greater wealth, power, and prestige. The same is true in Brazil.

Racial and ethnic awareness in the twentieth century has been linked to a wide variety of working-class, nationalist, separatist, and, more recently, feminist movements. The rise of Jamaican political parties and trade unions in the first part of the century was strongly influenced by black resentment of the white elite's persistent privileges. In Jamaica as well, the Rastafarian movement, initiated around 1930, has become internationally renowned through reggae music for its rejection of white European values. The French-speaking Caribbean gave rise to a literary and cultural movement known as "Negritude," whose focus on African cultural influences and colonial injustices inspired numerous black nationalist movements in other parts of the world (see reading 6.6).

The contrasting examples of Haiti and the Dominican Republic offer an excellent study in the complexities of contemporary race and ethnic relations in the Caribbean. Haiti's population paid a steep price for its revolution. Largely cut off from international markets, the economy turned inward and remained relatively stagnant. Social and political life was considerably more lively, since there was a continual contest for dominance between an urban mulatto population with a strong French cultural influence, and a black peasant majority descended from slaves. Black Haitians have developed one of the hemisphere's most vibrant African-American cultures, with a distinctive language (Creole), religion (voodoo), and pride in African heritage (see reading 6.7).

At the other end of the island, the Dominican Republic has evolved in a quite different manner. In the face of French colonial rule and subsequent incorporation into independent Haiti, the inhabitants of the eastern end of the island retained a distinctive Spanish identity. Their struggle to throw off Haitian rule, accomplished in 1844, was followed by formal independence from

Spain in 1865. The 22-year Haitian occupation left a significant impression on Dominican culture. With deep anti-Haitian sentiments still alive, the Dominican elite tended to emphasize its whiteness and European ties, as opposed to the blackness and African ties associated with Haiti.

This white Hispanic ideology, which contrasted sharply with the visible reality of a large mulatto and black majority among the Dominican population, reached its peak under the dictatorship of Rafael Trujillo, who ruled between 1930 and 1961. More recently, however, the growing presence of Haitian workers in the Dominican Republic and the greater visibility of African-influenced cultural expressions have contributed to a questioning of this national Hispanic ideology (see reading 6.8). The reality of the country's mixed racial and ethnic heritage is slowly making its way into the core of Dominican national consciousness.

Few generalizations can be made about contemporary Latin American and Caribbean social identities. Indian populations of the Andes and Mesoamerica have retained distinctive cultures and ethnic identities, but in forms differing sharply from those of their pre-Colombian ancestors. The small size of the Caribbean island states belies the extraordinary racial and ethnic diversity of their societies, which is the product of a tortuous plantation past, the various colonial and postindependence regimes, and migratory flows that have crisscrossed the region for centuries. For the Americas as a whole, patterns of racial and ethnic relations constitute a many-sided story that is continually being rewritten.

6.1 Indian Resistance to Encroachment

One of Peru's best-known writers, José Maria Arguedas published the novel
Yawar Fiesta *in 1941. In this work, set in a highland town in the 1920s,*
the author tells how the national government's attempt to suppress a ritual
Indian bullfight meets with varying responses from Indians, mestizos, and
the town's mistis *(upper-class whites). Despite their subordinate status, the*
Indians are able to exact concessions from the local elite because of their
cohesiveness, as the following selection from the novel's opening chapter
shows.

Puquio is a new town for the *mistis*. About 300 years ago, give or take
a little, the *mistis* came to Puquio from other towns where they had
mining business. Before that all of Puquio was an Indian town. In the
four *ayllus*[1] nobody but Indians lived. From time to time, the *mistis* would
come in search of peons for the mines, seeking provisions and women.

The other towns around Puquio are on mountainsides full of mine
shafts; along all of the streams that bring water to those towns old ore
mills are tumbling down; the old-timers milled silver there. Those towns
are named for saints; their streets are wide; their Plazas de Armas are
quite square and are in the middle of town; the churches are large,
with arched portals; the high altars of the churches are sometimes made
of carved wood, and their gilding is still visible. On the mountains around
Puquio there were no mines; that's why the *mistis* would arrive suddenly, have their party with the Indian women, recruit people willingly
or by force for the mines, and go away for a time.

But the mines gave out; mining was no longer profitable; then the
mistis scattered to all the Indian towns of the province. Their towns,
which had been named after saints, were almost emptied of gentlemen.
Now those little towns are tumbling down like the old ore mills; their
streets are being obliterated; the churches are also collapsing, the altars
are losing their gilt and are covered with dust.

Most of the *mistis* fell upon Puquio, because it was a big town, with
plenty of Indians for servants, with four irrigation ditches, one for each
ayllu, to bring water for their crops. Big town, in a good place.

Arguedas, José Maria. *Yawar Fiesta*, translated by Frances Horning Barraclough, 1–9.
Austin: University of Texas Press, 1985.

[1] An *ayllu* is an Indian neighborhood or community, and its members are called *comuneros*.

The *mistis* went with their priest, with their "foreigner" Child God; they made their Plaza de Armas on the edge of the town; they ordered a church to be built for them with arched portal and gilded altar; and from there, from their Plaza, like someone who is digging a ditch, they went on building their street, with no respect for the ownership claims of the *ayllus.*

"So what!"

It had to go in a straight line. *Misti* street is always straight.

In a short time, as soon as there were houses with balconies on Girón Bolívar, as soon as they could fit a few lanes onto one or the other side of Girón Bolívar, they moved the provincial capital to their new town.

And the plundering of the *ayllus* began. With the authorities' backing, the *mistis* began with the K'ollana neighborhood. K'ollana had good corn, barley, and wheat fields. The judges and the notaries signed papers of every description; that sufficed. After K'ollana came K'ayau. The lands with the most water were in those districts and they were closest to town. Next came Chaupi and Pichk'achuri. That's why Chaupi and Pichk'achuri own more land. In former times, it was the other way around.

From so much going into offices, from so much running to and fro about the documents with which their lands were being taken away, the Puquios learned to defend themselves in lawsuits, buying judges, court clerks, and notaries. Each Indian community rose up as a whole to defend its members. Every Sunday there would be council meetings in the *ayllus;* every Sunday the *comuneros* would come together to make decisions. And they put a stop to land-grabbing in the valley. By that time, the *mistis* had already become the owners of almost all of the cropland; by then, the K'ollanas and the K'ayaus were reduced to being mere field hands for the important people.

But the *ayllus* would not let go of the water.

The Indian staffbearers[2] schedule the irrigation water allotments, each in his own community, the same as in former times.

For that reason, at dawn on the days the water is being distributed, the *mistis* of Puquio go into the Indian communities to ask for water to irrigate their crops. Still shivering with cold, hiding their chins in their scarves, the prominent citizens go into a huddle with the neighborhood Indians and raise their hands and shout:

"Don[3] Gregorio! For my little patch of corn!"

In the early morning their blue and black overcoats, their straw hats, their "foreigner" cloth hats look like alien garb amid the red, yellow, and green ponchos of Puquio, among so many vicuña-colored Indian hats.

---

[2] Indian community leaders, or *varayok's;* they carry long staffs as symbols of authority. The highest rank is held by the *alcalde indio,* a Spanish term meaning mayor of the Indian community.— Trans.

[3] Spanish respectful title of address.—Trans.

Sometimes the sunlight has reached the mountaintops and the staff-bearing water distributor is still hearing:

"For my little wheat field in K'ellok'ello, for my corn patch at K'erok'ocha, for my barley at Cullahora! Don Gregorio!"

How many times have the *mistis* gone to the water distribution place, cracked their bullwhips, and taken the staffbearing leaders off to be shut up in the jail! But while the Chief Staffbearer was straining on the bar, the four *ayllus* would be all astir; Indians from K'ayau, from K'ollana, from Pichk'achuri, from Chaupi would go around to all the houses to notify the people. From Makulirumi Rock they'd sound the *wakawak'ra*[4] trumpets. Puquio would become as still and silent as it is in the darkness of the night.

On every street the *mistis* would fire their little bullets; on every street they'd get drunk and threaten the *comuneros*. They'd go into one house after another, kick the little children, and bloody the Indians' noses, mouths, and foreheads.

"Don't matter!"

You think *misti* knows how to irrigate? You think *misti* knows how to put up a wall? You think *misti* can weed wheat fields? Does *misti* mend road, make tiles and adobe bricks, slit sheep's throat? Well, who'd build the water intake points, who'd dig the ditches, who'd mend the dikes; who'd set the floodgates during the flashfloods of January and February, when the freshets that come down out of the mountains wash out the canals and fill up their intakes with stones, clods, and sand?

"Jajayllas!" [5]

Not even bullets, whipcracking, or the pleading of the *tayta*[6] Vicar could make the *comuneros* leave their *ayllus*.

"My eye first he'll take out! Like thieving sparrowhawk my eye first he'll eat! *Cumun yaku*[7] *jajayllas!*"

The Puquios knew that.

Then the *mistis* would be the first to humble themselves. In their minds they were really weeping with rage, but they'd get cane liquor from all the stores and with that they'd plead with the staffbearers and the elders. They'd go to the communities, whichever ones their property was located in, and enter the houses, sweet-talking, pledging friendship. . . .

Many of the mestizos become friendly with the Indian communities and speak up for their members. In the *ayllus* they are called Don Norberto, Don Leandro, Don Aniceto . . .

The Indians speak to them respectfully. But at fiestas they dance

---

[4] A trumpet made of bull's horn.—Trans.
[5] Quechua expression of scornful derision.—Trans.
[6] Father; also used as an affectionate and respectful form of address.—Trans.
[7] Community water.—Trans.

with them, equal to equal; when there is trouble, the mestizo friend gives them good advice and defends the *ayllus.*

That's how life is on Girón Bolívar and in the neighborhoods. That's how the *misti* strangers came to Puquio.

But when the Puquio people look down from above, from Sillanayok' Pass, from the top of Tayta Pedrork'o, when they see Girón Bolívar gleaming like a snake's back among the tiled roofs of the *ayllus,* they exclaim disgustedly:

"Atatauya Bolívar, street!"

When the Indians look down and speak that way, in their eyes another hope is glowing, their real soul is shining forth. They laugh loudly; they may be furious, too.

6.2 Bolivian Weavers

Indian communities have resorted to a variety of strategies to sustain themselves. This account of a woman from the Calcha, a Quechua-speaking ethnic group in the Bolivian highlands near the Argentine border, explores the role of women's weaving and shows how the craft helps create the group's identity. The woman's biography also makes clear how the increasing reliance of the community's male members on jobs in the capital of Buenos Aires has greatly altered family and community relationships. In other communities, it is often the women who migrate to the city to work as domestic servants or factory workers, while the men remain on the land (as shown in the previous chapter).

When she was a small girl, Doña Sara,* like all her kin and neighbors, had only the clothes that her mother had woven for her to wear. All the Calcha, a Quechua-speaking ethnic group in southern Bolivia, wore clothing woven by the women. They traded corn, the main crop of these subsistence farmers, for the wool of sheep raised in northern Ar-

Medlin, Mary Ann. "Doña Sara and Doña Juana: Two Bolivian Weavers." In *The Human Tradition in Latin America: The Twentieth Century,* edited by William H. Beezley and Judith Ewell, 219–29. Wilmington, Del.: Scholarly Resources, 1987.
*Doña Sara is a pseudonym.

gentina. Women and men worked together as members of families and settlements, doing all the tasks that needed to be done in order for their families to survive. Women and men worked at their distinctive tasks in the fields as they did in their household compounds. They still made their tools, houses, and clothing.

The Calcha have been an organized group living in southern Potosí, Bolivia, for hundreds of years. They felt the impact of the Inca conquest of their territory in the fourteenth century. In the sixteenth century, they were forced by the Spanish to supply labor for colonial silver mines and goods for the large, nearby mining city of Potosí. A Catholic church was established in the town, and there are records of baptisms and marriages from the 1700s. They were not isolated from the outside or from other ethnic groups with whom they had trade relationships. In the past, they met unavoidable demands from both Inca and colonial administrators. Today, they pay taxes and send their children to school and their young men to military service because they are required to by the state.

Doña Sara was born in 1914 into a household that worked to supply its own needs: family members grew their own food, traded with other groups, and processed raw materials into tools. As a young girl, she learned to weave by watching her mother, who wove clothing for her family and a very few gifts for individuals with close, long-term ties to her. By age ten Doña Sara had started her own first project, having already tried her hand at her mother's loom.

Doña Sara, as a teenager, wove all the textiles needed for a complete fiesta outfit. Respectable young women prepared their dress with care for the fiestas in the town. Young women and men from all of the dispersed hamlets attended the celebrations, which had four groups of musicians and dancers sponsored by the local political leaders. Crowds grew after dark and danced all night. Couples paired up late at night and evaluated one another as prospective marriage partners.

Youths attended with groups of cousins who could check on those thought to be attractive. They knew much about the families of those who were from nearby settlements, and many marriages were made with neighbors. Young men could also look at the fiesta dress of young women to get a good idea of the skill of the weaver, her industriousness, and the resources of her family, who had made weaving supplies available to her.

Doña Sara made a good marriage to a man who was one of five brothers. She inherited a small plot of land in a nearby settlement, which helped her new family, since her husband and his brothers had divided the little land their father had. One of her brothers decided to stay in Buenos Aires, where many young Calcha men went to work in construction. He arranged for Doña Sara and her husband to farm his land, so they had use of more land while the brother retained his right to the land in case he should return someday. . . .

Doña Sara gave birth to seven children, but today she has only one surviving son and one daughter. She wove all the clothing for the young children and continued to clothe them until, as the times changed, the young men left the region to work for wages and were able to buy manufactured clothing. When she still had two sons alive, the older, working in construction in Buenos Aires where his uncle found him a job, decided to stay in Argentina permanently. He married a young Bolivian woman who had migrated from rural Chuiquisaca with her brothers. Then his younger brother (Calcha families expect youngest sons to stay with their parents and take over their home) died in a truck accident. The son in Argentina returned to his parents with his wife and one son, who died soon after. Doña Sara's daughter-in-law says that the baby could not adjust to rural Bolivian life and food.

Doña Sara now lives with her surviving son, his wife, and their three children. The son says he wanted his children to be educated in Argentina rather than in rural Bolivian schools, but there was no one else to take care of his parents. Doña Sara occasionally goes to stay with her daughter in the town of Calcha when her son-in-law leaves to work in Buenos Aires. She helps with the care of her grandchildren and takes over household duties when they are born. . . .

Weaving for the women of Doña Sara's generation has changed: by the 1960s they no longer produced all of their families' clothing. First, young men who had changed back to Calcha clothing at the border when returning from wage labor stopped wearing Calcha dress daily. Next, young women were given manufactured clothing for daily use by their brothers and husbands, who had returned from wage labor. Then the older men put on the clothing their sons had given them after having stored it in suitcases for years. Finally, by 1982, the older women, including Doña Sara, had carefully stored their daily Calcha dress and put on the manufactured skirts and sweaters that their sons' wages had purchased.

Doña Sara, now in her sixties, is a widow dependent upon her son, but an important laborer in his household and the fields. She is able to continue to weave and has taught her daughter and her daughter-in-law to weave. She wears the manufactured clothing she had stored for many years and stores her Calcha clothing, including the complete outfit in which she will be buried. As her weaving was used less and less by her family in daily life, she spent more and more time in agriculture, because her husband and son were away in cities working to earn cash.

Today, the weaving of Calcha women is not used as daily dress. Their families are not naked, because they can and do buy manufactured clothing, although it is often bought secondhand. It is cheaper for them to wear purchased clothing. Both the materials needed for weaving and the time women must invest at the loom have become increasingly scarce as men leave the region for wage labor.

Women today, because of changes in economic and political relationships both within and outside of their ethnic group, have other essential tasks that occupy the time they once devoted to weaving. Now Calcha men, rather than make the trading trips that took them weeks in
the past, go to Argentina as wage laborers for months at a time. Women
more often have primary responsibility for, or share significant aspects
of the agricultural labor that must still be done in order for their families to eat. When men go to work, their wages do not pay all the expenses of their families. Their mothers, wives, and children, who remain in Calcha, must still labor to provide the food the family will eat.
Calcha women do weave the textiles that are necessary for their culture, but they must also see to it that other productive activities are
carried out.

Dramatic changes have occurred in Doña Sara's lifetime. Unlike her
mother, she does not weave to clothe her family, but the time she spent
in weaving in the past is not now free time. She works the long hours
that her mother did, but the particular tasks that supply her family's
needs have changed. She makes ethnic cloth for ceremonial and ritual
purposes, rather than for daily dress. She has a major role in supplying
her family's food. . . .

6.3 An Indian Conflict with Landowners

*Rigoberta Menchú grew up in a Mayan community of highland Guate-
mala during the 1960s and 1970s, a period of social ferment and political violence. The daughter of community leaders, she herself became a
leading figure in a revolutionary organization of Indian peasants following the murder of her parents by right-wing military forces. In this selection she describes how confrontations of Indian communities with ladino
(non-Indian) elites, such as local landowners and military officials, resulted in a spiral of official repression and growing radicalism within the
community.*

I, Rigoberta Menchú: An Indian Woman in Guatemala, edited by Elizabeth Burgos-Debray,
translated by Ann Wright, 102–16. London: Verso, 1984.

This was the first time my father went to prison. My brother said, "We don't know what to do for him because the lawyers say Papá will be in jail for eighteen years. We need money to get educated people to help us." In Guatemala this is what happens with the poor, especially Indians, because they can't speak Spanish. The Indian can't speak up for what he wants. When they put my father in jail, the landowners gave large amounts of money to the judge there. The judge in El Quiché, that is. There are several levels of authority. First, there is the Military Commissioner. He sometimes lives in the villages or is based in the town, and he tries to impose his own law. Then there is what we call the Mayor who represents the authorities which administer justice when they say someone has broken the law. Next come the Governors who govern the whole region, each province. And finally, there are the Deputies—God knows who they are! To get to see the Military Commissioner, you first have to give him a *mordida*, that's what we call a bribe in Guatemala. To see the Mayor, you have to get witnesses, sign papers and then give him a *mordida so* he will support your case. To see the Governor you need not only witnesses from the village, and money, but also lawyers or other intermediaries to talk for you. The Governor is a *ladino* and doesn't understand the language of the people. He'll only believe something if a lawyer or educated person says it. He won't accept anything from an Indian. The Mayor is a *ladino* too. But he's a *ladino* who's come from our people. The Military Commissioner is also a *ladino* although this varies a bit, because in some places the commissioners are Indians who have done military service and lived in the barracks. There comes a time when they return to their village, brutalized men, criminals.

My father fought for twenty-two years, waging a heroic struggle against the landowners who wanted to take our land and our neighbours' land. After many years of hard work, when our small bit of land began yielding harvests and our people had a large area under cultivation, the big landowners appeared: the Brols. It's said there that they were even more renowned criminals than the Martínez and García families, who owned a *finca* there before the Brols arrived. The Brols were a large family, a whole gang of brothers. Five of them lived on a *finca* they had taken over by forcibly throwing the Indians of the region off their land. . . .

The Government says the land belongs to the nation. It owns the land and gives it to us to cultivate. But when we've cleared and cultivated the land, that's when the landowners appear. However, the landowners don't just appear on their own—they have connections with the different authorities that allow them to manoeuvre like that. Because of this, we faced the Martínez family, the Garcías, and then the Brols arrived. This meant we could either stay and work as *peónes* or leave our land. There was no other solution. So my father travelled all over the place seeking advice. We didn't realize then that going to the Government authorities was the same as going to the landowners. They are the same. My father was tireless in his efforts to seek help. He went to other sectors, like the workers' unions. He asked them to help because we were already being thrown off our land.

The first time they threw us out of our homes was, if I remember rightly, in 1967. They turned us out of our houses, and out of the village. The Garcías' henchmen set to work with ferocity. They were Indians too, soldiers of the *finca*. First they went into the houses without permission and got all the people out. Then they went in and threw out all our things. I remember that my mother had her silver necklaces, precious keepsakes from my grandmother, but we never saw them again after that. They stole them all: They threw out our cooking utensils, our earthenware cooking pots. We don't use those sort of . . . special utensils, we have our own earthenware pots. They hurled them into the air, and, Oh God! they hit the ground and broke into pieces. All our plates, cups, pots. They threw them out and they all broke. That was the vengeance of the landowner on the peasants because we wouldn't give up our land. All the maize cobs they found in the *tapanco*, they threw away. Afterwards all the peasants had to work together to collect them up. We did it together and put them in another place. I remember it was pouring with rain, and we had nothing to protect ourselves from the rain. It took us two days to make a roughly built hut out of leaves. We only had those nylon sheets the peasants use to cover themselves in the rain. The first night we spent in the fields with streams of water running along the ground. It wasn't raining then but the ground was sodden.

Those few days confirmed my hatred for those people. I saw why we said that *ladinos* were thieves, criminals and liars. It was as our parents had told us. We could see that they were doing the same to us. They killed our animals. They killed many of our dogs. To us, killing an animal is like killing a person. We care for all the things of the natural world very much and killing our dogs wounded us very deeply. We spent more than forty days in the fields. Then the community held a meeting and said, "If they throw us out again, we will die of hunger." We had no utensils for cooking our *tortillas*, and no grinding stones. They'd been thrown away into the undergrowth. We organized ourselves, all of us, and said, "Let's collect our things together." We went looking for any of our things that were still more or less all right. My father said, "If they kill us they kill us, but we'll go back to our houses." Our people looked on my father as their own father, and so we went back to our houses. There was another village quite near ours and they helped us. People brought cooking pots and plates so that we could cook our maize and eat. So we went back to our houses. And the landowners came back again for what they called "collective negotiations." They told us we should resign ourselves to working as *peónes* because the land belonged to them. We could stay in our houses, but the land was not ours. If we didn't agree, they would throw us off again. But my father said: "We were the first families to come and cultivate this land and nobody can deceive us into thinking that this land is theirs. If they want to be the owners of more land, let them go and cultivate the mountains. There is more land but it is not land where things grow." Who knows, perhaps if the community had been alone, we would have become *peónes* and our land would now be part of a big *finca*. But my father would have none of it. He said, "Even if they kill us, we will do it." Of course, in those days we didn't have enough political clarity to unite with others and protest about our land. What we did we did as an individual community. So we went back to our homes and did not accept the landowners' deal. They left us alone for a month or two. Then there was another raid. All our things were broken for a second time, all the things our neighbours in the other village had given us. We couldn't stand what they were doing to us any longer and decided to go to the *finca*, abandoning our land. But we couldn't live in the *finca* all the time. What were we going to do? What would happen to us if we went to the *finca?* That's when we united and said: "We won't go!"

We love our land very much. Since those people tried to take our land away, we have grieved very much. My grandfather used to cry bitterly and say: "In the past, no one person owned the land. The land belonged to everyone. There were no boundaries." We were sadder still when we saw our animals going hungry because of us. If our animals went near our crops, they were killed by the Garcías' henchmen who were guarding them. . . . My grandfather said, "If they kill our animals, we must kill them." That was the idea that came to my grandfather. We spent about fifteen days away from our house after the second raid and our elders advised us to burn them and leave. But where to? We didn't know whether it was better to go to the *finca* or agree to be labourers on the landowner's estate. We couldn't decide. We discussed it with all our neighbours. Among the whole community. During all this time we couldn't celebrate our culture; none of our ceremonies. That's when my father took his stand. He said, "If they kill me for trying to defend the land that belongs to us, well, they'll have to kill me." . . .

6.4 Questions of Conquest

Whether and how Indian groups should be assimilated into national cultures has preoccupied Peru's leaders since colonial times. In the following essay, Mario Vargas Llosa, one of contemporary Latin America's outstanding literary figures and an unsuccessful candidate in the 1990 Peruvian presidential election, discusses the relationship between indigenous and national cultures. His conclusion that the country's economic and social modernization may depend on the complete assimilation of remaining Indian groups represents a familiar position in the historic debate over the issue. However, the difficulties faced by other Latin American countries without Indian minorities raises doubts as to whether such assimilation will indeed foster development.

. . . Why have the postcolonial republics of the Americas—republics that might have been expected to have deeper and broader notions of liberty, equality, and fraternity—failed so miserably to improve the lives of their Indian citizens? Even as I write, not only the Amazonian rain forests but the small tribes who have managed for so long to survive there are being barbarously exterminated in the name of progress.

To begin to answer these questions, we must put down our newspapers and open the pages of the books that allow us to see close up the era when the Europeans dared to venture to sea in search of a new route to India and its spices, and happened instead on an unspoiled continent with its own peoples, customs, and civilizations. . . .

Those who destroyed the Inca Empire and created that country called Peru, a country that four and a half centuries later has not yet managed to heal the bleeding wounds of its birth, were men whom we can hardly admire. They were, it is true, uncommonly courageous, but, contrary to what the edifying stories teach us, most of them lacked any idealism or higher purpose. They possessed only greed, hunger, and in the best of cases a certain vocation for adventure. The cruelty in which the Spaniards took pride, and the chronicles depict to the point of making us shiver, was inscribed in the ferocious customs of the times and was without doubt equivalent to that of the people they subdued and almost extinguished. Three centuries later, the Inca population had been reduced from twenty million to only six.

But these semiliterate, implacable, and greedy swordsmen, who even before having completely conquered the Inca Empire were already savagely fighting among themselves . . . represented a culture in which,

Vargas Llosa, Mario. "Questions of Conquest." *Harper's* 281 (December 1990): 45–53.

we will never know whether for the benefit or the disgrace of mankind, something new and exotic had germinated in the history of man. In this culture, although injustice and abuse often favored by religion had proliferated, by the alliance of multiple factors—among them chance— a social space of human activities had evolved that was neither legislated nor controlled by those in power. This evolution would produce the most extraordinary economic, scientific, and technical development human civilization has ever known since the times of the cavemen with their clubs. Moreover, this new society would give way to the creation of the individual as the sovereign source of values by which society would be judged.

Those who, rightly, are shocked by the abuses and crimes of the conquest must bear in mind that the first men to condemn them and ask that they be brought to an end were men, like Father Bartolomé de Las Casas, who came to America with the conquistadores and abandoned the ranks in order to collaborate with the vanquished, whose suffering they divulged with an indignation and virulence that still move us today.

. . . They fought against their fellow men and against the policies of their own country in the name of a moral principle that to them was higher than any principle of a nation or state. This self-determination could not have been possible among the Incas or any of the other pre-Hispanic cultures. In these cultures, as in the other great civilizations of history foreign to the West, the individual could not morally question the social organism of which he was a part, because he existed only as an integral atom of that organism and because for him the dictates of the state could not be separated from morality. The first culture to interrogate and question itself, the first to break up the masses into individual beings who with time gradually gained the right to think and act for themselves, was to become, thanks to that unknown exercise, freedom, the most powerful civilization in our world.

It seems to me useless to ask oneself whether it was good that it happened in this manner or whether it would have been better for humanity if the individual had never been born and the tradition of the antlike societies had continued forever. The pages of the chronicles of the conquest and discovery depict that crucial, bloody moment, full of phantasmagoria, when—disguised as a handful of invading treasure hunters, killing and destroying—the Judeo-Christian tradition, the Spanish language, Greece, Rome, the Renaissance, the notion of individual sovereignty, and the chance of living in freedom reached the shores of the Empire of the Sun. So it was that we as Peruvians were born. And, of course, the Bolivians, Chileans, Ecuadoreans, Colombians, and others.

Almost five centuries later, this notion of individual sovereignty is still an unfinished business. We have not yet, properly speaking, seen the light. We in Latin America do not yet constitute real nations. Our contemporary reality is still impregnated with the violence and marvels that those first texts of our literature, those novels disguised as history or historical books corrupted by fiction, told us about.

At least one basic problem is the same. Two cultures, one Western and modern, the other aboriginal and archaic, hardly coexist, separated from each other because of the exploitation and discrimination that the former exercises over the latter. . . .

Immense opportunities brought by the civilization that discovered and conquered America have been beneficial only to a minority, sometimes a very small one; whereas the great majority managed to have only the negative share of the conquest—that is, contributing in their serfdom and sacrifice, in their misery and neglect, to the prosperity and refinement of the westernized elites. One of our worst defects, our best fictions, is to believe that our miseries have been imposed on us from abroad, that others, for example, the conquistadores, have always been responsible for our problems. There are countries in Latin America— Mexico is the best example—in which the Spaniards are even now severely indicted for what they did to the Indians. Did they really do it? We did it; we are the conquistadores.

They were our parents and grandparents who came to our shores and gave us the names we have and the language we speak. They also gave us the habit of passing to the devil the responsibility for any evil we do. Instead of making amends for what they did, by improving and correcting our relations with our indigenous compatriots, mixing with them and amalgamating ourselves to form a new culture that would have been a kind of synthesis of the best of both, we, the westernized Latin Americans, have persevered in the worst habits of our forebears, behaving toward the Indians during the nineteenth and twentieth centuries as the Spaniards behaved toward the Aztecs and the Incas, and sometimes even worse. We must remember that in countries like Chile and Argentina, it was during the republic (in the nineteenth century), not during the colony, that the native cultures were systematically exterminated. In the Amazon jungle, and in the mountains of Guatemala, the exterminating continues.

It is a fact that in many of our countries, as in Peru, we share, in spite of the pious and hypocritical indigenous rhetoric of our men of letters and our politicians, the mentality of the conquistadores. Only in countries where the native population was small or nonexistent, or where the aboriginals were practically liquidated, can we talk of integrated societies. In the others, discreet, sometimes unconscious, but very effective apartheid prevails. Important as integration is, the obstacle to achieving it lies in the huge economic gap between the two communities. Indian peasants live in such a primitive way that communication is practically impossible. It is only when they move to the cities that they have the opportunity to mingle with the other Peru. The price they must pay for integration is high—renunciation of their culture, their language, their beliefs, their traditions and customs, and the adoption of the culture of their ancient masters. After one generation they become mestizos. They are no longer Indians.

Perhaps there is no realistic way to integrate our societies other than by asking the Indians to pay that price. Perhaps the ideal—that is, the preservation of the primitive cultures of America—is a utopia incompatible with this other and more urgent goal—the establishment of societies in which social and economic inequalities among citizens be reduced to human, reasonable limits and where everybody can enjoy at least a decent and free life. In any case, we have been unable to reach any of those ideals and are still, as when we had just entered Western history, trying to find out what we are and what our future will be.

If forced to choose between the preservation of Indian cultures and their complete assimilation, with great sadness I would choose modernization of the Indian population, because there are priorities; and the first priority is, of course, to fight hunger and misery. . . .

6.5 Racism in the Caribbean

Born in Trinidad, historian Eric Williams achieved fame in the 1940s with a series of scholarly publications analyzing the legacies of slavery and plantation systems in the Caribbean. By the following decade he had become one of the dominant political figures in the Caribbean as head of the People's National Movement in Trinidad. He became prime minister of Trinidad and Tobago upon its independence from Britain in 1962 and held that position until 1981. In his later years, Williams found his policies increasingly challenged by more radical black power advocates. In this selection he argues for an appreciation of the diverse consequences of colonial slave regimes.

The racial situation in the Caribbean is radically different from the racial situation in the United States and is thus rather incomprehensible to the native of the United States, black or white. It should first be clearly understood that there is no overt legal discrimination. The is-

Williams, Eric. *The Negro in the Caribbean*, 11–16, 62–66. Westport, Conn.: Negro Universities Press, 1942.

lands know neither Jim Crow nor lynching; there are neither separate schools, separate theaters, separate restaurants or special seats in public conveyances. Cases of rape of white women are unknown, and we have the testimony of an ex-governor of Jamaica as to the safety of white women, anywhere at any time. White, brown and black meet in the same churches in which pews, at a price, can be obtained by one and all. Graves of whites, browns and blacks are seen side by side in the cemeteries. The declaration of fundamental rights proclaimed by the Constituent Assembly of Cuba in 1940 may be taken as indicative of the legal situation in the Caribbean: "All Cubans are equal before the law. The Republic recognises no privileges. All discrimination because of sex, race, color, or class, or other affront to human dignity is declared illegal and punishable."

The racial consciousness which permeates the American Negro is also not found in the islands. This is a constant source of surprise and even exasperation to the American Negro visitor or student, who goes to the islands with his clichés and his prejudices, seeking for any violations of his own code of racial solidarity. It is annoying, for instance, to find the term "Negro" little used and almost an epithet of abuse or contempt, at least among intimate friends. The Haitians consider themselves "blacks," not Negroes. It is difficult, too, for the American Negro to realize that the term "colored" signifies a distinct group in the Caribbean. It is an old definition, dating back to the days of slavery. The English islands spoke of the "people of color"; in the French they were "gens de couleur"; in the Spanish "gente de color." One is not a mulatto in Cuba or Puerto Rico—one might be "pardo," or "moreno," or "trigueño," indicating different shades of brown.

If in the United States one drop of Negro blood makes a man a Negro, in the islands one is white or not according to the color of one's skin. If in the United States one is classified as a Negro if his Negro ancestry goes back to the fourth generation, then in the Caribbean one is considered white in the second generation. A common remark in the British West Indies of colored schoolboys to a companion of lighter skin whom they consider uppish is: "go home and look at your grandmother." There is a similar saying in Puerto Rico, in a popular song which says: "and your grandmother, where is she?"

Of overt legal discrimination, therefore, there is none in the Caribbean. Economic differences prevent the color question of the United States from arising. Only on the social level does racial prejudice present itself, but there in a radical form. A white skin, in a society still obsessed economically and therefore culturally by the slave tradition, is an indication of social status and the best passport to political influence. The nearer one is to the coveted white skin, the more likely is one to be accepted in society. If one is not fortunate enough to have a white skin, the next best thing is a partner with a white skin. Married to a white woman, a young Negro rapidly ascends the ladder of success.

How could it be otherwise? If the white skin means superiority, then the white woman, in the interest of white prestige, must be given an opportunity to live in a way and on a standard compatible with white dignity.

It is this high market value of a white skin, in addition to the stigma of past slavery and its consequences, which is responsible for those color distinctions for which the islands are notorious. These distinctions have the greatest effect in the lack of cohesion which exists among the middle classes. We have a picture of these color distinctions of middle class society in the British West Indies, drawn by a native Trinidadian. It may be taken as indicative of the colored middle class over the whole area. "Between the brown-skinned middle class and the black there is a continual rivalry, distrust and ill-feeling, which, skilfully played upon by the European people, poisons the life of the community. Where so many crosses and colors meet and mingle, the shades are naturally difficult to determine and the resulting confusion is immense. There are the nearly-white hanging on tooth and nail to the fringes of white society, and these, as is easy to understand, hate contact with the darker skin far more than some of the broader-minded whites. Then there are the browns, intermediates, who cannot by any stretch of imagination pass as white, but who will not go one inch toward mixing with people darker than themselves. And so on, and on, and on. Associations are formed of brown people who will not admit into their number those too much darker than themselves, and there have been heated arguments in committee as to whether such and such a person's skin was fair enough to allow him or her to be admitted, without lowering the tone of the institution. Clubs have been known to accept the daughter and mother, who were fair, but to refuse the father, who was black. A dark-skinned brother in a fair-skinned family is sometimes the subject of jeers and insults and open intimations that his presence is not required at the family social functions. Fair-skinned girls who marry dark men are often ostracised by their families and given up as lost. There have been cases of fair women who have been content to live with black men but would not marry them. Should the darker man, however, have money or position of some kind, he may aspire, and it is not too much to say that in a West Indian colony the surest sign of a man's having arrived is the fact that he keeps company with people lighter in complexion than himself. Remember, finally, that the people most affected by this are people of the middle class who, lacking the hard contact with realities of the masses and unable to attain to the freedoms of a leisured class, are more than all types of people given to trivial divisions and subdivisions of social rank and precedence." Prospective brides look for light-skinned men. They pray for "light" children, who might marry white. Expectant mothers abstain from coffee or chocolate. As the saying goes in Martinique, one who has reached the dining-room should not go back to the kitchen.

6.6 The Negritude Movement

Aimé Césaire is widely considered the foremost exponent of Negritude, an artistic and cultural movement that in the 1930s began to celebrate African roots of contemporary New World cultures and societies. His book Return to My Native Land *was one of the movement's first expressions. In this selection, Césaire is interviewed in 1967 by Haitian poet and militant René Depestre about the origins of the Negritude movement and its relation to Caribbean societies. The ideas associated with Negritude played a significant role in the genesis of the black power movements that emerged in many Caribbean countries in the 1960s and 1970s.*

[RENÉ DEPESTRE]: I would like to go back to the period in your life in Paris when you collaborated with Léopold Sédar Senghor and Léon Damas on the small periodical *L'Etudiant noir*. Was this first stage of the Negritude expressed in *Return to My Native Land*?

[AIMÉ CÉSAIRE]: Yes, it was already Negritude, as we conceived of it then. There were two tendencies within our group. On the one hand, there were people from the left, Communists at that time, such as J. Monnerot, E. Léro, and René Ménil. They were Communists, and therefore we supported them. But very soon I had to reproach them—and perhaps I owe this to Senghor—for being French Communists. There was nothing to distinguish them either from the French surrealists or from the French Communists. In other words, their poems were colorless.

R.D.: They were not attempting disalienation.

A.C.: In my opinion they bore the marks of assimilation. At that time Martinican students assimilated either with the French rightists or with the French leftists. But it was always a process of assimilation.

R.D.: At bottom what separated you from the Communist Martinican students at that time was the Negro question.

A.C.: Yes, the Negro question. At that time I criticized the Communists for forgetting our Negro characteristics. They acted like Communists, which was all right, but they acted like abstract Communists. I maintained that the political question could not do away with our condition as Negroes. We are Negroes, with a great number of historical peculiarities. I suppose that I must have been influenced by Senghor in this. At the time I knew absolutely nothing about Africa. Soon afterward I

Césaire, Aimé. *Discourse on Colonialism*, 65–77. New York: Monthly Review Press, 1972.

met Senghor, and he told me a great deal about Africa. He made an enormous impression on me: I am indebted to him for the revelation of Africa and African singularity. And I tried to develop a theory to encompass all of my reality. . . .

R.D.: How would you describe your encounter with Senghor, the encounter between Antillean Negritude and African Negritude? Was it the result of a particular event or of a parallel development of consciousness?

A.C.: It was simply that in Paris at that time there were a few dozen Negroes of diverse origins. There were Africans, like Senghor, Guianans, Haitians, North Americans, Antilleans, etc. This was very important for me.

R.D.: In this circle of Negroes in Paris, was there a consciousness of the importance of African culture?

A.C.: Yes, as well as an awareness of the solidarity among blacks. We had come from different parts of the world. It was our first meeting. We were discovering ourselves. This was very important.

R.D.: It was extraordinarily important. How did you come to develop the concept of Negritude?

A.C.: I have a feeling that it was somewhat of a collective creation. I used the term first, that's true. But it's possible we talked about it in our group. It was really a resistance to the politics of assimilation. Until that time, until my generation, the French and the English—but especially the French—had followed the politics of assimilation unrestrainedly. We didn't know what Africa was. Europeans despised everything about Africa, and in France people spoke of a civilized world and a barbarian world. The barbarian world was Africa, and the civilized world was Europe. Therefore the best thing one could do with an African was to assimilate him: the ideal was to turn him into a Frenchman with black skin. . . .

I still remember a poor little Martinican pharmacist who passed the time writing poems and sonnets which he sent to literary contests, such as the Floral Games of Toulouse. He felt very proud when one of his poems won a prize. One day he told me that the judges hadn't even realized that his poems were written by a man of color. To put it in other words, his poetry was so impersonal that it made him proud. He was filled with pride by something I would have considered a crushing condemnation.

R.D.: It was a case of total alienation.

A.C.: I think you've put your finger on it. Our struggle was a struggle against alienation. That struggle gave birth to Negritude. Because Antilleans were ashamed of being Negroes, they searched for all sorts of euphemisms for Negro: they would say a man of color, a dark-

complexioned man, and other idiocies like that. . . . That's when we
adopted the word *nègre,* as a term of defiance. It was a defiant name.
To some extent it was a reaction of enraged youth. Since there was
shame about the word *nègre,* we chose the word *nègre.* I must say that
when we founded *L'Etudiant noir,* I really wanted to call it *L'Etudiant
nègre,* but there was a great resistance to that among the Antilleans. . . .

R.D.: In *Return to My Native Land* you have stated that Haiti was the
cradle of Negritude. In your words, "Haiti, where Negritude stood on
its feet for the first time." . . . How have you applied the concept of
Negritude to the history of Haiti?

A.C.: Well, after my discovery of the North American Negro and my
discovery of Africa, I went on to explore the totality of the black world,
and that is how I came upon the history of Haiti. I love Martinique,
but it is an alienated land, while Haiti represented for me the heroic
Antilles, the African Antilles. I began to make connections between the
Antilles and Africa, and Haiti is the most African of the Antilles. It is
at the same time a country with a marvelous history: the first Negro
epic of the New World was written by Haitians, people like Toussaint
l'Ouverture, Henri Christophe, Jean-Jacques Dessalines, etc. Haiti is not
very well known in Martinique. I am one of the few Martinicans who
know and love Haiti. . . .

I would like to say that everyone has his own Negritude. There has
been too much theorizing about Negritude. I have tried not to overdo
it, out of a sense of modesty. But if someone asks me what my conception of Negritude is, I answer that above all it is a concrete rather than
an abstract coming to consciousness. What I have been telling you
about—the atmosphere in which we lived, an atmosphere of assimilation in which Negro people were ashamed of themselves—has great
importance. We lived in an atmosphere of rejection, and we developed
an inferiority complex. I have always thought that the black man was
searching for his identity. And it has seemed to me that if what we
want is to establish this identity, then we must have a concrete consciousness of what we are—that is, of the first fact of our lives: that we
are black; that we were black and have a history, a history that contains
certain cultural elements of great value; and that Negroes were not, as
you put it, born yesterday, because there have been beautiful and important black civilizations. At the time we began to write people could
write a history of world civilization without devoting a single chapter to
Africa, as if Africa had made no contributions to the world. Therefore
we affirmed that we were Negroes and that we were proud of it, and
that we thought that Africa was not some sort of blank page in the
history of humanity; in sum, we asserted that our Negro heritage was
worthy of respect, and that this heritage was not relegated to the past,

that its values were values that could still make an important contribution to the world.

R.D.: That is to say, universalizing values . . .

A.C.: Universalizing, living values that had not been exhausted. The field was not dried up: it could still bear fruit, if we made the effort to irrigate it with our sweat and plant new seeds in it. So this was the situation: there were things to tell the world. We were not dazzled by European civilization. We bore the imprint of European civilization but we thought that Africa could make a contribution to Europe. It was also an affirmation of our solidarity. That's the way it was: I have always recognized that what was happening to my brothers in Algeria and the United States had its repercussions in me. I understood that I could not be indifferent to what was happening in Haiti or Africa. Then, in a way, we slowly came to the idea of a sort of black civilization spread throughout the world. And I have come to the realization that there was a "Negro situation" that existed in different geographical areas, that Africa was also my country. There was the African continent, the Antilles, Haiti; there were Martinicans and Brazilian Negroes, etc. That's what Negritude meant to me. . . .

6.7　A Rainbow for the Christian West

The following selection is the opening passage from a long poem by René Depestre, a black Haitian poet and political activist who wrote mainly from exile after 1952. Written in 1967 and subtitled "Voodoo Mystery Poem" in its original form, the work upholds the values and beliefs of black Haitian culture against the racist and domineering tendencies of white culture. It presents the fantastic confrontation of a Haitian priest, fortified by the gods of voodoo, and a white racist judge and his family in Alabama. The rest of the poem goes on to narrate how the Haitian gods, once victorious over the false white gods, find themselves weak in the

Depestre, René. *A Rainbow for the Christian West*, 108–13. Amherst: University of Massachusetts Press, 1977.

face of North American technological power and the threat of nuclear war. It ends with an affirmation of a universal spirit that binds earthly and sacred forces together as humanity's hope for salvation.

Prelude

1

Yes I am a tempest-nigger
A nigger rooted in the rainbow
My heart grows tight as a fist
To strike at the false gods' face
At the end of my sadness
There are claws shooting forth
I blow up my shadows
Into a thousand lion-mornings.
I am the thunder on your roofs!
I am the wind shattering all!
I am the virus that does not spare!
I am the disasters at the Stock Exchange
Gladly my sun signs all your plagues!
I am a little girl
Crossing a torrent of gall
Every morning to go to school!
And like the black pastor who stirs up
The still living ashes of his church
I stir up the legends of my life
I will not build any new temples
I blow up my fear
I explode my biology
In a rain of stars upon your heads
I have come to stuff your dogs with straw
I have come to stuff your ferocious laws
I preserve your prayers in alcohol
Your tricks your taboos your white man's lies!
And the crown of thorns of which you are so proud
I put it on the head of my trained bear
Both of us will climb
On the next plane for London
Paris Rome Madrid Lisbon Brussels
Toronto Los Angeles Miami Capetown Sydney
The world will see what you have done
With the man who was crying under the olive trees!

2

I do not remain seated under a tree
Awaiting your miracles
The little Christ who was smiling in me
Last night I drowned him in alcohol
Likewise I drowned the Tablets of the Law
Likewise I drowned all your sacred sacraments
My collection of butterflies are monsters
That you loosed on my black man's dreams
Monsters of Birmingham monsters of Pretoria
I collect your hysterias
I collect your pale spirochetes
I devote myself to the stamp collecting of your cowardly acts
Here I am a brand new Black
I finally feel that I am myself
In my new solar geography
Me in the great joy of saying good-bye
To your ten commandments of God
To your hypocrisies to your bloody rites
To the brewing of your scandals!
Me in this fire of my veins
Who has never prayed
Me in this radium of my color
Who has never bent the knee
Me in this royal tree of my blood
Who has never turned towards the West
Leaves of submission
Me in the geometry of my lions
Me in the violence of my diamond
Me in the purity of my crystal
Me in the gaiety of rekindling life
For you volcano of my slave-compound!

3

I go forward barefoot
In the grass of my négritude
O sweet coolness under my savage stride!
From now on I know all that is dead in me
I am the collector of monsters
I also know the name of the wheat growing up through me

And the name of voodoo that stirs in my body
Great wings of innocence!
And I love these flames of mine
Their music marks the beat of all my impulses
I go forward all naked in the tunnel of my joy
To burn all that falls into my hands
I am of the great race of volcanos
When Memphis burns it will be me!
When Johannesburg burns it will be me!
I am a great oil-thrower over fire
Church fires family fires
Palace fires bank fires
I will proclaim your feasts at the edge of my nights!

It was a summer night in an Alabama city. I went forward all naked in the meadow of my misfortunes. Slave-ships furrowed in all directions through my sky. Somewhere inside me a loudspeaker recounted the childhood of my race. The words were falling in flames. The words were crackling, knocking against one another like blind sparrowhawks. Meanwhile they raised an intolerable hope in me. They laid before me a vast land of adventure. I had the feeling of walking towards a revelation called upon to change my life. It is tonight or never, I said to myself. And with a black-embers step I went into the drive leading to the home of the Whites. They were having dinner, the entire tribe. Everything in the house breathed affluence, charm, health, peace, light. Respectability beamed. I rubbed my eyes the better to believe it. This was truly the family in all their white fairyland. The captain of this luminous shore was a judge. He was the first one to notice my arrival. A giant wave of gall soon began to move, within the life of this righteous man of Alabama. And the whole table started to rock towards me. But not a single red globule vacillated in my body. I was a rock towering very high above this white tumult. . . .

6.8 The Merengue: Race, Class, Tradition, and Identity

Like many Latin American countries at the time, the Dominican Republic in the late 1960s and early 1970s was governed by an authoritarian regime, headed by Joaquín Balaguer. One of the forms of popular protest developed in this period was music, with the folk protests of the Nueva Cancíon *(New Song) movement at the forefront. In the 1970s the debates over popular music widened to include the long-suppressed issue of the country's African-American heritage. In the following selection, anthropologist Deborah Pacini Hernández recounts an evolving debate over the origins of the* merengue, *the country's most popular musical form.*

The energetic and brassy merengue is the Dominican Republic's most popular dance music and perhaps best-known cultural export. Merengue's long and rich history has reflected the country's attempts to come to grips with race, class, and cultural authenticity, issues which have been significant features of the country's evolving national identity. The origins of the dance music date to the time (1822–1844) when the Dominican Republic was occupied by its recently-independent neighbor to the west, Haiti. Dominican music historians ascribe the first danced merengue to one of the final battles of the Dominican struggle to expel Haitians from their territory. The story goes that a song ridiculing a wounded deserter emerged at a spontaneous victory celebration, and that merengue's particular dance step, in which one foot drags behind the other, was the result of revelers mimicking the injured coward's limping gait.

While colorful, this account more likely reflects both the desire to show the Haitian occupiers in an unfavorable light, and the Dominican urge to deny any Haitian influence on their music. Dominicans have never quite forgiven Haiti for an occupation that made the Dominican Republic the only country in Latin America to be subjugated by blacks; thus, the country's independence day, February 27th, does not commemorate independence from Spain, but from the 22-year occupation by Haiti.

The denial of the Dominican Republic's African heritage was solidified during the regime of the dictator Rafael Trujillo (1930–1961), whose racist policies—the 1937 massacre of thousands of persons of Haitian

Pacini Hernández, Deborah. "Race, Class, Tradition, and Identity in the Dominican Merengue." 1991. Original manuscript.

descent perceived to be encroaching on Dominican territory, and the prohibition of folk traditions with clear African or Haitian antecedents, for example—had made it impossible to affirm the country's African legacy in a positive way. Today, though 73% of the population are mulatto, 11% black, and 16% white, Dominicans often ignore or actively reject their African ancestry. Indeed, the sort of black pride or *negritude* movements in other Caribbean countries such as Haiti, Cuba, or Jamaica never emerged in the Dominican Republic.

Haitian music historians, on the other hand, assert that the Haitian meringue is the antecedent of merengue, and was in fact introduced to the Dominican Republic during the occupation. Complicating the issue even further, Cuba and Puerto Rico have also been cited as the birthplaces of merengue, with early published accounts from these islands mentioning the word *merengue* in evidence. Nevertheless, while the question of merengue's origins may never be resolved to everyone's satisfaction, there is no question that merengue has evolved and flourished most vigorously in the Dominican Republic.

Merengue was originally a rural music played by and for country people to enliven recreational events, from weddings and saint's day festivals to cockfights and informal Sunday get-togethers. The first merengues were played with stringed instruments, the *tambora* (a drum played sideways with the hand and a stick) and one or more of a variety of percussion instruments, and *guiro*, a hollowed, dried and striated calabash scraped rhythmically with a metal prong. In the late 1870's German merchants introduced the accordion to the country's prosperous north central region, known as the Cibao. The bright tones of the accordion were immediately appreciated by rural Cibaenos, and within a short time it had replaced the guitar as the lead instrument in merengue ensembles. Shortly afterwards the saxophone was introduced to merengue bands in the Cibao, although saxes did not become regular features until after 1910.

In addition to strictly recreational purposes, merengue songs also served as vehicles of social commentary for people who could neither read nor write, and therefore had no access to published information. Dalmaso Mercado, an elderly rural Dominican musician, pointed out: *El merengue ha sido siempre diremos el recuerdo de algún pasado histórico . . . es decir, que de cada acontecimiento que pasaba aquí salía a relucir un merengue.* ("The merengue has always been the recollection of a past occurrence. That is, from each event that took place here a merengue would result.")

At the turn of the century, the merengue, whether guitar or accordion-based, was still limited to rural contexts; the European-oriented Dominican elites shunned the merengue as a vulgar music form ill-suited to their social station. However, during the U.S. occupation of the Dominican Republic from 1916–1924, precisely because merengue was so rooted in vernacular culture, the merengue became a symbol of the country's beleaguered national identity, and was accepted for the first time in elite contexts. Nevertheless, in order for the merengue to be introduced into elite society, it needed to be "dressed up" appropriately. Dominican composers searched for a way to transform merengue from a rural folk form to urban salon music. In 1918 Juan Francisco García published the first merengue arrangement, although it was intended to be heard in a concert hall or salon rather than danced to. It was not until 1922 that Juan Espínola introduced a merengue— this time for dancing—into an elite social club in La Vega. But when the Marines withdrew from the country in 1924, the merengue was again relegated to rural contexts.

The next phase of merengue's evolution was influenced most dramatically by Rafael Trujillo, dictator of the Dominican Republic for 31 years. Trujillo, of lower middle class origins, liked popular music and dance. He astutely perceived merengue's potential as a vehicle for political propaganda, and more important, that it could serve as a symbol of national identity for a country long-fragmented by the rivalries of local political bosses. During his successful campaign for the presidency in 1930, Trujillo travelled the countryside accompanied by merengue ensembles who sang his praises and evoked the future glories his election would bring.

While the rural populace responded favorably to these merengues, the Dominican elite rejected Trujillo for his crude aggressiveness and vulgar customs, including his irritating insistence that merengue be played wherever he went. Dominican musician Luis Alberti recalls that in the early 1930's merengues were dutifully played and danced to in elite habitats while Trujillo was present, but that as soon as he turned his back, the merengue was forgotten. Nevertheless, supported by his immense wealth and power, Trujillo eventually inserted himself into Dominican high society—although he did not thereupon abandon his preference for merengue in favor of the elite's "refined" and international tastes. Instead, he decided to refashion the merengue so it would better reflect a more distinguished social context. He succeeded in turning it into a symbol of his regime's power and modernity.

In 1936, Trujillo hired the jazz band *Lira del Yaque*, led by the Cibaeñan Luis Alberti, took it to Santo Domingo and renamed it the *Orquesta Generalísimo Trujillo*. Trujillo generously provided Alberti funds to hire the best musicians so the band, the country's finest, could play for him at social functions. In the process, Alberti dropped the traditional accordion, and soon the merengue was transformed into something quite new and different: refined, sophisticated, and appropriate for the elite ballroom.

But more significantly, Trujillo's involvement in merengue profoundly changed merengue's function and content, which had heretofore been used as a vehicle for social commentary of all sorts. Though the merengue was refined and popularized under Trujillo's tutelage, in the process it lost its independence and became a mouthpiece for Trujillo's political agenda. No criticism of the regime, explicit or implicit, was tolerated in a music previously defined by the broad topicality of its lyrics. What was worse, musicians could not simply maintain a discreet silence, but instead, had to prove their loyalty to Trujillo by composing songs praising him and his every action. In the course of the 31-year Trujillo regime, thousands of merengues extolling the dictator and his activities were produced, not just by slavish followers, but by all Dominican musicians of any stature who did not go into exile. The titles of these songs reveal the depths of submission and triviality to which composers were forced to stoop: *Veneremos a Trujillo* (Let us venerate Trujillo), *Trujillo es grande e inmortal* (Trujillo is great and immortal), *Trujillo protector de choferes* (Trujillo protector of drivers). Other merengues served to publish the regime's views of national or world events, resulting in such forgettable titles as *El censo de 1950* (The census of 1950) or *La deuda interna* (The internal debt).

Remarkably, after Trujillo's death in 1961 the merengue was not discredited, but became a symbol of the Dominican society's new openness, and of modernity and progress. Johnny Ventura, one of the first and most successful of the new breed of *merengueros,* shed the elite ballroom character that had distinguished the merengue *orquestas* of the Trujillo regime, and pared the merengue ensemble down to a smaller and energetic *combo.* Influenced in part by U.S. rock and roll, Ventura's *combo* introduced glittery costumes, energetic choreography and spicy, satiric lyrics to the merengue performance, and was considered by young Dominicans to be more in tune with the decade of the 1960's. No longer threatened by the interference of Trujillo, merengue combos began recording and touring internationally, and by the late 1970s, merengue's popularity had spread far beyond the country's borders. Yet while the 1970s saw merengue become a successful and visible competitor in the international musical arena, at home merengue became contested terrain for an important national debate about the shape and content of the Dominican Republic's national identity.

A new generation of Dominican social scientists and folklorists provoked an impassioned public about Dominican national identity when they insisted on the country's African cultural heritage, thereby challenging the beliefs of the ruling elites, who for decades had insisted the country's culture was of purely Hispanic origins. A musical group called Convite made the most profound contribution to the debate by focusing on the relationship between the country's music and its national identity. Convite was not a musical ensemble in the usual sense of the word, but rather a loosely-structured group of musicians, folklorists and social scientists with a common desire to rediscover and reexamine the country's autochthonous musical traditions, particularly those with clear African roots which had been persistently ignored by cultural observers since the Trujillo era.

The assertion of African contributions to Dominican culture and music was not accepted easily. A declaration by folklorist Fradique Lizardo that merengue had African origins so horrified Luis Senior, a well-established merengue bandleader, that he wrote an article vehemently stating, "This outlandish statement is unpatriotic!"

These public debates culminated in two conferences on merengue held in Santo Domingo in the latter part of the 1970s. One, held in 1978 and entitled "Encounter with the merengue," focused specifically on race, which had become a major concern during the process of national redefinition. The musical group Tejeda, representing Convite, insisted on highlighting the importance of merengue's African roots, and asserted that Convite was contributing to the "rescue and diffusion of the Dominican musical patrimony" through music. This militant position was clearly an attempt to force those concerned with the country's national and cultural identity to squarely face the issue of race and racism. Asking the question, "Where did merengue come from" was clearly another way of asking, "Where did we Dominicans come from, and who are we?" Responding to the question forced cultural observers of all socio-political persuasions to acknowledge—or reject—the country's African heritage.

As the decade wore on, the merengue combos expanded in both spectacle and size—up to 12 or 15 musicians—including a front line of skillfully choreographed and flashily dressed vocalists who added a dynamic visual component to the performance. Composers and arrangers began to experiment with styles and instruments borrowed from abroad, and merengue's pace increased to almost breakneck speed. By the early 1980's, merengues had achieved an unprecedented international success, displacing salsa as the preferred dance music throughout the hemisphere. In the euphoria, the divisive discussions of merengue's African origins seem to have been forgotten. Today, cultural observers view merengue's new international popularity with trepidation, pleased with its success but concerned that international acceptance will dilute its quintessentially Dominican quality.

Another development in merengue signals profound changes in Dominican society: the active participation of women in merengue ensembles, not just as singers, but as musicians. Since the late 1970's several *orquesta* merengue ensembles have emerged (such as La Media Naranja, Las Chicas del Can), in which women play all the instruments—trombone, trumpets, bass, congas and synthesizers, instruments traditionally played only by men. Similarly, women accordianists such as Fefita la Grande are playing lead roles in *típico moderno* ensembles named after them. While many of the songs they perform have been written by men, others are composed by the women themselves and reflect the female point of view. These women musicians offer a highly potent image of changes in gender roles taking place in Dominican society.

In conclusion, merengue serves as a window onto the social changes transforming Dominican society since the 19th century. Initially a low-status music associated with the peasantry, merengue served as a symbol of national identity under U.S. occupation. Later it became a propaganda tool of a brutal dictatorship. After Trujillo's assassination in 1961, the issue of African contributions to Dominican culture—symbolized by merengue—became a major component in the struggle for national reconstruction and redefinition. More recently, merengue's international success has again raised questions of cultural authenticity, identity, and tradition. Moreover, an extraordinary variety of merengue styles continue to evolve simultaneously within their own regional and social contexts. These diverse developments have endowed the Dominican merengue with a richness and variety equalled by few Latin American musical genres.

7

In Women's Hands: The Changing Roles of Women

In Santiago, Chile, women led many of the protests against human rights violations committed by the Pinochet government, which held power between 1973 and 1990. © Steve Rubin/JB Pictures

Women have always played important roles in Latin American and Caribbean society, although they have often gone unnoticed. This has resulted in part from the scarcity of opportunities for women to be in the public eye, as well as from the tendency of historians to overlook them.

The lack of attention belies the achievements of those who have been at the forefront of the region's literary, artistic, and political life. Among the most renowned are Sor Juana Inés de la Cruz, a Mexican nun widely regarded as colonial Latin America's greatest poet; the Chilean writer Gabriela Mistral, the first Latin American to win a Nobel Prize in literature and one of only three women ever to earn this honor; and Frida Kahlo, the internationally acclaimed Mexican painter.

Latin American and Caribbean women have also achieved political prominence by serving in the highest offices in their nations. In Argentina, Isabel Perón, who had been vice president, succeeded her husband Juan Perón in the presidency following his death in 1974. Lydia Gueiller was elected president of Bolivia in 1979, and Violeta Chamorro was elected president of Nicaragua in 1990. In the Caribbean during the 1980s, Eugenia Charles of Dominica and Maria Liberia Peters of the Netherlands Antilles served as prime ministers of their respective countries.

Yet politically powerful women have not been the only ones to assume critical roles in their societies. Many women have joined armed rebellions against unpopular or repressive governments, as they did in the Mexican Revolution of 1910 and the Nicaraguan Revolution of 1979. Others have become community leaders pressuring the state to provide public services or protesting against unpopular policies. And millions of women have labored anonymously as professional, service, industrial, and agricultural workers.

Themes in Latin American Women's History

Of the hundreds of different indigenous cultures thriving before the Europeans arrived beginning in 1492, each had its own traditions defining women's roles and social participation. While all these societies were marked by some degree of gender inequality and limited public roles for women, they were characterized by more equitable gender relations than were Iberian societies of the same period.

The European conquest of the New World vastly altered the lives of indigenous women and set the pattern for their subordination, which persists up to the present. Women were among the spoils of victory for the conquerors. Since European women arrived as colonists only years after the initial invasions, the exploitation of Indian women continued in the form of labor, caretaking, and sexual gratification.

Elite Indian women were sometimes able to gain a somewhat privileged position through their liaisons with European men. As the era of military conquest ended, however, and more European women began to arrive in the New World, Indian women were confined to the bottom of the ethnic and class hierarchy. Nonetheless, they helped their cultures to adapt to the catastrophic effects of conquest through their day-to-day resistance to the dominant European culture and through their efforts to maintain a sense of identity and community. Similarly, African women, brought to the New World as slaves, also became guardians of tradition and supported their communities economically.

European women who came to the New World found their participation in society circumscribed by their role in maintaining the colonial empire's hierarchical structure. A particular concern of the colonists was that their "purity of blood" be preserved, meaning that no black or Indian people could enter into the family lineage. Women's behavior was thus carefully controlled. Under the regulation of *patria potestad,* women remained under the legal authority of their fathers until marriage, when authority was transferred to their husbands. This patriarchal arrangement gave rise to machismo, a cultural code of behavior emphasizing male superiority, virility, and control.

Outside these limitations, there were a few opportunities for wider roles for women. Widows and women who did not marry had more freedom to conduct commercial and legal affairs on their own. Also, women who chose to enter the convent were often able to pursue an education that might otherwise have been denied them, as was the case with Sor Juana in Mexico (see reading 7.1).

Women's participation in society changed to a degree during the nineteenth-century movements for Latin American independence, when their allegiance to the cause led them to be politically active and gained for them greater respect and recognition. Yet despite the activism of women during the independence period, their status hardly changed at all. Throughout the nineteenth century, women's participation in public life was limited and they remained legally minors. Gradual advances in education for women, however, did raise their literacy rates and allowed some to enter the professions. The greatest changes, perhaps, came through the alteration of civic codes, which ultimately abolished the *patria potestad* laws in many countries.

Latin American women entered the twentieth century with better educations and legal status but with still restricted roles. In some countries of the region, as reading 7.2 illustrates, women initiated campaigns for equal political and civil rights, including suffrage, legalized civil marriage, and the right to divorce. However, despite some gains, the contours of their lives continued to be shaped by machismo, motherhood, and the patriarchal family. Poor women faced the double duty of family and employment, while nonwhite women endured as the most impoverished and subordinated sector of society.

Contemporary Latin American Women—The Economy, Politics, and Society

Though Latin American and Caribbean women tend to share the traditional responsibilities of home management and child care, they are divided by class and ethnic differences. Many women from the upper classes seek work outside the home, both to enhance their family's income and to express their individual talent. Their freedom from household and family responsibilities, however, may be purchased at the expense of poor women who labor long days as domestic servants for very low pay. The exploitation faced by female domestics is one of the issues dividing Latin American women along class lines, as reading 7.3 describes.

Women from ethnic minorities often experience a dual discrimination based on gender and ethnicity. Rural women and those women who are Indian and black are particularly likely to be poor, and they are less likely to have access to education and adequate health care (see reading 7.4).

Significant developments, including most recently economic crises and the movement toward representative government, have changed the lives of Latin American women during the last few decades. In the economic realm, burdensome international debts, rising import and falling export prices, and government efforts to restructure national economies have threatened the well-being of many families and hampered their chances for upward mobility. The consequences include less adequate nutrition for low-income families and the loss of health insurance for many in the middle class.

The region's ongoing economic crisis has accelerated the process of women's incorporation into the labor force. To augment family income, poor women especially have sought employment outside the household as domestics, assembly plant workers, agricultural laborers, or prostitutes. They have also earned income in the informal economic sector as street vendors, small-scale peddlers, and scavengers. The popularity of *maquiladora* employment among women reflects the changing set of opportunities available to them—even in a context where the conditions of work in many of these assembly plants are unsanitary, unsafe, and low-paying, as described in Chapter 5.

Rural women have been affected by recent developments in the agrarian economy. Once well integrated into all aspects of family subsistence farming, especially in the Andean countries and Central America, women increasingly find themselves as low-wage laborers in large-scale export agriculture and related processing activities. As this shift has occurred, these women have lost valuable food resources and some control over their economic domain. Reading 7.5 describes the taxing physical and economic conditions they face.

The formal participation of women in the economy has also increased in the public sector. Although they still tend to hold lower-rank positions, women have a better chance of obtaining employment in government jobs than in the private sector.

Women have responded to these economic challenges with new forms of political activism. With their families and communities under siege, women have mounted various grass-roots movements to pool their resources or extract them from government. They have also strengthened ties of kinship, *compadrazgo* (godparenthood), and friendship among themselves to form networks of mutual aid. In Chile during the Pinochet years, for example, poor urban women organized mutual aid networks to collectivize food supplies in communal kitchens and feed entire neighborhoods.

Throughout Latin America, women have organized their communities to bring poverty and lack of public services to the attention of government officials. Much of the motivation for such political activity stems from their commitment to traditional roles as family and community caretakers. In their activism, they are reformulating the responsibilities of motherhood and expanding the boundaries of this role (see reading 7.6).

Women have staged protests, sent delegations, and formed alliances with political parties to get aid. In some instances, the grass-roots movements in which women participated have become influential in electoral politics, as in Fortaleza, Brazil, where such movements helped elect a feminist mayor in 1985. In Mexico City, popular organizations assisted in the formation of a new political party during the presidential campaign of 1988.

Women have also engaged in political protest against repressive regimes, especially during the last two decades. In Argentina, the Madres de la Plaza de Mayo (Mothers of the May Plaza) marched carrying pictures of relatives and friends who had been "disappeared" and demanded that the military government account for them. In Chile, women took a traditional female craft, *arpilleras* (appliquéd and embroidered wall hangings), and used them to tell the story of the state's increasing brutality against the people (see reading 7.7).

The expanded participation of women in economic and political activities has at times led to changes in their behavior within the traditional family. However, the changes often clash with the norms of machismo, for as women ask for democracy within society, they may also ask for it within the family. Consequently, relationships between women and men are being renegotiated, sometimes painfully, as reading 7.8 describes.

Movements that question machismo, patriarchal family structure, and traditional gender roles are not new on Latin America's social landscape. Feminist organizations have existed throughout the region since the early twentieth century. Latin American feminists usually focus on issues transcending class boundaries, such as sexuality, reproductive rights, and violence against women. Many feminists struggle with the contradictions of class and gender, particularly those involving the exploitation of poor women by middle- and upper-class women. The patriarchy that suffuses all aspects of life—from science and politics to life in the home—is also a key obstacle, as is discussed in reading 7.9.

Economic crisis, political change, and feminism all have challenged women to become active, creative participants in transforming Latin America and the Caribbean. Today, the region's women are becoming more influential and dynamic in their public participation than at any time in the past.

7.1 A Modern Voice from the Seventeenth Century

Born around 1650, Sor Juana Inés de la Cruz achieved fame at an early age in colonial Mexico for her poetry, plays, and scholarly brilliance. All her life, as she recounts below, she faced opposition to her desire to learn, and at one point she asked her mother to disguise her as a boy so that she might enter the university. At about 20 she entered a convent but continued to write on both religious and secular issues, to the growing distress of the Church hierarchy. The following excerpts are from a long letter she wrote in response to a bishop who criticized her writing as inappropriate for a nun. With characteristic energy and wit she defends the ability of women to excel in learning and suggests that the education of men is no guarantee of their good judgment.

I have never written of my own accord, but only when pressured by others . . . What is true and I will not deny . . . is that from my first glimmers of reason, my inclination to letters was of such power and vehemence, that neither the reprimands of others—and I have received many—nor my own considerations—and there have been not a few of these—have succeeded in making me abandon this natural impulse which God has implanted in me. . . .

To go on with the account of this strong bent of mine . . . when I was not yet three, my mother sent a sister of mine, older than I, to learn to read in one of those establishments called Amigas [girls' elementary schools], at which point affection and mischievousness on my part led me to follow her. Seeing that she was being given lessons, I became so inflamed with the desire to learn to read, that I tricked the mistress—or so I thought—by telling her that my mother had directed her to give me lessons. This was not believable and she did not believe me, but falling in with my little trick, she did give me lessons. I continued attending and she went on teaching me, no longer as a joke, since the event opened her eyes. I learned to read in so short a time that I already knew how when my mother found out, for the mistress kept it from her . . . I kept still, since I thought I would be whipped for having acted on my own initiative. . . .

. . . Afterward, when I was six or seven and already knew how to

de la Cruz, Sor Juana Inés. "The Reply to Sor Philothea." In *A Sor Juana Anthology*, translated by Alan S. Trueblood, 210–30. Cambridge, Mass.: Harvard University Press, 1988.

read and write, along with all the sewing skills and needlework that women learn, I discovered that in the City of Mexico there was a university with schools where the different branches of learning could be studied, and as soon as I learned this I began to deluge my mother with urgent and insistent pleas to change my manner of dress and send me to stay with relatives in the City of Mexico so that I might study and take courses at the university. She refused, and rightly so; nevertheless, I found a way to read many different books my grandfather owned, notwithstanding the punishments and reproofs this entailed . . .

. . . I became a nun because, although I knew that that way of life involved much that was repellent to my nature—I refer to its incidental, not its central, aspects—nevertheless, given my total disinclination to marriage, it was the least unreasonable and most becoming choice I could make to assure my ardently desired salvation. To which first consideration, as most important, all the other small frivolities of my nature yielded and gave way, such as my wish to live alone, to have no fixed occupation which might curtail my freedom to study, nor the noise of a community to interfere with the tranquil stillness of my books. . . . I thought I was escaping from myself, but, alas for me, I had brought myself along. In this propensity I brought my greatest enemy, given me by Heaven whether as a boon or a punishment I cannot decide, for, far from dying out or being hindered by all the exercises religion entails, it exploded like gunpowder. . . .

I went back (I misspeak: I had never stopped); I went on with the studious pursuit (in which I found relaxation during all the free time remaining from my obligations) of reading and more reading, study and more study, with no other teacher than books themselves. . . .

Even if these studies were to be viewed . . . as to one's credit (as I see they are indeed celebrated in men), none would be due me, since I pursue them involuntarily. If they are seen as reprehensible, for the same reason I do not think I should be blamed. . . .

The venerable Dr. Arce (in virtue and cultivation a worthy professor of Scripture) in his *Studioso Bibliorum*, raises this question: *An liceat foeminis sacrorum Bibliorum studio incumbere? eaque interpretari?* [Is it legitimate for women to apply themselves to study of the Holy Bible and to interpret it?] . . . He finally decides, in his judicious way, that to lecture publicly in the classroom and to preach in the pulpit are not legitimate activities for women, but that studying, writing, and teaching privately are not only allowable but most edifying and useful. Of course this does not apply to all women—only to those whom God has endowed with particular virtue and discernment and who have become highly accomplished and erudite, and possess the talents and other qualities needed for such holy pursuits. So true is this that the interpretation of Holy Scripture should be forbidden not only to women, considered so very inept, but to men, who merely by virtue of being men consider themselves sages, unless they are very learned and virtuous, with receptive and properly trained minds. Failure to do so, in my view, has given rise precisely to all those sectarians and been the root cause of all the heresies. For there are many who study in order to become ignorant, especially those of an arrogant, restless, and overbearing turn of mind . . .

7.2 The Suffrage Movement in Chile

In most Latin American countries women only achieved the right to vote after World War II. One of the earliest movements for women's suffrage in the region arose in Chile, but, as the following reading illustrates, it took more than three decades to succeed. The movement was led by Amanda Labarca, who in 1922 became the first female professor at the University of Chile, and in 1931 was named director of secondary education, the highest government post ever held by a woman at that time.

Women's emancipation in Chile was, from its beginnings, an activity that involved many women. There is, however, one woman who holds the undisputed place as the leader of feminism in Chile, and the movement for women's suffrage properly begins in 1915 when Amanda Labarca Hubertson founded a Círculo de Lectura (Women's Reading Circle) at which women met to study literary and philosophical works. The circle was not only the first club of its kind for women but also the first women's group to be organized through lay initiative and not under clerical sponsorship.

Women of the upper class immediately decided that they also wanted to organize, and at the end of the same year they formed a Club de Señoras [Women's Club] presided over by Delia Matte de Izquierdo; the two clubs began a more or less cordial collaboration and some women joined both groups.

The French writer Marcelle Auclair, who lived as a young woman in Santiago, recalls how the Círculo de Lectura "let a breath of fresh air

Chaney, Elsa M. *Supermadre: Women in Politics in Latin America,* 73–76. Austin: University of Texas Press, 1979.

into a closed, colonial Chile, with the best of thought, science, and literature." Juan de Soiza Reilly notes particularly the "anxiety felt by women of the higher class when they were confronted with the intellectual superiority of the 'little teachers' like Amanda Labarca." He quotes one of the founders of the Club de Señoras, Inés Echeverría de Larraín, who under the name "Iris" was to become the unofficial scribe of the emancipation movement: "To our great surprise, there appeared in Chile a middle class, and we had no idea how it came to be born . . . with the most perfectly educated women who had professional and teaching degrees, while we upper class women hardly knew the mysteries of the rosary."

As Amanda Labarca points out, the foundation of these clubs owed nothing to men and everything "to the leadership of the women themselves." Such groups, which also began to appear in pre–World War I Peru, thus had no connection with the salons of other epochs. Women from this time on met for intellectual and political discussion almost always with members of their own sex, as they do to this day. Even the political parties, with their sex-segregated women's sections, have not brought men and women together again to exchange ideas on political and social issues.

The salon had, of course, admitted only a small group of truly gifted and outstanding women, whereas the founders of women's groups after 1915 wanted to reach many more women and to awaken them to a more active intellectual and cultural (and later social and political) life. Perhaps for this reason, such women's groups were strongly opposed not only by men—particularly the clergy—but by the more conservative women. Says Amanda Labarca, recalling the pioneer years of the Reading Circle, which inevitably was attacked as "Masonic" and was identified with the secularizing principles of the Radical Party to which she and her husband belonged: "A simple Reading Circle was for the social and political bigots the incarnation of the devil, because without a doubt we would read books 'against morality and convention' whose very acquaintance would break down the family traditions so honorably preserved from colonial times."

If discussion of social and political ideas by women was not acceptable to Catholic conservative circles, the vote for women was anathema. When women's suffrage began to be discussed—and in 1917 when the youth section of the Conservative Party actually proposed that a bill be introduced to give women political emancipation—women who advocated such a measure were threatened with excommunication.

In 1919, members of the Reading Circle and the Women's Club joined forces to found the National Council of Women, which became the principal agitator for the feminist movement during the 1920s. Many other groups were formed between 1920 and 1940 specifically to work for women's rights, including associations of university women, leagues for civic action, and study groups. . . .

Amanda Labarca recounts how president after president, once in office, went back on promises to sponsor bills for women's emancipation because "they had no confidence in how women would use the vote." Even Pedro Aguirre Cerda, a member of Amanda Labarca's own Radical Party, who became president in 1938 as the candidate of the leftist Popular Front, went back on his word to promote national women's suffrage. She reports how the president made clear

> in our many conversations with him his doubt that the woman, having acquired the vote, would continue along the same line that had brought him to the Presidency of the Republic. That is, he didn't believe in the continuing leftism of the woman.
>
> In this, as a matter of fact, there was a basis in fact. The men—secularists, Masons, leftists, and even Socialists—simply didn't bother to orient their womenfolk toward their own political ideas.

Only in 1944, when the first National Congress of Women was held, did the movement for women's rights begin to awaken mass support. The Federation of Women's Organizations was formed as a result of this conference, with Amanda Labarca as its head. Despite the dissolution of the Popular Front in electoral politics, the women created a board of directors that incorporated leaders of all political ideologies from the extreme right to the extreme left . . .

Five years later, after much patient work on the part of a small group . . . women received the vote.

7.3 A Maid in the Capital

Rigoberta Menchú is an Indian woman from Guatemala who has become internationally famous as an activist and spokeswoman for her people. In this selection, she discusses her experiences as a domestic servant employed by a wealthy family in her nation's capital city. Her testimony describes the hardships she endured as a poor, newly arrived immigrant to the city, and reflects the deep divisions between Latin American women along class lines. The reading highlights the differences between life in the largely Indian countryside and that in the Spanish-speaking cities, and also shows the depth of ethnic and class prejudice.

I, Rigoberta Menchú: An Indian Woman in Guatemala, edited by Elizabeth Burgos-Debray, translated by Ann Wright, 91–101. London: Verso, 1984.

So we reached the capital. I remember that my clothes were worn out because I'd been working in the *finca:* my *corte* was really dirty and my *huipil* very old. I had a little *perraje*, the only one I owned. I didn't have any shoes. I didn't even know what wearing shoes was like. The master's wife was at home. There was another servant girl to do the cooking and I would have to do all the cleaning in the house. The other servant was also Indian, but she'd changed her clothes. She wore *ladino* clothes and already spoke Spanish. I didn't know any; I arrived and didn't know what to say. I couldn't speak Spanish but I understood a little because of the *finca* overseers who used to give us orders, bully us and hand out the work. Many of them are Indians but they won't use Indian languages because they feel different from the labourers. So I understood Spanish although I couldn't speak it. The mistress called the other servant: "Take this girl to the room in the back." The girl came, looked at me with indifference and told me to follow her. She took me to the other room. It was a room with a pile of boxes in the corner and plastic bags where they kept the rubbish. It had a little bed. They took it down for me and put a little mat on it, with another blanket, and left me there. I had nothing to cover myself with.

The first night, I remember, I didn't know what to do. That was when I felt what my sister had felt although, of course, my sister had been with another family. Then later the mistress called me. The food they gave me was a few beans with some very hard *tortillas*. There was a dog in the house, a pretty, white, fat dog. When I saw the maid bring out the dog's food—bits of meat, rice, things that the family ate—and they gave me a few beans and hard *tortillas*, that hurt me very much. The dog had a good meal and I didn't deserve as good a meal as the dog. Anyway, I ate it, I was used to it. I didn't mind not having the dog's food because at home I only ate *tortillas* with chile or with salt or water. But I felt rejected. I was lower than the animals in the house. . . .

At seven, the girl got up and came and told me: "Come here and wash the dishes." I went in my same clothes and the mistress came in and said: "How filthy! Get that girl out of here! How can you let her touch the dishes, can't you see how dirty she is?" The girl told me to leave the dishes, but she was upset too. "Here's the broom, go and sweep up," the mistress said. I went out to sweep the yard. "Water the plants," she said, "that's your job. And then come here and do the washing. Here are the clothes, but mind you wash them properly or I'll throw you out." . . .

At about half past eleven, she called me again and took me into a room. She said: "I'm going to give you two month's pay in advance and you must buy yourself a *huipil*, a new *corte*, and a pair of shoes, because you put me to shame. My friends are coming and you're here like that. What would that look like to my friends? They are important people so you'll have to change your ways. I'll buy you these things but you stay here because I'm ashamed to be seen with you in the market. Here's your two month's pay." Well, I didn't know what to say because I didn't know enough Spanish to protest or say what I thought. But in my mind I insulted her. I thought, if only I could send this woman to the mountains and let her do the work my mother does. I don't think she'd even be capable of it. I didn't think much of her at all.

She went off to market. She came back with a *corte*. It was about a couple of yards long. The simplest there was. She also brought a simple *huipil* which must have cost her two fifty or three *quetzals*. She didn't buy me another belt, I had my old one. And she said she didn't buy me shoes because two month's pay wasn't enough. Then she gave me the *corte*. I had to tear it into two so that I could keep one of them to change into. I tore it into two parts. . . . the mistress said, "When you've changed, go to my room and make my bed." I went to change, and she made me have a bath. I came back and started making her bed. When I'd finished she came to check my work and said, "Do this bed again, you didn't make it properly." And she began scolding the other girl: "Why didn't you show her how to do it? I don't want mobs of people here who can't earn their keep." We started to make the bed again. I didn't know how to dust because I'd never done it, so the other girl taught me how to dust, and how to clean the toilets. . . .

I learned to dust, wash and iron very quickly. I found ironing the hardest because I'd never used an iron before. I remember how the washing and ironing used to pile up. The landowner had three children and they changed their clothes several times a day. All the clothes they left lying around had to be washed again, and ironed again, and then hung up in the right place. The mistress used to watch me all the time and was very nasty to me. She treated me like . . . I don't know what . . . not like a dog because she treated the dog well. She used to hug the dog. . . .

I didn't go out either although on Saturdays the mistress said I had to go out: "Come on, out of here. I'm fed up with servants hanging around." That made me very angry because we worked, we did everything. We probably didn't work as hard for our parents as we did for that rich old woman. But on Saturdays, she'd say: "Out of here. I don't want to see heaps of maids around." That's what happens to Indian girls in the capital. On Saturdays we were allowed out in the evenings, but it was preparing their maids for prostitution because we were ordered out and then we had to find somewhere to sleep. We went out on Saturdays and came back on Sundays. Thank Heavens the other girl was really decent. She said, "I've got some friends here. We'll go to their house." I went with her. But what if I'd been on my own? I wouldn't have had anywhere to stay, only the street, because I couldn't even speak to the mistress to tell her not to throw me out. I couldn't find my way around the city either. So the other girl took me to her friend's house. We went there every Saturday to sleep. . . .

There were times we'd really had enough. One day the other maid and I agreed we'd start being difficult. She said, "If the mistress complains, let her complain." And we stopped doing certain things just to annoy her. So she got up and shouted at us, but the more she shouted the more stubborn we became and she saw that that wasn't any use. The other maid said: "Come on, let's leave and find another job." But I was worried because I couldn't just decide like that; I didn't know the city and if I counted on her, she might take me somewhere worse. What was I to do? Soon I realized that the mistress spurned this girl because she wouldn't become the boys' lover. She told me later: "That old bag wants me to initiate her sons. She says boys have to learn how to do the sexual act and if they don't learn when they're young, it's harder for them when they're older. So she put in my contract that she'd pay me a bit more if I taught her sons." . . .

After eight months Christmas came and we had a lot to do, because the mistress told us we were going to make two hundred *tamales*. We had to make two hundred because her friends were coming and she'd promised to make *tamales* for them all. So the other maid told her that if she wanted them she'd better set to work herself because we weren't going to do anything. . . .

But I was anxious. I couldn't do it then, perhaps because of the way my parents had brought me up. I was incapable of disobedience. And those employers exploited my obedience. They took advantage of my innocence. Whatever it was, I did it, as my duty. My friend had plans but the mistress realized that we were making a real fool of her and she threw her out. She threw her out just before Christmas. She also did it so that I couldn't leave; but even if I had left, I wouldn't have known where to go. I still didn't know anyone. I didn't know the city. . . . I had to do all the work. The mistress made me serve everything, and she had to work a bit too to make all the *tamales* she'd promised. I hardly slept. We made the *tamales* and we did all the other jobs in the house. But the washing piled up and the house was dirty because there wasn't time to clean it. . . .

Then the mistress said: "Here's a *tamal* for you so you can try out my handiwork." And she left me a *tamal*. I was so angry I couldn't bear it, I didn't even bother to look at the *tamal* she'd left me on the stove.

7.4 Life in the Favela

Carolina Maria de Jesus is a poor African-American woman who lived in an urban favela *(shantytown) earning her living by picking over trash and doing odd jobs. She came to the* favela *as a migrant from northeast Brazil after her boyfriend and employers deserted her when she became pregnant. Her story is unusual because the publication of her diary documenting life among the impoverished earned her an income that enabled her to move her family out of poverty. Her story tells of the violence, squalor, indignity, and drudgery of* favela *life—and also of her undaunted perseverance. A sensation when first published in Brazil, the diary conveys the toll of discrimination based not only on gender, but on ethnicity and rural background as well. The diary has subsequently been translated into dozens of languages and has a worldwide audience.*

May 23, 1958 . . . The sky is beautiful, worthy of contemplation because the drifting clouds are forming dazzling landscapes. Soft breezes pass by carrying the perfume of flowers. And the sun is always punctual at rising and setting. The birds travel in space, showing off in their happiness. The night brings up the sparkling stars to adorn the blue sky. There are so many beautiful things in the world that are impossible to describe. Only one thing saddens us: the prices when we go shopping. They overshadow all the beauty that exists.

Theresa, Meryi's sister, drank poison. And for no reason. They say she found a note from a woman in her lover's pocket. It ate away her mouth, her throat, and her stomach. She lost a lot of blood. The doctors say that even if she does get well she will be helpless. She has two sons, one four years old and the other nine months.

May 26 At dawn it was raining. I only have four cruzeiros, a little food left over from yesterday, and some bones. I went to look for water to boil the bones. There is still a little macaroni and I made a soup for the children. I saw a neighbor washing beans. How envious I became. It's been two weeks that I haven't washed clothes because I haven't any soap. I sold some boards for 40 cruzeiros. The woman told me she'd pay today. If she pays I'll buy soap.

For days there hasn't been a policeman in the favela, but today one came because Julião beat his father. He gave him such a violent blow that the old man cried and went to call the police.

de Jesus, Carolina Maria. *Child of the Dark*, translated by David St. Clair, 44–45, 57–58, 97–98. New York: Dutton, 1962.

May 27 It seems that the slaughterhouse threw kerosene on their garbage dump so the *favelados* would not look for meat to eat. I didn't have any breakfast and walked around half dizzy. The daze of hunger is worse than that of alcohol. The daze of alcohol makes us sing, but the one of hunger makes us shake. I know how horrible it is to only have air in the stomach.

I began to have a bitter taste in my mouth. I thought: is there no end to the bitterness of life? I think that when I was born I was marked by fate to go hungry. I filled one sack of paper. When I entered Paulo Guimarães Street, a woman gave me some newspapers. They were clean and I went to the junk yard picking up everything that I found. Steel, tin, coal, everything serves the *favelado*. Leon weighed the paper and I got six cruzeiros.

I wanted to save the money to buy beans but I couldn't because my stomach was screaming and torturing me.

I decided to do something about it and bought a bread roll. What a surprising effect food has on our organisms. Before I ate, I saw the sky, the trees, and the birds all yellow, but after I ate, everything was normal to my eyes.

Food in the stomach is like fuel in machines. I was able to work better. My body stopped weighing me down. I started to walk faster. I had the feeling that I was gliding in space. I started to smile as if I was witnessing a beautiful play. And will there ever be a drama more beautiful than that of eating? I felt that I was eating for the first time in my life. . . .

June 13, 1958 I dressed the boys and they went to school. I went to look for paper. At the slaughterhouse I saw a young girl eating sausages from the garbage.

"You should get yourself a job and you'd have a better life."

She asked me if looking for paper earned money. I told her it did. She said she wanted to work so she could walk around looking pretty. She was 15 years old, the age when we think the world is wonderful. The age when the rose unfolds. Later it falls petal by petal and leaves just the thorns. For those who tire of life . . . there is suicide. Others steal. I looked at the face of the girl. She had blisters all over her mouth.

The prices mount up like waves of the sea. Each one is stronger. Who fights with waves? Only the sharks. But the strongest shark is the thinking one. He walks on earth. He is the merchant.[1]

Lentils are 100 cruzeiros a kilo, a fact that pleases me immensely. I danced, sang and jumped and thanked God, the judge of kings! Where am I to get 100 cruzeiros? It was in January when the waters flooded

---

[1] In Portuguese slang, shark is the name given to anyone who tries to make high or illicit profits from others.

the warehouses and ruined the food. Well done. Rather than sell the things cheaply, they kept them waiting for higher prices. I saw men throw sacks of rice into the river. They threw dried codfish, cheese, and sweets. How I envied the fish who didn't work but lived better than I. . . .

August 14, 1958 Ditinho, Lena's boy, is a veteran of the favela. But he's bald and never learned to read, never learned a trade. Only learned to drink *pinga*. Lena has a nicely built shack on Port Street. But Tuburcio tricked poor Lena. They traded shacks and he gave her a badly built one and kept hers. Afterward he sold it for 15,000 cruzeiros.

I went to the junk yard and got 15 cruzeiros. I passed by the shoemaker to tell him to fix Vera's shoes. I kept hurrying up streets. I was nervous because I had very little money and tomorrow is a holiday. A woman who was returning from market told me to go and look for paper at Porto Seguro Street, the building on the corner, fourth floor, apartment 44.

I went up in the elevator, Vera and I. But I was so frightened that the minutes I stayed inside the elevator seemed to me like centuries. When I got to the fourth floor I breathed easier. I had the impression that I was coming out of a tomb. I rang the bell and the lady of the house and the maid appeared. She gave me a bag of paper. Her two sons took me to the elevator. The elevator, instead of going down, went up two more floors. But I was accompanied, I wasn't frightened. I kept thinking: people claim they aren't afraid of anything but at times they are frightened by something completely harmless.

On the sixth floor a man got into the elevator and looked at me with disgust. I'm used to these looks, they don't bother me.

He wanted to know what I was doing in the elevator. I explained to him that the mother of those two boys had given me some newspapers. And that was the reason for my presence in his elevator. I asked him if he was a doctor or a Congressman. He told me he was a Senator.

The man was well dressed. I was barefoot. Not in condition to ride in his elevator.

I asked a news vendor to help me put the sack on my back, and that the day that I was clean I would give him an embrace. He laughed and told me:

"Then I know I'm going to die without getting a hug from you, because you never are clean."

He helped me put the rest of the paper on my head. I went in a factory and later I went to see Senhor Rodolfo. I earned 20 more cruzeiros. Afterward I was tired. I headed toward home. I was so tired that I couldn't stand up. I had the impression that I was going to die. I thought: if I don't die, I'll never work like this again. I could barely breathe. I got 100 cruzeiros.

I went to lie down. The fleas didn't leave me in peace. I'm so tired of this life that I lead. . . .

7.5 Women of El Salvador

In El Salvador, as throughout Latin America, the family farming economy is being displaced by large agricultural businesses that grow crops for export. Although the industries provide employment for large numbers of people, they also have some negative consequences. Workers receive minimum wages for laboring under physically difficult and unhealthy conditions, either in the fields or in processing plants. The following selections are the personal accounts of three women who work in the expanding agribusiness. The first woman discusses the difficulty displaced peasants confront in finding work. The second describes conditions in a processing plant, and the third deals with the economic disparity between the wages women earn and the cost of living.

At the age of 16, I started to work in all kinds of crop harvesting, coffee, maize and sugarcane. I lived in the Department of Sonsonate but we went all over the place looking for work. Almost all our village would go—brothers, sisters, relatives and friends, arriving home every fortnight, unless we had the good fortune to be working nearby.

We'd pick coffee from October to January, but January is called the stagnant month. We would glean the last of the coffee but hardly got paid anything. You had to search through half the estate to gather a pound of coffee for 2 colones. Or we would go to the coast to pick cotton, which is really exhausting. The fields there are a source of a lot of sickness, particularly with the pollution. The poisons they use in the fields are very strong and we're always having to take people off to the hospital. They'd give you two and a half sacks as a quota for every day and if you didn't manage it, they didn't pay you anything. Men have always been paid 5 colones more than women or children and we all do exactly the same work. When the rains come in May, there's work sowing maize, fertilizing the coffee plants or making irrigation ditches: you do this until October when you start with the coffee crop again.

I wanted to find a better job, but for a factory you need to have finished school and in the coffee processing industries they ask for ninth grade. On the estates, they don't make so many demands, but even there, it's not easy to find work. I have been living in the city for three years and if I were to go to the estates now they wouldn't give me work. In 1979, they were hiring less people, giving jobs to men rather than women. Things are much worse now.

—San Salvador, April 1983

. . . There were many departments where the work was very heavy. In the sections where maize and bananas were cooked, we worked in front of a blazing open fire all day long. The ventilation was very bad too. Many contracted lung diseases, rheumatism and allergies from the acidic ingredients they touched. The noise levels were deafening and you came off work feel-

Thomson, Marilyn. *Women of El Salvador*, 16, 18. Philadelphia: Institute for the Study of Human Issues, 1986.

ing your head would explode. There were dangerous jobs and little in the
way of safety precautions. One woman had her finger cut off in a slicing
machine and never received any compensation. Or rather, her only compensation was receiving the sack.

The supervisors constantly bothered the women, making insulting remarks
and insinuating things. In many cases, in order to obtain a loan, the women
would have to go to bed with one of the supervisors or the boss.

—Mexico, May 1982

Cecilia works in a small coffee factory in Ilopango which employs 118
women out of a total of 280 employees. The women work exclusively
in the packing department, putting coffee into different size packets.
It is the worst paid department in the entire factory:

> I was earning 4 colones a day when the cost of a kilo of meat was between 2
> or 3 colones. Now, because of the decree laws, the situation is worse. Salary
> increases over 10% are forbidden. In 1981 the government declared a 10%
> increase in those factories where it was economically viable, but we only re-
> ceived a 5% rise and our factory was very well off in economic terms. After
> the nationalization of the coffee industry in 1979, the company made a good
> deal with INCAFE, the state marketing board. They had no problem with
> the supply of raw materials and their market was guaranteed by the govern-
> ment. In 1982, we were given another 5% rise although inflation was well
> over 50%. Since then we have had no more increases. We earn 300 colones
> a fortnight and my husband, two children and I spend 150 colones on food
> alone. We can only afford to eat meat twice a week, the rest of the time it's
> beans and rice. The rent for our house, which only has two small rooms, is
> 250 colones. Since the elections, our situation has become even worse. There's
> no longer money to buy clothes. A pair of trousers now costs 95 colones.

—San Salvador, April 1983

7.6 The Peasant Women's Organization in Bolivia

*In the following selections, Bolivian anthropologist Rosario Leon traces
the history of a peasant women's federation in the Bolivian highlands from
1974 to 1984. The organization was named after Bartolina Sisa, the*

Leon, Rosario. "Bartolina Sisa: The Peasant Women's Organization in Bolivia." In *Women
and Social Change in Latin America*, edited by Elizabeth Jelin, 135, 136, 138, 142, 148–49.
London: Zed Books, 1990.

woman who was the partner of the Indian leader, Tupac Katari, in the eighteenth-century wars for independence. The author notes how the deteriorating economy spurred women to take action to safeguard their families and communities. As the women's organizing efforts matured, they began to recognize the common problems they faced as women, not just as housewives and mothers. As they became more politically savvy, they resisted efforts by other organizations to subvert them and their political agenda. The Bartolina Sisa activists did, however, unite with other women's groups. The selection also notes that the women's Indian background was an integral part of their consciousness as activists trying to improve their economic and political conditions.

The literature on social movements in Bolivia makes almost no reference to the participation of women. This attitude is in contradiction to the very clear presence of women in the popular movement: women have not only been present in the struggles but in recent years they have organized themselves independently—although not in isolation—from the predominantly male organizations.

An important example of women's presence on the socio-political stage is that of rural women and their main organization, the Bartolina Sisa Federation of Peasant Women. This organization has, perhaps, established and consolidated its own identity to a greater degree than any other women's organization in Bolivia. . . .

The continuity and unity between these women's domestic and productive roles have bridged the apparent gap between the private sphere of the family and the public sphere of politics, and have established the specificity of the female situation within the peasant movement. Their socio-political activity is based on their social condition as women, which is defined by their role as consumers, administrators of peasant production, as the principal traders in rural markets, as mothers, wives and daughters of peasants. In carrying out these roles they experience the contradictions of the market system in a number of different ways. Nevertheless, insofar as they do not enjoy several of the "benefits" that are the rights of citizenship, they are at the opposite extreme from urban culture. Illiteracy and, in many cases, speaking only their own indigenous language, limit their capacity to negotiate with a Westernized society that stigmatizes their cultural differences and very low standard of living. The participation of peasant women in an organized way within the peasant and popular movement, therefore, through the demands they make, integrates the class, nationality, gender and ethnic contradictions to which they are subjected.

The Experience of Participation and Awareness

. . . The economic crisis had a very particular effect on the role of women. As housewives they were faced by shortages and dwindling purchasing power for even basic consumption items. Faced by the critical situation with respect to basic supplies, which forced women to seek alternative survival strategies that involved an intensification of their "domestic" time, women learned to collectively express their problems and worries from their basis in the domestic sphere.

In their role as workers, peasant women in the Andean region are responsible for marketing their output; rural markets are predominantly women's domain. During this period peasant women were faced with a drastic prices policy. As the prices of peasant output were frozen and the cost of rural transport more than doubled, there was an alarming decline in peasant income.

Peasant women's experience of participation in different organizations and in collective events helped to increase the value attributed to their economic, social and political functions. . . .

. . . We want to be valued as women, as people. Also this democracy, which didn't come about just like that, even now that we have democracy we still can't live in peace. We have to continue to make our voices heard. Just because we are peasant women doesn't mean that we have no value, we should be valued. And we also have to teach our little ones, we must begin to organize from there. These are the demands of peasant women. . . .

So, little by little, we are opening our eyes because we are breaking away from our husbands' chain. It is very difficult for a married woman to leave the house because they say: "What are women going to do, they only know how to sit and wet themselves, so what are they going to do?" They don't value us, because of machismo, all that male chauvinism. Just when peasant women want to assert themselves, the men say, "She won't pay any attention to me, she's going to do what she pleases, that's no good for us." . . . The more politically active ones say, "You don't want to get into that union, that's political. When the repression comes, they'll catch all of you!"

(. . . 1985; interview with Fernanda Sostres)

The peasant women's activities in the Federation, the fact of having their own organization and a collective identity, which they established during the First Congress, led peasant women to begin to express their rights and political possibilities more explicitly. Gender demands began to appear once they had discovered their right to a public life and to engage in public actions. . . .

. . . Many peasant women were firmly opposed to the plan to unite the men's and women's peasant movements around the Confederation:

. . . Men always win, in those joint meetings we are afraid to speak out. But when we women meet alone, we have a good discussion, we are not afraid of throwing out ideas. We understand each other more quickly, without so many words and we also speak about women's things which we couldn't discuss in front of men. But in meetings of men and women together we stay silent. Now we know what we would lose if they join us together again with the men. This is why we are going to struggle so that we don't lose what we have gained.

([Interview with] Florentina Alegre). . . .

On the other hand, the demands expressed by the Federation are also part of women's demands in other sectors, such as those of domestic workers and housewives in the outlying poor neighbourhoods. They also unite with women from the mines in other, more political ways.

Very often people are confused because women from the poor neighbourhoods and peasant women are very different. But we are aware that we have the same blood, that we are the granddaughters and great-granddaughters of peasant women who migrated to the city and have to live in poor neighbourhoods on the outskirts—we are their daughters. So that is why I embrace all our women in sisterhood.

. . . We follow their example because our blood cries out that the time has arrived for women to organize, to end this marginalization we have endured for years, for centuries.

Our peasant sisters are not alone. I want to tell them, they are no longer alone, as when they were thrown out of their own federation, or when they went on hunger strike. At the time we were still not aware, but now we are in solidarity with them and if at any moment they need our support, we are here. The Housewives of the Popular Neighbourhoods are ready to carry on the struggle and we hope they carry on, because they are an example for us to follow just like the women miners, who are also daughters of peasant women. Peasant blood is everywhere, tell me where it cannot be found. . . .

([Interview with] Dominga Velasquez, Executive Secretary of the Federation of Housewives from Popular Neighbourhoods)

7.7 Embroidery as Protest

This selection is the anonymous account of a middle-class Chilean woman who was involved in establishing workshops of arpilleras—*appliquéd wall hangings—during the politically repressive Pinochet regime of the 1970s and 1980s. Under the auspices of the Roman Catholic Church, these workshops were set up to provide material aid and emotional support to*

Agosin, Marjorie. *Scraps of Life*, 93–99. Trenton, N.J.: Red Sea Press, 1987.

women whose relatives and neighbors had been "disappeared" by the government. Creating a traditional Chilean household craft became a way for women to "sew" their protests against the regime's human rights abuses. The arpilleras' *subsequent exhibition outside Chile brought international attention to government violations against its citizens. Particularly evident in this account is the critical reflection these women used to analyze their reality. The reading also describes how women pooled resources during the country's economic crisis of the time.*

Testimony #1

. . . I was born in Chile, a country of mountains, three hundred years of struggle did not save us from the conquest and independence from Spain did not save us from madness.

My interest in art arose naturally from my contact with other students, in the face of family opposition I entered the school of Fine Arts in the University and there became involved in movements interested in working with community groups, in literacy work in marginal sectors of the city, finding for the first time the gratifying sensation of giving something and not only that but contributing something of great value to others, such as the ability to read and write. . . .

Slowly I entered a period of personal confrontation with myself, of questioning. Trying to be aware above all of the fact of being a woman, I began to work with women.

Together we began the search for our own cultural roots . . .

But we are not only our origins, we are our origins plus everything that happens in our history, we are the result of three hundred years of struggle, we are the result of the cultural influence and the slow impoverishment of our land, of the importation of luxurious goods that we don't need, of the propaganda that transforms us into a society that consumes products that we don't make, of seeing every day on televisions a luxurious and exotic life that we try to imitate and in that way we again repeat the cycles of our earlier history when we embraced foreign cultures and values instead of treasuring our own. . . .

And here I wish to speak about a part of my work, the arpilleras. Their beginning, their expression, their possibilities and their future.

After the military coup I was out of a job like so many others, in a short time the Pro-Paz committee asked me to develop some craft work projects with women, the first group assigned to me were women of families of the detained-disappeared: mothers, wives, sisters. At the end of my first interview with them, it was clear to me that in their state of anxiety they would not be able to concentrate on anything except their own pain, I went back to my house, their anxiety embedded in me, I could hardly believe what I had heard, sons, husbands, brothers snatched with blows and threats to their families, pregnant women carried off, couples including their small children, all disappeared for weeks and even months, with nobody knowing anything about them, not even about the newborns or the older children and even less about the adults.

Everything I had been thinking of doing with these women was useless, since the future work we would undertake together ought to serve as a catharsis, every woman began to translate her story into images and the images into embroidery, but the embroidery was very slow and their nerves weren't up to that, without knowing how to continue I walked, looked and thought and finally my attention was attracted by a Panamanian *mola*, a type of indigenous tapestry, I remembered also a foreign fashion very much in vogue at that time: "patchwork." Very happy with my solution the very next day we began collecting pieces of fabric, new and used, thread and yarn, and with all the material together we very quickly assembled our themes and the tapestries, the histories remained like a true testimony in one or various pieces of fabric, it was dramatic to see how the women wept as they sewed their stories, but it was also very enriching to see how in some way the work also afforded happiness, provided relief, happiness to see they were capable of creating their own testimony, relief simply from the fact of being together with others, talking together, sewing, being able to show that by means of this visual record others would know their story.

This *collage* of fabric, mixture of *mola* and patchwork, was not, as a technique, new, but we all liked it and were satisfied with it. Some visitors and foreign journalists saw the result and took them away, other people, all motivated by our problems, acquired them and they began to be in demand inside the country as well as abroad, the demand for arpilleras had begun.

Two months after beginning this work . . . unemployment was going up, imported goods arrived by the tons, propaganda helped turn us into a grossly overblown importer-country. And with this primitive streak that still remains in us to be dazzled by glass beads of beautiful colours, we bought and bought without realizing that by doing so we were closing down our own industry, and as our factories closed there were hundreds and thousands of unemployed workers and the workers had wives and children and all of them needed to eat.

The Church assumed a historic role, opening its doors and taking on as its own the problems of the most needy. In a desperate attempt to stave off malnutrition the first childfeeding projects were begun in various churches. The mothers in the communities organized, going out every morning to collect left-over foodstuffs, from stores, private houses, restaurants, in produce markets, even going out into the countryside and there gathering produce of poor quality that could not be sold in the markets, it was painful to see how few resources they had to work with, many times, the good half of a half-rotten tomato was used, and the same thing went for potatoes and other vegetables and fruits, it was an impressive effort to cook something with the poor and miserable things they were able to collect.

Then we saw heartbreaking situations when women recently confronted by the drama of hunger would arrive at the church dining rooms for the first time with their children, only to find all the places taken, but it never failed that some woman would give up her place to the newcomer saying "My child ate yesterday and the day before, let your child eat now." . . .

Also there were anguished women, another kind of anguish, first of all, hunger, and another equally painful, to see a child slowly becoming thinner and thinner, slowly being consumed, not having means to go to a hospital, nothing with which to buy medicine, is always painful. And with these groups the story of the arpilleras continued.

The women didn't know how to begin, one of my volunteer companions, Gloria Torres, a lawyer, suggested to the children that they draw the dining rooms, new collages of fabrics appeared with enormous pots, enormous tables filled with children and long lines awaiting their turn, these were the things they began to tell in different arpilleras, then they began to make their own drawings, mamas collecting foodstuffs, cooking, serving steaming hot plates, mamas waiting. We should add here that the only income some of these women received at all was from the sale of arpilleras. . . .

Our little chapel served us as child-care centre, dining room, as a place for mass, for the catechism, for baptisms, as a meeting place, as a place to ease one's sorrows.

One of the groups of women had formed a little laundry service when their husbands lost their jobs, washing clothes is work that women in our shantytowns know how to do well, with no washing machines washing is done by hand in a tub, it is also very common that the houses have no running water and water has to be carried in buckets from some nearby faucet, the children are expert water carriers and the women too have very strong backs for carrying loads. The laundry business didn't go very well because by now the men of the middle class were starting to lose their jobs and their wives had to take on the domestic chores, so that with the increase in unemployment the numbers of women wanting work washing clothes went up while the clientele went down. In view of this situation I was called in to see what I could do with this group, and other arpilleras appeared telling other stories. These women were very imaginative and began the evolution of the arpilleras, incorporating volume and other materials to the work, it was very heart-warming to see reflected in the new arpilleras the very busy little chapel, and so much laundry hanging on the line. In addition to picturing the stories of the women washing clothes they told how their husbands had lost their jobs when the factories and plants had closed, of the interminable treks that the men made in search of work, of how they slowly used up their few possessions, of the solidarity that developed around the common soup pots.

. . . They also speak of the history of the workshops and their organization, of that organization that has changed their lives, that has converted them all into individuals, of that organization that changed them into a self-run enterprise, that manages three commercial outlets, that lets them face life in a different way, freer, more independent, with fewer economic problems; and the most important is that the organization made them discover the value and strength of a community.

7.8 Taming Macho Ways

Elvia Alvarado is a Honduran campesina (rural peasant woman) who became a community activist through her involvement in the Roman Catholic Church. Like Rigoberta Menchú, she is well known for her work in organizing campesinas. This chapter from her autobiography describes the conflicts that exist between women and men because of the patriarchal social structure and the pressures of poverty. As Alvarado notes in this selection, women are not passive in the face of male violence. In closing her chapter, she offers recommendations for change.

When I started working with the mothers' clubs in the Catholic church, it was the first time I realized that we women work even harder than the men do.

We get up before they do to grind the corn and make tortillas and coffee for their breakfast. Then we work all day—taking care of the kids, washing the clothes, ironing, mending our husband's old rags, cleaning the house. We hike to the mountains looking for wood to cook with. We walk to the stream or the well to get water. We make lunch and bring it to the men in the field. And we often grab a hoe and help in the fields. We never sit still one minute.

It's true that there are some jobs that require a lot of strength and that women can't do as well as men. For example, when we have to clear a piece of forest, it's the men who go out with the axes and cut

Alvarado, Elvia. *Don't Be Afraid, Gringo,* edited and translated by Medea Benjamin, 51–56. New York: Harper & Row, 1987.

down the trees. Other work we consider "men's work" is chopping fire-wood and plowing the land with a team of oxen. These are things that men do better than women, because they're stronger. I don't know if it's a physical difference from birth, but the fact is that here in Hon-duras women are usually either pregnant or nursing, and that takes a lot of energy out of you.

Men may be out working during the day, but when they come home they usually don't do a thing. They want their meal to be ready, and after they eat they either lie down to rest or go out drinking. But we women keep on working—cooking the corn and beans for the next day's meal, watching the children.

Even when we go to sleep, we don't get to rest. If the babies wake up crying, we have to go take care of them—give them the breast if they're still breast-feeding, give them medicine if they're sick. And then if our husbands want to make love, if they get the urge, then it's back to work again.

The next morning, we're up before the sun, while our husbands are still sleeping. . . .

I have a friend in the city who works in a factory. If he comes home from work and the meal isn't ready—maybe his wife is busy watching the children or washing clothes—he just grabs the pots and pans and gets to work. I've seen it with my own eyes. He actually cooks the meal for the whole family. You'd never see that in a campesino house!

I don't think it's fair that women do all the work. Maybe it's because I've been around more and I've seen other relationships. But I think that if two people get together to form a home, it should be because they love and respect each other. And that means that they should share everything.

The problem some campesina women have is even worse. Not only do their husbands refuse to help, but they don't even support the family. They don't give her money to put food on her children's plates.

When the men find work, they earn a few dollars a day. The cam-pesino with better habits gives all his money to his wife; maybe he keeps 50 cents to buy cigarettes. The campesino with bad habits gives his wife less. If he earns $2.50, he gives her one dollar and keeps $1.50 for himself. . . .

That's why so many campesina women have to work. They fatten pigs or raise chickens, bake bread or sell tortillas in the market—any-thing to make a few pennies to feed their children. . . .

Another problem women have is that their husbands often beat them. Say a campesino comes home late after drinking or sleeping with a woman he has on the side. If his wife yells at him, he hits her. Some-times he leaves her all black and blue or with a bloody nose, a black eye, or a busted lip.

The neighbors can hear everything. But since it's a fight between the two of them, no one interferes. Unless the woman starts to yell, "Help! So-and-so's trying to kill me." Then the neighbors come over and tell him to stop hitting the poor woman. . . .

He usually stops hitting her when the neighbors get involved. But if no one comes to help her, she wakes up the next morning all black and blue.

The woman never says what really happened. She's too embarrassed. So she says she fell down or had an accident. She doesn't even tell her friends or her own mother what happened. Because if she tells her mother, her mother says, "You knew what he was like when you went to live with him. So why did you go with him in the first place?" Or if the mother tells her to come home and live with her and she does, a few days later they get back together again and the mother's the one that looks bad.

If the woman can't take it any more, she leaves him. But even after the woman leaves, the man usually follows her and keeps harassing her.

We know it's against the law to beat someone like that, but the police don't get involved in fights between couples. They say it's none of their business. They say it's something for the man and wife to figure out by themselves.

Machismo is a historical problem. It goes back to the time of our great-grandfathers, or our great-great-grandfathers. In my mind, it's connected with the problem of drinking. Drinking is man's worst disease. When men drink, they fight with everyone. They hit their wives and children. They offend their neighbors. They lose all sense of dignity.

How are we going to stop campesinos from drinking? First of all, we know the government isn't interested in stopping it, because it's an important source of income. Every time you buy a bottle of liquor, part of that money goes to the government.

That's why the government doesn't let the campesinos make their own liquor, because the government doesn't make any money off homemade brew. . . .

If we're ever going to get campesinos to stop drinking, we first have to look at why so many campesinos drink. And for that we have to look at what kind of society we have. We've built up a society that treats people like trash, a society that doesn't give people jobs, a society that doesn't give people a reason to stay sober. I think that's where this vice comes from.

I've seen what happens when campesinos organize and have a plot of land to farm. They don't have time for drinking any more, except on special occasions. They spend the day in the hot sun—plowing, planting, weeding, irrigating, cutting firewood for the house, carrying the produce to market. Most of them are very dedicated to their work and their families.

So I've noticed that once the campesinos have a purpose, once they have a way to make a living and take care of their families, they drink less. And they usually stop beating their wives, too. And I've seen that once the women get organized, they start to get their husbands in line.

I know that changing the way men and women treat each other is a long process. But if we really want to build a new society, we have to change the bad habits of the past. We can't build a new society if we are drunks, womanizers, or corrupt. No, those things have to change.

But people *can* change. I know there are many things I used to do that I don't do any more, now that I'm more educated. For example, I used to gossip and criticize other women. I used to fight over men. But I learned that gossip only destroys, it doesn't build. Criticizing my neighbors doesn't create unity. Neither does fighting over men. So I stopped doing these things.

Before, whenever I'd see the slightest thing I'd go running to my friends, "Ay, did you see so-and-so with what's-his-face?" I'd go all over town telling everyone what I saw. Now I could see a woman screwing a man in the middle of the street and I wouldn't say anything. That's her business.

If someone is in danger, then, yes, we have to get involved. For example, I heard a rumor that a landowner was out to kill one of the campesino leaders I work with. I made sure to warn the campesino so he'd be careful. That kind of rumor we tell each other—but not idle gossip.

I also used to flirt with married men, just for the fun of it and to make their wives jealous. Now I'm much more responsible, much more serious. That doesn't mean I don't joke around and have a good time. I just make it clear that we're friends.

We all have to make changes. Campesino men have to be more responsible with their women. They have to have only one woman. Because they have a hard enough time supporting one family, let alone two. Campesinos who drink have to stop drinking. And campesinos who fight with their wives have to stop fighting. Our struggle has to begin in our own homes.

7.9 Feminist Movements in Latin America

Silvia Chester is an Argentine feminist who chronicles in this selection the history of the feminist movement in her country. She notes the important role of Eva Perón, who during her lifetime was regarded as one of the most powerful women in Latin America. She was an activist on behalf of women and the poor, and as the wife of President Juan Perón, she was able to influence state policy. In some respects, the Argentine feminist movement is similar to North American feminism in its middle-class base, its stress on the importance of political power, and its focus on legal means as a remedy for gender inequality. Chester also notes that the concern with violence against women, basic human rights, and the importance of creating spaces for women are as important in Argentine feminism as they are in other Latin American feminist movements. Even though in nations like Chile the women's movement came out of a multiclass and politically diverse alliance, in Argentina the feminist movement was much like that of the United States.

Feminism is not a new phenomenon in Argentina. As early as 1900, women were making demands for equal political and civil rights, access to education, equality at work and, though to a lesser extent, campaigning for the right to divorce, peace and the need for an end to prostitution. By 1920 the emphasis had shifted away from these last three concerns (mainly the preoccupation of socialist and anarchist groups) into the political arena, namely women's right to vote and to be elected on an equal platform with men.

The right to vote was finally won in 1947, much helped by strong support from Eva Perón. Once the Peronist government had passed the law granting women equal political rights with men, women's participation in politics reached unprecedented heights: women were elected to public office, a women's branch of the party was formed and a number of legal reforms introduced to improve conditions for women workers. . . .

The 1970s saw the emergence of a new kind of women's liberation movement that was much more questioning of male power, sex-role definitions and the fundamental roots of women's oppression. It chal-

Chester, Sylvia. "The Women's Movement in Argentina: Balance and Strategies." In *The Latin American Women's Movement*, edited and translated by Miranda Davies and Ana Maria Portugal, 15–19. Rome and Santiago: Isis International, 1986.

lenged prevalent concepts of sexuality and the role of the family, questioned the obligatory nature of motherhood, and raised issues of abortion (still illegal in our country), divorce and sexual violence. In other words, feminists began to recognize that, in spite of women's early achievements in terms of equal rights and legal reforms, certain basic inequalities between the sexes continued to persist.

The feminist organizations which emerged in the 1970s tended to be small and closed, focusing on internal work and with only very limited outreach into the wider community of women. The unleashing of repression in 1975, followed a year later by the military dictatorship, meant that feminists had little opportunity to extend their activities beyond organizing a few consciousness-raising and study groups. In the early years of this decade, however, at least three organizations deserve mention: Union Feminista Argentina [The Feminist Union], Movimiento de Liberación Femenina [The Women's Liberation Movement] and Frente de Lucha de la Mujer [Front for Women's Struggle].

The Feminist Union, founded in 1970, was the most important in terms of numbers, though it mainly attracted middle-class and professional women. Its main priorities were consciousness-raising, the organization of debates and the dissemination of propaganda. Many present-day militant feminists came to feminism through the Union, which disappeared in 1976.

The Women's Liberation Movement was founded in 1971 and disappeared four years later, to re-emerge in 1980 as the Feminist Organization of Argentina. This group publishes the magazine *Persona* and spreads information in other ways, keeping in touch with international women's organizations. Since 1984 it has been most well-known for campaigns against violence against women, under the name Tribunal de Violencia Contra la Mujer.

In 1975 feminist organizations, independent feminists and women from political parties grouped together to form Frente de Lucha de la Mujer (Front for Women's Struggle), outlining a series of demands, many of which form the basis for the present program. These are: reform of the law concerning childcare facilities, equality at work and in education, abolition of the decree prohibiting the distribution of contraceptives, free and legal abortion, wages for housework, repression of the white slave trade, recognition of paternal responsibility for children, protection for single mothers, abolition of the law which obliges a woman to follow her husband to the home of his choice, and protection for working mothers.

Feminism in the 1980s

Since 1980 there has been a resurgence of feminist activity, much of it extending beyond the usual focus on consciousness-raising. One example is the campaign to change the law of *patria potestad* (paternal authority) whereby the man has all the rights over his offspring with none of the obligations to look after them. This demand for the equal sharing of parental responsibilities became a rallying point for independent feminists and women from quite diverse organizations, some of which are briefly described below.

• *Atem, 25 de Noviembre* organizes talks, debates, conferences and study days on themes such as sexuality and violence.

• *Alternativa Feminista* focuses above all on the revision of sex roles. These two organizations produce their own publications aimed at encouraging a wider diffusion of feminist ideas and activities.

• *Lugar de Mujer* (A Women's Place), founded in August 1983, calls itself a pluralist organization and carries out ongoing work through a women's house—the only one in the country. The house, run by a collective of 14 women, is open every day for various activities. These include: conferences, exhibitions, literary readings, video, theater and cinema shows: closed consciousness-raising groups; advice on legal, psychological and sexual matters; the running of self-help groups for battered women; and theoretical discussion in the form of round tables, debates and conferences. The house also has a feminist bookshop, library and bar. . . .

• *Multisectorial de la Mujer* is a national alliance of women from different political parties, cultural groups, feminist associations and trade unions, who mobilized together for the first time on International Women's Day in 1984. In a document drawn up for that day they expressed the importance of unifying women across ideological and political boundaries. They also outlined the following demands: ratification of the United Nations Convention on the Elimination of All Forms of Discrimination Against Women; equal protection for children under the law; modification of the law concerning "paternal authority"; accomplishment of the law granting equal pay for equal work; regulation of the law concerning childcare facilities; pension rights for housewives; and the creation of a Ministry for Women. . . .

In spite of the existence of feminist organizations since the beginning of the century, feminism in Argentina is weak and cannot be compared to the development of the women's movement in other Latin American countries this last decade. Our organizations are small and, for them to grow, we clearly need to make the dissemination of feminist ideas one of our main priorities.

Up until now, feminism has reached only small numbers of women from the middle and working classes, but its impact shouldn't just be measured in terms of organizational development or the amount of actions carried out. The influence of feminism is evident in other less direct ways, such as use of the term in newspapers and magazines, on radio programs and in cultural gatherings. The elaboration of different ways of expressing women's oppression is central to feminist thought and so, clearly, the more widely it features, especially in professional and political circles, the better.

Since the 1983 elections, in which women played a significant role, there has been a definite growth in feminist consciousness. Although women's issues were raised on the electoral platform, many were dissatisfied and unhappy about the limited channels of communication provided by existing institutions. It may have been a negative experience, but it gave them the strength to forge their own path towards the achievement of women's demands.

The reluctance of women in political parties to support feminist slogans stems partly from a lack of consciousness of feminist issues. However, even when the consciousness is there they have great trouble trying to make such issues a priority within their parties. Divorce, an age-old feminist demand, first raised in 1902, may be recognized as a problem by many political parties, but not one is prepared to include it as part of their political campaign. Inevitably, the reason given is simply that other problems are more important, despite a strong consensus of support for the issue. Themes such as divorce and sexual violence remain completely taboo within political parties.

In terms of how the politics of feminist organizations relate to the work of political parties, there is no one common attitude. Many feminists accept the need to work in political organizations, although the majority are not prepared to compromise, arguing that it is very hard to work in organizations governed by authoritarian values or for which they simply don't have the necessary competitive and aggressive attitudes. Those who do make the compromise usually operate a form of double militancy.

In the current development of feminism in Argentina autonomous organization is a necessity for survival. Our struggle will never be recognized if we let it be diluted within organizations with other priorities. Only through developing our own strength can we ever be ready to link up with the general struggle against injustice and oppression being carried out by other organizations, from political, union and human rights groups to neighborhood associations.

It cannot be said that feminism in Argentina is an unknown phenomenon, but it is certainly unfamiliar and the prejudices against it are many. However, it is important to bear in mind that the feminist activity that began in the early seventies more or less disappeared for several years, only to re-emerge at the beginning of 1980. The dominance of the military dictatorship throughout the last decade prevented any public activity, leaving women isolated both among themselves and from what was happening in other countries.

Other obstacles lie in the unshakeable hold of authoritarian ideas and the strength of patriarchal ideology. The latter permeates every area from "scientific knowledge" to interpretations of ideology and psychoanalysis, but its weight is probably most felt in the influence of the Catholic Church which relegates women to the family, exalting their role as mothers and subordinating their sexuality to that of men. Yet another manifestation of patriarchy is the tendency to regard as synonymous feminism and lesbianism.

8

Miracles Are Not Enough: Continuity and Change in Religion

This Holy Week celebration in Nicaragua illustrates the enduring relevance of religion to people in the Americas. © Claude Constant/ JB Pictures

Religion in the Americas reflects an ongoing process of integrating the traditional with the new in a dynamic pattern of continuity and change. Religion in the region has been formed by a complex array of indigenous beliefs blended with faiths brought by waves of immigrants, beginning with the Spanish conquest. Africans introduced Yoruba and other African belief systems; nineteenth-century European immigrants brought Kardecian spiritism. More recently Islam, Hinduism, and Pentecostalism have become part of the religious landscape. Most Latin Americans, however, identify themselves as Christians, with Catholics predominating. Many do not practice their religion, and their belief systems adapt to changing circumstances and evolve over time.

In Latin America during the last fifty years political, economic, and social changes have stimulated substantial religious innovations. These innovations are the product of theological, clerical, pastoral, and liturgical experimentation, and the growth of non-traditional religions such as Rastafarianism in Jamaica, spiritism in Brazil, and Pentecostalism in Guatemala. The result has been a much greater variety of religions, as well as more differentiation within religions, particularly Catholicism and mainline Protestantism, which together claim approximately 90 percent of Latin Americans.

Religion in Precolonial and Colonial America

Religion has played a major role in Latin America since well before the arrival of Christopher Columbus. Belief in the divine and an afterlife was common among indigenous peoples, and the Aztec, Incan, and Mayan civilizations each had religions that gave meaning to life and legitimized political, economic, social, and cultural systems (see reading 8.1). Their high degree of centralization helped facilitate Hispanic and Christian penetration, particularly of the Aztec and Incan empires. Less centralized, more tribal cultures were not as easily dominated by Catholicism.

The Catholic Church was deeply involved in the Portuguese and Spanish exploration and conquest of the Western Hemisphere. As early as 1493, Pope Alexander VI issued the bull *Inter Caetera,* granting all lands 100 leagues west and south of the Azores and Cape Verde Islands to the Spanish monarchs. Such action was justified on the grounds that the inhabitants were pagans and therefore could legitimately be made subjects of Catholic monarchs. The grant carried with it the obligation to convert indigenous peoples, and Christianization became an integral part of conquest and colonization.

But moral issues about the nature and treatment of indigenous peoples and enslaved Africans did cause tensions throughout the colonial period. The conquistador turned Dominican friar, Bartolomé de Las Casas, lobbied the Spanish Crown to create special laws to protect indigenous peoples from exploitation by Europeans. His efforts eventually led to the New Laws (1543) and to a formal debate at the Royal Court at Valladolid in 1550 concerning the rights of Native Americans (see reading 8.2). Such pleas, as well as royal laws, did not prevent the exploitation, but they do illustrate the role of clerics in raising moral issues in Latin America.

The Valladolid debate epitomized the diversity of views that existed, not only within the Catholic Church but also among colonial elites, concerning the legitimacy of Spanish and Portuguese conquest and exploitation of Indian labor. The disparity of views on basic issues has been characteristic of Latin American clergy and laity up to the present.

The enslavement of Africans was another source of tension within the Catholic Church and among religious and secular elites. While slavery was widely accepted, it was questioned throughout the colonial period by some sectors of society, particularly clerics, although some religious institutions owned slaves. In addition, there was ongoing pressure on the Spanish and Portuguese monarchies to accord slaves certain rights, including to purchase their own freedom. Some successful court cases were initiated by slaves or former slaves, attesting to the fact that such laws were occasionally implemented. Nevertheless, attitudes toward Africans did reflect the era's prejudices. Like the Indians, Africans were exploited and had to struggle to enjoy minimal rights. Such moral issues permeated the colonial period.

Overall, however, the Catholic Church in colonial Latin America helped reinforce Iberian control. This resulted largely from the *Patronato Real,* a system of royal patronage that emerged in the Iberian peninsula between 1031 and 1492. Under this system, the Spanish and Portuguese Crowns were granted privileges regarding church appointments, finances, and discipline, in return for assuming some obligations for maintaining and spreading

Catholicism. This church-state alliance proved problematic since it tended to result in overlapping jurisdictions, causing disputes.

Schools were largely the responsibility of the Catholic Church and were a prime means of inculcating Christianity; they also provided colonial society with an intellectual and technical elite. By the end of the eighteenth century there were 25 universities and more than 50 secondary schools in Spanish America, exclusively for males. Females had less access to education, although many convents served as centers of learning and artistic production for women.

In the eighteenth century, many Church intellectuals became imbued with Enlightenment thought, which challenged divine right monarchy and the Crown's right to empire. This was particularly true of the Jesuits, regarded as the wealthiest and most politically independent religious order. Their liberalism was among the reasons that led to their expulsion from Brazil in 1759 and from the Spanish colonies in 1767.

A major issue that became increasingly contentious, particularly during the eighteenth century, was the wealth of some church institutions and religious orders. Such riches were substantial, although often exaggerated, and frequently went to provide social services (see reading 8.3). Wealth also took artistic and intellectual form in the cathedrals, mission churches, convents, schools, and libraries throughout the colonies that constituted extraordinary treasures. Many of the artists and artisans were Native Americans, mestizos, or Africans, and the treasures produced reflect a blend of cultures and styles uniquely Latin American.

The Catholic Church played a complex role in Latin America's independence movement, which was fueled by discontent among many segments of society, particularly the Creole merchant elite. Tension and conflict between church and state under the Spanish Bourbons (1700–1822) helped erode royal control over the colonies. Although in the end the Catholic Church as an institution supported the Crown, some clerics, including the Bishop of Quito and the Mexican priests Miguel Hidalgo and José Maria Morelos, actively encouraged and some even participated in the independence movements. Following independence, most of the new republican governments shared a desire to reduce the power and the influence of the Church. In Brazil, where a dynasty of Portuguese origin ruled until 1889, tensions between civil and ecclesiastical authorities helped contribute to the monarchy's downfall.

After independence, liberals argued for separation of church and state, and in some countries, such as Mexico, succeeded in forcing the Catholic Church to divest itself of its landholdings. This had the unexpected result of the Church becoming one of the chief sources of investment capital in the second half of the nineteenth century in Mexico. Elsewhere, as in Colombia, the Catholic Church was able to sustain the alliance of church and state well into the twentieth century.

Religion and Social Change

Within the Catholic Church, some individuals and religious orders have always been concerned with the poor and exploited, although the Latin American church is traditionally viewed as a supporter of the status quo. Different theological and political tendencies have historically existed within the Church. As early as 1891 Pope Leo XIII, in his encyclical *Rerum Novarum*, focused on the condition of workers under capitalism. While strongly critical of exploitation resulting from industrial capitalism's excesses, the pope was also critical of elements of socialism, particularly the concepts of class warfare and the dictatorship of the proletariat. Nevertheless, he considered broad-based political participation essential for legitimate economic and political systems, but warned against confrontational tactics such as strikes.

In the 1920s and 1930s, groups such as Catholic Action, Young Catholic Workers, and Christian Democratic parties were promoted by the Church to increase popular participation in political and economic decision making in both the public and the private sectors, and to compete with Marxist labor unions and political parties.

After World War II, the rapidly accelerating pace of political, economic, and social change in the Americas challenged traditional Church strategies and objectives. Industrialization, rural-urban migration, and intellectual ferment were set against a background of greater restiveness among the lower and middle classes. In the face of increased pressures for societal change, experimentation with theological and pastoral models began. These efforts were directed toward making the Catholic Church more responsive to contemporary problems, especially poverty, exploitation, and violence. Mainline Protestant denominations moved in the same direction, while fundamentalist groups were inclined to be more politically conservative and less socially active. The fundamentalists experienced strong growth, beginning in the 1950s and 1960s, particularly in Brazil. In recent years some Pentecostal churches have grown rapidly in countries such as Guatemala and El Salvador, where they offer stable communities in the midst of escalating societal conflict.

The increase of progressivism was reinforced by the Second Vatican Council (1962–65), the Latin American bishops' conference in Medellín, Colombia, in 1968, and the Protestants' Evangelical Assembly in Oaxtepec, Mexico, in 1978. These meetings discussed the promotion of peace, justice, and human rights as principal objectives of the churches, as described in reading 8.4, and encouraged greater activism on the part of the churches and the faithful. Because of the ideological and political diversity within the churches at all levels, progressivism also intensified debate, particularly in the Catholic Church and in Protestant denominations such as the Presbyterian, Methodist, Lutheran, and Episcopal.

During the 1960s and 1970s, new theological formulations emerged, the most prominent of which was liberation theology. Its conception of salvation required the faithful to struggle for social justice and to identify with the poor and oppressed. Borrowing from the social sciences, liberation theologians used some aspects of dependency theory, as well as Marxism. They criticized capitalism as it had evolved in Latin America and regarded socialism as preferable (see reading 8.5). Over time liberation theology has become more analytically complex, in part, in response to critiques of its more radical versions. In 1984 and 1986 the Vatican formally criticized liberation theology's emphasis on class struggle and called for more attention to social reconciliation. Today liberation theology continues to evolve and is most influential among Church intellectuals and activists, as well as university students.

Religious Experimentation

Another major development was the emergence of base Christian communities (also known as CEBs, after their Spanish and Portuguese acronyms). The CEBs are small groups of church-people who meet regularly to discuss the relevance of scripture and Church doctrine to their daily lives. Organized by Catholics and some Protestant denominations, in part as a response to the scarcity of clerical vocations and increased competition from fundamentalist religions, CEBs have been thought by some to have superseded traditional congregations and to be universally progressive. In reality, they range across the spectrum politically and theologically, and incorporate less that 1 percent of Latin Americans. Some recent studies suggest they are growing more slowly than spiritism and Pentecostalism because they are less responsive to people's needs (see reading 8.6).

Progressivism within churches grew in reaction to the excesses of authoritarian governments in the region. After military coups in Brazil (1964), Uruguay and Chile (1973), and Argentina (1976), government repression stimulated Church activism. In Guatemala and El Salvador, Church activists took strong positions against violence, and consequently they became targets themselves. The escalating repression of both clergy and lay leaders in these two countries resulted in a wave of assassinations, including Salvadoran archbishop Oscar Romero and four U.S. women missionaries in 1980, as well as six Jesuits in 1989.

In the Caribbean, religion has often been a political force, as leaders identified with various beliefs have used religion to mobilize supporters. In the 1950s François (Papa Doc) Duvalier aligned himself with vodun practitioners to help capture the presidency in Haiti. Rastafarian symbols became influential in Jamaican politics in the 1960s, and in 1990 a Muslim group attempted to overthrow the government of Trinidad and Tobago.

A good number of religious people in Latin America today strongly support greater socioeconomic justice, peace, and human rights. This commitment requires change in existing political, economic, and social structures. How to accomplish this is intensely debated within churches. In addition, many believers are also attempting to reform their institutions and deal with the racism and sexism within them. The result is a high degree of religious ferment within societies already under intense pressure for change.

Although churches in Latin America today are generally poor, they have rarely been as influential. Their participation in modern Latin American societies is so extensive they have become arenas of authentic political, economic, social, and ideological struggles.

8.1 The Mayan Book of the Dawn of Life

This reading recounts the Quiché Mayan version, from the sacred book Popol Vuh, *of the creation of the natural world and the birth of humans. The Mayan emphasis on the natural world and the cyclical pattern of history is highlighted. It is important to note that the* Popol Vuh *was likely written after the conquest in the early sixteenth century by descendants of the preconquest Quiché Maya leadership. Consequently, it has probably been influenced to some degree by Christianity, as evidenced by the similarity between the creation story in the* Popol Vuh *and that of Genesis in the Christian Bible.*

There is not yet one person, one animal, bird, fish, crab, tree, rock, hollow, canyon, meadow, forest. Only the sky alone is there; the face of the earth is not clear. Only the sea alone is pooled under all the sky; there is nothing whatever gathered together. It is at rest; not a single thing stirs. It is held back, kept at rest under the sky.

Whatever might be is simply not there: only the pooled water, only the calm sea, only it alone is pooled.

Whatever there is that might be is simply not there: only murmurs, ripples, in the dark, in the night. Only the Maker, Modeler alone. Sovereign Plumed Serpent, the Bearers, Begetters are in the water, a glittering light. They are there, they are enclosed in quetzal feathers, in blue-green.

Thus the name, "Plumed Serpent." They are great knowers, great thinkers in their very being.

And of course there is the sky, and there is also the Heart of Sky. This is the name of the god, as it is spoken.

And then came his word, he came here to the Sovereign Plumed Serpent, here in the blackness, in the early dawn. He spoke with the Sovereign Plumed Serpent, and they talked, then they thought, then they worried. They agreed with each other, they joined their words, their thoughts. Then it was clear, then they reached accord in the light, and then humanity was clear, when they conceived the growth, the generation of trees, of bushes, and the growth of life, of humankind, in the blackness, in the early dawn, all because of the Heart of Sky,

"Popol Vuh." In *The Definitive Edition of the Mayan Book of the Dawn of Life and the Glories of Gods and Kings,* translated by Dennis Tedlock, 21, 72–84. New York: Simon & Schuster, 1985.

named Hurricane. Thunderbolt Hurricane comes first, the second is Newborn Thunderbolt, and the third is Raw Thunderbolt.

So there were three of them, as Heart of Sky, who came to the Sovereign Plumed Serpent, when the dawn of life was conceived:

"How should it be sown, how should it dawn? Who is to be the provider, nurturer?"

"Let it be this way, think about it: this water should be removed, emptied out for the formation of the earth's own plate and platform, then comes the sowing, the dawning of the sky-earth. But there will be no high days and no bright praise for our work, our design, until the rise of the human work, the human design," they said.

And then the earth arose because of them, it was simply their word that brought it forth. For the forming of the earth they said "Earth." It arose suddenly, just like a cloud, like a mist, now forming, unfolding. Then the mountains were separated from the water, all at once the great mountains came forth. By their genius alone, by their cutting edge alone they carried out the conception of the mountain plain, whose face grew instant groves of cypress and pine.

And the Plumed Serpent was pleased with this:

"It was good that you came, Heart of Sky, Hurricane, and Newborn Thunderbolt, Raw Thunderbolt. Our work, our design will turn out well," they said.

And the earth was formed first, the mountain-plain. The channels of water were separated; their branches wound their ways among the mountains. The waters were divided when the great mountains appeared.

Such was the formation of the earth when it was brought forth by the Heart of Sky, Heart of Earth, as they are called, since they were the first to think of it. The sky was set apart, and the earth was set apart in the midst of the waters.

Such was their plan when they thought, when they worried about the completion of their work.

Now they planned the animals of the mountains, all the guardians of the forests, creatures of the mountains: the deer, birds, pumas, jaguars, serpents, rattlesnakes, yellowbites, guardians of the bushes.

A Bearer, Begetter speaks:

"Why this pointless humming? Why should there merely be rustling beneath the trees and bushes?"

"Indeed—they had better have guardians," the others replied. As soon as they thought it and said it, deer and birds came forth.

And then they gave out homes to the deer and birds:

"You, the deer: sleep along the rivers, in the canyons. Be here in the meadows, in the thickets, in the forests, multiply yourselves. You will stand and walk on all fours," they were told.

So then they established the nests of the birds, small and great: . . .

When Hurricane had spoken with the Sovereign Plumed Serpent, they invoked the daykeepers, diviners, the midmost seers:

"There is yet to find, yet to discover how we are to model a person, construct a person again, a provider, nurturer, so that we are called upon and we are recognized: our recompense is in words.

> Midwife, matchmaker,
> our grandmother, our grandfather,
> Xpiyacoc, Xmucane,
> let there be planting, let there be the dawning
> of our invocation, our sustenance, our recognition
> by the human work, the human design,
> the human figure, the human mass.

So be it, fulfill your names:

> Hunahpu Possum, Hunahpu Coyote,
> Bearer twice over, Begetter twice over,
> Great Peccary, Great Tapir,
> lapidary, jeweler,
> sawyer, carpenter,
> Maker of the Blue-Green Plate,
> Maker of the Blue-Green Bowl,
> incense maker, master craftsman,
> Grandmother of Day, Grandmother of Light.

You have been called upon because of our work, our design. Run your hands over the kernels of corn, over the seeds of the coral tree, just get it done, just let it come out whether we should carve and gouge a mouth, a face in wood," they told the daykeepers.

And then comes the borrowing, the counting of days; the hand is moved over the corn kernels, over the coral seeds, the days, the lots.

Then they spoke to them, one of them a grandmother, the other a grandfather.

This is the grandfather, this is the master of the coral seeds: Xpiyacoc is his name.

And this is the grandmother, the daykeeper, diviner who stands behind others: Xmucane is her name.

And they said, as they set out the days:

> "Just let it be found, just let it be discovered,
> say it, our ear is listening,
> may you talk, may you speak,
> just find the wood for the carving and sculpting
> by the builder, sculptor.
> Is this to be the provider, the nurturer
> when it comes to the planting, the dawning?

> You corn kernels, you coral seeds,
> You days, you lots:
> may you succeed, may you be accurate,"

they said to the corn kernels, coral seeds, days, lots. "Have shame, you up there, Heart of Sky; attempt no deception before the mouth and face of Sovereign Plumed Serpent," they said. Then they spoke straight to the point:

"It is well that there be your manikins, woodcarvings, talking, speaking, there on the face of the earth."

"So be it," they replied. The moment they spoke it was done: the manikins, woodcarvings, human in looks and human in speech.

This was the peopling of the face of the earth:

They had come into being, they multiplied, they had daughters, they had sons, these manikins, woodcarvings. But there was nothing in their hearts and nothing in their minds, no memory of their mason and builder. They just went and walked wherever they wanted. Now they did not remember the Heart of Sky.

And so they fell, just an experiment and just a cutout for humankind. They were talking at first but their faces were dry. They were not yet developed in the legs and arms. They had no blood, no lymph. They had no sweat, no fat. Their complexions were dry, their faces were crusty. They flailed their legs and arms, their bodies were deformed.

And so they accomplished nothing before the Maker, Modeler who gave them birth, gave them heart. They became the first numerous people here on the face of the earth.

8.2 The Great Debate

Las Casas's concern over abuse of the Indians catalyzed a controversy in Spain during the mid-1500s about the justness of war against them. In a famous debate with the theologian Juan Ginés de Sepúlveda at Valladolid,

Ginés de Sepúlveda, Juan. "Tratado sobre las justas causas de la guerra contra los indios" (Mexico, 1941). In *Readings in Latin American Civilization: 1492 to the Present*, 4th ed., edited by Benjamin Keen, 105–13. Boulder, Colo.: Westview Press, 1986.

de las Casas, Bartolomé. "Apologética historia de las Indias" (Madrid, 1909). In *Readings in Latin American Civilization: 1492 to the Present*, 4th ed., edited by Benjamin Keen, 128–29. Boulder, Colo.: Westview Press, 1986.

> *Spain, in 1550, Las Casas affirmed the oneness of humankind and the equality of all races. His argument resulted in some protective royal orders and as a result, Las Casas is generally regarded as the best-known champion of Indians in the New World. The actual debate was held before a board of theologians convened by Charles V in 1550. On the first day, Sepúlveda spoke for three hours; on the second day, Las Casas presented his views. The debate lasted five days. Portions of the debate are presented below in the original order.*

[Juan Ginés Sepúlveda:] Now compare these [Spanish] traits of prudence, intelligence, magnanimity, moderation, humanity, and religion with the qualities of these little men in whom you will scarcely find even vestiges of humanity; who not only are devoid of learning but do not even have a written language; who preserve no monuments of their history, aside from some vague and obscure reminiscence of past events, represented by means of certain paintings; and who have no written laws but only barbaric customs and institutions. And if we are to speak of virtues, what moderation or mildness can you expect of men who are given to all kinds of intemperance and wicked lusts, and who eat human flesh?

And do not believe that before the coming of the Christians they lived in that peaceful reign of Saturn that the poets describe; on the contrary, they waged continuous and ferocious war against each other, with such fury that they considered a victory hardly worth while if they did not glut their monstrous hunger with the flesh of their enemies, a ferocity all the more repellent since it was not joined to the invincible valor of the Scythians, who also ate human flesh. For the rest, these Indians are so cowardly that they almost run at the sight of our soldiers, and frequently thousands of them have fled like women before a very few Spaniards, numbering less than a hundred. . . .

Could one give more convincing proof of the superiority of some men to others in intelligence, spirit, and valor, and of the fact that such people are slaves by nature? For although some of them display a certain talent for craftsmanship this is not proof of human intelligence, for we know that animals, birds, and spiders do certain work that no human industry can completely imitate. And as regards the mode of life of the inhabitants of New Spain and the province of Mexico, I have already said that they are considered the most civilized of all. They themselves boast of their public institutions, for they have cities constructed in an orderly fashion, and kings, not hereditary but elected by popular vote; and they carry on commerce among themselves in the manner of civilized people.

But see how they deceive themselves, and how much I disagree with their opinion, for in these same institutions I see proof on the contrary of the rudeness, the barbarism, and the inherently slavish nature of these people. For the possession of habitations, of a fairly rational mode of life, and of a kind of commerce is something that natural necessity itself induces, and only serves to prove that they are not bears or monkeys and are not completely devoid of reason. But on the other hand, they have no private property in their state, and they cannot dispose of or bequeath to their heirs their houses or fields, since they are all in the power of their lords, whom they improperly call kings, at whose pleasure, rather than at their own, they live, attentive to their will and caprice rather than to their own freedom. And the fact that they do all this in a voluntary and spontaneous manner and are not constrained by force of arms is certain proof of the servile and abased spirit of these barbarians. . . .

Such, in sum, are the disposition and customs of these little men—barbarous, uncivilized, and inhumane; and we know that they were like this before the coming of the Spaniards. We have not yet spoken of their impious religion and of the wicked sacrifices in which they worshipped the devil as their God, believing that they could offer no better tribute than human hearts. . . . How can we doubt that these peoples, so uncivilized, so barbarous, contaminated with so many infidelities and vices, have been justly conquered by such an excellent, pious, and just king as the late Ferdinand the Catholic, and the present Emperor Charles, and by a nation that is most humane and excels in every kind of virtue?

[Bartolomé de las Casas:] From these examples, both ancient and modern, it is clear that no nation exists, no matter how rude and uncivilized, barbarous, gross, savage or almost brutal it may be, that cannot be persuaded into a good way of life and made domestic, mild, and tractable—provided that diligence and skill are employed, and provided that the method that is proper and natural to men is used: namely, love and gentleness and kindness. . . .

For all the peoples of the world are men, and the definition of all men, collectively and severally, is one: that they are rational beings. All possess understanding and volition, being formed in the image and likeness of God; all have the five exterior senses and the four interior senses, and are moved by the objects of these; all have the natural capacity or faculties to understand and master the knowledge that they do not have; and this is true not only of those that are inclined toward good but of those that by reason of their depraved customs are bad; all take pleasure in goodness and in happy and pleasant things; and all abhor evil and reject what offends or grieves them. . . .

Thus all mankind is one, and all men are alike in what concerns their creation and all natural things, and no one is born enlightened. From this it follows that all of us must be guided and aided at first by those who were born before us. And the savage peoples of the earth may be compared to uncultivated soil that readily brings forth weeds and useless thorns, but has within itself such natural virtue that by labor and cultivation it may be made to yield sound and beneficial fruits.

8.3 The Wealth of the Church

Throughout its history in America, the Roman Catholic Church has faced questions about its alleged wealth. According to some critics, its wealth is a contradiction of its religious mission. Defenders of the Church point out that its resources were often used for charitable and educational purposes; possessing wealth was thus not inconsistent with its calling. The following selection discusses the merits of such arguments in terms of the Latin American Catholic Church in colonial times.

That the increase of the monasteries in wealth and numbers tended to be out of all proportion to the needs of the new American settlements, and was inconsistent with conditions of life in pioneer, New World communities, was early sensed by Spaniards both in Europe and in America. As early as 1535, the crown decreed that lands in New Spain might be bestowed on *conquistadores* and other worthy settlers only on condition that they were never alienated to an ecclesiastic, a church, or a monastery. In 1559 it was decreed that monasteries outside the cities must be at least 6 leagues apart. As many of the establishments had only a few inmates although possessing considerable revenues, and as these were increasing in number, Pope Paul V in 1611 issued a bull suppressing all not occupied by at least 8 resident friars. At this time, according to the ecclesiastical writer Gerónimo de Mendieta, the Franciscans alone in New Spain had 166 religious houses. And besides these there were the houses of the Dominicans, Augustinians, and other Orders. In Lima at the same time, a city of some 26,500 inhabitants, with 19 churches and monasteries, a census revealed that 10 per cent of the population were priests, canons, friars, or nuns. Moreover, the erection of these countless churches and monasteries, their upkeep, and the

Haring, Clarence. "The Wealth of the Church." In *The Roman Catholic Church in Colonial Latin America,* edited by Richard E. Greenleaf, 177–81. New York: Knopf, 1971.

maintenance of so numerous a clergy, rested chiefly if not wholly upon the labor of the Indians. The clergy shared in the use of forced labor in the form of the *mita* or the *repartimiento* as did other Spaniards, and often only served to increase the heavy burdens upon the miserable aborigines.

The colonists themselves felt the inconveniences of this state of affairs, as when in 1578 the *cabildo*[1] of Mexico City urged the viceroy to limit the acquisition of land by the Church. Again in 1644 the *cabildo* of the same city petitioned the king to this effect, and also requested that no more convents or monasteries be founded, that no more friars be sent to New Spain, and that the bishops be restricted in the number of clergy they might ordain.

Not until the eighteenth century, under the new Bourbon dynasty, was any real effort made by the Spanish government to remedy this situation. A decree of 15 March 1717 declared that the number of friars was a burden upon the land, hindered the cultivation of the fields and the increase of public wealth, and that thereafter no conventual establishments were to be created in the Indies. In 1734 the crown ordered, with the approval of Rome, that for ten years no one in New Spain be admitted under any pretext to a religious Order. Twenty years later, in 1754, the king expressly forbade any member of a religious Order to interfere in the drawing up of wills. The extensive domains of the monasteries were generally acquired by bequest, for, as the Chilean historian Barros Arana remarked, "a will which did not include some legacy in favor of the monasteries passed for an act against religion." But although in 1775 a decree was again issued forbidding confessors or their convents to be heirs or legatees, the policy of the crown was not always consistent, nor were its decrees enforced. When the great German scientist Baron von Humboldt visited New Spain in the opening years of the nineteenth century, he found in Mexico City 23 monasteries and 15 nunneries with over 3,300 inmates in a population of perhaps 100,000.

Whatever may have been the services of the Church in maintaining and spreading the Christian religion . . . there can be little doubt that in certain respects the ecclesiastical establishment, as the royal decree of 1717 declared, was an economic burden upon the colonies. These were chiefly two: the acquisition of so much of the best agricultural land by way of benefactions, purchase, or mortgage, and the system of ecclesiastical taxation, especially the tithe. The tithe amounted to a ten per cent income tax collected at the source on agricultural and pastoral industries. While this assessment was common throughout European Christendom, its effect must have been prejudicial to the progress and prosperity of a young, frontier, agricultural society. The gross amount of tithes collected in New Spain in the decade 1769–79 was nearly thir-

[1] Town or city government.—Trans.

teen and a half million pesos. In the following decade, it rose to nearly eighteen and a half million.

The engrossing of much of the best land by the Church was unfortunate for the colonies in that it aggravated the evils of the system of large estates. The church was not responsible for the *latifundia*[2] nor were all the *latifundia* in the hands of the church. But the concentration of so much land in the control of one great corporation, or group of allied corporations, intensified the drawbacks of the system in the American colonies. For in most pioneering countries relatively small landed holdings and the stimulus of private ownership by many individuals are generally needed to encourage immigration and secure the most profitable and economical use of the soil. In the case of ecclesiastical lands the outlook was the more hopeless because the "dead hand" of the Church prevented properties from changing owners or being redivided and distributed.

The amount of ecclesiastical property in the Spanish American colonies controlled by the secular Church or by the Orders, in estates and in mortgages, has been variously estimated. Humboldt wrote, in his description of New Spain at the beginning of the nineteenth century, that in some of the provinces four-fifths of the land was held in mortmain. The estimate must have included lands on which ecclesiastical societies held heavy mortgages, for the Mexican historian Alamán, a not unfriendly writer, tells us that there was scarcely an estate in New Spain that was not so encumbered, and that at least half of the landed wealth was controlled by the Church. At the end of the colonial period the aggregate value of agricultural property belonging to the Church and to pious endowments in what is now the Republic of Mexico was probably in the neighborhood of fifty million pesos. Indeed the property and wealth of the Church, and the political influence which such wealth enabled it to exercise, constituted one of the most troublesome problems bequeathed to the nascent republics of the nineteenth century.

The prevalence of ecclesiastical mortgages arose from two circumstances typical of Spanish colonial society. Agriculture was not a capitalistic enterprise that endeavored to produce a surplus of liquid capital for investment. In fact there was little opportunity for investment except in land or mines, and of land the great proprietors already had a great sufficiency. The colonies were not industrialized communities. On the other hand, the Spanish American landed aristocracy in general inherited a tradition of prodigality and extravagance that may be said to have come down to them from the feudal society of medieval times.

As there was little surplus liquid capital, there was little need of organized banking until near the close of the colonial era. In 1716 the viceroy Linares reported that there were only two banks in Mexico City,

---

[2] Large landholdings, plantations.—Trans.

one under control of the Tagle family, the other belonging to Isidro
Rodríguez. It was not until the time of Matlas de Gálvez (viceroy, 1783–
4) that the celebrated Bank of San Carlos was founded. Consequently,
when the improvident landowner needed to borrow, he applied to the
monasteries. For they alone, generally less prodigal and extravagant
than the private landowners, had an accumulated surplus to invest. They
were in a sense the banks of Spanish colonial America.

There is, however, another side to the picture. Virtually all of the
social services of the community in colonial days were the peculiar and
exclusive domain of the clergy. They created and managed the schools,
hospitals, and asylums. They administered the numerous pious funds
established by devout laymen or ecclesiastics. Private philanthropy was
as common in Spanish colonial society as it is in these more modern
times, perhaps more so than has been customary in the Spanish republics of today. But in a society so completely suffused with ecclesiasti-
cism, in which education, science, and letters were largely dominated
by the clergy, and charitable activities were entirely in their hands, private beneficence was canalized in the direction of the Church. A repen-
tant millionaire, instead of endowing private colleges, laboratories, or
museums, built a chapel or a monastery or gave money to the Church
to be administered for the poor and infirm. This not only brought great
wealth to the Church, but also imposed vast responsibilities upon it.
Consequently its social and charitable contributions to society in the
colonies were quite as important as its religious ministrations.

8.4 The Catholic Church in Support of Human Rights and Justice

*The Second Annual Conference of the Latin American Bishops (CELAM
II) in 1968 attempted to apply general directives to Latin America resulting from the worldwide meeting of Catholic bishops in 1962–65 known
as Vatican II. Vatican II's emphasis on church support for peace, justice,
and human rights contributed to extensive discussions of the exploitation*

"The Church in the Present Day Transformation of Latin America in the Light of the
Council." Excerpts from *The Second Annual Conference of the Latin American Bishops*
(CELAM II),vol. 2, 58–64. Bogotá: Secretariat of CELAM, 1968.

of workers, government repression, and acute poverty. Solutions, the bishops asserted, required intensifying evangelization to promote the biblical message of love for one's neighbor. Both liberal capitalism and Marxism were criticized for dehumanizing workers. Capitalistic reform was regarded as essential and should involve increased worker participation in decision making. Emphasis should be on promoting the common good rather than class conflict. The bishops also argued that economic development, properly managed, should contribute to raising the standard of living, particularly of the poor, and that rich nations have an obligation to assist poorer nations. The following selection includes excerpts from the CELAM II and deals with the doctrinal bases for action.

II. Doctrinal Bases

. . .

3. The Latin American Church has a message for all men on this continent who "hunger and thirst after justice."

. . . For our authentic liberation, all of us need a profound conversion so that "the kingdom of justice, love and peace," might come to us. The origin of all disdain for mankind, of all injustice, should be sought in the internal imbalance of human liberty, which will always need to be rectified in history. The uniqueness of the Christian message does not so much consist in the affirmation of the necessity for structural change, as it does in the insistence on the conversion of men which will in turn bring about this change. We will not have a new continent without new and reformed structures, but, above all, there will be no new continent without new men, who know how to be truly free and responsible according to the light of the Gospel.

4. . . . Love, "the fundamental law of human perfection, and therefore of the transformation of the world," is not only the greatest commandment of the Lord; it is also the dynamism which ought to motivate Christians to realize justice in the world, having truth as a foundation and liberty as their sign.

5. This is how the Church desires to serve the world, radiating over it a light and life which heals and elevates the dignity of the human person, which consolidates the unity of society and gives a more profound reason and meaning to all human activity. . . .

The Christian quest for justice is a demand arising from biblical teaching. All men are merely humble stewards of material goods. In the search for salvation we must avoid the dualism which separates temporal tasks from the work of sanctification. Although we are encompassed with imperfections, we are men of hope. We have faith that our love for Christ and our brethren will not only be the great force liberating us from injustice and oppression, but also the inspiration for social justice, understood as a whole of life and as an impulse toward the integral growth of our countries.

III. Projections for Social Pastoral Planning

6. Our pastoral mission is essentially a service of encouraging and educating the conscience of believers, to help them to perceive the responsibilities of their faith in their personal life and in their social life. This Second Episcopal Conference wishes to point out the most important demands, taking into account the value judgment which the latest Documents of the Magisterium of the Church have already made concerning the economic and social situation of the world of today and which applies fully to the Latin American continent.

Direction of Social Change

7. The Latin American Church encourages the formation of national communities that reflect a global organization, where all of the peoples but more especially the lower classes have, by means of territorial and functional structures, an active and receptive, creative and decisive participation in the construction of a new society. Those intermediary structures—between the person and the state—should be freely organized, without any unwarranted interference from authority or from dominant groups, in view of their development and concrete participation in the accomplishment of the total common good. They constitute the vital network of society. They are also the true expression of the citizens' liberty and unity.

(a) The Family

8. . . . Latin American families ought to organize their economic and cultural potential so that their legitimate needs and hopes be taken into account, on the levels where fundamental decisions are made, which can help or hinder them. In this way they will assume a role of effective representation and participation in the life of the total community.

Besides the dynamism which is generated in each country by the union of families, it is necessary that governments draw up legislation and a healthy and up-to-date policy governing the family.

(b) Professional Organization

9. The Second Latin American Episcopal Conference addresses itself to all those who, with daily effort, create the goods and services which favor the existence and development of human life. We refer especially to the millions of Latin American men and women who make up the peasant and working class. They, for the most part, suffer, long for and struggle for a change that will humanize and dignify their work. Without ignoring the totality of the significance of human work, here we refer to it as an intermediary structure, inasmuch as it constitutes the function which gives rise to professional organization in the field of production.

(c) Business Enterprises and the Economy

10. . . . The system of Latin American business enterprises, and through it the current economy, responds to an erroneous conception concerning the right of ownership of the means of production and the very goals of the economy. A business, in an authentically human economy, does not identify itself with the owners of capital, because it is fundamentally a community of persons and a unit of work, which is in need of capital to produce goods. A person or a group of persons cannot be the property of an individual, of a society, or of the state.

The system of liberal capitalism and the temptation of the Marxist system would appear to exhaust the possibilities of transforming the economic structures of our continent. Both systems militate against the dignity of the human person. One takes for granted the primacy of capital, its power and its discriminatory utilization in the function of profit-making. The other, although it ideologically supports a kind of humanism, is more concerned with collective man, and in practice becomes a totalitarian concentration of state power. We must denounce the fact that Latin America sees itself caught between these two options and remains dependent on one or other of the centers of power which control its economy.

Therefore, on behalf of Latin America, we make an urgent appeal to the businessmen, to their organizations and to the political authorities, so that they might radically modify the evaluation, the attitudes and the means regarding the goal, organization and functioning of business. All those financiers deserve encouragement who, individually or through their organizations, make an effort to conduct their business according to the guidelines supplied by the social teaching of the Church. That the social and economic change in Latin America be channeled towards a truly human economy will depend fundamentally on this.

11. On the other hand this change will be essential in order to liberate the authentic process of Latin American development and inte-

gration. Many of our workers, although they gradually become conscious of the necessity for this change, simultaneously experience a situation of dependence on inhuman economic systems and institutions: a situation which, for many of them, borders on slavery, not only physical but also professional, cultural, civic and spiritual.

With the clarity which arises from the knowledge of man and of his hopes, we must reiterate that neither the combined value of capital nor the establishment of the most modern techniques of production, nor economic plans will serve man efficiently if the workers, the "necessary unity of direction" having been safeguarded, are not incorporated with all of the thrust of their humanity, by means of "the active participation of all in the running of the enterprise, according to ways which will have to be determined with care and on a macro-economic level, decisive nationally and internationally."

(d) Organization of the Workers

12. Therefore, in the intermediary professional structure the peasants' and workers' unions, to which the workers have a right, should acquire sufficient strength and power. Their associations will have a unified and responsible strength, to exercise the right of representation and participation on the levels of production and of national, continental and international trade. They ought to exercise their right of being represented, also, on the social, economic and political levels, where decisions are made which touch upon the common good. Therefore, the unions ought to use every means at their disposal to train those who are to carry out these responsibilities in moral, economic, and especially in technical matters.

(e) Unity of Action

13. Socialization understood as a socio-cultural process of personalization and communal growth, leads us to think that all of the sectors of society, but in this case, principally the social-economic sphere, should, because of justice and brotherhood, transcend antagonisms in order to become agents of national and continental development. Without this unity, Latin America will not be able to succeed in liberating itself from the neo-colonialism to which it is bound, nor will Latin America be able to realize itself in freedom, with its own cultural, socio-political and economic characteristics.

(f) Rural Transformation

14. The Second Episcopal Conference wishes to voice its pastoral concern for the extensive peasant class . . . If it is true that one ought to consider the diversity of circumstances and resources in different coun-

tries, there is no doubt that there is a common denominator in all of them: the need for the human promotion of the peasants and Indians. This uplifting will not be viable without an authentic and urgent reform of agrarian structures and policies. This structural change and its political implications go beyond a simple distribution of land. It is indispensable to make an adjudication of such lands, under detailed conditions which legitimize their occupation and insure their productivity for the benefit of the families and the national economy. This will entail, aside from juridical and technical aspects not within our competence, the organization of the peasants into effective intermediate structures, principally in the form of cooperatives; and motivation towards the creation of urban centers in rural areas, which would afford the peasant population the benefits of culture, health, recreation, spiritual growth, participation in local decisions, and in those which have to do with the economy and national politics.

(g) Industrialization

15. . . . Industrialization will be a decisive factor in raising the standard of living of our countries and affording them better conditions for an integral development. Therefore it is indispensable to revise plans and reorganize national macro-economies, preserving the legitimate autonomy of our nation, and allowing for just grievances of the poorer nations and for the desired economic integration of the continent, respecting always the inalienable rights of the person and of intermediary structures, as protagonists of this process.

8.5 Liberation Theology

Though early formulations of liberation theology antedate Vatican II (1962–65) and the Latin American Bishops Conference held in Colombia in 1968, the theology did not begin to gain wide attention until after the Bishops Conference. The writings of Gustavo Gutierrez were particularly influential in liberation theology's early dissemination, particularly his 1971 book,

Gutierrez, Gustavo. *A Theology of Liberation: History, Politics and Salvation*, edited and translated by Sister Caridad, Inda Eagleson, and John Eagleson, 272–79. Maryknoll, N.Y.: Orbis Books, 1973.

A Theology of Liberation, *excerpted below, in which he supported socialism and accepted class struggle as a reality. His more recent writings, such as* The Truth Shall Make You Free *(1986), reflect some changes in his thinking, with increased emphasis on liberty as well as justice. In recent publications he has called for an equilibrium among private, social, and state property, and denounced the violence of such groups as Sendero Luminoso, a guerrilla group in Peru, in addition to state terror.*

Human brotherhood, which has as its ultimate basis our sonship before God, is built in history. Today history is characterized by conflict which seems to impede this building of brotherhood. There is one characteristic in particular which holds a central place: the division of humanity into oppressors and oppressed, into owners of the means of production and those dispossessed of the fruit of their work, into antagonistic social classes. But this is not all; the division brings with it confrontations, struggles, violence. How then are we to live in evangelical charity in the midst of this situation? How can we reconcile the universality of charity with the option for a particular social class? Unity is one of the notes of the Church and yet the class struggle divides men; is the unity of the Church compatible with class struggle?

These questions are being posed to the Christian conscience with a growing insistence. On them depend very concretely the meaning of the presence of the Church in the world, a central theme of the Council. In the case of Latin America this means a presence in a world in revolutionary turmoil and in which violence takes on the most varied forms, from the most subtle to the most open.

The Council broke open a new path on which there is no turning back: openness to the world. In the conciliar texts this world appears above all in its positive and irenic aspects, but gradually the Church became more clearly aware of the conflicts and confrontations involved in it. The class struggle is one of the cardinal problems of the world today which challenge the life and reflection of the Christian community and which can no longer be avoided.

It is undeniable that the class struggle poses problems to the universality of Christian love and the unity of the Church. . . .

Recognition of the existence of the class struggle does not depend on our religious or ethical options. There are those who have claimed that it is something artificial, foreign to the norms which guide our society, contrary to the spirit of "Western Christian civilization," and the work of agitators and malcontents. Perhaps in spite of those who think this way, there is one thing that is true in this viewpoint: oppression and exploitation, and therefore the experience of the class struggle, are endured and perceived first of all by those who have been marginated by that civilization and do not have their own voice in the Church. . . . The class struggle is the product of demented minds only for those who do not know, or who do not wish to know, what is produced by the system. . . .

Those who speak of class struggle do not "advocate" it—as some would say—in the sense of creating it out of nothing by an act of (bad) will. What they do is to recognize a fact and contribute to an awareness of that fact. And there is nothing more certain than a fact. To ignore it is to deceive and to be deceived and moreover to deprive oneself of the necessary means of truly and radically eliminating this condition—that is, by moving towards a classless society. Paradoxically, what the groups in power call "advocating" class struggle is really an expression of a will to abolish its causes, to abolish them, not cover them over, to eliminate the appropriation by a few of the wealth created by the work of the many and not to make lyrical calls to social harmony. It is a will to build a socialist society, more just, free, and human, and not a society of superficial and false reconciliation and equality. To "advocate" class struggle, therefore, is to reject a situation in which there are oppressed and oppressors. But it is a rejection without deceit or cowardliness; it is to recognize that the fact exists and that it profoundly divides men, in order to be able to attack it at its roots and thus create the conditions of an authentic human community. To build a just society today necessarily implies the active and conscious participation in the class struggle that is occurring before our eyes.

In the second place, we must see clearly that to deny the fact of class struggle is really to put oneself on the side of the dominant sectors. Neutrality is impossible. It is not a question of admitting or denying a fact which confronts us; rather it is a question of which side we are on. The so-called "interclassist doctrine," writes Girardi in a well-known article on this question, "is in fact very classist: it reflects the point of view of the dominant class." When the Church rejects the class struggle, it is objectively operating as a part of the prevailing system. By denying the existence of social division, this system seeks to perpetuate this division on which are based the privileges of its beneficiaries. It is a classist option, deceitfully camouflaged by a purported equality before the law. The history of this refusal is long, and its causes many and complex. But the ever more acute awareness that the oppressed have of their situation and the increasing participation of Christians in the class struggle are raising new questions in the Church which are more authentic and real. . . .

The Gospel announces the love of God for all people and calls us to love as he loves. But to accept class struggle means to decide for some people and against others. To live both realities without juxtapositions is a great challenge for the Christian committed to the totality of the process of liberation. This is a challenge that leads him to deepen his faith and to mature in his love for others.

The universality of Christian love is only an abstraction unless it becomes concrete history, process, conflict; it is arrived at only through particularity. To love all men does not mean avoiding confrontations; it does not mean preserving a fictitious harmony. Universal love is that which in solidarity with the oppressed seeks also to liberate the oppressors from their own power, from their ambition, and from their selfishness: "Love for those who live in a condition of objective sin demands that we struggle to liberate them from it. The liberation of the poor and the liberation of the rich are achieved simultaneously." One loves the oppressors by liberating them from their inhuman condition as oppressors, by liberating them from themselves. But this cannot be achieved except by resolutely opting for the oppressed, that is, by combatting the oppressive class. It must be a real and effective combat, not hate. This is the challenge, as new as the Gospel: to love our enemies. This was never thought to be easy, but as long as it was only a question of showing a certain sweetness of character, it was preached without difficulty. The counsel was not followed, but it was heard without any uneasiness. In the context of class struggle today, to love one's enemies presupposes recognizing and accepting that one has class enemies and that it is necessary to combat them. It is not a question of having no enemies, but rather of not excluding them from our love. But love does not mean that the oppressors are no longer enemies, nor does it eliminate the radicalness of the combat against them. "Love of enemies" does not ease tensions; rather it challenges the whole system and becomes a subversive formula.

Universal love comes down from the level of abstractions and becomes concrete and effective by becoming incarnate in the struggle for the liberation of the oppressed. . . . Our love is not authentic if it does not take the path of class solidarity and social struggle. To participate in class struggle not only is not opposed to universal love; this commitment is today the necessary and inescapable means of making this love concrete. For this participation is what leads to a classless society without owners and dispossessed, without oppressors and oppressed. In dialectical thinking, reconciliation is the overcoming of conflict. The communion of paschal joy passes through confrontation and the cross.

The fact of class struggle also challenges the unity of the Church and demands a redefinition of what we understand by this unity.

The Church is in a world divided into antagonistic social classes, on a universal scale as well as at the local level. Because it is present in our society, the Church cannot attempt to ignore a fact which confronts it. What is more, this fact exists within the Church itself. Indeed, Christians belong to opposing social classes, which means that the Christian community itself is split by this social division. It is not possible to speak of the unity of the Church without taking into account its concrete situation in the world.

To try piously to cover over this social division with a fictitious and formalistic unity is to avoid a difficult and conflictual reality and definitively to join the dominant class. It is to falsify the true character of the Christian community under the pretext of a religious attitude which tries to place itself beyond temporal contingencies. In these conditions, to speak, for example, of the priest as "the man of unity" is to attempt to make him into a part of the prevailing system. It is to attempt to make him a part of an unjust and oppressive system, based on the exploitation of the great majorities and needing a religious justification to preserve itself. This is especially true in places like Latin America, where the Church has a great influence among the exploited masses.

Understood in this way, the unity of the Church is rightly considered by Althusser as a myth which must disappear if the Church is to be "reconverted" to the service of the workers in the class struggle: "For this to happen," he asserts, "it would be necessary that the myth of the 'Christian community' disappear, for it prevents the recognition of the division of society into classes and the recognition of class struggle. One can foresee serious divisions occurring in the Church precisely around the theme of the *recognition* and the *understanding* of social classes and the class struggle, the recognition and the understanding of a reality which is incompatible with the *peculiarly religious* myth of the 'community of the faithful' and the (catholic) universality of the Church." The author does not seem very convinced of the possibility for this "reconversion." Nevertheless there are growing numbers of Christians who challenge the mythical notion of the Christian community alluded to by Althusser and who believe that the authentic unity of the Church necessarily implies the option for the oppressed and exploited of this world.

Unity is a gift of God and a historical conquest of man. Unity is not something already given. It is a process, the result of overcoming all that divides men. The promise of unity is at the heart of the work of Christ; in him men are sons before the Father and brothers among themselves. The Church, the community of those who confess Christ as their Lord, is a sign of unity among men *(Lumen gentium,* no. 1). The unity of the Church is not truly achieved without the unity of the world. In a radically divided world, the function of the ecclesial community is to struggle against the profound causes of the division among men. It is only this commitment that can make of it an authentic sign of unity. Today, in Latin America especially, this unity implies the option for the oppressed; to opt for them is the honest, resolute way to combat that which gives rise to this social division. The Church itself will become more and more unified in this historical process and commitment to the liberation of the marginated and exploited. Unity will thus be forged not among those who only say, "Lord, Lord," but among those who "do the will of the Father." For the ecclesial community to recognize the fact of class struggle and to participate actively in it will not be therefore a negation of the message of unity which it bears; rather it will be to discover the path by which it can free itself from that which now prevents it from being a clear and true sign of brotherhood.

This perspective is, among other things, changing the focus of the concerns of ecumenism. Christians of different confessions are taking similar positions regarding the misery and injustice in Latin America, and this unites them more strongly than intraecclesial considerations. Christian unity thus begins to present questions very different than those we receive from Europe. Because of a more realistic focus for its presence in the world and its commitment to the disinherited, Christians in Latin America are united and divided in ways and for reasons very different than in past years. The paths which lead to accepting the gift of unity in Christ and his Spirit in history are going through unecclesiastical places. A new kind of ecumenism is being born. . . .

8.6 The Role of Religion in Daily Life

This selection explores the interplay of base Christian communities (CEBs), spiritism, and Pentecostalism in urban Brazil, and reveals the variety of motives influencing the choice of one over the others. It also indicates the degree to which adherents of one religion may be involved in another. The reading describes the appeal of various religions to women, who constitute Latin America's most active believers, and suggests how religious practices are molded by the realities of daily life, particularly among the poor. Finally, it offers some reasons for the recent growth of Pentecostalism and spiritism in Latin America.

What about the product of the post-Conciliar, and especially of the post-Medellín, progressive Church, the Bible reflection group [within the CEB program]? A generation of young priests and pastoral agents . . . conceive the Bible circle as a small, neighborhood-based group that nurtures trust and intimacy. As the priest explained,

> The Bible circle creates more effective friendship ties, even more effective religious ties. To the extent that these people are meeting each other, by locale, where they live, by street, you know? So the Bible circle will strengthen people in their feeling of fraternity, of being followers of that doctrine, that faith.

Burdick, John. "Gossip and Secrecy: Women's Articulation of Domestic Conflict in Three Religions of Urban Brazil." *Sociological Analysis* 51:2 (1990): 153–70.

It is within this supposed space of trust and friendship that progressive priests hope that neighbors will reflect upon the Bible and make a connection between faith and life (*ligar fé e vida*). In particular, the progressive Church hopes that participants will develop a more critical social and political consciousness. But that is not all. As the priest pointed out, "The Bible circle should try to focus on all the dimensions of life, on the dimensions of neighborhood, family, community, survival." In practice, however, people virtually never speak about their own domestic tensions within the reflection groups. In my weekly attendance at various Bible circles in São Jorge, I never heard such talk, and I never once heard a request for a prayer related to a specific domestic conflict. On the few occasions that talk did turn to family problems, it was about *other* people's (non-group members') problems, and this gossip left many participants visibly uneasy. The most common type of talk in the circles is moral exhortation to follow Christ's example: to be charitable, loving, faithful, committed, and so forth. Never did I (nor to the best of my knowledge, did my informants) witness the Bible circle used to discuss and work out a personal problem using public discourse. Indeed, participants explicitly claim that the circles neither are nor should be used for this purpose: "In the groups, people don't talk about their current problems, no they don't. The group isn't for that. They don't talk about problems, but about the things they have learned from the Gospel, or of what ought to be learned from the Gospel" (group coordinator, a woman in her fifties). I asked another longstanding participant in the groups, a widowed woman, whether a woman might complain about her husband within the group. "Never! There, if you talk about that, you're not connecting life with the Bible. Because the connection between life and the Bible doesn't mean things about husbands and wives, about children, or the problems we have."

Why are domestic issues taboo in the reflection groups? We may approach a partial answer by considering the fact that group participants are recruited primarily through ties of *neighborhood* (as inhabitants of a specific street or block) and *common prior religious identity* (as Catholics). The reflection groups may thus be considered "local cults" . . . a religious group that recruits its participants through *place* and *prior identity*, thus transferring and extending prior social roles to the religious space. . . . As a local cult, participants in the reflection groups see other members in the same social roles they occupy outside the circle: they are, above all, *neighbors,* and relations between neighbors, as any anthropologist or small-town dweller knows, are fraught as much with tension as they are blessed with trust. Thus, the fear of being judged by neighbors inhibits revealing domestic tensions within the local cult. Outside the Bible circle, neighbors judge each other all the time; within the group, this tendency is reinforced by Catholic moral ideology, an ethic that emphasizes human responsibility and a direct relationship between human agency and sin. This emphasis has been deepened by post-Conciliar and post-Medellín teaching. . . . But . . . diagnoses of domestic conflict that allocate responsibility in human terms will tend to open the floodgates of judgment, advice, and taking of sides: in short, of gossip. . . .

Of course, a crucial source of inner strength for many Catholic women in dealing with the pressures of the domestic realm is devotion to the Virgin Mary. As one leader of the CEB (a woman with a highly problematic marriage) confided, "When he arrives at home drunk, you know, swearing, I think of Our Lady, because didn't she also suffer? So there, I can suffer a little too." On the other hand, Marian devotion leaves a woman isolated, with resignation her only comfort. For many devout Catholic women, this is enough. But in the context of competition by cults of affliction that promise a change of life and social support through adversity, Marian devotion may begin to appear a weak alternative, especially for younger women who have had little experience of it. . . .

Many Catholic women come to a healer or prayer-meeting, receive the prayer and even the blessing they seek, yet make no further commitment to the church. For others, these prayers are a first step toward conversion and membership. In general, women who do not become members are seeking mainly a place to *articulate* a domestic problem; those who convert find in pentecostalism the long-term *resolution* of their domestic difficulties. . . . Here I wish to focus on the several ways pentecostalism helps women to achieve long-term resolution of domestic conflict. First, it defines in unequivocal fashion proper wifely conduct inside and outside the home, thus eliminating uncertainty about the female role, and sacralizing female submissiveness by appealing to the Pauline epistles. As a presbyter of the Assembly of God assured me, household conflict was usually due to female pride:

> When a woman doesn't want to submit to the order of the husband, that's the start of a fight, right? But if the woman is a true Christian, she is going to want to obey. For the Apostle Paul said: Women must obey their husbands. Like it or not, she has to obey, if she wants to be a good Christian, she has to obey her husband.

It may be that in the context of male dominance and the machismo complex, many women find greater domestic tranquillity by accepting a clearly subordinate role, rather than flirting with the progressive Catholic Church's call for greater equality between the sexes. . . .

Yet there is an important twist to the gender identity offered to women by the Assembly of God. If on the one hand the church teaches women to submit, on the other it provides them with new spiritual resources: the authority to speak in the name of God, the support and collective prayers of other members, and the general strength derived from the conviction of being one of God's chosen. Carolina, before converting to the Assembly, was always fighting with her husband because of his drinking; but the more she tried to "correct" him, the more he drank.

> After becoming a *crente*, I didn't fight anymore, because I had more strength to speak about things, without having to fight. You feel there is always someone praying for you. . . . [After conversion] I'd talk with him with authority, and he would cry. I would talk, quietly, that it wasn't right for us to waste the small salary we had on things that weren't bread, because that's Biblical. . . . Being a member of the church gave me more authority to talk like this at home.

And Nena, facing the increased disobedience of her children, found in pentecostalism the strength she needed to cope: "After becoming a *crente*, my children started obeying me more. [Why?] Because instead of correcting them, you know, directly, by giving them a smack, I would kneel and pray. With prayer, Jesus liberates any type of disobedience." . . .

. . . Pentecostalism rejects the machismo complex as the work of the Devil and subjects men to discipline or exclusion from the church should they indulge repeatedly in any of the elements of that complex (alcohol, cigarettes, gambling, womanizing, swearing, fighting). A crucial source of this control is the presence of the Holy Spirit within the church: this gives members gifts of prophecy and vision that are in constant vigil over the behavior of *crentes*. A man will think twice about partaking in a secret affair when he imagines the possibility of a prophet denouncing him during a church service. (This has indeed happened several times.) This sanction may also come in the form of dreams. One man had been flirting with the idea of seeing on the sly an old flame from outside the town. While he was considering it, he was approached by a female prayer specialist who told him she had had a dream, in which she saw him about to do something against God's will. This, of course, settled things: the man dropped the idea of a tryst at once.

Whenever it becomes known that a *crente* couple is fighting, the pastor calls them into his office. He reminds the woman of her Biblical duty and the husband of his. Because he speaks with the authority not only of the Word and the Holy Spirit, but also as a family man himself, these consultations are often quite effective. . . .

Domestic Conflict and Umbanda

The explanation given for feeling free to articulate personal issues in a pentecostal church is remarkably similar to that of Naomi, a leader of the CEB who frequents an *umbanda* center from time to time:

There, in the center, no one gossips, no one criticizes. There everything is secret. ["Secret"?] You see, son, everyone is there because of their problems. They aren't going to talk about other people's problems, because if they did, aren't they going to have to say why they were there, too?

To the extent that an active Catholic usually visits an *umbanda* center clandestinely, the confidentiality of what one says there is virtually guaranteed.

There is a good deal of variation in the ritual practice of Brazilian mediumship religions. In particular, there is the important contrast between mediums who receive spirits who demand food or drink, and those who receive spirits who do not. One of the things these different cults have in common is that they are all well-suited to the public or private articulation of domestic issues. In one *umbanda* center I visited, one after another of the women present approached the medium and told him their tale of domestic woe, in a voice loud enough for all to hear. As a cult of affliction, this center made possible the public airing of these issues. Further, the idiom this medium used to describe how his spiritual guide *(guia)* helps people with their problems is that it "visits" each afflicted person's home to "see what's going on there." The *guia* visits the homes of people even if they do not report domestic conflict as their affliction. . . . The idiom of response to all affliction here is thus eminently domestic: all ills begin and end in the home.

Those mediumship practices that are directed toward spirits who eat and drink tend to focus on the private, one-on-one articulation of personal affliction, rather than encourage the public airing of one's troubles. They also legitimate the expression of resentment and the desire for vengeance (phrased as "justice"). Here the key to the therapy is in part the secrecy guaranteed by the spirit, in part the possibility that justice according to human criteria will be done. Geraldinha identifies herself as a Catholic, but is developing her mediumship in an *umbanda* center. She recounted her participation in *umbanda:*

> When [my husband] Dico became unemployed, I never spoke about it in the Catholic Church. You know, in the Church many say: "He has to assume his duties." They criticize, and I was ashamed. So I began to consult with Fidelio. I thought at first he was just a *rezador,* later I found out he dealt with *orixás* [spirits]. [Why didn't you feel ashamed with Fidelio?] Because I was talking with the *orixás.* I couldn't speak about these things with human beings. With people, they comment to each other; but with an *orixá,* the thing stays with it alone.

This last example reminds us that just as in pentecostalism there exists the contrast between frequenters and members, so in *umbanda* there are people who come simply to consult with the spirits and those who come to develop more complicated and permanent relationships of exchange and mediumship with them. Such relationships, like pentecostal membership, may be considered from the angle of how they help forge long-term domestic tranquillity. . . .

The Contrast Between Pentecostalism and Umbanda

For the woman who is either merely requesting a prayer or becoming a member, either only consulting a medium or becoming a medium herself, both pentecostalism and mediumship religion locate the source of domestic trouble outside the Self. But whereas the moral world of pentecostalism is absolute and dichotomized, that of *umbanda* is ambiguous and multifaceted. Whereas pentecostalism embraces a vision of human weakness overcome by total submission to God, in mediumship cults humans can influence and exchange with spirits. Manuel, the prayer-healer, concisely defined his religion's difference from *umbanda* by saying, "God doesn't do anyone any favors": that is, *umbanda* sees God as a distributor of privileges, but for pentecostalism He is a lawgiver.

While pentecostalism deals with domestic conflict by interpreting it as part of the general project of the Devil, mediumship cults attribute it to spiritual power at the service of some evil or disobedient human will: the ultimate source of such conflict is in the will of an enticing woman, a selfish or careless husband, an irascible wife. The rituals and language of *umbanda* are flexible enough that one can always find a culprit other than the self—indeed, *umbanda*'s power resides precisely in this—but the culprit is always human. Spirits are blameless: their power may be used for good or ill, at the command of those who call upon them. . . . For pentecostalism evil is always beyond the ken of human power and justice; it can be overcome only by recognizing one's powerlessness and submitting to divine justice. For *umbanda,* evil always originates in a human Other, and hence may be dealt with by using spiritual means to achieve human justice.

This contrast partly accounts for why a woman sometimes asks for help in more than one place. It is not simply that she is somehow "hedging her bets" or "shopping around," as the supermarket model would have it. In each place she can articulate her predicament in a slightly different way, emphasizing different aspects of the problem. In Catholicism, the emphasis is on her own guilt and resigning herself to adversity. Pentecostalism, meanwhile, proclaims the power of faith to move mountains. There she may recognize a human perpetrator of evil, but since he is a mere tool of the Devil, she may only feel pity toward him and the desire that God touch his heart to save him from damnation; there she must reject resignation and call upon God to transform the situation. In *umbanda* she may express anger and resentment, and impose remedies fashioned on human rather than divine justice. Catholicism nurtures perseverance; pentecostalism, "letting go," and *umbanda*, self-help. . . .

CEB Catholicism is organized on the basis of neighborhood rather than affliction, and articulates domestic tensions in terms of the Self; hence talk about such tensions naturally spills into gossip. Mediumship cults and pentecostalism, meanwhile, both articulate domestic conflict in terms of a spiritual or human Other. . . . [T]he peculiar spiritual discourses and affliction-centeredness of both pentecostalism and mediumship cults limit the space for gossip. This is one of the deep reasons why the Catholic Church is shrinking in Brazil today while pentecostalism and *umbanda* continue to grow.

9

Builders of Images: Writers, Artists, and Popular Culture

Two of Puerto Rico's most prominent artists, writer Luis Rafael Sánchez and painter Nick Quijano, are concerned with the balance between local and international influences in Latin American culture today. © Juan Mandelbaum

Is there such a thing as a common Latin American culture? Yes and no. The very term *Latin America* was invented in France in the nineteenth century to include the former Portuguese, Spanish, and French colonies. There are some common cultural patterns and concerns. For instance, writers and artists, often privileged members of their societies, nevertheless have responded to injustice, ethnic diversity, and the call for social change.

Yet nowhere is the diversity and innovation characteristic of Latin America better illustrated than through its culture. Since the colonial period, cultural expression has been marked by an ongoing tension between the indigenous and the colonial, native and European, national and international. In addition to national cultures, "Latin America" embraces a complexity of vernacular ethnic, rural, and urban cultures that defy any idea of a homogeneous national culture. Even with the variations, most countries of the Americas have encountered tensions and conflict over the struggle to reconcile competing tendencies: the development of cultural identity around strictly national values and forms of expression, versus the growing internationalization of Latin American expression.

Artists and Intellectuals

Latin American artists and intellectuals traditionally have had a keen sense of responsibility toward the social needs of their countries. They have played a critical role in the struggle to shape and craft unique forms of cultural expression. Some have relied on traditional forms, such as poetry or literature, to convey social concerns. Others have found new and ingenious ways to express culture in response to changing international currents that affect intellectual and popular life.

The economic boom of Latin America between the 1890s and the 1920s coincided with the emergence of the modernist period in Latin American literary expression. Although strongly influenced by literary developments in France, modernism was the first literary movement to have its origin in the Americas. Rubén Darío, a Nicaraguan, is the best Spanish American modernist poet. Like many Spanish Americans who had initially been more interested in Europe, Darío gradually developed an awareness of and wrote about Spanish America's problems, as reading 9.1 illustrates.

Another outstanding poet of the era, the Cuban José Martí, was deeply involved in his island's struggle for independence from Spain. He drew on popular Hispanic ballads for some of his poetry. Although a nationalist, Martí developed a new interpretation of a unified Spanish America he called *Nuestra America,* which continues to have validity (see reading 9.2). Like Darío, he was pragmatic and not simply an imitator of European or North American styles. Both asserted the Latin American presence on the cultural scene, and saw the region as participating in a common culture.

A key concern throughout much of the twentieth century in the cultural expression of the Americas had to do with national identity and the celebration of originality. This was often fostered through direct state involvement. Following its revolution in 1910, Mexico entered the 1920s as a leader of innovation in the region. During this period, Mexico's minister of education developed an ambitious plan to educate the masses; one of his chosen media was painting.

From this experiment emerged the Mexican mural movement, led by three great Mexican painters, Diego Rivera, David Alfaro Siqueiros, and José Clemente Orozco, whose work drew worldwide attention to Latin American art. The three artists differed in their politics, but shared a large-scale nationalist vision of Mexican history and society. Their art transcended national boundaries, and each worked periodically outside Mexico. For example, Rivera painted murals of the U.S. automobile industry at the Detroit Institute of Arts.

In Brazil, the modernist movement differed from its Spanish American counterparts. Initiated by the Modern Art Week of 1922 in São Paulo, this new form of cultural expression launched a period of experimentation that emphasized the esthetic and human values peculiar to modern Brazil. Brazilian modernists demanded that Brazilian writers use the Portuguese spoken in the country—emphasizing a colloquial, even slangy style. For example, Mario de Andrade, a Brazilian modernist, used poetry to express his enthusiasm for São Paulo.

Parallel to the celebration of urban life was a strong regionalist movement influenced by the writings of sociologist Gilberto Freyre, who stressed the importance of African elements and the traditional Brazilian family. Regionalist novels by Graciliano Ramos, who wrote *Barren Lives* (see reading 9.3), and J. Lins do Rego and Jorge Amado, are set in the Brazilian northeast and often depict rural life or the lives of the working classes.

Poetry was the most innovative genre during this period. Poets such as the Chilean Pablo Neruda broke from the elitism of the modernists. He created new publics for poetry and used it as a vehicle to communicate to ordinary people, especially the working class. For Neruda, poetry was a public and political experience, as reading 9.4 illustrates. Another great poet of the period, the Peruvian César Vallejo, believed that the language of poetry should approximate the human condition and often focused on such themes as sexuality and existential despair. Saint Lucian poet Derek Walcott, whose epic poem *Omeros* received the U.S. National Book Award, celebrates the music of West Indian dialect and African storytelling, while drawing on the literary traditions of Europe and the United States (see reading 9.5).

Poetry was also a major form of women's literary expression in this period. Gabriela Mistral, a Chilean, first won a prize for her poetry in 1914 and received the Nobel Prize in 1945. Mistral's poems are marked by themes of love, idealism, and nature, as illustrated in reading 9.6.

The Changing Novel

Throughout the first half of the century Latin American novelists tended to focus on the region as a "green continent," where nature dominated the individual, and the picturesque and the violent clashed. The anthology of writings *The Green Continent,* published by the Colombian Germán Arciniegas, is an example of this genre.

One writer departing from this tradition was the Argentine short story writer Jorge Luis Borges. Emphasizing themes such as the infinite and the universe as a chaotic labyrinth, Borges often abstracted story plots from regional and local reference (see reading 9.7) and set them in the past or in places such as China or Muslim Spain, remote from the reader's frame of reference. Borges believed the writer could freely appropriate any aspect of world culture without being bound to national or local traditions. His spare prose set him apart from many other writers in the region, whose literary style tended to be more elaborate and complex.

Although still writing about rural or indigenous themes, novelists such as the Peruvian José Maria Arguedas, the Mexican Juan Rulfo, and the Guatemalan Miguel Angel Asturias, who wrote during the 1950s and 1960s, developed innovative styles with debts to oral tradition and indigenous myth. Their works usually focused on the resistance of indigenous and provincial culture to capitalism's spread.

In the 1960s, writers such as the Peruvian Mario Vargas Llosa and the Colombian Gabriel García Márquez juxtaposed colonial customs against modern life and combined fantasy with historical reality to break with the novel's traditional evolutionary style. Vargas Llosa created a variety of characters within a geography that ranged from jungle outposts to city squatter settlements, from church convents to military barracks. García Márquez focused on the theme of "one hundred years of solitude," the eccentric and contradictory result of isolation and uneven development that allowed Latin American countries to develop idiosyncratic politics and culture. From the Caribbean came the magical realism of Cuba's Alejo Carpentier and the historically grounded fiction of Trinidad's V. S. Naipaul.

These writers and others conceived of themselves as political gadflies.

Latin America's rapid urbanization and the general growth of the middle class throughout the region expanded the literary audience. As Latin American writers raised their readers' level of sophistication, literary tastes developed beyond the social protest novels then dominating the book market.

The authors' readerships gave them international exposure and fame, and made more visible their efforts to mix literature with political discourse. Vargas Llosa firmly believed in the right of the novelist to act as a social and political critic. His campaign for the Peruvian presidency in 1989, though abortive, illustrates his involvement in social action. García Márquez has been an advocate for the world's downtrodden, as conveyed in reading 9.8. His continuing support for Fidel Castro's revolution indicates his commitment to anti-imperialism. That Vargas Llosa and García Márquez differ significantly in their political ideology reflects a larger reality: writers of this genre are united only in the most general sense and have little in common except their dedication to literary innovation.

Popular Culture

The spread of technology and literacy throughout the Americas led to other forms of cultural expression. Mass culture was first introduced in Latin America in the early twentieth century through music halls and the popular press. Although Mexico and Argentina developed their own film industries, Hollywood films tended to dominate Latin American film markets. The spread of radio throughout the region helped Latin American musicians, such as Carlos Gardel, develop a continental following.

With the rise in literacy and the spread of technology, a mass culture had emerged by the 1950s. Television and new forms of popular culture, such as the photonovel and the comic strip novel, burst on the scene. In contrast to Cuba, where the postrevolutionary literacy campaign had been followed up by the publication of classical Latin American and foreign texts, along with the prose of contemporary Cuban writers, the rest of Latin America was exposed largely to the attractions of consumer culture, such as the music of the Beatles and reruns of popular U.S. television series, including "Lassie," "Bonanza," and "The Lone Ranger."

The diffusion of North American popular culture throughout the Southern Hemisphere reached its peak in the 1960s. The initial reaction among leaders of the Latin American literary community was defensive. Charges of "cultural imperialism" were periodically raised. Local Latin American artists, for example, were often pressured to reject foreign influences such as electric musical instruments.

But, as in other areas of life, adaptation and innovation flourished. A Peruvian soap opera, "Simplemente María," gained a continent-wide audience in the 1960s. Brazil and Mexico developed their own mass media empires. In Brazil, Rede Globo—a conglomerate including TV, radio, and newspapers—has exported its programs throughout the world. Mexico's Televisa network mass-produces telenovelas (drama-serials) and broadcasts Spanish-language news throughout the United States.

Some popular programs have extolled nonnational values and style, as well as consumerism. However, the serialized formats of radio, television, and mass literature have developed communities of viewers and readers, giving them a common cultural point of reference. Throughout the Americas radio has also been an important educational instrument, widely relied upon especially by those living in rural isolation or burdened by illiteracy. Many television dramas downplay local differences so they can be marketed outside the country in which they are produced. Mass culture on international lines has developed.

Mass literature of the comic strip variety often promotes and reinforces positive messages—family preservation, environmental protection, and personal hygiene. However, comic strips have also been appropriated for progressive or oppositional causes. Comics drawn by Rius in Mexico, for example, have been critical of the governing party. The National Autonomous University of Honduras published an antigovernment magazine, *Tornillo sin fin* (The Endless Screw), throughout the 1970s. *Humor,* an Argentine weekly, satirized the repressive military government.

Music produced in the Americas tends to blend elements of the three dominant cultures: indigenous Indian, colonizing Hispanic, and transported African. However, the African influence on music has had a major impact on dance styles, from merengue to samba. Afro-Cuban traditions have also strongly influenced Latin music, and are the source of many influential and popular dance forms, including the habanera, rumba, bolero, mambo, conga, cha-cha, as well as the more contemporary crossover music of Gloria Estefan and the Miami Sound Machine. From Colombia, the cumbia, like its Cuban counterparts, exhibits many African features in its choreography. In recent music, eclectic strands have come together in salsa. Musicians such as Paul Simon and David Byrne have spread and popularized music with Afro-Brazilian roots throughout Europe and the United States.

As in so many other dimensions of life, cultural expression in the Americas is a hybrid of competing forces, often under difficult conditions, as reading 9.9 illustrates. Early concerns with expressing national identity have been largely replaced by the emergence of a cross-national culture that selectively articulates broader values and concerns. While many Latin American and Caribbean writers and artists emphasize the celebration of local values, others have fully embraced a cosmopolitan style and form. In some cases, the significance of their work has found wider acceptance in the international marketplace of contemporary art and ideas.

9.1 Poetry of Rubén Darío

Rubén Darío was a poet, journalist, critic, short story writer, and diplomat. Born in Nicaragua in 1867, Darío began his literary career as a journalist and soon published prose and verse in newspapers throughout the Americas. Darío's writing reflected the French literary style of the period, including romanticism, Parnassianism, and symbolism. Darío lived in Paris and Madrid, where he met some of Europe's most influential writers. Spain's defeat following U.S. intervention in the 1898 war for Cuban independence fostered a realization among many, including Darío, of the United States' growing importance in the Western Hemisphere. Darío, however, refused to accept the perceived second-class status of Spanish American culture, as the following poem suggests.

To Roosevelt

The voice that would reach you, Hunter, must speak
in Biblical tones, or in the poetry of Walt Whitman.
You are primitive and modern, simple and complex;
you are one part George Washington and one part Nimrod.
    You are the United States,
future invader of our naive America
with its Indian blood, an America
that still prays to Christ and still speaks Spanish.

You are a strong, proud model of your race;
you are cultured and able; you oppose Tolstoy.
You are an Alexander-Nebuchadnezzar,
breaking horses and murdering tigers.
(You are a Professor of Energy,
as the current lunatics say).

You think that life is a fire,
that progress is an irruption,
that the future is wherever
your bullet strikes.

            No.

Darío, Rubén. "To Roosevelt." In *Selected Poems of Rubén Darío*, translated by Lysander Kemp, 69–70. Austin: University of Texas Press, 1965.

The United States is grand and powerful.
Whenever it trembles, a profound shudder
runs down the enormous backbone of the Andes.
If it shouts, the sound is like the roar of a lion.
And Hugo said to Grant: "The stars are yours."
(The dawning sun of the Argentine barely shines;
the star of Chile is rising . . .) A wealthy country,
joining the cult of Mammon to the cult of Hercules;
while Liberty, lighting the path
to easy conquest, raises her torch in New York.

But our own America, which has had poets
since the ancient times of Nezahualcóyotl;
which preserved the footprints of great Bacchus,
and learned the Panic alphabet once,
and consulted the stars; which also knew Atlantis
(whose name comes ringing down to us in Plato)
and has lived, since the earliest moments of its life,
in light, in fire, in fragrance, and in love—
the America of Moctezuma and Atahualpa,
the aromatic America of Columbus,
Catholic America, Spanish America,
the America where noble Cuauhtémoc said:
"I am not on a bed of roses"—our America,
trembling with hurricanes, trembling with Love:
O men with Saxon eyes and barbarous souls,
our America lives. And dreams. And loves.
And it is the daughter of the Sun. Be careful.
Long live Spanish America!
A thousand cubs of the Spanish lion are roaming free.
Roosevelt, you must become, by God's own will,
the deadly Rifleman and the dreadful Hunter
before you can clutch us in your iron claws.

And though you have everything, you are lacking one thing:
    God!

9.2 José Martí's Concept of Spanish America

Born in Havana in 1853, José Martí was first imprisoned in Cuba by the Spanish government in 1870 because he wrote a letter critical of its rule. In exile from the island colony a few years later, Martí continued his attack in Madrid through newspaper letters and essays. Following brief stays in Mexico and Guatemala, Martí returned to Cuba but was once again cast into exile by the Spaniards. From 1880 to 1895, Martí lived in New York City. Throughout this period he was a dedicated revolutionary while at the same time developing widely recognized skills as a master poet and writer. Traveling along the Atlantic coast, Martí organized Cuban exiles in Key West, Tampa, and New York. He was selected president of the newly formed Cuban Revolutionary Party in 1892. During this time, he wrote that Cuba should develop its own governing institutions based on native traditions rather than on externally imposed forms. Joining with other revolutionaries in early 1895, Martí called for a revolutionary uprising in Cuba. He returned to the island to fight the Spaniards but was killed in battle on May 19, 1895. A dedicated writer, Martí wrote letters and in his diary until the day before he was killed. Although a Cuban patriot, Martí was committed to the broader concept of Spanish America, as the following essay suggests.

. . . The hour is fast approaching when our America will be confronted by an enterprising and energetic nation seeking close relations, but with indifference and scorn for us and our ways. And since strong countries, self-made by the rifle and the law, love, and love only, strong countries; since the hour of recklessness and ambition, of which North America may be freed if that which is purest in her blood predominates, or on which she may be launched by her vengeful and sordid masses, her tradition of expansion or the ambition of some powerful leaders, is not so near at hand, even to the most timorous eye, that there is not time to show the self-possessed and unwavering pride that would confront and dissuade her; since her good name as a republic in the eyes of the world puts on the America of the North a brake which cannot be removed even by the puerile grievances, the pompous arrogance, or parricidal discords of our American nations, the pressing need for our America, is to show herself as she is, one in soul and

Martí, José. "Our America." In *The America of José Martí,* translated by Juan de Onis, 148–51. New York: Noonday Press, 1953.

purpose, swift conqueror of a suffocating tradition, stained only by the blood drawn from hands that struggle to clear away ruins, and the scars left us by our masters. The scorn of our formidable neighbor, who does not know us, is the greatest danger for our America; and it is imperative that our neighbor know us, and know us soon, so she shall not scorn us, for the day of the visit is at hand. Through ignorance, she might go so far as to lay hands on us. From respect, once she came to know us, she should remove her hands. One must have faith in the best in men and distrust the worst. If not, the worst prevails. Nations should have a pillory for whoever fans useless hates; and another for whoever does not tell them the truth in time. . . .

But as nations take shape among other different nations, they acquire distinctive and vital characteristics of thought and habit, of expansion and conquest, of vanity and greed, which from the latent state of national preoccupation could be converted in a period of internal unrest, or precipitation of the accumulated character of the nation, into a serious threat to the neighboring countries, isolated and weak, which the strong country declares perishable and inferior. The thought is father to the deed. But it must not be supposed, from a parochial animus, that there is a fatal and ingrained evil in the blond nation of the continent, because it does not speak our tongue, nor see the world as we do, nor resemble us in its political faults, which are of a different order, nor favorably regard the excitable, dark-skinned people, nor look charitably, from its still uncertain eminence, on those less favored by History, who climb the road of republicanism by heroic stages. The self-evident facts of the problem should not be obscured for it can be resolved, to the benefit of peaceful centuries yet to come, by timely study and the tacit, immediate union of the continental soul. The hymn of oneness sounds already; the actual generation carries a purposeful America along the road enriched by their sublime fathers; from the Rio Grande to the straits of Magellan, the Great Semi, seated on the flank of the condor, sows the seed of a new America through the romantic nations of the continent and the sorrowful islands of the sea!

9.3 Graciliano Ramos: Barren Lives

Graciliano Ramos, born in 1892 in the Brazilian northeast, worked as a civil servant in small towns of the region. Like other novelists from the area, he had a deep interest in the area's economic and social problems. His style, vision, and psychological insight make him one of Brazil's most admired novelists. He is known in particular for his austere creations. His book Barren Lives, *first published in 1938 and later made into a film, describes the difficulties of surviving in the drought-ridden northeast. The book graphically conveys both the parched environment and its effects on its inhabitants. It is composed of thirteen short sequences about a herdsman, Fabiano, his wife, Vitória, and their family, who drift through an arid land and whose actions are guided by instinct rather than thought. This chapter is about the family's dog.*

The Dog

The dog was dying. She had grown thin and her hair had fallen out in several spots. Her ribs showed through the pink skin and flies covered dark blotches that suppurated and bled. Sores on her mouth and swollen lips made it hard for her to eat and drink.

Fabiano, thinking she was coming down with rabies, tied a rosary of burnt corncob about her neck. The dog, however, only went from bad to worse. She rubbed against the posts of the corral or plunged impatiently into the brush, trying to shake off the gnats by flapping her dangling ears and swishing her short, hairy tail, thick at the base and coiled like a rattlesnake's.

So Fabiano decided to put an end to her. He went to look for his flintlock, polished it, cleaned it out with a bit of wadding, and went about loading it with care so the dog wouldn't suffer unduly.

Vitória shut herself up in the bedroom, dragging the children with her. They were frightened and, sensing misfortune, kept asking, "Is the dog going to be hurt?"

They had seen the lead shot and the powder horn, and Fabiano's gestures worried them, causing them to suspect that the dog was in danger.

She was like a member of the family. There was hardly any differ-

Ramos, Graciliano. *Barren Lives*, translated by Ralph Edward Dimmick, 86–92. Austin: University of Texas Press, 1973.

ence to speak of between her and the boys. The three of them played together, rolling in the sand of the riverbed or in the loose manure, which, as it piled up, threatened to cover the goat pen.

The boys tried to push the latch and open the door, but Vitória dragged them over to the bed of tree branches, where she did her best to stop their ears, holding the head of the older between her thighs and putting her hands over the ears of the younger. Angry at the resistance they offered, she tried to hold them down by force, grumbling fiercely the while.

She too had a heavy heart, but she was resigned. Obviously Fabiano's decision was necessary and just. The poor dog!

Listening, she heard the noise of the shot being poured down the barrel of the gun, and the dull taps of the ramrod on the wadding. She sighed. The poor dog!

The boys began to yell and kick. Vitória had relaxed her muscles, and the bigger one was able to escape. She swore.

"Limb of Satan!"

In the struggle to get hold of the rebel again she really lost her temper. The little devil! She gave him a crack on the head, which he had plunged under the bedcovers and her flowered skirt.

Gradually her wrath diminished and, rocking the children, she began grumbling about the sick dog, muttering harsh names and expressions of contempt. The sight of the slobbering animal was enough to turn your stomach. It wasn't right for a mad dog to go running loose in the house. But then she realized she was being too severe. She thought it unlikely that the dog had gone mad and wished her husband had waited one more day to see whether it was really necessary to put the animal out of the way.

At that moment Fabiano was walking in the shed, snapping his fingers. Vitória drew in her neck and tried to cover her ears with her shoulders. As this was impossible, she raised her arms and, without letting go of her son, managed to cover a part of her head.

Fabiano walked through the lean-to, staring off toward the brauna trees and the gates, setting an invisible dog on invisible cattle.

"Sic 'em, sic 'em."

Crossing the sitting room and the corridor, he came to the low kitchen window, from which, on examining the yard, he saw the dog scratching herself, rubbing the bare spots of her hide against the Jerusalem thorn. Fabiano raised the musket to his cheek. The dog eyed her master distrustfully and slipped sulkily around to the other side of the tree trunk, where she crouched with only her black eyes showing. Bothered by this maneuver on her part, Fabiano leaped out the window and stole along the corral fence to the corner post, where he again raised the arm to his cheek. As the animal was turned toward him and did not offer a very good target, he took a few more steps. On reaching the catingueira trees, he adjusted his aim and pulled the trigger. The load hit the dog in the hindquarters, putting one leg out of action. The dog began to yelp desperately.

Hearing the shot and the yelps, Vitória called upon the Virgin Mary, while the boys rolled on the bed, weeping aloud. Fabiano withdrew.

The dog fled in haste. She rounded the clay pit, went through the little garden to the left, passed close by the pinks and the pots of worm-wood, slipped through a hole in the fence, and reached the yard, run-ning on three legs. She had taken the direction of the shed but, fearing to meet Fabiano, she withdrew toward the goat pen. There she stopped for a moment, not knowing where to go, and then set off again, hop-ping along aimlessly.

In front of the oxcart her other back leg failed her, but, though bleeding profusely, she continued on her two front legs, dragging her hindquarters along as best she could. She wanted to retreat under the cart, but she was afraid of the wheel. She directed her course toward the jujube trees. There under one of the roots was a deep hole full of soft dirt in which she liked to wallow, covering herself with dust against the flies and gnats. When she would arise, with dry leaves and twigs sticking to her sores, she was a very different-looking animal.

She fell before reaching this distant refuge. She tried to get up, rais-ing her head and stretching out her forelegs, but her body remained on its flank. In this twisted position she could scarcely move, though she scraped with her paws, digging her nails into the ground, pulling at the small pebbles. Finally, she dropped and lay quiet beside the heap of stones where the boys threw dead snakes.

A horrible thirst burned her throat. She tried to look at her legs but couldn't make them out, for a mist veiled her sight. A desire came over her to bite Fabiano. She set up a yelp, but it was not really a yelp, just a faint howl that grew weaker and weaker until it was almost impercep-tible.

Finding the sun dazzling, she managed to inch into a sliver of shade at the side of the stones.

She looked at herself again, worried. What was happening to her? The mist seemed ever thicker and closer.

A good smell of cavies* drifted down to her from the hill, but it was faint and mingled with that of other creatures. The hill seemed to have grown far, far away. She wrinkled her muzzle, breathing the air slowly, desirous of climbing the slope and giving chase to the cavies, as they jumped and ran about in freedom.

She began to pant with difficulty, feigning a bark. She ran her tongue over her parched lips, but felt no relief. The smell was ever fainter: the cavies must certainly have fled.

She forgot them and once more had the desire to bite Fabiano, who

---

* Guinea pigs.—Trans

appeared before her half-glazed eyes with a strange object in his hand. She didn't recognize it, but she began to tremble, sure that it held a disagreeable surprise for her. She made an effort to avoid it, pulling in her tail. Deciding it was out of harm's way, she closed her leaden eyes. She couldn't bite Fabiano; she had been born near him, in a bedroom, under a bed of tree branches, and her whole life had been spent in submission to him, barking to round up the cattle when the herdsman clapped his hands.

The unknown object continued to threaten her. She held her breath, covered her teeth, and peered out at her enemy from under her drooping eyelids. Thus she remained for some time, and then grew quiet. Fabiano and the dangerous thing had gone away.

With difficulty she opened her eyes. Now there was a great darkness. The sun must certainly have disappeared.

The bells of the goats tinkled down by the riverside; the strong smell of the goat pen spread over the surroundings.

The dog gave a start. What were those animals doing out at night? It was her duty to get up and lead them to the water hole. She dilated her nostrils, trying to make out the smell of the children. She was surprised by their absence.

She had forgotten Fabiano. A tragedy had occurred, but the dog did not see in it the cause of her present helplessness nor did she perceive that she was free of responsibilities. Anguish gripped at her small heart. She must mount guard over the goats. At that hour there should be a smell of jaguars along the riverbanks and in the distant tree clumps. Fortunately the boys were sleeping on the straw mat under the corner shelf, where Vitória kept her pipe.

A cold, misty, winter night enveloped the little creature. There was no sound or sign of life in the surroundings. The old rooster did not crow on his perch, nor did Fabiano snore in the bed of tree branches. These sounds were not in themselves of interest to the dog, but when the rooster flapped his wings and Fabiano turned over, familiar emanations let her know of their presence. Now it seemed as if the ranch had been abandoned.

The dog took quick breaths, her mouth open, her jaw sagging, her tongue dangling, void of feeling. She didn't know what had happened. The explosion, the pain in her haunch, her difficult trip from the clay pit to the back of the yard faded out of her mind.

She was probably in the kitchen, in among the stones on which the cooking was done. Before going to bed, Vitória raked out the coals and ashes, swept the burnt area of the earthen floor with a broom, and left a fine place for a dog to take its rest. The heat kept fleas away and made the ground soft. And when she finally dozed off, a throng of cavies invaded the kitchen, running and leaping.

A shiver ran up the dog's body, from her belly to her chest. From her chest down, all was insensibility and forgetfulness, but the rest of her body quivered, and cactus spines penetrated the flesh that had been half eaten away by sickness.

The dog leaned her weary head on a stone. The stone was cold; Vitória must have let the fire go out very early.

The dog wanted to sleep. She would wake up happy, in a world full of cavies, and would lick the hands of Fabiano—a Fabiano grown to enormous proportions. The boys would roll on the ground with her in an enormous yard, would wallow with her in an enormous goat pen. The world would be full of cavies, fat and huge.

9.4 Pablo Neruda: Memoirs

Chilean poet Pablo Neruda published his first poems in 1921 at the age of 17. He served Chile as a consul, first in the Far East and then in Spain, from 1934 to 1938. He lived for a short period in Mexico and then returned to Chile as a member of the Communist Party. He dabbled in the country's politics and was elected to the Chilean Senate in 1945; because of his political affiliations he went into exile in 1948. He did not return to Chile until 1953, two years after he had been awarded the Stalin Peace Prize for his poetry. Two years before his death in 1973, he was honored with the Nobel Prize for literature. Some of Neruda's poetry was written under the tensions of ideological conflict and political crisis. Neruda believed that art and literary expression were related to historical and political contexts. He was firmly committed to sharing his poetry with the common, working man, as this reading illustrates.

The Power of Poetry

It has been the privilege of our time—with its wars, revolutions, and tremendous social upheavals—to cultivate more ground for poetry than anyone had ever imagined. The common man has had to confront it, attacking or attacked, in solitude or with an enormous mass of people at public rallies.

When I wrote my first lonely books, it never entered my mind that,

Neruda, Pablo. *Memoirs*, 253–55. New York: Penguin, 1978.

with the passing years, I would find myself in squares, streets, factories, lecture halls, theaters, and gardens, reading my poems. I have gone into practically every corner of Chile, scattering my poetry like seed among the people of my country. . . .

How should I handle this audience? What could I speak to them about? What things in my life would hold their interest? I could not make up my mind, but disguising my desire to run out of there, I took the book I was carrying with me and said to them: "I was in Spain a short time back. A lot of fighting and a lot of shooting were going on there. Listen to what I've written about it."

I should explain that my book *España en el corazón* has never seemed to me an easy book to understand. It tries to be clear, but it is steeped in the torrent of overwhelming and painful events.

Well, I thought I would just read a handful of poems, add a few words, and say goodbye. But it didn't work out that way. Reading poem after poem, hearing the deep well of silence into which my words were falling, watching those eyes and dark eyebrows following my verses so intently, I realized that my book was hitting its mark. I went on reading and reading, affected by the sound of my own poetry, shaken by the magnetic power that linked my poems and those forsaken souls.

The reading lasted more than an hour. As I was about to leave, one of the men rose to his feet. He was one of those who had a sack knotted around his waist. "I want to thank you for all of us," he spoke out. "I want to tell you, too, that nothing has ever moved us so much."

When he finished talking, he couldn't hold back a sob. Several others were also weeping. I walked out into the street between moist eyes and rough handclasps.

Can a poet still be the same after going through these trials of fire and ice?

9.5 Derek Walcott: A Sea Chantey

Born on January 23, 1930, in Castries on the island of Saint Lucia, Derek Walcott was educated at St. Mary's College there and at the University of West Indies in Jamaica. He worked as a teacher in Jamaica,

Walcott, Derek. "A Sea-Chantey," in *Derek Walcott, Collected Poems, 1948–1984*, 44–46. New York: Farrar, Straus & Giroux, 1986.

*Saint Lucia, and Grenada before settling in Trinidad. Walcott is gener-
ally regarded as the Caribbean's most notable playwright/poet; his writings
emphasize an important dimension of the cultural and historical evolution
of the Caribbean: its polychromatic ethnic and cultural diversity. The following poem expresses Walcott's appreciation for the "rosary" of the ar-
chipelago islands.*

A Sea Chantey

> *Là, tout n'est qu'ordre et beauté,*
> *Luxe, calme, et volupté.*
> —Baudelaire

Anguilla, Adina,
Antigua, Cannelles,
Andreuille, all the *l*'s,
Voyelles, of the liquid Antilles,
The names tremble like needles
Of anchored frigates,
Yachts tranquil as lilies,
In ports of calm coral,
The lithe, ebony hulls
Of strait-stitching schooners,
The needles of their masts
That thread archipelagoes
Refracted embroidery
In feverish waters
Of the seafarer's islands,
Their shorn, leaning palms,
Shaft of Odysseus,
Cyclopic volcanoes,
Creak their own histories,
In the peace of green anchorage;
Flight, and Phyllis,
Returned from the Grenadines,
Names entered this Sabbath,
In the port clerk's register;
Their baptismal names,
The sea's liquid letters,
Repos donnez à cils . . .
And their blazing cargoes
Of charcoal and oranges;
Quiet, the fury of their ropes.

Daybreak is breaking
On the green chrome water,
The white herons of yachts
Are at Sabbath communion,
The histories of the schooners
Are murmured in coral,
Their cargoes of sponges
On sandpits of islets,
Barques white as white salt
Of acrid St. Maarten,
Hulls crusted with barnacles,
Holds foul with great turtles,
Whose ship-boys have seen
The blue heave of Leviathan,
A seafaring, Christian,
And trepid people.

Now an apprentice washes his cheeks
With salt water and sunlight.

In the middle of the harbour
A fish breaks the Sabbath
With a silvery leap.
The scales fall from him
In a tinkle of church bells;
The town streets are orange
With the week-ripened sunlight,
Balanced on the bowsprit
A young sailor is playing
His grandfather's chantey
On a trembling mouth organ;
The music curls, dwindling
Like smoke from blue galleys,
To dissolve near the mountains.
The music uncurls with
The soft vowels of inlets,
The christening of vessels,
The titles of portages,
The colours of sea grapes,
The tartness of sea-almonds,
The alphabet of church bells,
The peace of white horses,
The pastures of ports,
The litany of islands,
The rosary of archipelagoes,
Anguilla, Antigua,

Virgin of Guadeloupe,
A stone-white Grenada
Of sunlight and pigeons,
The amen of calm waters,
The amen of calm waters,
The amen of calm waters.

9.6 Poetry of Gabriela Mistral

Gabriela Mistral was the first Latin American writer to be awarded the Nobel Prize for literature, in 1945. Born in 1889 in Chile, Mistral spent her early years as a teacher in the countryside. When she was 25 her poems began to gain fame. Some had been published in a French fashion magazine, Elegancias, *whose editor was Rubén Darío. In 1922 a Mexican government official, José Vasconcelos, invited Mistral to Mexico to help him develop an ambitious program of educational reform that included teaching Indian adults and rural children. Mistral combined her literary energy with an intense commitment to improving elementary and secondary education throughout Latin America. In fact, her last public appearance, shortly before her death in 1957, was at a high school on Long Island, New York, where she spoke informally with U.S. students studying Spanish. Today, many schools throughout the region are named after her. Mistral's poetry—its rhythm, music, and imagery—was unique in its time. Another unique aspect of her work was the diversity of themes, ranging from school and children to nature, time, and sorrow. The following poem illustrates the vigor she brought to her poetry.*

Morning

She has returned! She has returned!
Each morning the same and new.
Awaited every yesterday,
she must return this morning.

Mistral, Gabriela. "Morning." In *Selected Poems of Gabriela Mistral*, edited and translated by Doris Dana, 162. Baltimore: Johns Hopkins University Press, 1971.

Mornings of empty hands
that promised and betrayed.
Behold this new morning unfold,
leap like a deer from the East,
awake, happy and new,
alert, eager and rich with deeds.

Brother, raise up your head
fallen to your breast. Receive her.
Be worthy of her who leaps up,
soars and darts like a halcyon,
golden halcyon plunging earthward singing
Alleluia, alleluia, alleluia!

9.7 The Shape of the Sword

Jorge Luis Borges's literary creativity found its primary expression in the short story. Born in 1899, he was educated in Geneva and then lived in Spain for a period before returning to his native country. Although Argentine by birth, Borges had a consuming interest in universal literature and was widely read throughout the world. Indeed, his work was often criticized by fellow countrymen as non-Argentine. Borges's fiction focuses on the process of striving, which leads to discovery and insight. Unlike the writing of many Latin Americans of his time, much of Borges's work has been translated into English, including the passage that follows.

A spiteful scar crossed his face: an ash-colored and nearly perfect arc that creased his temple at one tip and his cheek at the other. His real name is of no importance; everyone in Tacuarembó called him the "Englishman from La Colorada." Cardoso, the owner of those fields, refused to sell them: I understand that the Englishman resorted to an unexpected argument: he confided to Cardoso the secret of the scar. The Englishman came from the border, from Río Grande del Sur; there are many who say that in Brazil he had been a smuggler. The fields were overgrown with grass, the waterholes brackish; the Englishman,

Borges, Jorge Luis. "The Shape of the Sword." In *Labyrinths: Selected Stories and Other Writings*, 67–72. New York: New Directions, 1964.

in order to correct those deficiencies, worked fully as hard as his labor-ers. They say that he was severe to the point of cruelty, but scrupu-lously just. They say also that he drank: a few times a year he locked himself into an upper room, not to emerge until two or three days later as if he from a battle or from vertigo, pale, trembling, confused and as authoritarian as ever. I remember the glacial eyes, the energetic lean-ness, the gray mustache. He had no dealings with anyone; it is a fact that his Spanish was rudimentary and cluttered with Brazilian. Aside from a business letter or some pamphlet, he received no mail.

The last time I passed through the northern provinces, a sudden overflowing of the Caraguatá stream compelled me to spend the night at La Colorada. Within a few moments, I seemed to sense that my ap-pearance was inopportune; I tried to ingratiate myself with the En-glishman; I resorted to the least discerning of passions: patriotism. I claimed as invincible a country with such spirit as England's. My com-panion agreed, but added with a smile that he was not English. He was Irish, from Dungarvan. Having said this, he stopped short, as if he had revealed a secret.

After dinner we went outside to look at the sky. It had cleared up, but beyond the low hills the southern sky, streaked and gashed by light-ning, was conceiving another storm. Into the cleared up dining room the boy who had served dinner brought a bottle of rum. We drank for some time, in silence.

I don't know what time it must have been when I observed that I was drunk; I don't know what inspiration or what exultation or tedium made me mention the scar. The Englishman's face changed its expres-sion; for a few seconds I thought he was going to throw me out of the house. At length he said in his normal voice:

"I'll tell you the history of my scar under one condition: that of not mitigating one bit of the opprobrium, of the infamous circumstances."

I agreed. This is the story he told me, mixing his English with Span-ish, and even with Portuguese.

"Around 1922, in one of the cities of Connaught, I was one of the many who were conspiring for the independence of Ireland. Of my comrades, some are still living, dedicated to peaceful pursuits; others, paradoxically, are fighting on desert and sea under the English flag; another, the most worthy, died in the courtyard of a barracks, at dawn, shot by men filled with sleep; still others (not the most fortunate) met their destiny in the anonymous and almost secret battles of the civil war. We were Republicans, Catholics; we were, I suspect, Romantics. Ireland was for us not only the utopian future and the intolerable pre-sent; it was a bitter and cherished mythology, it was the circular towers and the red marshes, it was the repudiation of Parnell and the enor-mous epic poems which sang of the robbing of bulls which in another incarnation were heroes and in others fish and mountains . . . One afternoon I will never forget, an affiliate from Munster joined us: one John Vincent Moon.

"He was scarcely twenty years old. He was slender and flaccid at the same time; he gave the uncomfortable impression of being invertebrate. He had studied with fervor and with vanity nearly every page of Lord knows what Communist manual; he made use of dialectical materialism to put an end to any discussion whatever. The reasons one can have for hating another man, or for loving him, are infinite: Moon reduced the history of the universe to a sordid economic conflict. He affirmed that the revolution was predestined to succeed. I told him that for a gentleman only lost causes should be attractive . . . Night had already fallen; we continued our disagreement in the hall, on the stairs, then along the vague streets. The judgments Moon emitted impressed me less than his irrefutable, apodictic note. The new comrade did not discuss; he dictated opinions with scorn and with a certain anger.

"As we were arriving at the outlying houses, a sudden burst of gunfire stunned us. (Either before or afterwards we skirted the blank wall of a factory or barracks.) We moved into an unpaved street; a soldier, huge in the firelight, came out of a burning hut. Crying out, he ordered us to stop. I quickened my pace; my companion did not follow. I turned around: John Vincent Moon was motionless, fascinated, as if eternized by fear. I then ran back and knocked the soldier to the ground with one blow, shook Vincent Moon, insulted him and ordered him to follow. I had to take him by the arm; the passion of fear had rendered him helpless. We fled, into the night pierced by flames. A rifle volley reached out for us, and a bullet nicked Moon's right shoulder; as we were fleeing amid pines, he broke out in weak sobbing.

"In that fall of 1923 I had taken shelter in General Berkeley's country house. The general (whom I had never seen) was carrying out some administrative assignment or other in Bengal; the house was less than a century old, but it was decayed and shadowy and flourished in puzzling corridors and in pointless antechambers. The museum and the huge library usurped the first floor: controversial and uncongenial books which in some manner are the history of the nineteenth century; scimitars from Nishapur, along whose captured arcs there seemed to persist still the wind and violence of battle. We entered (I seem to recall) through the rear. Moon, trembling, his mouth parched, murmured that the events of the night were interesting; I dressed his wound and brought him a cup of tea; I was able to determine that his 'wound' was superficial. Suddenly he stammered in bewilderment:

" 'You know, you ran a terrible risk.'

"I told him not to worry about it. (The habit of the civil war had incited me to act as I did; besides, the capture of a single member could endanger our cause.)

"By the following day Moon had recovered his poise. He accepted a cigarette and subjected me to a severe interrogation on the 'economic resources of our revolutionary party.' I told him (truthfully) that the situation was serious. Deep bursts of rifle fire agitated the south. I told Moon our comrades were waiting for us. My overcoat and my revolver were in my room; when I returned, I found Moon stretched out on the sofa, his eyes closed. He imagined he had a fever; he invoked a painful spasm in his shoulder.

"At that moment I understood that his cowardice was irreparable. I clumsily entreated him to take care of himself and went out. This frightened man mortified me, as if I were the coward, not Vincent Moon. Whatever one man does, it is as if all men did it. For that reason it is not unfair that one disobedience in a garden should contaminate all humanity; for that reason it is not unjust that the crucifixion of a single Jew should be sufficient to save it. Perhaps Schopenhauer was right: I am all other men, any man is all men, Shakespeare is in some manner the miserable John Vincent Moon.

"Nine days we spent in the general's enormous house. Of the agonies and the successes of the war I shall not speak: I propose to relate the history of the scar that insults me. In my memory, those nine days form only a single day, save for the next to the last, when our men broke into a barracks and we were able to avenge precisely the sixteen comrades who had been machine-gunned in Elphin. I slipped out of the house towards dawn, in the confusion of daybreak. At nightfall I was back. My companion was waiting for me upstairs: his wound did not permit him to descend to the ground floor. I recall him having some volume of strategy in hand, F. N. Maude or Clausewitz. 'The weapon I prefer is the artillery,' he confessed to me one night. He inquired into our plans; he liked to censure them or revise them. He also was accustomed to denouncing 'our deplorable economic basis'; dogmatic and gloomy, he predicted the disastrous end. *'C'est une affaire flambée,'* he murmured. In order to show that he was indifferent to being a physical coward, he magnified his mental arrogance. In this way, for good or for bad, nine days elapsed.

"On the tenth day the city fell definitely to the Black and Tans. Tall, silent horsemen patrolled the roads; ashes and smoke rode on the wind; on the corner I saw a corpse thrown to the ground, an impression less firm in my memory than that of a dummy on which the soldiers endlessly practiced their marksmanship, in the middle of the square . . . I had left when dawn was in the sky; before noon I returned. Moon, in the library, was speaking with someone; the tone of his voice told me he was talking on the telephone. Then I heard my name; then, that I would return at seven; then, the suggestion that they should arrest me as I was crossing the garden. My reasonable friend was reasonably selling me out. I heard him demand guarantees of personal safety.

"Here my story is confused and becomes lost. I know that I pursued the informer along the black, nightmarish halls and along deep stairways of dizzyness. Moon knew the house very well, much better than I. One or two times I lost him. I cornered him before the soldiers stopped me. From one of the general's collections of arms I tore a cutlass: with that half moon I carved into his face forever a half moon of blood. Borges, to you, a stranger, I have made this confession. Your contempt does not grieve me so much."

Here the narrator stopped. I noticed that his hands were shaking.

"And Moon?" I asked him.

"He collected his Judas money and fled to Brazil. That afternoon, in the square, he saw a dummy shot up by some drunken men."

I waited in vain for the rest of the story. Finally I told him to go on. Then a sob went through his body; and with a weak gentleness he pointed to the whitish curved scar.

"You don't believe me?" he stammered. "Don't you see that I carry written on my face the mark of my infamy? I have told you the story thus so that you would hear me to the end. I denounced the man who protected me: I am Vincent Moon. Now despise me."

To E. H. M.

Translated by D. A. Y.

9.8 Gabriel García Márquez: Nobel Speech

Gabriel García Márquez, born in Aracataca, Colombia, in 1928, was the oldest of 16 children. His experiences in the small town served as the inspiration for Macondo, a village in which fantasy and reality intermingle in his most famous novel, One Hundred Years of Solitude. *A journalist by vocation, García Márquez began his writing career at the newspaper* El Espectador, *in Bogotá. He later resigned in protest over military interference in his journalistic work, moved to Mexico in 1961, and later to Spain. A political activist, García Márquez has been a strong supporter of Fidel Castro and an advocate for social justice in Latin America.*

García Márquez, Gabriel. "The Solitude of Latin America." In *Lives on the Line: The Testimony of Contemporary Latin American Authors,* translated by Marina Castañeda and edited by Doris Meyer. Berkeley: University of California Press, 1988.

In 1982 he was awarded the Nobel Prize for literature, the fourth Latin American author to be so honored. The following reading is his acceptance speech, in which he supports the cause of self-determination and encourages the region's efforts to eradicate injustice.

Antonio Pigafetta, a Florentine navigator who went with Magellan on the first voyage around the world, wrote, upon his passage through our southern lands of America, a strictly accurate account that nonetheless resembles a venture into fantasy.

In it he recorded that he had seen hogs with navels on their haunches, clawless birds whose hens laid eggs on the backs of their mates, and others still, resembling tongueless pelicans, with beaks like spoons. He wrote of having seen a misbegotten creature with the head and ears of a mule, a camel's body, the legs of a deer and the whinny of a horse. He described how the first native encountered in Patagonia was confronted with a mirror, whereupon that impassioned giant lost his senses to the terror of his own image.

This short and fascinating book, which even then contained the seeds of our present-day novels, is by no means the most staggering account of our reality in that age.

The Chroniclers of the Indies left us countless others. El Dorado, our so avidly sought and illusory land, appeared on numerous maps for many a long year, shifting its place and form to suit the fantasy of cartographers. In his search for the fountain of eternal youth, the mythical Alvar Núñez Cabeza de Vaca explored the north of Mexico for eight years, in a deluded expedition whose members devoured each other and only five of whom returned, of the 600 who had undertaken it. One of the many unfathomed mysteries of that age is that of the 11,000 mules, each loaded with 100 pounds of gold, that left Cuzco one day to pay the ransom of Atahualpa and never reached their destination. Subsequently, in colonial times, hens were sold in Cartegena de Indias that had been raised on alluvial land and whose gizzards contained tiny lumps of gold. One founder's lust for gold beset us until recently. As late as the last century, a German mission appointed to study the construction of an inter-oceanic railroad across the Isthmus of Panama concluded that the project was feasible on one condition: that the rails not be made of iron, which was scarce in the region, but of gold.

Our independence from Spanish domination did not put us beyond the reach of madness. General Antonio López de Santana, three times dictator of Mexico, held a magnificent funeral for the right leg he had lost in the so-called Pastry War. General Gabriel García Moreno ruled Ecuador for sixteen years as an absolute monarch; at his wake, the corpse was seated on the presidential chair, decked out in full-dress uniform and a protective layer of medals. General Maximiliano Hernández Martínez, the theosophical despot of El Salvador who had 30,000 peasants slaughtered in a savage massacre, invented a pendulum to detect poison in his food, and had street lamps draped in red paper to defeat an epidemic of scarlet fever. The statue to General Francisco Morazán erected in the main square of Tegucigalpa is actually one of Marshal Ney, purchased at a Paris warehouse of second-hand sculptures.

Eleven years ago, the Chilean Pablo Neruda, one of the outstanding poets of our time, enlightened this audience with his words. Since then, the Europeans of good will—and sometimes those of bad, as well—have been struck, with ever greater force, by the unearthly tidings of Latin America, that boundless realm of haunted men and historic women, whose unending obstinacy blurs into legend.

We have not had a moment's rest. A promethean president, entrenched in his burning palace, died fighting an entire army, alone; and two suspicious airplane accidents, yet to be explained, cut short the life of another great-hearted president and that of a democratic soldier who had revived the dignity of his people.

There have been 5 wars and 17 military coups; there emerged a diabolic dictator who is carrying out, in God's name, the first Latin American ethnocide of our time. In the meantime, 20 million Latin American children died before the age of one—more than have been born in Europe since 1970. Those missing because of repression number nearly 120,000, which is as if no one could account for all the inhabitants of Uppsala. Numerous women arrested while pregnant have given birth in Argentine prisons, yet nobody knows the whereabouts and identity of their children, who were furtively adopted or sent to an orphanage by order of the military authorities. Because they tried to change this state of things, nearly 200,000 men and women have died throughout the continent, and over 100,000 have lost their lives in three small and ill-fated countries of Central America: Nicaragua, El Salvador, and Guatemala. If this had happened in the United States, the corresponding figure would be that of 1,600,000 violent deaths in four years.

One million people have fled Chile, a country with a tradition of hospitality—that is, 10 percent of its population. Uruguay, a tiny nation of two and a half million inhabitants, which considered itself the continent's most civilized country, has lost to exile one out of every five citizens. Since 1979, the civil war in El Salvador has produced almost one refugee every 20 minutes. The country that could be formed of all the exiles and forced emigrants of Latin America would have a population larger than that of Norway.

I dare to think that it is this outsized reality, and not just its literary expression, that has deserved the attention of the Swedish Academy of Letters. A reality not of paper, but one that lives within us and determines each instant of our countless daily deaths, and that nourishes a source of insatiable creativity, full of sorrow and beauty, of which this roving and nostalgic Colombian is but one cipher more, singled out by fortune. Poets and beggars, musicians and prophets, warriors and scoundrels, all creatures of that unbridled reality, we have had to ask but little of imagination, for our crucial problem has been a lack of conventional means to render our lives believable. This, my friends, is the crux of our solitude.

And if these difficulties, whose essence we share, hinder us, it is understandable that the rational talents on this side of the world, exalted in the contemplation of their own cultures, should have found themselves without a valid means to interpret us. It is only natural that they insist on measuring us with the yardstick that they use for themselves, forgetting that the ravages of life are not the same for all, and that the quest of our own identity is just as arduous and bloody for us as it was for them. The interpretation of our reality through patterns not our own serves only to make us ever more unknown, ever less free, ever more solitary.

Venerable Europe would perhaps be more perceptive if it tried to see us in its own past. If only it recalled that London took 300 years to build its first city wall, and 300 years more to acquire a bishop; that Rome labored in a gloom of uncertainty for 20 centuries, until an Etruscan king anchored it in history; and that the peaceful Swiss of today, who feast us with their mild cheeses and apathetic watches, bloodied Europe as soldiers of fortune as late as the sixteenth century. Even at the height of the Renaissance, 12,000 lansquenets in the pay of the imperial armies sacked and devastated Rome and put 8,000 of its inhabitants to the sword.

I do not mean to embody the illusions of Tonio Kroger, whose dreams of uniting a chaste north to a passionate south were exalted here 53 years ago by Thomas Mann. But I do believe that those clear-sighted Europeans who struggle, here as well, for a more just and humane homeland could help us far better if they reconsidered their way of seeing us. Solidarity with our dreams will not make us feel less alone, as long as it is not translated into concrete acts of legitimate support for all the peoples that assume the illusion of having a life of their own in the distribution of the world.

Latin America neither wants, nor has any reason, to be a pawn without a will of its own; nor is it merely wishful thinking that its quest for independence and originality should become a Western aspiration. However, the navigational advances that have narrowed such distances between our Americas and Europe seem, conversely, to have accentuated our cultural remoteness.

Why is the originality so readily granted us in literature so mistrustfully denied us in our different attempts at social change? Why think that the social justice sought by progressive Europeans for their own countries cannot also be a goal for Latin America, with different methods for dissimilar conditions? No: The immeasurable violence and pain of our history are the result of age-old inequities and untold bitterness, and not a conspiracy plotted 3,000 leagues from our homes. But many European leaders and thinkers have thought so, with the childishness of old-timers who have forgotten the fruitful excesses of their youth as if it were impossible to find another destiny than to live at the mercy of the two great masters of the world. This, my friends, is the very scale of our solitude.

In spite of this, to oppression, plundering and abandonment, we respond with life. Neither floods nor plagues, nor famines nor cataclysms, nor even the eternal wars of century upon century have been able to subdue the persistent advantage of life over death. An advantage that grows and quickens: Every year, there are 74 million more births than deaths, a sufficient number of new lives to multiply, each year, the population of New York sevenfold. Most of these births occur in the countries of least resources—including, of course, those of Latin America. Conversely, the most prosperous countries have succeeded in accumulating powers of destruction such as to annihilate, a hundred times over, not only all the human beings that have existed to this day but also the totality of all living beings that have ever drawn breath on this planet of misfortune.

On a day like today, my master William Faulkner said, "I decline to accept the end of man." I would feel unworthy of standing in this place that was his if I were not fully aware that the colossal tragedy he refused to recognize 32 years ago is now, for the first time since the beginning of humanity, nothing more than a simple scientific possibility. Faced with this awesome reality that must have seemed a mere utopia through all of human time, we, the inventors of tales, who will believe anything, feel entitled to believe that it is not yet too late to engage in the creation of the opposite utopia. A new and sweeping utopia of life, where no one will be able to decide for others how they die, where love will prove true and happiness be possible, and where the races condemned to one hundred years of solitude will have, at last and forever, a second opportunity on earth.

9.9   Art Thrives amid Violence

Despite terrorism and the threat of violence resulting from narcotics traf-
fickers in Colombia, cultural activity in the country has markedly in-
creased. Driven in part by growing literacy and urbanization, as well as
by the quality of the arts, Colombian citizens are responding in their own
unique ways to the daily tension provoked by violence, as this article illus-
trates.

Undeterred by threats from Colombia's drug lords to explode a car
bomb with five tons of dynamite in a crowded place, Bogotá is preparing to open some of the largest theater, book and visual arts festivals
ever in Latin America.

The inaugural Friday of the II Ibero-American Theater Festival, expected to draw more than one million people to downtown theaters
and open-air arenas, illustrates a bright side of Colombia that is little-
known—and seldom written about—abroad.

While Colombia is the most violent society in the Western Hemisphere—there have been about 80,000 homicides over the past four
years—it also is one of Latin America's premiere cultural centers. Colombia's theater, arts and literature are thriving as never before.

"In the face of so much violence, this is our best therapy," Fanny
Mikey, the theater festival's director, said in an interview this week.
"We take refuge in art to escape this gruesome reality we live in."

An "epidemic of culture" has overtaken Colombia in the past three
years, Mikey said. Indeed, the country has become Latin America's
leading book exporter and a major center for visual and performing
arts. Colombia's first theater festival two years ago attracted 1.2 million
people.

Among the most prominent visiting groups will be East Germany's
Berliner Ensemble, founded by playwright Bertold Brecht in 1946, which
will perform Brecht's Three Penny Opera; Hungary's Katona Jozsef
group, which will perform a play by Anton Chekhov; and Moscow's
Satyricon Company, which will present a Jean Genet play.

There will be four U.S. groups, one from Cuba—Teatro Irrumpe—
and one each from Britain, Denmark, France, Spain and most South
American countries. In all, they will perform 300 shows, most in downtown Bogotá theaters, with a few also in public squares.

Oppenheimer, Andres. "Culture, Arts, Thrive in Violence: Capital Takes Refuge in a
Renaissance." *Miami Herald,* April 5, 1990.

Despite widespread fears of a new wave of narco-terrorism this week, none of the theater groups has called off its visit, Mikey said.

Colombia's most powerful drug traffickers, in a weekend communique, threatened to explode a car bomb with five tons of dynamite "in an oligarchic neighborhood of Bogotá: as a response to the government's extradition of a drug smuggler to the United States last week."

The drug traffickers' announcement came after a reported break in indirect peace talks between officials of President Virgilio Barco's government and the drug barons.

Mikey, an Argentine-born actress who has lived in Colombia for more than three decades, said that the festival will not be canceled under any circumstances. More than 1,000 police officers will protect the visiting performers, and the public will be frisked at the entrance of theaters before every show.

A bomb explosion during Colombia's first theater festival two years ago did not keep people from attending subsequent shows, Mikey said.

"On the contrary, we had more people coming to the festival after the bomb than before," she said. "We have faith in this country. We want to demonstrate that we want to help this country go forward."

The performing-arts extravaganza is largely funded by ticket sales, relying on government funds for only 20 percent of its budget. Organizers cite this as evidence that the theater craze is a legitimate artistic phenomenon, and not an artificial event sponsored by the government to help lift public morale.

Unrelated to the theater festival but also opening this week in Bogotá is the 50th anniversary show of the National Artists' Exhibit, which will assemble the largest collection of Colombian art to date.

One thousand works of art from 455 Colombian artists—including Fernando Botero, Latin America's best-known living painter and sculptor—will be shown at the exhibit. The artwork will occupy 10,000 square yards of Bogotá's International Convention through May 4.

The third major cultural event scheduled to open this month will be the International Book Fair, expected to draw 120 publishing houses from more than a dozen countries. Organizers expect more than 150,000 people to visit the fair, which starts April 27.

Alejandro Reyes, a sociologist with Colombia's National University, said the cultural explosion results from a growing trend toward a more literate, urban society over the past two decades.

Unlike most other Latin American countries, Colombia's economy has not suffered from the foreign-debt crisis of the 1980s. While deep poverty is still visible, illiteracy rates are dropping, the number of university graduates is rising, and more low-income workers are buying their first homes.

10

Get Up, Stand Up: The Problems of Sovereignty

In their music, reggae poets like Mutabaruka express Jamaica's powerful sense of national identity. Courtesy Shanachie Recording Artist

Latin American and Caribbean countries, despite considerable diversity in their size, history, and cultural attributes, have all sought to establish their sovereignty. Components of sovereignty in the Americas include independence and nonintervention from external powers, and state control over the national territory.

In practice, major external and internal constraints have hampered the exercise of sovereignty in the region. Political and diplomatic aspects of sovereignty intermix with economic and cultural issues. Can a country establish itself economically and forge a unique identity based on cultural attributes defined by national boundaries and history?

Sovereignty and Nonintervention

Sovereignty as a major national concern in Latin America emerged only after numerous efforts to unify the region during and after independence from Spain in the early 1800s. The most articulate proponent of this vision was Simón Bolívar, independence leader in the northern part of the continent. In his famous "Jamaica Letter" of 1815, which is included in Chapter 2, Bolívar argued for three Spanish American federations (Mexico and Central America; the Spanish countries of northern South America, Peru, and Bolivia; and the countries of southern South America). A decade later Bolívar called for a total unification of Spanish America. Yet by that time strong nationalist sentiments favored the creation of self-governing and independent republics.

Nonintervention as a basic element of sovereignty emerged in the late nineteenth century in response to Latin America's fear of European intervention to collect public and private debts. Opposition to foreign intervention was heightened and redirected throughout Latin America when it became obvious that the United States would use the Monroe Doctrine to justify its intervention in Latin America's internal affairs (see reading 10.1). Issued in 1823 by President James Monroe as a warning to European powers not to invade Latin America, the document lay dormant until the late nineteenth century. Then, U.S. interest in the Caribbean began to increase in response to complex motives, including the search for overseas markets and a strong cultural mission that embraced a sense of divine responsibility to spread good government and superior political culture. Latin America, however, never accepted the legitimacy of the Monroe Doctrine, as reading 10.2 illustrates.

Direct U.S. intervention to foster Panama's independence from Colombia in 1903, and the enunciation one year later of the Roosevelt Corollary justifying U.S. involvement in Latin America's domestic affairs (see reading 10.3), sent a clear message that Latin America and the United States differed significantly in their conceptions of sovereignty. The antagonisms and conflicts generated by these important differences have been repeatedly highlighted in the twentieth century by U.S. interventions in Panama, Haiti, Cuba, Mexico, the Dominican Republic, Nicaragua, Guatemala, and Grenada (see reading 10.4).

Throughout the first decade of the twentieth century, Latin American countries used a range of international forums through the Pan-American movement, a regionwide alliance of Latin American countries, to press for a legal U.S. commitment to nonintervention, as reading 10.5 illustrates. At the Montevideo Conference of 1933, the United States finally ratified a nonintervention treaty consistent with the new, more conciliatory approach to the region. The United States explicitly agreed that "no state has the right to intervene in the internal or external affairs of another."

Following World War II, Latin American countries and the United States reconfirmed their commitment to sovereignty and nonintervention as signatories to the charter of the Organization of American States (OAS). Article 3 of the 1948 charter states that "[i]nternational order consists essentially of respect for the personality, sovereignty, and independence of States . . ." Article 18 explicitly warns that "[n]o State or group of States has the right to intervene directly or indirectly, for any reason whatever in the internal or external affairs of any other State." The article further "prohibits not only armed force but also any other form of interference or attempted threat against the personality of the State or against its political, economic and cultural elements."

Contemporary Constraints on Sovereignty

In practice, however, sovereignty has proved to be a relative concept. Through overt and covert means and a mix of economic and military assistance, the United States has used its power and resources to intervene in the internal and external affairs of many Latin American and Caribbean countries during the post–World War II period, often violating its neighbors' sovereign rights.

In most instances, the justification for such intervention was framed by the Cold War—the struggle for ideological, economic, and political influence between the United States and the Soviet Union—which waned in the late 1980s. The Cold War tended to obscure the national and domestic sources of political instability in Latin America, but the U.S. tendency toward intervention has generally been justified in this era by fears of Soviet expansion in the Western Hemisphere.

Examples abound. During the mid-1950s, the U.S. government sponsored a covert operation in Guatemala that toppled the reform-minded government there. In the early 1960s, the United States supported an expeditionary force to overthrow the pro-Soviet revolutionary government of Fidel Castro in Cuba. In 1965 Pres. Lyndon B. Johnson sent U.S. Marines to the Dominican Republic to stop a civil war he perceived to be heading in the direction of a "new Cuba." In the early 1970s the United States actively sought to undermine the socialist government of Chile's Salvador Allende. A U.S. military force intervened on the Caribbean island of Grenada in 1983 to restore order following a deadly struggle between rival socialist factions then governing the country.

Resistance to U.S. intervention has been most forcefully expressed in the Cuban Revolution. Sovereignty has come to be defined there as successful opposition to the "colossus of the North" (see Chapter 11). Similarly, a major feature of Nicaragua's new nationalism after the 1979 revolution was anti-imperialism. Throughout much of the 1980s, the Nicaraguan government was engaged in a military struggle with counter-revolutionaries financed by the U.S. government and private groups.

Jamaica's Michael Manley made another important effort to assert sovereignty. From his post as prime minister (1972–80), Manley promoted a new nationalism featuring greater control by Jamaica over its national resources—including most importantly bauxite, Jamaica's key export. His policies also stressed economic independence from outside powers and an independent foreign policy (as conveyed in reading 10.6). During this period, there was a resurgence of national pride and popular culture. However, Jamaica could not overcome its vulnerability in the international economy and hostility from foreign powers, such as the United States. Manley's experiment in "democratic socialism" ended, as he and his party were voted out of office in the country's 1980 elections. But there were gains: a strong national identity was created, and Jamaica acquired a majority stake in its bauxite industry.

Although the United States has been the dominant external actor in the region during the twentieth century, other powers exercised considerable influence. The Cuban government under Fidel Castro, for example, forged close links with the Soviet Union in the 30-year period between 1960 and 1990.

Numerous Caribbean countries still maintain direct ties with their European colonizers. For example, British military forces have been encamped in Belize (formerly British Honduras) throughout much of the country's 20 years of independence because of Guatemala's claim over Belizean territory. It is likely that the British will stay until an agreement between Belize and Guatemala can be achieved.

Several Caribbean islands, including Puerto Rico, maintain special relations with larger, more industrialized countries. Guadeloupe and Martinique are still formally departments of France.

The continuing presence of the British in the South Atlantic was most sharply contested during the Malvinas/Falkland Islands War with Argentina in 1982, as was described in Chapter 3.

Sovereignty concerns based on territorial debates continue to be contentious issues between neighboring countries in Latin America. El Salvador and Honduras have not been able to resolve a lingering debate over disputed border areas which led to war in 1969. Colombia and Venezuela periodically threaten conflict over territorial limits. Deep hostilities exist between Ecuador and Peru over border areas held commonly by both countries. Venezuela and Guyana have still not resolved their differences over areas of the Orinoco Valley.

New Challenges to Sovereignty

But not all threats to sovereignty are external. In many Latin American and Caribbean countries the challenges to sovereignty come from powerful groups and individuals who question the legitimacy of state authority.

In some areas of Colombia, for instance, guerrilla groups control and govern large territorial expanses, challenging the authority of a government that they see as having failed to meet the needs of the people. In other areas, such as the poor neighborhoods of Medellín there is growing chaos and violence from gangs whose members are known as *sicarios,* often at the service of drug lords—powerful traffickers of cocaine who have amassed enormous wealth and influence.

Drug cartels threaten and use violence and corruption against government officials to undermine the legal system's authority and legitimacy. Strenuous efforts are being made to limit the influence of such groups. As reading 10.7 illustrates, a very high price has been paid by judges, political leaders, and the police, who have been on the retaliatory end of traffickers' violence, particularly in Colombia. Many Latin Americans argue that the problem of drugs is caused by demand in the United States and Europe, and that the United States is asking them to resolve a problem that is not theirs.

U.S. antinarcotics policies in Latin America often have led to charges of U.S. intervention in the internal affairs of countries most frequently associated with trafficking. For example, the U.S. military invasion of Panama, reflecting multiple motives, was partially justified on the basis of deposing a group of military officers tied to drug trafficking, as is described in reading 10.8. Far more frequent, however, is the intense U.S. pressure on Latin American countries to extradite their own citizens to face trafficking charges in U.S. courts. In response, in many countries a backlash rejecting U.S. demands and a resurgence of nationalism have emerged.

Countries of the Americas are caught in a double bind: allowing drug traffickers to subvert the state and bring about national disintegration, or permitting violations of their sovereignty by allowing the United States to conduct its war on drugs freely. This dilemma illustrates the continuing search to balance sovereignty and autonomy with the realities of international power and the occurrence of new domestic threats.

10.1 The Monroe Doctrine

The Monroe Doctrine is the first formal statement of interest in Latin America by the United States. Issued by U.S. President James Monroe in a message to Congress in December 1823, the statement reflected growing concern in the United States that European powers would encourage Spain to reimpose its rule over newly independent Latin American countries. In practice, the declaration had no direct impact because the United States had little military capability to extend its influence. However, it was an early statement of U.S. intentions to constrain Latin America's independence, and it was later used to justify U.S. intervention in Latin America.

A precise knowledge of our relations with foreign powers as respects our negotiations and transactions with each is thought to be particularly necessary. . . .

At the proposal of the Russian Imperial Government, made through the minister of the emperor residing here, full power and instructions have been transmitted to the minister of the United States at St. Petersburg to arrange by amicable negotiation the respective rights and interests of the two nations on the northwest coast of this continent. A similar proposal had been made by His Imperial Majesty to the government of Great Britain, which has likewise been acceded to. The government of the United States has been desirous, by this friendly proceeding, of manifesting the great value which they have invariably attached to the friendship of the emperor and their solicitude to cultivate the best understanding with his government.

In the discussions to which this interest has given rise and in the arrangements by which they may terminate the occasion has been judged proper for asserting, as a principle in which the rights and interests of the United States are involved, that the American continents, by the free and independent conditions which they have assumed and maintain, are henceforth not to be considered as subjects for future colonization by any European powers. . . .

It was stated at the commencement of the last session that great effort was then making in Spain and Portugal to improve the condition of the people of those countries and that it appeared to be conducted with extraordinary moderation. It need scarcely be remarked that the

Monroe, James. "The Monroe Doctrine." In *The Evolution of Our Latin American Policy: A Documentary Record,* edited by James W. Gantenbein, 323–25. New York: Columbia University Press, 1950.

result has been so far very different from what was then anticipated. Of events in that quarter of the globe with which we have so much intercourse and from which we derive our origin, we have always been anxious and interested spectators. The citizens of the United States cherish sentiments the most friendly in favor of the liberty and happiness of their fellowmen on that side of the Atlantic. In the wars of the European powers in matters relating to themselves we have never taken any part, nor does it comport with our policy to do so. It is only when our rights are invaded or seriously menaced that we resent injuries or make preparation for our defense.

With the movements in this hemisphere we are of necessity more immediately connected, and by causes which must be obvious to all enlightened and impartial observers. The political system of the allied powers is essentially different in this respect from that of America. This difference proceeds from that which exists in their respective governments; and to the defense of our own, which has been achieved by the loss of so much blood and treasure, and matured by the wisdom of their most enlightened citizens, and under which we have enjoyed unexampled felicity, this whole nation is devoted. We owe it, therefore, to candor and to the amicable relations existing between the United States and those powers to declare that we should consider any attempt on their part to extend their system to any portion of this hemisphere as dangerous to our peace and safety.

With the existing colonies or dependencies of any European power we have not interfered and shall not interfere. But with the governments who have declared their independence and maintained it, and whose independence we have, on great consideration and on just principles, acknowledged, we could not view any interposition for the purpose of oppressing them, or controlling in any other manner their destiny, by any European power in any other light than as the manifestation of an unfriendly disposition toward the United States. In the war between those new governments and Spain we declared our neutrality at the time of their recognition, and to this we have adhered, and shall continue to adhere, provided no change shall occur which, in the judgment of the competent authorities of this government, shall make a corresponding change on the part of the United States indispensable to their security.

The late events in Spain and Portugal show that Europe is still unsettled. Of this important fact no stronger proof can be adduced than that the allied powers should have thought it proper, on any principle satisfactory to themselves, to have interposed by force in the internal concerns of Spain. To what extent such interposition may be carried, on the same principle, is a question in which all independent powers whose governments differ from theirs are interested, even those most remote, and surely none more so than the United States.

Our policy in regard to Europe, which was adopted at an early stage of the wars which have so long agitated that quarter of the globe, nevertheless remains the same, which is not to interfere in the internal concerns of any of its powers; to consider the government de facto as the legitimate government for us; to cultivate friendly relations with it, and to preserve those relations by a frank, firm, and manly policy, meeting in all instances the just claims of every power, submitting to injuries from none. But in regard to those continents, circumstances are eminently and conspicuously different. It is impossible that the allied powers should extend their political system to any portion of either continent without endangering our peace and happiness; nor can anyone believe that our southern brethren, if left to themselves, would adopt it of their own accord.

It is equally impossible, therefore, that we should behold such interposition in any form with indifference. If we look to the comparative strength and resources of Spain and those new governments, and their distance from each other, it must be obvious that she can never subdue them. It is still the true policy of the United States to leave the parties to themselves, in the hope that other powers will pursue the same course.

10.2 In Opposition to Monroe

The Monroe Doctrine was formulated in 1823 as a warning to Europeans not to intervene in the Western Hemisphere. In subsequent years, however, the United States used the statement as a means to justify U.S. involvement in Latin American affairs. This address, by Roque Saenz Peña, was delivered in 1898 in response to U.S. involvement in the Spanish-Cuban war, and is typical of Latin American responses to the U.S. violation of sovereignty. Roque Saenz Peña was a well-known and highly respected South American political leader who later became president of Argentina (1910–14).

The Doctrine of President Monroe, contained in the message of December [1823], was a declaration against intervention; but that decla-

Saenz Peña, Roque. "A Doctrine of Intervention." In *Latin America: Yesterday and Today*, edited by John Rothchild, 383–85. New York: Bantam, 1973.

ration contained mental reservations which rendered its objectives doubtful and its effects pernicious; in principle it condemned European interventions, but in fact it did not oppose American interventions, which means that it is not a general, scientific doctrine with unity of concept and principle but rather a national, specific act. It appears to the world as the whim of a strong and invincible power. . . .

That Doctrine in my opinion is the cause and origin of the present perversions of public law. The Mackinley *[sic]* doctrine is simply the fjlatest chapter in the Monroe Doctrine and the Polk doctrine; they are not three doctrines, they are three acts sanctifying a single usurpation: the intervention of the United States in the destinies and life of the people of the Americas.

When the divine-right governments of Europe were threatening to spread their system over this continent, the declaration of the United States was justified on political grounds, however much justification it may have lacked on juridical grounds: it was an arbitrary act opposing an illegal act. But in the present posture of law, diplomacy, and humanity both the arbitrary and the illegal ought to disappear. No American nation exists nor ever has existed with sufficient political and international capacity to assume to represent the entire continent and to serve as the spokesman for its free peoples; just as there never has existed a single foreign chancellery for the New World, so also there is no single sovereign for the hemisphere.

President Monroe's claims to authority were not only debatable: they were fictitious because no American state had delegated nor alienated its authority to determine its relations with other nations of the world. The warnings which Monroe directed toward Europe were not ratified by the new nations in whose name he spoke and whose destinies he undertook to dispose of; the so-called Doctrine did not emerge from the halls of Congress but remained an internal action without diplomatic or international ramifications. The essence of that Doctrine in fact was unacceptable not only to Europe, where it evoked protests from Russia and later from Great Britain, but also to the free nations of this continent. To condemn European interventions while at the same time reserving an American right of intervention and to exercise such a right unilaterally and without consultations is not in fact to censure intervention but rather to claim a monopoly of it. . . .

The position of the Latin-American states *vis à vis* a government which has taken over the officious management of the New World in relation to Europe is to ask: From what source did you obtain your solicitorship? Whence came your police authority and your inquisitorial powers over independent states which are no less inviolable than those of Europe? Will we have to search for them in the right of primogeniture, which is an accident of birth rather than law? Will we find them in the right of geographical proximity, which is an accident of nature and not reason?

We will have to conclude finally and emphatically that force creates doctrine, that the army establishes rights.

The Latin-American republics must vindicate, both by honor and title, the generous force of a new doctrine—a doctrine which was consecrated by Bolívar in convoking and organizing the Panama Congress. Bolívar possessed a sure insight into the future and was able to foresee from a distance that [Monroe's] message of December had its Achilles heel. . . .

The theme which Bolívar stressed in convoking that Congress consecrated the doctrine of non-intervention not against Europe but against every foreign power; that was the doctrine in its juridical and universal character; that was the true policy to which the peoples of the Americas aspired to in order to become sovereign and free not only in relation to Europe but in relation to all nations. But that redemptive doctrine of free nations which clipped the wings of the eagles of the Capitol provoked the discontent of the Cabinet in Washington to such an extent that the United States was not represented at Panama; one of its delegates arrived late and ill, and the other never arrived because he died on the way. Bolívar proposed not only to establish the true doctrine but also to elevate the stature of these republics by correcting the inert plasticity to which they had been reduced by the message of December 2; he wished to give them political capacity so that they could act of their own accord and strength when deciding their destinies or speaking in the name of America, or working under the care of the United States. . . .

10.3   The Roosevelt Corollary

U.S. intentions to intervene in Latin America evolved from the defensive claims of the Monroe Doctrine into the more aggressive interpretation of the Roosevelt Corollary, issued to the U.S. Congress in 1904 by Pres. Theodore Roosevelt. Conferring on the United States the role of international policeman and debt-collecting agency in the Western Hemisphere, the corollary provided a policy mandate for U.S. intervention in the

Roosevelt, Theodore. "The Roosevelt Corollary." In *A Compilation of the Messages and Speeches of Theodore Roosevelt*, vol. 2, edited by A. H. Lewis, 857. Washington: Bureau of National Literature and Art, 1906.

Caribbean and in Central America and directly challenged regional notions of sovereignty. Instances of this intervention include U.S. control
over the fiscal affairs of the Dominican Republic from 1905 to 1941, as
well as military intervention there from 1916 to 1924; the U.S. military
occupation of Haiti from 1915 to 1934; and the U.S. military occupation
of Nicaragua from 1912 to 1925 and from 1927 to 1933.

. . . If a nation shows that it knows how to act with reasonable effi-
ciency and decency in social and political matters; if it keeps order and
pays its obligations, it need fear no interference from the United States.
Chronic wrongdoing or an impotence which results in a general loos-
ening of ties of civilized society, may in America, as elsewhere, ultimately require intervention by some civilized nation, and in the Western Hemisphere the adherence of the United States to the Monroe
Doctrine may force the United States, however reluctantly, in flagrant
cases of such wrongdoing or impotence, to the exercise of an international police power. . . . It is a mere truism to say that every nation,
whether in America or anywhere else, which desires to maintain its
freedom, its independence must ultimately realize that the right of such
independence cannot be separated from the responsibility of making
good use of it.

10.4 In Defense of Monroe

U.S. and Latin American conceptions of sovereignty have differed mark-
edly in the twentieth century. Elihu Root, who served as secretary of war
(1899–1904) under President McKinley and as secretary of state (1905–
9) during the presidency of Theodore Roosevelt, enunciated the U.S. gov-
ernment's pro-Monroe position. A recognized legal scholar, Root was se-
lected by McKinley to administer a burgeoning colonial empire stretching
from the Philippines and Guam to Cuba and Puerto Rico. Under Presi-
dent Roosevelt, he helped craft U.S. policies promoting and justifying U.S.
intervention throughout the region. Years later, when he was president of
the American Society of International Law, Root provided the following

Root, Elihu. "The Real Monroe Doctrine." *American Journal of International Law* (1914):
427–42.

elaborate interpretation of the Monroe Doctrine, which linked indepen-
dence with sovereignty, but which acknowledged that size differences among
the region's states could result in the larger state's assuming "superior
authority."

As the particular occasions which called it forth have slipped back into
history, the declaration itself [the Monroe Doctrine], instead of being
handed over to the historian, has grown continually a more vital and
insistent rule of conduct for each succeeding generation of Americans.
Never for a moment have the responsible and instructed statesmen in
charge of the foreign affairs of the United States failed to consider
themselves bound to insist upon its policy. Never once has the public
opinion of the people of the United States failed to support every just
application of it as new occasion has arisen. Almost every President and
Secretary of State has restated the doctrine with vigor and emphasis in
the discussion of the diplomatic affairs of his day . . .

It seems fair to assume that a policy with such a history as this has
some continuing and substantial reason underlying it; that it is not out-
worn or meaningless or a purely formal relic of the past, and it seems
worth while to consider carefully what the doctrine is and what it is
not.

No one ever pretended that Mr. Monroe was declaring a rule of international law or that the doctrine which he declared has become international law. It is a declaration of the United States that certain acts
would be injurious to the peace and safety of the United States and
that the United States would regard them as unfriendly. The declaration does not say what the course of the United States will be in case
such acts are done. . . .

The Doctrine is not international law but it rests upon the right of
self-protection and that right is recognized by international law. The
right is a necessary corollary of independent sovereignty. It is well
understood that the exercise of the right of self-protection may and
frequently does extend in its effect beyond the limits of the territorial
jurisdiction of the state exercising it.

. . . The centuries of struggle to preserve the balance of power in
Europe all depend upon the very same principle which underlies the
Monroe Doctrine; that is to say, upon the right of every sovereign state
to protect itself by preventing a condition of affairs in which it will be
too late to protect itself. Of course each state must judge for itself when
a threatened act will create such a situation. If any state objects to a
threatened act and the reasonableness of its objection is not assented
to, the efficacy of the objection will depend upon the power behind it.

. . . Yet it is to be observed that in reference to the South American
governments, as in all other respects, the international right upon which
the declaration expressly rests is not sentiment or sympathy or a claim
to dictate what kind of government any other country shall have, but

the safety of the United States. It is because the new governments cannot be overthrown by the allied powers "without endangering our peace and happiness" that "the United States cannot behold such interposition in any form with indifference."

The Monroe Doctrine does not assert or imply or involve any right on the part of the United States to impair or control the independent sovereignty of any American state. In the lives of nations as of individuals, there are many rights unquestioned and universally conceded. The assertion of any particular right must be considered, not as excluding all others but as coincident with all others which are not inconsistent. The fundamental principle of international law is the principle of independent sovereignty. Upon that all other rules of international law rest. That is the chief and necessary protection of the weak against the power of the strong. Observance of that is the necessary condition to the peace and order of the civilized world. By the declaration of that principle the common judgment of civilization rewards to the smallest and weakest state the liberty to control its own affairs without interference from any other Power, however great.

The Monroe Doctrine does not infringe upon that right. It asserts the right. The declaration of Monroe was that the rights and interests of the United States were involved in maintaining a condition, and the condition to be maintained was the independence of all the American countries. It is "the free and independent condition which they have assumed and maintained" which is declared to render them not subject to future colonization. It is "the governments who have declared their independence and maintained it and whose independence we have on great consideration and on just principles acknowledged" that are not to be interfered with . . .

10.5 Latin America in Caricature

In the early 1900s, Latin American countries participated in a variety of international forums to push the United States to adopt a nonintervention policy. Within the United States, Latin America was frequently the target of cartoonists' humor and cynicism. The first cartoon depicts one cartoonist's view of U.S.–Latin American relations in mid-1906 shortly after the United States intervened in Panama and in the Dominican Republic. The idea for the cartoon was derived from U.S. participation in the Third International Conference of American States in Rio de Janeiro in 1906.

Guarding the Basket

Darling, J.N. "Ding." "Guarding the Basket." In *Latin America in Caricature*, John J. Johnson, p. 65. Austin: University of Texas Press, 1980.

The cartoon below depicts President Roosevelt's secretary of state Elihu Root, who ignores anti-intervention pleas from Latin American countries, the birds. At left is a cartoon interpretation of the results of the Sixth International Conference of American States, which met in Havana in early 1928. Here the head of the U.S. delegation is depicted as stopping an effort by Latin American countries to approve an anti-intervention resolution. The resolution was later adopted during the 1933 conference.

When the Pie was Open'd the Birds Began to Sing

Warren, Garnett. "When the Pie was Open'd the Birds Began to Sing." In *Latin America in Caricature*, John J. Johnson, p. 47. Austin: University of Texas Press, 1980.

10.6 Michael Manley on the Bauxite Production Levy

Many small states throughout Latin America and the Caribbean have been fundamentally concerned with the political and economic difficulties of establishing a unique national identity free of foreign intervention. In Jamaica, the bauxite industry was the largest center of capital investment, and it paid more in taxes than any island industry. However, it was entirely foreign owned and tended to pursue its own corporate objectives rather than Jamaica's national interests. During the 1970s, Michael Manley's party, the People's National Party, called for a policy of democratic socialism focusing on the importance of national sovereignty and local control over natural resources, including bauxite. In this selection, Manley explains the logic behind his government's effort to mobilize Jamaican nationalism by exercising sovereign rights over bauxite production.

We developed a policy with four main objectives. First, we were determined to increase drastically the revenue from the mining of bauxite and the production of alumina. Although we were mining 14 millions tons of raw bauxite a year and producing some 2½ million tons of alumina, the total revenues to the Jamaican government were only $25 million per annum. Some of the new alumina plants, which had been built in the late 1960s, had agreements under which they were paying virtually no revenue to the government at all. Clearly this had to be stopped. We decided to base taxation policy on a new concept. Bauxite was a commodity which we had to sell and which had a value. This value was to be derived from the total value of the aluminum ingot which is made from the bauxite. Taxation was to reflect a reasonable share of this total value accruing to the bauxite raw material. Further, if world inflation increased the price of the finished product, then the value of our bauxite was to increase accordingly and our tax revenue likewise.

Second, we were going to recover the use of our ore; under a series of complex laws and agreements, the multinational corporations acting in Jamaica had total control over the use of the one and a half billion tons of proven bauxite deposits in the island. They alone could decide the rate at which these deposits were used and the government had no

Manley, Michael. *The Politics of Change: A Jamaican Testament*, 258–62. Washington: Howard University Press, 1975.

rights whatsoever in this regard. This was an intolerable situation. . . .

Third, we were determined to re-acquire all the lands owned by the bauxite corporations. Some 200,000 acres of land had been sold outright to these companies which had complete surface rights. This made national agricultural planning difficult as it involved the tying up of major areas of agricultural land in foreign hands. Fourth, we intended to commence the process by which the bauxite industry could be brought under national majority ownership and control.

We were determined to avoid any political confrontations with either the United States of America or Canada when starting negotiations with the Aluminum Company of Canada, the Aluminum Company of America, the Kaiser Bauxite Corporation, the Reynolds Metal Corporation, the Revere Corporation, and the Anaconda Corporation. Consequently, I visited Pierre Trudeau, Prime Minister of Canada, and Dr. Henry Kissinger, Secretary of State of the United States, to explain our purpose in the bauxite negotiations and to assure them that the action which we proposed to take implied no political hostility towards our North American neighbours and friends. I explained in detail to both these distinguished leaders the economic rationale of what we were about to do. We then called in the presidents of all the corporations involved so that I could explain the new policies to them. Then the negotiations commenced. We decided to deal with the question of revenue first, but after nine weeks of bargaining, we could reach no agreement. It seemed that the corporations did not understand that we were serious and were reluctant to admit the reasonableness of our case. In the end, we were asking for an increase in tax revenue which would have added, if passed fully on to the consumer, six per cent to the price of aluminum ingot. We were seeking this when we had been required to pay more than 200 per cent increase for wheat. Our position seemed reasonable to us, but our view was not shared by the corporations. Consequently, they left us no choice but to act unilaterally and to impose the new taxation by legislation. I did this with considerable protest from the corporations.

There were muffled threats about the danger of American reprisals, to say nothing of the imminent collapse of the aluminum industry. However, confident that we were right, we hewed to our course and made it clear that no compromise was possible. What we had imposed was a production levy on all bauxite mined in Jamaica and tied this to a minimum level of annual production for each company so as to discourage tricks like cutting back production as an act of reprisal. The net effect of the levy in 1974 was to increase our revenue from the industry from $25 million a year to $200 million. This levy was based on a charge of 7½ per cent of the price of a ton of aluminum ingot as the share to be received for mining bauxite. Previously, Jamaica had been receiving an average of about one per cent of the value of aluminum ingot for each ton of bauxite mined. When it is recognized that it takes slightly less than five tons of bauxite to make a ton of aluminum ingot it can be readily seen that the former arrangement was less than fair. The new arrangement created a far more reasonable relationship between the value of the finished product and the benefit available to Jamaica for the use of the bauxite. Even as this postscript is being written, we have moved on from the production levy to the negotiation of the other items of our claim in the industry, and we are as determined as we were in the matter of taxation.

There were three major consequences of the negotiations for the Bauxite Production Levy, two intended and one arising because the situation ended as it did. The new revenue put us in a position to help finance the war on poverty and helped us turn the corner of the balance of payments crisis. Most of the money, however, is being put into a Capital Development Fund, since we regard this as a patrimony that must not be squandered but rather must be used to lay the economic and social foundations of a viable, independent nation. Then again the negotiations provided a great opportunity to practice the politics of participation. To begin with, the Bauxite Negotiating Team was comprised of a remarkable mixture of civil service, university, business, and legal talent. . . . Not only was this a first-class team, but in its very composition it symbolized a coming together of all of the intellectual and professional resources of the society. Apart from the team itself, which worked closely under the direction of the Sub-Committee of the Cabinet headed by me, we conducted elaborate briefing sessions for the trade unions, worker delegates, and shop stewards in the bauxite industry, with the members of the press and the information media generally, and amongst the institutional leaders such as the Jamaica Council of Churches, the Jamaica Manufacturers Association, the Jamaica Exporters Association, and the Chamber of Commerce. By the time the negotiations came to the breaking point, we had effectively mobilized the entire society behind our efforts. Thus, when the final moment of decision came, I was not alone. The decision to break the existing contracts with the companies and to impose a settlement unilaterally by legislative action was not an easy one to make. Contracts are binding, and the North American economic community is powerful; but contracts make little sense if they operate in changed circumstances to the avoidable disadvantage of either of the contracting parties; our case was just, our needs clear, and our duty wider than to ourselves alone. We were very conscious of a responsibility to the hopes of the Third World in what we did.

Whichever way the negotiations happened to go, they provided a magnificent opportunity for participatory politics. However, it is only because our talks broke down and we had the courage to act unilaterally that the third and last consequence could arise. This was the bringing into play for the first time in Jamaican experience all that range of emotions which are associated with the exercise of sovereignty. I have often felt that the Jamaican people lacked a heroic image of themselves and their own capabilities because we achieved independence rationally and without any real struggle. All the great chapters of our history in which the courage of the Jamaican people has been demonstrated are lost in the confused clouds that obscure the memory of slavery. The British can trace their courage from Agincourt through Waterloo to El Alamein. America's tradition stretches from Valley Forge through the Alamo to Iwo Jima. Our battles were fought by slaves and produced stories of epic courage, but we have yet to learn to remember them. Terrible as war and conflict are, the recollection of them can help to form a people's opinion of themselves. When we faced the multinational corporations and imposed our Production Levy, we were acting as a sovereign nation; we were risking whatever consequences might follow and the pulse of every Jamaican quickened a little bit, even if only for a short while. We were part of a new experience, an experience in which we had weighed all the odds and taken all the precautions, considered our course of action, known it to be just, faced the possibility of dire consequences, and, with our courage in our hands, had acted. Whatever else the future holds, the Jamaican people at the moment when I announced the Production Levy in the sovereign Parliament of our country knew what it was to be citizens of a sovereign, independent nation.

10.7 The Colombian Justice System

By the mid-1980s, the nations of the Americas were enjoying a rebirth of democracy. For most countries of the region, economics, foreign debt, and the threat of direct U.S. intervention in Central America were major concerns. Then came the challenge of drugs. At first, it seemed the drug trade was mainly a problem for the United States, where expanded awareness of the widespread use of drugs gradually became a national political issue. Soon, however, it became clear that the vast monies of the drug economy were overtaking and perverting Latin American countries. Drug cartels placed themselves outside the law, regularly challenging nations' ability to govern and provide minimal levels of law and order. Nowhere is this situation better illustrated than in Colombia, where a full-blown war between the government and drug traffickers began in 1986. Many of the country's politicians felt trapped between U.S. demands to extradite traffickers to the United States and the requirements of personal and national survival. Innovative policies were forged to respond to the twin pressures, as this newspaper account illustrates.

Colombia's ambitious effort to put drug traffickers on trial at home rather than extradite them has run into a persistent problem: how to protect judges against some of the globe's richest, most violent criminals?

Colombian officials in recent weeks have been unable to hide their elation over the apparent success of a new judicial program intended to curb drug trafficking. Seven drug suspects, including two Medellín cartel leaders, turned themselves in under an official offer of leniency, including guarantees of no extradition and reduced prison sentences.

The surrenders vindicated President César Gaviria Trujillo's policy of coaxing traffickers into jail through legal concessions, the officials said. Mr. Gaviria himself assured skeptics that surrendering traffickers would serve significant jail time in Colombia.

Then came the system's first failure. One trafficking suspect who surrendered under the plan was tried, sentenced—and released.

A judge in the western city of Manizales last week sentenced the suspect, Gonzalo Mejía Sanín, to 36 months in jail. The judge then suspended the sentence and quickly resigned. Mr. Mejía Sanín, wanted in the United States on cocaine trafficking charges, was paroled.

Yarbro, Stan. "Colombian Justice System Falters." *Christian Science Monitor*, January 24, 1991, p. 3.

The tale is an old one in Colombia, where traffickers have proven their ability to kill any judge they can neither bribe nor threaten into a favorable verdict.

Colombian officials were obviously embarrassed by the verdict, refusing to confirm it for several days. Attorney General Carlos Arrieta said the judge's decision in the Mejía Sanín case was a "rotten precedent" for the leniency program and pledged to investigate the judge for misconduct.

Mr. Arrieta said the suspect may find himself jailed again if an appeals court overturns the judge's decision as expected. But foreign officials say they worry more light sentences for drug traffickers will follow, despite Colombia's vague assurances that the judicial system has been strengthened.

"The government's efforts to prove that it hasn't sold out to the traffickers hinges on the functioning of the justice system," says a Western diplomat. "I'm pessimistic because judges are obviously still exposed to bribery and intimidation."

Of particular concern is the pending trial of Jorge Luis Ochoa, the Medellín cartel's No. 2 man, who turned himself in to court officials on Jan. 15.

Mr. Ochoa, wanted in the United States on cocaine distribution and murder charges, had already been incarcerated twice in Colombia. On both occasions he was released by judges who were subsequently dismissed on misconduct charges.

"Ochoa has already bribed himself out of prison twice," says a Colombian attorney specializing in international criminal law. "What makes the government think he won't do it again?"

The lawyer, speaking on condition of anonymity, adds that extradition should be applied in Ochoa's case. "If you want that guy to spend significant time in jail, the only thing to do is to stick him on a plane headed north."

Ochoa's younger brother Fabio was the first cartel leader to take advantage of the government's offer when he surrendered in December. Both suspects went before a judge and confessed a crime. The government has not said what the crimes are, but many people doubt the offenses will carry weighty sentences.

"I cannot see any way under Colombian law that any of these suspects will receive more than eight years," says the Western official. "The question is whether Colombia can justify those results to officials in the United States, where people are serving life sentences for similar crimes."

Even more dangerous than the Ochoa brothers is Pablo Escobar, the cartel leader alleged to have masterminded its terrorist campaign. . . .

The cartel boss recently said he, too, would consider surrendering if the government granted him more concessions, including forming a state council to negotiate with traffickers. The cartel leader has apparently not abandoned his quest to be treated as a political criminal similar to the country's leftist guerrillas, who receive amnesty when they disarm.*

Justice Minister Jaime Giraldo Angel pledged last week to make no more reconciliation gestures to traffickers and exhorted them to submit themselves to the revamped judicial system.

Mr. Giraldo is architect of a new jurisdictional system of 82 judges charged with putting the Ochoas and other drug and terrorist suspects on trial. The judges' identities are to be kept secret under the plan.

But several legal analysts and judges say the plan will not work for the most basic of reasons.

"The suspects who have the influence and money to uncover judges' identities are the drug traffickers . . . who have killed scores of judicial officials in the past," says Maria Consuelo del Rio, a Bogotá human rights lawyer who has made an extensive study of the judicial reform.

Adds Gregorio Oveido, a Bogotá criminal court judge, "The government has put the new system in place as part of negotiations with drug traffickers, not to protect judges."

Though he is not one of the 82 special judges, Mr. Oveido says he knows many of them who are scared. "They know that if they sentence one of the [cocaine bosses] to 20 years, they run the risk of being killed," he says.

Government officials, particularly those in the president's inner circle, are sensitive to such criticism. Colombian officials rebuffed requests for an interview on the new judicial system.

10.8　Between Dependence and Sovereignty in Panama

The U.S. invasion of Panama in December 1990 introduced a new concern in the Americas: the United States seemed willing to disregard the sovereignty of the hemisphere's nations in order to fight the war on drugs. Although the Panamanian invasion contained elements of past U.S. interventions in the Americas, the December military action placed in power a group of civilian leaders who had been denied electoral victory by a

---

*After a constitutional convention in 1991 prohibited extradition, drug cartel leader Pablo Escobar gave himself up. (Ed.)

Krauss, Clifford. "Dependence and Sovereignty Pull at Panama's Equilibrium." *New York Times,* February 11, 1991, p. 1.

military dictator with links to international drug traffickers. This New York Times *article illustrates the difficulties and complexities of establishing and maintaining sovereignty, even after a military dictatorship was replaced by civilian governors.*

Thirteen months after the United States invaded Panama and arrested Gen. Manuel Antonio Noriega, most of the problems that have plagued the nation for years remain. Panama is still searching for its own identity and seems linked more than ever to Washington.

The economy here has rebounded and political freedoms have expanded since General Noriega's ouster, arrest and extradition to Florida to face trial on drug trafficking charges. But cocaine continues to be smuggled through Panama on its way to the United States and other destinations.

Popular support for the Government has weakened, as have the cheers for the American invasion. And President Guillermo Endara, who was installed on the day of the invasion, remains highly dependent on the 10,000 American troops in the country, relying on them, as he did two months ago, to thwart attempts by some in the security forces to retake power.

Panamanian officials say they want to assert an independent identity, but their failure to construct an effective and popular Government appears to insure that Washington will not be able to withdraw the shadow it casts over this small nation of 2.3 million people any time soon. . . .

With its many glistening shopping centers, banks, high-rise condominiums and Dairy Queen drive-ins, Panama City could be a city in Florida.

The resemblance is more than cosmetic. In its essential political character, Panama has not changed since President Theodore Roosevelt, seeking a subservient country in which to dig a transoceanic canal, encouraged the rebellion that separated the isthmus from Colombia.

Just as the first President of Panama was installed by United States forces, so was President Endara. Panama's unit of currency remains the United States dollar.

Local Sovereignty vs. Relying on U.S.

Mr. Endara conceded that democracy in Panama is weak, but said it is "getting stronger by the day." He said it would be more stable if the $461 million aid program from the United States had only come through faster to "jump start" the economy.

Even while the Endara Government affirms its dependency, it must assert its autonomy to obtain popular support. In this vein, as the United

States demands tougher enforcement against drugs and money-laundering, Panama officials say such demands are intrusions on their sovereignty.

Sniping between Panama City and Washington has risen to the point that Foreign Minister Julio Linares and the United States Ambassador, Deane Hinton, engaged in a public shouting match over a proposed money-laundering enforcement agreement at a recent party at the Vatican embassy.

Washington has frozen $84 million in aid for agriculture, education and health until Panama agrees to open Panamanian bank accounts to United States officials investigating money-laundering, much of it related to drug trafficking. Mr. Endara says he has no objection to provisions of the Mutual Legal Assistance Agreement to fight money-laundering, but says provisions to combat insider trading and tax evasion offend his nation's sovereignty. . . .

Ghosts of Past Haunt Endara

More friction has been caused by Panama's refusal to sign an agreement providing joint naval patrols to stop drug trafficking in Panamanian waters. United States officials said that, while Panamanian drug arrests have increased, Panama City alone cannot control the increased amounts of cocaine being shipped through Panama and Central America now that international law enforcement has improved in Caribbean waters.

"Their dignity is intact," Ambassador Hinton commented sarcastically, "but the drugs continue to pour in."

"I think the frictions come from too high expectations by the United States of what the Panamanians were going to do, and too high expectations by the Panamanians of what the United States was going to do," he said.

Mr. Endara said the Governments would work out their differences. His more serious task, he said, is to guarantee that democratically elected civilians succeed him. . . .

The fragility of Panama's democracy and the persistence of its dependence were revealed Dec. 4, when 50 former members of the Panama Defense Force of General Noriega revolted and First Vice President Ricardo Arias Calderon called the American military for help in putting down the rebellion, centered on the Tinajitas barracks outside Panama City.

Col. James Steele of the United States Army, then commander of the United States Military Support Group, instructed the civilian commander of the Public Force to surround and retake Tinajitas. But the Panamanian commander found that most officers either tacitly supported the uprising or sat on the fence. The rebels then occupied the Public Force national headquarters, where they were resisted only by Colonel Steele and other American military advisers.

Hundreds of American troops put down the rebellion. . . .

People Reassess U.S. Invasion

In the rundown Colón slum of El Vaticano, where the overcrowded wooden Victorian-style tenements are sagging from rot, local Roman Catholic priests say that increasing family violence, alcoholism, and drug abuse are symptoms of growing alienation.

"Endara said he was going to give us jobs with help from the American Government," said Robert Anthony Simons, a 33-year-old unemployed dock worker of Jamaican descent. "But now all he does is fire us." Sidestepping children playing barefoot in a stream of raw sewage, he recalled, "People here voted for Endara in 1989 because we wanted to get rid of Noriega, but we wouldn't now."

"If we ever rose up, Endara would simply call in the Rangers," he said, referring to the United States Army.

The perceived failures of the Endara Government are rubbing off on the Bush Administration, and some Panamanians are reassessing their once unquestioning support for the 1989 invasion.

Late last year, a musical opened in Panama City entitled "Maestra Vida" (Teacher Life). In one scene an invading unit of American soldiers offered first aid to some Panamanians wounded in the rocketing of the El Chorrillo barrio. At the opening performance, the audience began to jeer at the actors. "People cried," recalled Norman Douglas, the director, "because they felt impotent."

The playwright adjusted the script to satisfy his audience. For the next six weeks of the performances, the same American troops roughed up the Panamanians. The show was a hit.

11

Fire in the Mind: Revolutions and Revolutionaries

This soldier is part of the forces of Cuba's Fidel Castro, who led the first socialist revolution in the Americas. © Alberto Korda, Havana/ Courtesy Center for Cuban Studies

A successful revolution requires a fundamental transformation of the political, economic, and social relations of a society. The political history of Latin America has been characterized by rebellions, coups, chronic instability, and violence; however, revolutionaries have been successful in gaining power in only a few nations, most notably Mexico, Cuba, and Nicaragua.

If poverty, oppression, economic inequality, and dictatorship were sufficient conditions for revolution, the phenomenon would be far more common in the Americas. But the region's history shows that revolutionary movements have coincided with economic modernization and development rather than the absence of it. The region's integration into the modern world economy increased social dislocations and political tensions. Popular expectations and aspirations for democratic government have grown even as the ability and disposition to meet these expectations has not kept pace. Revolutionary leadership usually emerges from the ranks of the dominant elite—individuals dissatisfied with the existing order who seek rapid and violent change if other paths are blocked.

The Haitian Revolution (1791–1804) was the first successful effort in Latin America to break with the existing social and political order. Inspired by the French Revolution of 1789, the slaves of Saint Domingue, led by François Toussaint L'Ouverture, rose against their French masters and later fought invading French, Spanish, and British forces to gain their freedom and independence. In the process, the plantation system was destroyed, whites and mulattos were killed or fled, and the colonial regime was swept away.

On the heels of the United States' struggle for independence and the French Revolution, the Haitian Revolution sent a powerful message to independence-minded leaders throughout the Americas. However, the fear of social transformation and the memory of Haiti's violent experience tended to retard independence efforts. Local leaders were interested in wresting control from imperial masters, but were less keen on social and political transformations that could jeopardize their privileged social and political position.

Thus, from the first, the wars for independence had a major impact on the rest of the region, though not exactly the revolutionary effect expected or feared.

Twentieth-Century Revolutions

Latin America's most noteworthy revolutions of the twentieth century have occurred in Mexico (1910), in Cuba (1959), and in Nicaragua (1979). In each case, economic and social dislocations, resulting in part from modernization and frustrated economic expectations, increased pressures for radical change. Like the Haitian Revolution before them, these uprisings had a major impact on the region, challenging the hemispheric status quo and the United States' preeminence. They have served as models to be emulated by the region's revolutionaries, as symbols to be sustained by nationalists elsewhere in Latin America and the Caribbean, and as threats to be countered by governments in power.

In each case where revolution occurred, the event was triggered by dictatorial abuses that blocked avenues to socioeconomic and political change, as reading 11.1 illustrates. The old regime's inherent weakness, its linkage to foreign interests, and the gradual narrowing of support led to its collapse and the consequent ascendancy of the revolutionaries. Yet the defeat of the old regime did not end the struggle for power. Revolutionary movements tended to be coalitions whose source of cohesion was usually based on opposition to the corrupt and repressive governments they sought to replace. Most movements, however, were characterized by competing visions of the new society they hoped to create.

In each of the revolutions, struggles over power and policy ensued once the old regime was ousted, as reading 11.2 demonstrates. The winner was usually the party able to attract the widest possible support. However, each revolution has taken its own distinctive directions. In Mexico, a mass party emerged to embody the revolutionary spirit. Although many claim that this revolutionary spirit has been eroded, the party of the revolution, or PRI, continues to dominate the country's political life, as reading 11.3 illustrates. In Cuba, the leadership of Fidel Castro dominated the island's experience of socialism and polarized the Cuban population. In Nicaragua, despite ambitious social and economic reforms, revolutionary consolidation proved virtually impossible because of mismanagement, a faltering economy, and the opposition of the United States, including U.S. financing of an exile army, the Contras.

Each revolution has served as a potent catalyst to other nations in the Americas seeking change. The Mexican experience emphasized nationalistic assertions of popular culture, agrarian reform, and expropriations of foreign enterprises. It gave confidence to would-be revolutionaries and reformers in El Salvador, Nicaragua, Peru, Venezuela, and Costa Rica. The Cuban example sent a strong message throughout the region that revolution was attainable and even likely unless reform of the old undemocratic and inegalitarian structures was achieved (see reading 11.4). Revolutionary leaders in countries such as Argentina, Brazil, Colombia, Peru, and Venezuela were inspired and encouraged—and in some cases directly aided—by Castro, and used guerrilla warfare to gain popular support for their efforts and to undermine the existing governments.

Nicaragua's revolution in 1979 emphasized nationalism and anti-imperialism (see reading 11.5). It also emboldened reform-minded leaders in nearby El Salvador and Guatemala to push for changes. In El Salvador, the military initiated modest reforms in an attempt to preempt an emerging revolutionary force inspired in part by the successful ouster of the old Nicaraguan regime (see reading 11.6). El Salvador was devastated by civil war in the 1980s, and sporadic peace efforts were unsuccessful. Ultimately both sides agreed that neither side could win a military victory, and the United Nations successfully brokered a peace accord signed in 1992.

In the early 1980s, Guatemalan revolutionary leaders accelerated their efforts to topple a military-dominated government that was abusive of human rights and repressive in predominantly Indian rural areas (see reading 11.7). Despite a return to civilian rule in the mid-1980s, guerrillas continued their militant opposition through the early 1990s, when the United Nations' mediation efforts were underway.

The U.S. Response

The United States has played an important and complex role in response to these revolutionary movements. It found itself in a contradictory position early in the Mexican revolution, at first supporting reformers and then becoming the target of nationalists seeking to expropriate U.S.-owned assets in the 1930s.

The U.S. response to revolutionary change in Cuba and Nicaragua was heavily influenced by the U.S. relationship to its great-power rival—the Soviet Union. In Cuba, U.S. opposition to the revolution was galvanized by Cuba's decisions to expropriate U.S. properties, to seek direct economic and military support from the Soviet Union, and eventually to install a Communist political system. Indeed, perceiving a major threat to U.S. interests, Pres. John Kennedy (1961–63) launched his ambitious Alliance for Progress (see Chapter 4), which was designed to encourage social and political reform and forestall Communist revolutions throughout the region.

U.S. concerns about the Cuban threat to the Americas coincided with similar apprehensions among Latin American governments, many of which voted to expel Cuba from the Organization of American States in 1962. As a result, Cuba was isolated from much of the Americas—except from Mexico—until the late 1970s, when it resumed relations with most nations in the hemisphere except the United States.

U.S. tolerance of Nicaragua's revolutionary government turned to overt hostility in the early 1980s. The Sandinistas' attempt to impose a one-party system, their close ties to Cuba and revolutionaries in neighboring states, and Soviet and Eastern European aid to the country fed U.S. fears that Nicaragua could become "another Cuba" (reading 11.8).

However, much of Latin America did not share those concerns about Nicaragua; and most opposed U.S. intervention in Nicaraguan internal affairs. Indeed, numerous peacekeeping initiatives were undertaken in the 1980s by Latin American countries in response to U.S. covert activities intended to destabilize Nicaragua's revolutionary government. First, Venezuela, Colombia, Mexico, and Panama formed the so-called Contadora Group to promote an end to armed conflict in Nicaragua, El Salvador, and Guatemala. Then, in 1987, the Central American countries themselves agreed to an initiative put forward by Costa Rican president Oscar Arias to cease fighting in Nicaragua (see reading 11.9). Known informally as the Arias Peace Plan, this effort was in direct opposition to continuing U.S. support for anti-Sandinista Contras in Nicaragua and for the military in El Salvador.

A growing sense of national and regional sovereignty is an important development in the Americas. The Mexican Revolution was a single country's challenge to U.S. hemispheric dominance. Cuba's revolution and its alliance with the Soviet Union dramatically altered traditional patterns of inter-American relations. Central American efforts to bring about peace took the diplomatic initiative away from the United States. It is clear that Latin American and Caribbean nations will increasingly develop and articulate their own policies and priorities, at times in opposition to those of the United States.

With the collapse of Communist rule in Eastern Europe and the changes in the Soviet Union, Latin American revolutionaries will face new challenges in the 1990s. They will have to either seek new international allies and sources of support to sustain their "armed struggle" for power, or involve themselves in non-violent competitive politics, including elections (see reading 11.10).

11.1 Plan of San Luis Potosí

Mexico experienced rapid economic growth during the latter part of the nineteenth century. Economic progress was accompanied by growing political centralization. Gen. Porfirio Díaz, in power since 1876, had alieniated intellectuals and powerful sectors of Mexico's elites who wanted greater economic and political participation. Following fraudulent elections in 1910, through which Díaz was reelected, Francisco Madero led the movement to oust the dictator. The son of a family that had made its wealth in cattle and mining, Madero issued a call for armed resistance against the government. His Plan of San Luis Potosí was issued from a jail cell, where he was imprisoned for protesting the rigged elections. One year later, the Díaz government collapsed and the dictator went into exile. Madero's subsequent election as president marked the first stage of one of Latin America's preeminent revolutions of the twentieth century.

5 October, 1910

I have designated Sunday, the 20th of next November, from six o'clock in the afternoon and thereafter in all the towns of the Republic, that [the people] should arise in arms under the following Plan:

1st. The elections for President and Vice-President of the Republic, for magistrates of the Supreme Court of the Nation, for deputies and senators as celebrated in June and July of the current year are declared null.

2nd. The present Administration of General Díaz is repudiated, as well as the officials whose power ought to spring from the will of the People, because besides not having been elected by the People they have lost whatever title they could have had of legality, committing and assisting with all the elements which the People put at their disposition for the defense of their interests the most scandalous electoral fraud ever registered in Mexican history.

3rd. In order to avoid in so far as possible the disturbances inherent in any revolutionary movement, all laws promulgated by the present administration and the regulations appertaining thereto are declared in effect while intending in due course to revise constitutionally and by constitutional means those which require reform, while excepting those

"The Plan of San Luis Potosí." In *The Political Plans of Mexico*, Thomas B. Davis and Amado Ricon Virulegio, 588–94. Lanham, Md.: University Press of America, 1987.

which obviously are not found contrary to the principles proclaimed in this Plan.

Through the abuse of the Law of Public Lands numerous small proprietors, the majority of them indigenous Indians, have been despoiled of their lands through agreement with the Secretary of Development *[fomento]* or through decisions of the courts of the Republic. It being no more than justice to the former owners of the land of which they have been robbed in so arbitrary a fashion that such dispositions and decisions are declared subject to revision, and it will be required of those who acquired [the lands] in so immoral a manner, or of their heirs, that they restore them to the original owners to whom they shall also pay indemnities for the damages suffered. . . .

4th. In addition to the Constitution and the laws now in force, the principles of no re-election of the President and Vice-President of the Republic, of governors of the States and of presidents of municipalities is declared the Supreme Law of the Republic until the respective constitutional reforms can be effected.

5th. I assume the position of provisional President of the United Mexican States with the necessary powers to make war on the usurper government of General Díaz. As soon as the capital of the Republic and more than half of the states of the Federation are in possession of the forces of the People, the provisional President shall issue a call for special general elections for the month thereafter and he will deliver the power to the President who may have been elected as soon as the results of the election have been determined.

6th. The provisional President, before surrendering power, shall give an account to the Congress of the Union of the use he has made of the powers which the present Plan confers upon him.

7th. On the 20th of November after six o'clock and thereafter all citizens of the Republic will take up arms in order to throw out of office the authorities who are presently in office. The people who may be deprived of means of communication shall so act after sunset.

8th. When authorities offer armed resistance, they will be required by force of arms to respect the popular will, but in this case the laws of war will be rigorously observed; their attention is called to [the prohibitions against] the shooting of prisoners. Also, attention is called in respect to the duty of every Mexican to respect foreigners in regard to their persons and their property.

9th. The authorities who offer resistance to the realization of this Plan will be sent to prison in order that they may be tried by the courts of the Republic when the revolution shall have ended.

Since it is an indispensable requisite in the laws of warfare that belligerent troops should wear some uniforms or distinctive mark, and since it would be difficult to uniform the numerous forces of the people who are going to take part in the struggle, a three-colored ribbon worn on the hat or tied around the arm will be adopted as the distinctive [identification] of the liberating forces, whether they be volunteers or of the regular military establishment.

FELLOW CITIZENS: If I call upon you to take up arms and to overthrow the Government of General Díaz, it is not only for the crimes which he has committed during the latest election, but also to save the country from the dark future which awaits it under the dictatorship and under the Administration of the nefarious scientific oligarchy which without scruple and so rapidly are absorbing and destroying the national resources, and if we permit them to continue in power in a very short time they will have completed their work: they will have sucked up all its riches and have left it in utmost misery; they will have caused the bankruptcy of the Fatherland, so that weak, impoverished, and shackled, it will find itself helpless to defend its frontiers, its honor, and its institutions.

As for myself, I have a tranquil conscience and no one can accuse me of promoting a Revolution for personal advantage because it is common knowledge that I did everything possible to arrive at a peace-candidacy provided that General Díaz would have permitted the Nation to designate who should be the Vice-President of the Republic. But dominated by incomprehensible pride and by an unheard of haughtiness, he was deaf to the voice of the Fatherland, and he preferred to precipitate it into a Revolution rather than concede the least point, rather than return to the people an atom of their rights . . .

He himself justified the present Revolution when he said, "Let no citizen impose himself and perpetuate himself in the exercise of power and this will be the last revolution."

If the interests of the Fatherland had weighed more in the mind of General Díaz than the sordid interests of himself and of his counsellors, this Revolution would have been avoided by making some concessions to the people, but he has not done so. So much the better!—the change will be more rapid, more radical, because the Mexican people, instead of crying like a coward, will accept the challenge like a brave man, and while General Díaz pretends to help himself by use of brute force to impose an ignominious yoke, the people will take recourse to this same force in order to shake off that yoke and to toss this dismal man from power and to reconquer its freedom.

San Luis Potosí.
Francisco I. Madero
Effective suffrage to Re-election

11.2 The Ayala Plan

*Although Francisco Madero had an important role in initiating the Mex-
ican revolution, he helped unleash forces he could not control. Madero
faced the opposition of the old Díaz army, which he had not disbanded.
Rebel leaders, like Emiliano Zapata, had little patience for Madero. Their
concern was to recover land they had lost, primarily during the years of
the Díaz dictatorship. When Madero showed little sympathy for their land
demands, Zapata and others initiated their own antipresidential revolt in
their Plan de Ayala, excerpted below. Madero managed to stay in office
for two more years—but was assassinated by one of his military commanders in 1913. The revolutionary effort then gained momentum as
rebel leaders fought against Madero's assassins and then against one another. Following four years of bloody civil war, a new constitution was
written in 1917, firmly enshrining the principles of "no re-election" and
setting the basis for expanded participation in the country's political and
economic life.*

28 November, 1911

We, the Undersigned, organized as a Revolutionary body *[Junta]* in order to support and bring to realization the Revolutionary promises made
the 10th of November last, declare solemnly before the civilized world
which judges us and before the Nation to which we belong and which
we love the propositions which we have formulated in order to bring
an end to tyranny which oppresses us. [These propositions] are set forth
in the following Plan.

. . .

Art. 2. Commandante Francisco I. Madero is repudiated as chief of
the Revolution as well as President of the Republic for reasons heretofore expressed and which have brought about the overthrow of this
functionary.

Art. 3. The Eminent Commander General Pascual Orozco, second in
command of the Leader Francisco I. Madero is recognized as Chief of
the Revolution; and in case he may not be able to accept this delicate
post, then Commandante Emiliano Zapata will be recognized as Chief
of the Revolution.

Art. 4. The Revolutionary Committee *[Junta]* of the State of Morelos
declares to the Nation under formal protestation: that it accepts as its

"Plan of Ayala." In *The Political Plans of Mexico,* Thomas B. Davis and Amado Ricon
Virulegio, 606–10. Lanham, Md.: University Press of America, 1987.

own the Plan of San Luis Potosí with the additions expressed below, for the benefit of oppressed towns, and it makes itself defender of the principles which it will defend either to victory or death.

Art. 5. The Revolutionary Committee of the State of Morelos does not accept either the transactions of political compromises which did not lead to the overthrow of the dictatorial forces of Porfirio Díaz and Don Francisco I. Madero, because the Nation is tired of deceitful men and traitors who make promises as liberators, but on gaining power forget them and set themselves up as tyrants.

Art. 6. As an additional part of the Plan which we support, we make the following declaration: that the lands, mountains, and waters and all landed properties which the big landowners [hacendados], that fancy politicians [científuecos] or the political hacks [caciques] under shadow of tyranny and of venal justice usurped will be turned over at once to the towns or to the citizens who have proper titles to these properties, [property] of which they have been dispoiled through the bad faith of our oppressors, these [citizens and towns] maintaining by all means, arms in hand, this said possession, and the usurpers who may consider that they have equal rights with them may present their case before special tribunals which will be established on the triumph of the Revolution.

Art. 7. By virtue of the fact that the immense majority of the towns and Mexican Citizens are no longer owners of the soil which they set foot upon, suffering the horrors of poverty without being able to improve their social condition in the least, neither by turning to industry nor to agriculture, for both lands, mountains and waters are monopolized by a restricted number of people. For this reason one-third of these monopolies will be expropriated by prior indemnification to the powerful owners in order that the towns and the citizens of Mexico may obtain public lands [ejidos], new lands, rural property for towns, and fields for sowing or for cultivation, and in all ways may improve that which was lacking for the prosperity and well-being of all Mexicans.

Art. 8. The big landowners, fancy politicians, or party hacks who directly or indirectly may oppose this present Plan shall have their property nationalized and two-thirds of what belongs to them will be destined for war indemnities, pensions to widows and orphans of the victims who succumbed in the fight for the present Plan.
 . . .

Art 10. The insurgent Military Commanders of the Republic who rose up with arms in hand at the call of Don Francisco I. Madero in order to defend the Plan of San Luis Potosí and who now are opposing this present Plan with armed force will be judged as traitors to the cause which they we[re] defending and to the Fatherland . . .

Art. 12. Once the Revolution which we have brought to the point of realization has triumphed, a Committee *[Junta]* of the principal revolutionary leaders *[jefes]* of the various states will name or designate an interim President of the Republic who will call for elections in order to form a new Congress of the Union, and this [body] then will call for election for the organization of the other federal branches.
. . .

Art 14. If President Madero and the other dictatorial elements of the present and former regime desire to avoid the terrible misfortunes which afflict the Fatherland, let them immediately renounce the offices which they now hold, and with their act they will somewhat close the great wounds which they have opened in the breast of the Fatherland, for if they do not do this then on their heads will flow the blood poured out by our brothers. . . .

Ayala, November 28, 1911.

(Signed)
Emiliano Zapata and others

11.3 The Mexican Revolution Is Dead

After the violence of the Mexican Revolution finally subsided in 1920, successive revolutionary leaders used the revolution's symbols to consolidate their power over the country's politics and economy. Until Marxist economist Jesús Silva Herzog wrote this article in 1949, few had dared challenge the prevailing myth that the Mexican revolution was ongoing and vibrant. His statement about the crisis in Mexican government and politics in the 1940s explicitly said that the revolution had ceased to exist. His

Silva Herzog, Jesús. "The Mexican Revolution Is Now a Historical Fact." In *Is the Mexican Revolution Dead?* edited by Stanley R. Ross, 99–103. New York: Knopf, 1966.

criticism of the revolution is still frequently repeated by those who believe that the dominant party, the Institutional Revolutionary Party (PRI), is unrepresentative and antidemocratic, and has lost its commitment to social reform.

More than six years ago I wrote that the Mexican Revolution, one of the three most profound events in the independence history of Mexico, was suffering a moral and ideological crisis of the greatest gravity. I believed then that it could be saved and could continue its forward march for the benefit of the Mexican people. Now, after time has passed, I feel with true sadness and sense distinctly that the Mexican Revolution no longer exists. It ceased to be, died quietly, without anyone taking note of it; with no one, or almost no one, noting it yet.

What has happened? The reply is obvious: nothing extraordinary. Here I do not wish to refer to any sociologist, historian, economist, or political scientist. I simply wish to recall the phrase of a poet, changing but a single word: we revolutions also are mortal.

Revolutions are not immortal. They leave a profound impression on the heart of posterity as do the great thinkers. . . . But the moment always arrives when revolutions lose currency and cease to be because they exhaust their creative vitality, because they realize their task in history, or because there are new forces which restrain or overcome them. Revolutions are historical facts and everything historical involves, necessarily, transitoriness. History means movement, constant change, eagerness, and intention of human betterment. History is the drama of man, and revolutions are episodes in some of the acts of the drama. Episodes and acts pass and are followed by other acts and episodes, and the tragedy, always old and always new, continues unfolding on the stage of the world.

Is there anyone who maintains in this year of 1949 that the Independence Revolution of the United States is not a thing of the past but rather something alive, or would affirm an analogous view of the French Revolution? It is evident that everything substantive is stored in the memory of men and influences their conduct and their essential knowledge; but what is preserved in the memory of men is neither history nor biography. It is something that was and which no longer is, past rather than present. . . . Why, then, should the Mexican Revolution have been eternal, an exception to the universal law of constant change? Valid arguments which prove the contrary—namely, the perpetuity of our latest great social movement—to my knowledge do not exist. . . .

On the other hand, I am perfectly aware that there will be those who say that my thesis is dangerous and inopportune from the political point of view because it will be used by the reactionary parties which are enemies of the Revolution and of every progressive idea. I do not share such views. The thesis which I advance and which I believe is true will serve honest revolutionaries rather than professional demagogues or profiteers of the Revolution. The lie on occasion is useful to the evil politician, but not for the good policy which invariably must rest on the truth. Only with the truth, as I said on another occasion, can the people be truly served. . . .

When the armed conflict ended, the Revolution became government, and the revolutionary governments began their political and administrative effort. Some have objected to the joining of these two terms because they think that governing is the opposite of rebelling. They think, with apparent reasonableness, that two antithetical terms are involved. Nevertheless, the designation is correct. With all propriety one can and must label those administrations as revolutionary governments. The reason is that in their action they were farther to the left than the Constitution. They were more radical than the fundamental law of the Republic in regard to agrarian reform, defense of subsoil resources, and labor legislation. . . . Cárdenas gave the greatest advance possible on behalf of popular interests and the economic independence of Mexico. During his administration, in 1938, the Mexican Revolution reached its culmination. Afterwards came descent, crisis, agony and death.

The Mexican Revolution accomplished great things. It is worthwhile trying to point these out, at least in part.

It finished with the remains of feudalism or, rather, with a certain type of feudalism inherited from the colonial era and facilitated the development of capitalism or precapitalism. In round numbers it distributed land totaling something more than thirty million hectares to 1,700,000 peasant families. It organized cheap agricultural credit for *ejidatarios* and small farmers, although without meeting all rural needs. It began the construction of huge irrigation systems which have brought under cultivation a million hectares of previously seasonally usable, grazing, or wooded land. It united extensive zones of the country by means of highways. It established a Central Bank and recognized the national credit system on entirely new bases. It made possible the organization of labor unions and the promulgation of one of the most humane and advanced protective labor codes in the world. It promoted public education, establishing many rural schools throughout the nation, as well as secondary, normal, and technical schools. It exalted the personality of inhabitants of the Indian race, erasing the remains of a positive discrimination which the old semifeudal aristocracy and some families of the middle class still felt and practiced. It aided the great Mexican painters in their definitive formation, creating a climate favorable to the realization of their masterpieces. It provided asylum for anyone persecuted for political reasons, and such refugees found means of livelihood and affection within our borders. It respected human life during its later years and consecrated freedom of thought as an irrevocable principle to such an extent that it could be affirmed proudly that in this regard no country surpassed us. . . . Its international conduct was always enlisted in the service of peace and in defense of good causes. In addition, it expropriated the property of foreign petroleum companies when they declared themselves in rebellion by refusing to obey a decision of the nation's Supreme Court of Justice. This was a significant step toward the achievement of our economic independence.

It is evident that not everything the Mexican Revolution did was perfect. It was a human undertaking, and more than a few errors were committed. But there was creative impulse of profound character in the desire and effort to improve the living conditions of the great masses of the population.

If the facts are analyzed calmly, it is impossible to deny the positive results achieved in the social and economic spheres. However, the same cannot be said for the political progress of the country. In this respect the conclusions are negative, and honesty requires the admission that the Revolution has failed.

11.4 Fidel Castro's "Second Declaration of Havana"

On December 2, 1956, Fidel Castro, a young lawyer, landed at the foothills of the Sierra Maestra with 81 companions to initiate a guerrilla war against the dictatorial government of Fulgencio Batista. His efforts culminated in the Cuban Revolution of January 1, 1959. Castro initiated sweeping domestic reforms on the island, expanded Cuba's foreign policy initiatives, and actively promoted revolutionary change in Latin America and in the Third World. Castro's revolution was a major event in the twentieth century because it offered a potent example of how political and economic change could take place in the Western Hemisphere, even in opposition to powerful U.S. interests. In the early 1960s, with their power at home increasingly secure, the leaders of the Cuban Revolution began to pay more attention to the rest of Latin America and the Caribbean. They held up their struggle as a model for social change in the region and as a direct challenge to U.S. imperialism, as can be seen in this February 1962 speech by Fidel Castro. A generation of Latin American and Caribbean

Castro, Fidel. "Second Declaration of Havana." In *Fidel Castro's Personal Revolution in Cuba: 1959–1973*, edited by James Nelson Goodsell, 263–68. New York: Knopf, 1975.

revolutionaries was nurtured by the rhetorical and material support pro-
vided by Castro and his government.

What is Cuba's history but that of Latin America? What is the history
of Latin America but the history of Asia, Africa, and Oceania? And
what is the history of all these peoples but the history of the cruelest
exploitation of the world by imperialism?

At the end of the last century and the beginning of the present, a
handful of economically developed nations had divided the world among
themselves, subjecting two thirds of humanity to their economic and
political domination. Humanity was forced to work for the dominating
classes of the group of nations which had a developed capitalist economy.

The historic circumstances which permitted certain European countries and the United States of North America to attain a high industrial
development level put them in a position which enabled them to subject and exploit the rest of the world.

What motives lay behind this expansion of the industrial powers?
Were they moral, "civilizing" reasons, as they claimed? No. Their motives were economic. . . .

Since the end of the Second World War, the Latin American nations
are becoming pauperized constantly. The value of their capita income
falls. The dreadful percentages of child death rate do not decrease, the
number of illiterates grows higher, the peoples lack employment, land,
adequate housing, schools, hospitals, communication systems and the
means of subsistence. On the other hand, North American investments
exceed 10 billion dollars. Latin America, moreover, supplies cheap raw
materials and pays high prices for manufactured articles. Like the first
Spanish conquerors, who exchanged mirrors and trinkets with the Indians for silver and gold, so the United States trades with Latin America. To hold on to this torrent of wealth, to take greater possession of
America's resources and to exploit its long-suffering peoples: this is
what is hidden behind the military pacts, the military missions and
Washington's diplomatic lobbying. . . .

As to the accusation that Cuba wishes to export its revolution, we
reply: Revolutions are not exported; they are made by the peoples.

What Cuba can give and has already given to the peoples is its example.

And what does the Cuban Revolution teach: that revolution is possible, that the peoples can make it, that in today's world there is no
force strong enough to impede the peoples' liberation movements.

Our victory would never have been possible if the revolution itself
had not been inexorably destined to arise from the conditions which
existed in our economic-social reality, a reality which pertains even to
a greater degree in a goodly number of Latin American countries.

It happens inevitably that in those countries where Yankee monop-
olist control is strongest, where exploitation by the reigning few is most
unrestrained and where the conditions of the masses of workers and
peasants are most unbearable, the political power becomes more vi-
cious, states of siege become habitual, all expression of mass discontent
is suppressed by force, and the democratic channels are closed off,
thereby revealing more plainly than ever the kind of brutal dictatorship
assumed by the dominating classes. That is when the peoples' revolutionary breakthrough becomes inevitable.

And while it is true that in America's underdeveloped countries the
working class is in general relatively small, there is a social class which
because of the sub-human conditions under which it lives constitutes a
potential force which—led by workers and the revolutionary intellectuals—has a decisive importance in the struggle for national liberation:
the peasantry.

In our countries two circumstances are joined: underdeveloped industry and an agrarian regime of a feudal character. That is why no
matter how hard living conditions of the workers are, the rural population lives under even more horrible conditions of oppression and exploitation. But, with few exceptions, it also constitutes the absolute majority, sometimes more than 70 percent of Latin American populations.
. . .

Wherever roads are closed to the peoples, where repression of workers and peasants is fierce, where the domination of Yankee monopolies
is strongest, the first and most important lesson is to understand that it
is neither just nor correct to divert the peoples with the vain and fan-
ciful illusion that the dominant classes can be uprooted by legal means
which do not and will not exist. The ruling classes are entrenched in
all positions of state power. They monopolize the teaching field. They
dominate all means of mass communication. They have infinite financial resources. Theirs is a power which the monopolies and the ruling
few will defend by blood and fire with the strength of their police and
their armies.

The duty of every revolutionary is to make revolution. We know that
in America and throughout the world the revolution will be victorious.
But revolutionaries cannot sit in the doorways of their homes to watch
the corpse of imperialism pass by. The role of Job does not behoove a
revolutionary. Each year by which America's liberation may be has-
tened will mean millions of children rescued from death, millions of
minds freed for learning, infinitudes of sorrow spared the peoples. Even
though the Yankee imperialists are preparing a bloodbath for America
they will not succeed in drowning the peoples' struggle. They will evoke
universal hatred against themselves. This will be the last act of their
rapacious and cave-man system.

No one people of Latin America is weak, because all are part of a
family of 200 million brothers who suffer the same miseries, harbor the

same sentiments, face the same enemy. All dream alike of a happier fate, and all can count on the solidarity of all honorable men and women throughout the world.

The epic of Latin America's independence struggles was great, and the fight was a heroic one. But today's generation of Latin Americans is summoned to write a greater epic, one even more decisive for humanity. The earlier fight was to free ourselves from Spanish colonial power, from a decadent Spain which had been invaded by Napoleon's armies. Today the liberation struggle confronts the strongest imperial land in all the world, the most significant power of the world imperialist system. Thus we perform an even greater service for humanity than did our ancestors.

This struggle, more than the first, will be conducted by the masses, by the peoples. The people will play a far more important role than they did then. Individual leaders matter less in this fight than in that.

This epic we have before us will be written by the hungry masses of Indians, of landless peasants, of exploited workers. It will be written by the progressive masses, the honest and brilliant intellectuals of whom we have so many in these suffering lands of Latin America. A battle of masses and ideas, an epic borne onward by our peoples who have been ignored until today and who now are beginning to make imperialism lose its sleep. They thought us to be an impotent, submissive herd, but now they are beginning to fear that herd. It is a thundering herd of 200 million Latin Americans among whom Yankee monopoly capital already spies its gravediggers. . . .

11.5 In Defense of the Sandinista Revolution

In July 1979, the Somoza dynasty in Nicaragua was ousted after 41 years in power. The multiclass revolutionary forces that toppled the dictatorship were led by the Marxist-dominated Frente Sandinista de Liberación Na-

Borge, Tomás. "This Revolution Was Made to Create a New Society." In *Nicaragua: The Sandinista People's Revolution: Speeches by Sandinista Leaders*, 22–38. New York: Pathfinder Press, 1985.

cional (FSLN), a revolutionary movement bent on restructuring the country. The FSLN embraced the anti-imperialism of Augusto César Sandino, a Nicaraguan revolutionary who fought against U.S. forces occupying Nicaragua in the late 1920s and early 1930s. Anti-imperialistic and pro-Cuban, the FSLN set forth an ambitious plan to reorganize Nicaraguan society, consciously favoring working-class and peasant interests. In foreign policy, the Sandinistas sought support from Cuba, the Soviet Union, and Eastern European countries and backed struggling revolutionaries in other Central American nations. The following reading is an excerpt from a 1982 speech by Tomás Borge, a founder of the FSLN, delivered to a crowd of 100,000 Managuans in a May Day celebration. First jailed by the Somoza government at the age of 16, Borge served as the Sandinista minister of the interior. His speech outlines his concerns over the problems of revolutionary consolidation as well as the growing hostility with the United States and neighboring Honduras.

What is the difference between yesterday and today? Who are the ones who complain about the Sandinista People's Army (EPS), the Sandinista Police, the organs of State Security—apart from some justified complaints against isolated cases of abuse which, though less each day, unfortunately are still committed? . . .

Those who complain are the ones who in the past had an unrestricted instrument for repressing workers and peasants; those who complain are the great landowners and the big industrialists and the tiny groups that still allow themselves to be confused by counterrevolutionary preaching. And the reason is very simple. While yesterday the industrialists and the landowners had an army and a police like the National Guard and an office of security serving their interests, today the workers and the peasants, all the working people, the ordinary people of Nicaragua, have at their wholehearted service the Sandinista People's Army, the Sandinista Police, and the organs of State Security.

One would really have to be an idiot or a victim of delusion, or both things at once, to ask for the support of the people in order to give back the lands that were taken away from the landowners, or to return the holdings that were confiscated from the *somocistas*. . . .

With the victory of the revolution, a new phase begins. It is still necessary to unite the widest possible strata of Nicaraguan society to confront the common enemy of all Nicaraguans, which is U.S. imperialism. This means that this new phase, after victory, puts the main emphasis on the defense of the nation, on the struggle to have our national sovereignty respected, on the right of self-determination, and on the need to unite all Nicaraguan patriots to confront a huge and cruel enemy.

But in this new phase, serious internal contradictions begin to come to the surface, when the revolution is forced—by its own dynamic and to remain in harmony with the political, economic, and social principles that were its reason for being—to determine which social sectors shall be given priority within the revolutionary process. Our people already know who the privileged ones were yesterday, and our people already know which classes have priority today, for whom this revolution was made. . . .

This new phase, however, is extraordinarily complex, because on one side we have the interests of the workers and peasants, the backbone of the revolution. And on the other side there are those capitalist sectors that the revolution wants to keep on its side, even giving them economic incentives. But at the same time these sectors are torn apart by the dashing of their political hopes, and because the umbilical cord that ties them to imperialism, due to their antipatriotic traditions, refuses to disappear. . . .

Experience tells us that on one hand, a certain number of elements belonging to these social groups cannot resign themselves to the new reality, and that even within the revolution, there are those who believed that ultimately the dreams of the workers and peasants would end in a nightmare and the dreams of the bosses as a class would end in paradise.

Experience has also shown that there are capitalist sectors who are ready to work with the revolution, and that broad middle strata and the majority of small and medium agricultural producers have incorporated themselves into the revolutionary process. . . .

This revolution was made, not to reaffirm the old society, but to create a new society. . . .

Therefore, the Sandinista front was the living instrument for the conquest of power by the workers, and the living instrument for the consolidation of the power of the workers.

What does this mean? Just like the human body needs vitamins and protein to nourish itself and develop, the Sandinista front needs to draw its sustenance from the working class. The vitamins and protein of the Sandinista front are the Nicaraguan workers and peasants. The intellectuals, professionals, and other sectors of society who want to identify with the Sandinista people's revolution, must identify with the interests of the workers and peasants. And the capitalists, regardless of their ideological conceptions of the Nicaraguan workers and peasants, have to identify with the patriotism of the peasants and workers if they are to remain in Nicaragua. . . .

The Sandinista front is the vanguard of the workers and peasants, and is the vanguard of these social sectors; the Sandinista front is the living instrument of the revolutionary classes, the guide leading toward a new society.

To sum up, all our efforts are directed toward destroying the negative habits that are a part of the *somocista* inheritance so that those habits enter a crisis simultaneously with the breakdown of imperialist domination in Central America. This domination started to break down when the Sandinista people's revolution triumphed, and the process was speeded up with the development of revolutionary struggle in Central America. . . .

We reiterate our policy of peace toward the United States and our proposals to Honduras. This policy and these proposals reject the offensive and arrogant language that scarcely deigns to hide its aim of blocking any understanding.

But it is this arrogance I refer to. Nicaragua, they say, has become a threat to peace in Central America. This is a situation, they say, that they don't want and will not tolerate. What do they mean by that? That they neither want nor will tolerate. . . What are they going to do to us? More than they have done to us already? We are ready to receive not only their insolent blustering, we are ready to meet with them too, so they will know what we are going to do. . . .

Of course, we are still in favor of peace, but peace must begin with mutual respect, and not with insolent messages that injure our dignity. Although we have told you that apparently that prospect has been defeated, does this mean that imperialism has given up all ideas of direct aggression against Central America and Nicaragua? It does not mean this. It means that they have given up, for the moment, perhaps, on direct aggression. But we would be naive dreamers, we would be stupid if we believed that imperialism had already given up on wiping out our revolution. . . .

It is trying to develop even further the tactics of destabilization used against our revolution. Internal corrosion within the vanguard is one objective. It wants to sow mistrust and internal violence inside Nicaragua. To give priority to the technical capacity and firepower of the counterrevolutionary bands, especially in the northern areas of the country. They propose to increase sabotage, assassination attempts, and other forms of terrorism. They will try to disorient the people, encouraging ideological confusion, manipulating the religious feelings of the Nicaraguan people, and exploiting the consequences of our economic difficulties. . . .

I believe that those who have conceived this plan are going to live and die deceived. . . . Here, during the Spanish conquest, they deceived the Indians with little glass marbles and mirrors. Those who dream of overthrowing the revolutionary government and its political leadership have not yet realized that the time of the conquistadors had gone, and that here the only thing we will conquer will be the establishment of a new and higher society.

11.6 A Call to Revolution

The Nicaraguan Revolution of 1979 gave a new surge of optimism to Central American revolutionaries intent on deposing entrenched military governments. In an effort to undercut armed struggle in El Salvador, a group of reformist military officers, in alliance with civilian groups, toppled a highly repressive conservative military government in October 1979. The new government faltered almost immediately, with civilian members resigning by January 1980. Guerrilla forces stepped up their activities and repression increased. In March 1980 the People's Revolutionary Army (ERP), the most militaristic and radical of the rebel groups, issued the statement that follows, which rejected nonviolence and called for unity among revolutionary forces. A Marxist-Leninist organization, the ERP then formed a unified revolutionary command structure, the Farabundo Martí National Liberation Front (FMLN). In emulation of the Sandinista victory some 18 months earlier, the unified command in early 1981 led a so-called final offensive, which was unsuccessful in toppling the government. During the 1980s, the civil war between the government and the guerrillas claimed more than 80,000 lives.

The Salvadorian people are at present confronting a crucial moment in history, in search of their final liberation. The struggle that is now taking place in our country expresses a people's right to be the author of its own destiny. . . .

It is in this general context that our country, El Salvador, has suffered almost half a century of criminal and pitiless repression at the hands of murderous military dictatorships, which have protected the interests of American Imperialism and of the Salvadorian Oligarchy, while keeping our people submerged in a terrible drama of poverty which ranks us among the countries with the highest indices of illiteracy, malnutrition, lack of housing, infant mortality, etc., in the world.
. . .

. . . [W]hile the Oligarchy hold the economic power, there will be neither peace nor justice for our nation, and any government that does not have the popular sectors as the fundamental base for military, economic and political change, is a government condemned sooner or later to defeat. . . .

There is only one solution: that the people take in their hands what

"People's Revolutionary Army (ERP): Statement on FMLN Unity." In *The Central American Crisis Reader,* edited by Robert S. Leiken and Barry Rubin, 401–6. New York: Summit Books, 1987.

legitimately belongs to them, the huge plantations of coffee, sugar, cotton; the huge factories, the banks and all the properties of the oligarchy; this is the definitive solution and no other that would keep us subjected to poverty and permanent repression is acceptable.

Now, the sectors of the murderous and reactionary right wing attribute all the problems to communist subversion. . . .

The reactionary and fascist right is accustomed to seeing the workers as sheep and slaves to whom they do not give the right to think and to organize. And so they invent the story about subversives who want to cheat the people. They are mistaken. The workers are no longer the same submissive people who used to put up with these humiliations, not saying anything and bowing their heads. Now they are getting ready to take what is rightfully theirs.

Those people who, from the comfort of the residential suburbs, of multiple economic resources, have not sensed the grave problems of unemployment and misery; don't know what it is to live in a village with the ever-present fear that the National Guard will arrive and rape the women, kill the men and steal what little they have; do not understand that the war is not just now beginning, but the war against the people began a long time ago, and that for that reason the only path open to the people is to defend themselves with all their strength.

The assassins of the Right raise the banners of Fatherland, Liberty, God and Work, talking about the Democratic and Representative Republic. But the Fatherland they defend belongs to fourteen families; their Liberty, the exploitation and humiliation of the workers; their God, the god of money, to buy consciences and corrupt the work of slavery and misery. . . .

The Christian Democratic Party in our country is a group of corrupt petty politicians that does not have the least amount of popular support. . . . The People's Revolutionary Army (ERP) constitutes part of the most advanced sectors of the population that are struggling for liberation of our country, and that have resolutely taken up arms in this war of legitimate defense against the oppressors of our people.

In recent months our military forces have intensified their actions, taking towns, villages, cantons, suburbs and sections of cities, preparing the people for the tasks of insurrection.

More than 75 military operations have been carried out in recent days, and dozens of persons responsible for repression in different parts of the country have been executed; patrols of the National Guard, the National Police and the Treasury Department Police have been attacked . . .

As part of our military activity we have captured elements of the oligarchy in order to oblige them to pay war-tax in exchange for their freedom. Regarding this, the reactionary right has tried to discredit the revolutionary organization by constantly asking, "What do the subversives do with the money from the kidnappings?" and they make accounts over what they have paid to the organizations, trying in this way to say that it has been squandered. The answer to this question is simple: the people also need money in order to wage war, and what we have done is to recuperate part of the money that belongs to our people—which for the moment is in the hands of the oligarchy—in order to convert it into better organization, more arms, more propaganda, and in this way cover all the costs implied in the process of the People's Revolutionary War. The changes implemented by the Popular Democratic Government will embrace every aspect of the . . . economic structure. . . .

• Expropriation without right to indemnization of all properties in the hands of the Oligarchy in different economic levels, and their subsequent re-distribution as collective, communal, or state properties. This measure infers the realization of Agrarian, Industrial and Urban Reforms, without affecting the small and middle businessmen to whom incentives and support are offered.

• Expropriation of all Imperialist enterprises, and the abandonment of all treaties which subject our country to economic dependence.

• Management of the national economy on the basis of a system of national planning which embraces all branches, sectors and regions.

• Organization of an economic system based on collective property, communal property, state property, and private holdings of small and medium size.

• Nationalization of the export of coffee, cotton, sugar and other products.

• Nationalization of the financial and banking system.

• Nationalization of the production of electrical energy and the refinement of petroleum. . . .

11.7 Guatemala's Indian Wars

Guatemala, a country with a population of 8 million located in Central America, has one of Latin America's worst records of human rights violations. There is a tradition of abuse of the largely Indian rural popula-

Krauss, Clifford. "Background to Repression: Guatemala's Indian Wars." *The Nation,* March 14, 1981, p. 212.

tion. Disappearances, torture, and assassination became routine occurrences in the country's urban areas during the mid-1970s. Guatemala had one of the earliest known "death squads"—paramilitary organizations formed to murder government opposition figures, labor and student leaders, and anyone else who might question the established order. The cycle of violence was accelerated by left-leaning guerrilla leaders seeking to overthrow the government. During the early 1980s, when the following account was written, the government of Gen. Romeo Lucas García actively engaged in a deliberate policy of torture and repression toward opposition leaders and rural villagers. After hundreds of reports about this situation and a worldwide outcry against these repressive conditions, General Lucas García was deposed in a military coup that brought into office a tough law-and-order leader who was even more repressive, particularly toward the indigenous rural peoples.

Under the cover of predawn darkness last July 28, a Guerrilla Army of the Poor (E.G.P.) commando team raided an army outpost on a bluff overlooking the Ixil Indian town of San Juan Cotzal. The integrated Ladino and Indian force surprised the soldiers and killed several before retreating into the Guatemalan highlands. After the army's *orejas* (ears) in the village told the commander of the outpost that certain civilians knew of the impending raid but had refused to warn the soldiers, flak-jacketed troops, many of them Indians, forced open the doors of dozens of homes, rounded up about sixty young males, executed them and buried them in common graves.

Leftist rebellion and rightist reaction are nothing new to Guatemala. Since Col. Jácobo Arbenz and his left-leaning regime fell to a Central Intelligence Agency-financed coup in 1954, more than 35,000 Guatemalans have died in political violence. Guerrilla groups have come and gone—victims of army counterinsurgency as well as their own ideological bickering and strategic blunders. Rightist death squads have changed their names a half-dozen times.

Nor is repression and exploitation of the Indian majority a recent development. As soon as the Spanish swept through Guatemala in 1524, thousands of Mayas were mobilized as unpaid labor to produce cocoa, indigo, leather, gold and silver. Today the goods are different but the system largely remains: A half-million Indians are forced into what amounts to debt peonage every year and compelled to migrate hundreds of miles to toil at substandard wages on southern coastal plantations.

What is new to Guatemala is the burgeoning activism of thousands of Indians within the last year. That's bad news for the Ladino elite, and the rightist regime that serves their interests has stepped up repression. Thirty Quiché peasants and students occupied the Spanish Embassy in Guatemala City in January 1980, taking thirty-one hostages. They demanded an investigation into the alleged army killing of dozens of farmers around the town of Uspantan in Quiché. When police climbed onto the embassy roof and attempted to break in, a militant threw a Molotov cocktail. The entire building exploded in flames and twenty-nine militants, seven Spanish diplomats, a former Guatemalan Vice President, a foreign minister who had taken sanctuary in the embassy and a Guatemalan secretary were killed.

A less dramatic though potentially more important development soon followed. Exploiting widespread discontent over low wages, crowded housing, DDT poisoning and tropical disease among workers at the southern coastal plantations, the Guerrilla Army of the Poor had organized 75,000 Indian migrants through its labor wing, the Peasant Unity Committee (C.U.C.). Last February, the workers struck for seventeen days and won their first raise since 1972—a 186 percent hike that brought their minimum daily wage to $3.20. One hundred peasants suspected of taking part in the work action disappeared in June, presumably the victims of the death squads. Despite the loss of life, the C.U.C. strike was considered the most successful union action in years. The Government took notice and began broadcasting patriotic announcements in Indian languages defending the army and extolling the virtues of peace. . . .

In war or peace, the plight of the Guatemalan Indians is bleak. Illiteracy in the countryside reaches 80 percent. Indian infant mortality exceeds 100 per 1,000 live births. Hunger, underemployment, mental retardation and alcoholism are endemic. To escape the misery of the fields, thousands of Indians reject their ancestral dress and migrate to the cities where they live in ragtag slums without running water.

The struggle for existence becomes acute in November throughout the highlands. In Santa Catarina Palopo, a town squeezed between steep mountains and the banks of moody Lake Atitlan, 1,500 Cakchiquel Indians barely eke out a subsistence ten months a year. When the rainy season ends in October, leaving the smell of rotting corn behind, families begin to run out of food and money. Out of desperation, about 400 Santa Catarina Palopo men join hundreds of thousands of their countrymen and migrate to cotton, coffee and sugar plantations on the sweltering southern coast. "My family doesn't have enough land," complained Manuel Gonzalez, a 28-year-old migrant of the town who clings to his Cakchiquel tongue and wears traditional striped culottes. Gonzalez must share an acre of exhausted soil with three generations of his family. "There is much pain on the coast and it is very hot. Sometimes it makes me mad but I have no choice but to go," Gonzalez added. Gonzalez hires out to contractors who offer him loans of between $5 and $15 to feed his family in exchange for a month or two of work on the plantations. His advance is taken out of his daily salary; when he returns to his farm in February he is often penniless or still in debt. . . .

One Government rural credit spokeswoman explained with a shrug that public efforts to aid the Indians had little impact because of "the low cultural level of the indigenous population." A more systematic analysis would demonstrate that Government policy is directly responsible for the forced migrations. After all, cheap Indian labor gives Guatemalan produce a competitive edge on the world market. "The politicians believe that if the Indians do better they will not work on the plantations. That is the sad truth," said a Government official responsible for Indian affairs. A list of the country's most powerful politicians and generals would duplicate a Who's Who of the Guatemalan landowning class. Jorge García Granados, private secretary and business partner of President Lucas García, is the second largest cotton planter in the country. Lucas García himself is a cattle rancher who owns at least 25,000 acres in the Transversal Strip region, where valuable oil deposits have been found. Over the last twenty years of strong economic growth, low business taxes and conservative monetary policies have succeeded in keeping inflation—and the Indian—down.

President Lucas García characterizes his Government as "center-left" and spends thousands of quetzals publicizing a $19 million program funded by the U.S. Agency for International Development to settle 5,000 landless families in the Transversal Strip and the projects of Bandesa, the public rural credit bank. But the Government's own statistics belie the promises officials have made in an attempt to avert a Sandinist-style revolution. Two percent of Guatemala's 7.2 million people own 70 percent of the nation's cultivable land. Some 200,000 peasant families own no land at all. Meanwhile, a few large landholders, who let as much as 30 percent of their land go unused, increased their acreage from 5.5 million to 6.7 million between 1964 and 1979. . . .

One of the worst massacres took place on the morning of May 29, 1978, when 700 Kekchi Indians gathered in the town square of Panzos, a village eighty miles northeast of Guatemala City, to give the mayor a petition demanding the return of lands taken from them by rich Ladinos. They were met by a large army detachment with automatic weapons at the ready. An Indian leader began shouting and swinging his machete at the soldiers, as if to beckon the unarmed peasants to attack them. The soldiers lost control of the situation and finally cleared the square in a frenzy of gunfire—leaving 114 men, women and children dead. E.G.P. guerrillas were quick to take revenge and blew up an army truck, killing seventeen soldiers.

The massacre, called "Guatemala's My Lai" by one local newspaper, climaxed two years of "disappearances" and evictions in the isolated northern province of Alta Verapaz. For centuries the indigenous Kekchi Indians lived there peacefully in communes, because the Ladinos had little use for property in an upland jungle region without roads. But a decade ago, oil and nickel deposits were discovered and the Government built a highway, which made the area attractive to cattle ranchers. Well-connected Ladino businessmen, generals and politicians found the National Property Registry only too happy to write them deeds to land that the Indians had occupied for centuries. The Indians could do nothing through the legal channels; they had no titles recognized by Ladino authorities. "The large landholders are not capitalists," explained a Government official active in Indian affairs. "They are rich people with a colonialist mentality. And they always say the Indians are at fault for the country's poverty."

That same attitude legitimizes the forced induction of thousands of Indians into the army every year. Soldiers commonly surround the markets of villages and kidnap young men, tie them up for days, force them repeatedly to insult their Indian customs and train them to kill. The army recently began to recognize that the program was counterproductive and modified it. But there continue to be reports of recruits who choose to commit suicide (particularly in the southeastern Jutiapa army camp) rather than kill their brothers.

The guerrillas are fast becoming the only significant political force in the country committed to improving conditions among Indians. Rightwing hit men, who function without fear of Government reprisal, have systematically gunned down moderate leaders who campaign for land reform and gradual social change. Vice President Francisco Villagran Kramer, the most influential liberal in the Government, resigned last September following several death threats.

Growing Indian and liberal support does not assure a final leftist victory in a country with the strongest army in the area and a considerable middle class that has a stake in the status quo. In fact, in the last election, Lucas García only won by defrauding an even more conservative candidate. And although there is growing evidence that the four guerrilla groups in the country have begun a dialogue, sectarianism divides them. The Rebel Armed Forces (F.A.R.), whose worker and student members specialize in urban guerrilla warfare, broke away from the thirty-one-year-old Communist Guatemalan Workers Party (P.G.T.). O.R.P.A. and E.G.P., in turn, split from the F.A.R. But even if the guerrillas were united, their fight against the 18,000-man army would be decidedly uphill. . . . Even those who have automatic rifles are no match for soldiers armed with Israeli-made Galil assault rifles and supported by 105-millimeter howitzers. . . .

11.8 U.S. Presidential Report on Central America

Following the Sandinista Revolution in 1979 in Nicaragua and the elec-
tion of Ronald Reagan to the U.S. presidency in 1980, Central America
became a major issue in U.S. foreign policy. There was little consensus in
the United States over the exact nature of the problem or the policies to
follow. President Reagan's policy—supporting elections and enhancing
military capacity in Honduras and El Salvador against externally directed
subversion—accelerated public debate on the issue. A major theme of the
debate centered around the "home-grown" or foreign nature of the poten-
tial or actual subversion. In July 1983 the president established the Na-
tional Bipartisan Commission on Central America to examine the region's
political, economic, and social conditions and to provide advice that could
contribute to a comprehensive U.S. policy for Central America. The com-
mission's final report, an excerpt of which follows, forcefully argued that
Soviet and Cuban objectives for revolutionary struggle coincided in Cen-
tral America, and that Nicaragua served as an important stepping-stone
for the insurgency efforts of the two countries.

In retrospect it is clear that Castro's communization of Cuba was a sem-
inal event in the history of the Americas—a fact appreciated almost
immediately by the Soviet Union. It prompted Khrushchev to declare
in 1960 that the Monroe Doctrine had "outlived its times" and had died
"a natural death."

Soviet policy in this hemisphere has followed the pattern of Soviet
policy elsewhere in the world: Moscow has exploited opportunities for
the expansion of Soviet influence. In the aftermath of the Cuban Missile Crisis, the Soviets concentrated on expanding their diplomatic, economic and cultural ties in Latin America and on strengthening the influence of local communist parties in broad electoral fronts, trade unions
and the universities. In this respect they differed from Castro, who
continued to support a course of armed struggle in Venezuela, Colombia, Guatemala, and several other countries. But later the fall of
Allende in Chile and the subsequent right-wing takeovers in Uruguay,
Argentina and Bolivia discredited the Soviet expectation of the "peaceful path" to communism in Latin America.

In the 1970s, a number of other developments combined to shift the

National Bipartisan Commission on Central America. *The Report of the President's Na-*
tional Bipartisan Commission on Central America, 105–9. New York: Macmillan, 1984.

Soviet Union toward a more adventurous approach, including support for revolutionary armed struggle in Central America.

One of these developments was the triumph of Soviet-backed forces in Indochina, Angola, Mozambique, Ethiopia and South Yemen. This seemed to reward a more aggressive Soviet policy toward the Third World generally, in keeping with the perception in Moscow that the "correlation of forces" had shifted dramatically against the West. The result was a very significant strengthening of the Soviet military capability in the Caribbean. This included a dramatic build-up in the size and sophistication of the Cuban Armed Forces, not least their air and naval components; an enlarged direct Soviet military presence in Cuba, with regular port calls by Soviet naval task forces and nuclear missile submarines; and the deployment of advanced reconnaissance aircraft; increased numbers of Soviet military advisers; and close operational collaboration between Soviet and Cuban forces, as, for example, when Russian pilots were sent to Cuba in 1976 and 1978 to replace Cuban pilots aiding pro-Soviet regimes in Angola and Ethiopia.

This coincided with a reduction in the U.S. military presence in the Caribbean Basin (from over 25,000 in 1968 to under 16,000 in 1981), in the wake of Vietnam and in a climate of public hostility to U.S. security concerns, especially in the Third World. Finally, the 1970s saw the sharpening of the social, economic, and political crisis in Central America—a development extensively dealt with elsewhere in this report—which made the region an inviting target for insurgency.

The success of the revolution in Nicaragua in 1979, like Castro's own accession to power a decisive event, accelerated the revision of Soviet policy toward revolution in Central America. The President of the Soviet Association of Friendship with Latin American countries, Viktor Volski, called the armed victory in Nicaragua a "model" to be followed in other countries . . .

Cuban and Soviet perceptions began to merge again. The new line was quickly accepted by the Communist Party of El Salvador (PCES), which had previously described the country's insurgent groups as "adventurist" and "bound to fail," and had been accused, in turn, of "decadence" and "revisionism." The PCES now made a complete about-face and turned toward armed struggle. . . .

The revolutionary strategy pursued in 1978–79 by Cuba in Nicaragua has since been attempted in El Salvador, Guatemala, and Honduras. Traditionally splintered insurgent groups were required to unify as a condition for increased Cuban and other Soviet bloc military support. This creation of a unified military front allowed Cuba to exercise greater control over the uprising. Meanwhile, a separate political front was created—a "broad coalition," led by the extreme left but including some elements of the noncommunist opposition. Such a political front allowed the guerrillas to co-opt some noncommunist leaders and to neutralize them as rival alternatives to the existing government. . . .

The commitment to the promotion of armed struggle was further backed up by a dramatic increase in Soviet arms deliveries to Cuba. They grew from an average of 15,000 tons a year in the 1970s—roughly equal to current deliveries to Nicaragua—to 66,000 tons in 1981, and about the same amount in each of the following two years. Cuba's armed forces currently total 227,000, a fivefold increase over 1960, and this figure does not include paramilitary and reserve organizations of 780,000. Cuban forces are well equipped with sophisticated weaponry supplied by Moscow, have extensive combat experience on foreign soil, and are well trained. In addition, the Soviets provide a brigade of approximately 3,000 men stationed near Havana, as well as an additional presence of 2,500 military advisers and 8,000 civilian advisers.

The Cuban Air Force now has more than 200 combat jet aircraft, including three squadrons of MiG-23's, as well as Mi-X helicopter gunships and Mi-24 assault helicopters. AN-26 and other transport aircraft give Cuba a logistic capability much greater than it had at the time of the airlift to Angola in 1975. An expansion of the Cuban Navy which began in the 1970s has continued with the acquisition of two Foxtrot submarines, a Koni-class frigate, minesweepers, and landing craft, and an upgrading of the naval base at Cienfuegos, which services nuclear submarines.

All this makes Cuba no less than the second military power in Latin America after Brazil, a country with twelve times Cuba's population. And some experts put Cuba ahead of even Brazil in terms of modern military capabilities. Cuba's island geography complicates its sponsorship of subversion. But Nicaragua suffers no such limitation. From there, men and materiel destined for El Salvador can be transported overland through remote areas by routes that are almost impossible to patrol on a constant basis, or by sea to isolated beaches, or by air at night to remote bush strips along the coast or farther inland. Furthermore, Cuba, with Soviet aid, has built a powerful radio communication center that is now being used to relay the orders of insurgent leaders based in Nicaragua to their troops in the field, thus making the Salvadoran guerrillas far more effective than would otherwise be possible.

As a mainland platform, therefore, Nicaragua is a crucial stepping-stone for Cuban and Soviet efforts to promote armed insurgency in Central America. Its location explains why the Nicaraguan revolution of 1979, like the Cuban revolution 20 years earlier, was a decisive turning point in the affairs of the region. With the victory of the Sandinistas in Nicaragua, the levels of violence and counter-violence in Central America rapidly increased, engulfing the entire region.

11.9 The Arias Peace Plan

Following efforts by a coalition of Latin American countries to develop a peace plan for Central America during the mid-1980s, the president of Costa Rica, Oscar Arias, crafted a proposal in 1987 known informally as the Arias Peace Plan. The plan, signed by all of Central America's presidents, outlined mechanisms to conciliate contending forces throughout the isthmus. Principally aimed at Nicaragua, the agreement served as an alternative to continued U.S. unilateral measures supporting armed opposition to the Sandinista government, and earned President Arias a Nobel Peace Prize in 1987. Excerpts of the plan are featured in the following reading.

7 August 1987

The governments of the Republics of Costa Rica, El Salvador, Guatemala, Honduras and Nicaragua, determined to achieve the objectives and to develop the principles established in the United Nations Charter and the Charter of the Organization of American States. . .

National Reconciliation

Dialogue

To urgently carry out, in those cases where deep divisions have resulted within society, steps for national reconciliation which would allow for popular participation with full guarantees in authentic political processes of a democratic nature based on justice, freedom, and democracy. Towards this end, to create those mechanisms which, in accordance with the law, would allow for dialogue with opposition groups. For this purpose, the corresponding governments will initiate a dialogue with all unarmed internal political opposition groups and with those who have availed themselves of the amnesty.

Amnesty

In each Central American country, except those where the International Commission of Verification and Follow-up determines that such a measure is not necessary, an amnesty decree will be issued containing

"The Esquipulas II Agreement, 7 August 1987." In *Latin America and Caribbean Contemporary Record, 1987–88,* edited by James M. Malloy and Eduardo A. Gamarra, C3–C7. New York: Holmes & Meier, 1990.

all the provisions for the guarantee of the inviolability of life; as well as freedom in all its forms, property and the security of the persons to whom these decrees apply. Simultaneous with the issuing of the amnesty decree by the government, the irregular forces of the respective country will place in freedom all persons in their power.

National Reconciliation Commission

In order to verify the compliance with the commitments that the five Central American governments subscribed to by the signing of this document, concerning amnesty, cease-fire, democratization and free elections, a National Reconciliation Commission will be established whose duties will be to verify the actual carrying out in practice of the national reconciliation process, as well as the full exercise of all civil and political rights of Central American citizens guaranteed in this document. . . .

Democratization

The governments commit themselves to promote an authentic democratic, pluralist and participatory process that includes the promotion of social justice; respect for human rights, [state] sovereignty, the territorial integrity of states and the right of all nations to freely determine, without outside interference of any kind, its economic, political, and social model; and to carry out in a verifiable manner those measures leading to the establishment, or in their instances, the improvement of representative and pluralist democratic systems which would provide guarantees for the organization of political parties, effective popular participation in the decision making process, and to ensure free access to different currents of opinion, to honest electoral processes and newspapers based on the full exercise of citizens' rights.

For the purpose of verifying the good faith in the development of this democratization process, it will be understood that there shall exist complete freedom of press, television, and radio. This complete freedom will include the opening and maintaining in operation of communications media for all ideological groups, and the operation of this media without prior censorship. . . .

Cessation of Assistance to Irregular Forces or Insurrectionist Movements

The governments of the five Central American states shall request the governments of the region, and the extra-regional governments which openly or covertly provide military, logistical, financial, propagandistic aid in manpower, armaments, munitions and equipment to irregular forces or insurrectionist movements to cease this aid, as an indispensable element for achieving a stable and lasting peace in the region. . . .

Refugees and Displaced Persons

The governments of Central America commit themselves to give urgent attention to the groups of refugees and displaced persons brought about by the regional crisis, through protection and assistance, particularly in areas of education, health, work and security, and whenever voluntary and individually expressed, to facilitate in the repatriation, resettlement and relocation [of these persons]. They also commit themselves to request assistance for Central American refugees and displaced persons from the international community both directly through bilateral or multilateral agreements, as well as through the United Nations High Commissioner for Refugees and other organizations and agencies. . . .

We, the presidents of the five states of Central America, with the political will to respond to the longings for peace of our people, sign this [document] in the City of Guatemala, on the seventh day of August of 1987.

Oscar Arias Sánchez
José Napoleón Duarte
Vinicio Cerezo Arévalo
José Azcona Hoyo
Daniel Ortega Saavedra

11.10 About-Face for Salvador Rebel Leader

During the course of the decade-long war in El Salvador, the country's political system began to open up to incorporate previously excluded political interests. In addition, the military's strength and impunity seemed to grow in direct proportion to the massive U.S. military assistance it received to support its antiguerrilla efforts. By the end of the 1980s, it appeared that neither the guerrillas nor the military could win a decisive victory. This view was furthered by world political events: the collapse of Communist governments throughout Eastern Europe; the new pragmatism in

Uhlig, Mark A. "Top Salvador Rebel Alters His Goals." *New York Times*, March 7, 1991.

Soviet foreign policy, and the increasing weakness of the Cuban model of revolutionary change. This helped encourage compromise and negotiations on the part of the government and of the guerrillas. The reading below provides a glimpse into the changing position of a leader of the guerrilla force, the FMLN, as he attempted to adjust his movement to the new conditions of the 1990s.

MEXICO CITY, March 6—Moving away from his coalition's ideological roots, the senior military commander of the Salvadoran rebel army asserted this week that his group could no longer be considered a Marxist movement, and added that one-party rule in El Salvador would be "absurd."

In his first major public comments since the collapse of the Soviet bloc, the commander, Joaquín Villalobos, said that his coalition's goals would not be achieved through armed revolution, but through participation as an unarmed political movement in a pluralistic, "competitive" democracy.

Describing what he termed an important transformation in the rebels' thinking in the wake of recent world events, Mr. Villalobos said the guerrilla coalition had moved beyond Marxism, which he called "just one more political theory, like any other." He said its military goals had shifted from defeating or reforming the Salvadoran Army to winning a permanent disarmament of both sides under the supervision of the United Nations.

Portraying orthodox Communism as an extreme position comparable to El Salvador's right wing, Mr. Villalobos said his coalition, the Farabundo Martí National Liberation Front, now hoped to model El Salvador's future on such prominent capitalist countries as Germany, Japan and nearby Costa Rica, which has no army and is closely tied to the United States economy.

"Cut off the Extremes"

"In El Salvador there is a need to isolate or cut off the extremes," Mr. Villalobos said. "In our case that means the thinking of dogmatic Stalinism and traditional, classic Communism. At the other extreme, it is the orthodox right wing, which in El Salvador is something from the Stone Age."

Mr. Villalobos' comments, made in an unusual set of interviews here over recent days, came amid continued news of guerrilla attacks and military clashes in El Salvador as the country moved toward municipal and legislative elections on Sunday. During the last week, guerrillas briefly took over part of the exclusive residential section of Escalón in the capital and attacked the country's main hydroelectric plant in the northern province of Chalatenango, leaving 23 people dead.

The nature and timing of the remarks suggested the possibility that they were designed to appeal to the guerrillas' foreign critics and to present an image of moderation on the eve of the coming elections, which the rebels have pledged not to interrupt.

But the statements marked a striking departure from the traditional revolutionary positions of Mr. Villalobos' coalition, which has long taken such doctrine with deadly seriousness and has been considered one of the most ideologically rigid guerrilla movements in the region.

The remarks also appeared to underline what the guerrilla commander described as the "new political reality" that his movement now faces after 18 months of dramatic political upheaval affecting its key international supporters. Those developments have included wholesale change in the Soviet Union, the Eastern bloc nations and Nicaragua, and deepening crisis in Cuba, which has long been a principal ally of the Salvadoran guerrilla cause.

Compromise Now His Objective

Believed to be about 40 years old, Mr. Villalobos rarely grants interviews and has spent most of the last decade living secretly abroad or in the hills of El Salvador, directing rebel forces against the Salvadoran army and its American military advisers. But he and other members of the guerrilla high command have devoted increasing effort to talks with the Salvadoran Government toward a negotiated compromise that he said is now the principal objective of the insurgent movement.

12

The Americans: Latin American and Caribbean Peoples in the United States

There are 20 million people from Latin America and the Caribbean in the United States. Early in the next century, they will bypass African-Americans to become the country's largest minority. © Diana Walker/Gamma Liaison

Visible throughout its history as a beacon for immigrants from around the globe, the United States has experienced a new wave of immigration since the 1960s. Within that wave, migrant and refugee groups from Latin America and the Caribbean have been among the most prominent new neighbors. In Chapter 5 we saw the range of forces and motivations spurring this migration and the issues it poses for those countries. This chapter focuses on the diverse experiences of immigrant groups in the United States, as well as their impact on U.S. society and culture.

Old Roots and New Branches

In reality, the Latin American and Caribbean presence in the United States is older than the country itself. The Southwest formed part of the Spanish Empire and then Mexico until 1848, when the territory was expropriated by the United States following the war with Mexico. In that region, soon after the turn of the twentieth century, descendants of the original Spanish and Mexican settlers were joined by immigrant Mexican laborers recruited to work in agriculture and mining, and on the railroads. Elsewhere, on a much smaller scale, Cubans had begun to relocate in South Florida around 1860, while Puerto Ricans established communities in New York after the island became a U.S. territory in 1901.

Nonetheless, the large numbers and diverse origins of contemporary immigrants have given them a heightened visibility in much of the rest of the country. As of 1990 the number of Hispanics had reached 20.1 million, or almost 10 percent of the total population. The high concentration of those groups within large cities and particular regions, reinforced continually as new immigrants make use of the social networks created by previous arrivals, has also contributed to their increased sense of presence.

By virtue of its size and proximity, Mexico continues to account for the majority of Latin American and Caribbean people in the United States. The Census Bureau reported that individuals of Mexican origin numbered 12.6 million in 1990. The actual number may in fact be considerably higher, as Mexicans also constitute the overwhelming majority of illegal or undocumented immigrants. Though Mexican immigrants are widely dispersed across the Southwest and Midwest, the largest contingents have settled in Los Angeles, Chicago, and several border cities.

As U.S. citizens, Puerto Ricans who have moved to the mainland are not immigrants in the formal sense, but as native Spanish-speakers rooted in a Caribbean culture, they have considerably augmented the Hispanic presence in the United States. Around 2.3 million Puerto Ricans now reside on the mainland, primarily in East Coast cities, with the largest concentration still in New York.

Impelled by the 1959 revolution and subsequent policies of Fidel Castro's regime, Cubans have migrated en masse to the United States over the last three decades. Now numbering in excess of 1 million, the U.S. Cuban population is the most highly concentrated immigrant group in terms of location, with more than 60 percent residing in metropolitan Miami.

Several other countries from Latin America and the Caribbean have also contributed to the recent migratory boom in the United States. Immigrants from the Dominican Republic have become one of the largest minority communities in New York, while Jamaican workers are an important East Coast presence in both urban and agricultural enterprises. Fleeing both political repression and economic hardship, Haitians have migrated on a large scale and formed sizable communities in New York and Miami.

Meanwhile, from war-torn Central America, some 500,000 Salvadorans, Guatemalans, and Nicaraguans have sought political refuge in the United States. As a result, large Salvadoran populations have clustered in California, Texas, and Washington, D.C.; whole villages of Guatemalan Indians are now working as migratory agricultural laborers in Florida and elsewhere, and a cross section of Nicaraguan society has been repositioned alongside the Cuban enclave in Miami.

The Challenge of "Making It" in the United States

Despite the history and image of the United States as a land of immigrants, newly arriving groups have almost always been greeted by a mixture of fear, suspicion, and resentment by the descendants of earlier immigrant groups. The current boom, composed in large measure of nonwhite immigrants from Third World countries, is no exception. From political debates to popular entertainment, numerous expressions of concern have surfaced about such consequences as unemployment for the native born, overcrowding in schools and excess demand for other public services, cultural fragmentation, rising crime rates, and environmental degradation. Reading 12.1 exemplifies this viewpoint.

Responding to such fears, summed up by the notion that the United States had "lost control of its borders," Congress passed the Immigration Reform and Control Act in 1986. Among other measures, the bill sought to cut back on illegal immigration by imposing stiff penalties on firms that hired undocumented workers.

While few would argue that the United States should simply abandon all efforts to control immigration, researchers have found that most of the common fears about immigration are groundless or highly exaggerated. Much of their work has focused on the diverse characteristics and achievements of Latin American and Caribbean immigrants.

For a variety of reasons—Third World origins, perceptions of nonwhite racial characteristics, and concentration in low-status jobs, among others—recent immigrants have been popularly thought to represent the overflow of the poor and destitute from underdeveloped countries. Survey after survey has found, however, that Latin American and Caribbean immigrants arriving in the United States, whether of legal, undocumented, or refugee status, have above-average levels of education and occupational skills compared with the general population of the countries they left behind. Legal immigrants, moreover, compare quite favorably to overall U.S. standards.

Once in the United States, though, immigrants usually find that linguistic and cultural barriers initially confine them to jobs that are low paying, low status, and lacking in security or prospects for advancement. The experiences recounted in readings 12.2 and 12.3 are not atypical in this regard, as a Cuban judge and a Puerto Rican teacher find their first jobs as a maid in Miami and as a seamstress in the Northeast, respectively. These stories also reveal, however, how immigrants confront their new circumstances by embracing hard work and high ambitions.

Not all immigrants find their dreams within reach, of course. In large measure, the immigrant experience follows the established pattern of social mobility in the United States: the higher the level of parents' education and occupational status, the higher an individual's educational achievement, which in turn ultimately leads to higher occupational status and income.

Nevertheless, Latin American and Caribbean immigrants are far from uniform in their experiences in the United States. In recent decades Puerto Ricans have consistently experienced higher unemployment rates, lower occupational status, and lower income levels than other Hispanic groups, with averages similar to those of black Americans. Mexicans have fared somewhat better but are still relatively underprivileged. At the other extreme, Cubans have in general overcome the initial disadvantages of immigration to achieve socioeconomic standards comparable to those of nonimmigrant white Americans.

These variations are not so much a matter of cultural distinctions as of differences in the historical context of the reception that the various immigrant groups have encountered. The differences include the degree of acceptance and support accorded a particular immigrant group by the U.S. government; the economic and social characteristics of the labor market in the cities or regions where a particular group settles; and the nature of the ethnic community formed by previous immigrants from that group.

Thus, the relative success of Cuban Americans is in part the result of the dynamic entrepreneurial community of Cuban Miami, which has offered both initial employment and avenues of advancement, as well as the favorable treatment accorded them by the government as refugees from a Communist country. Puerto Ricans in the Northeast, by contrast, form a largely working-class population in a region that has suffered industrial decline and significant job loss since the 1970s. They may also be subject to racial discrimination if they are perceived as black, a factor weighing heavily on the experience of migrants from other Caribbean countries, such as Haiti, Jamaica, and the Dominican Republic (see reading 12.4).

A major source of tension between immigrant and native-born populations in the United States centers on the immigrants' cultural assimilation and integration into the U.S. mainstream, especially with regard to language. The fear that other languages will displace or eclipse English has greeted virtually every new immigrant group in the country's history, and has proved unfounded just as often.

Spanish-speaking immigrants from Latin America have discovered no less quickly that mastering English is an important key to social, economic, and political advancement, even if it is unnecessary for getting along in the ethnic urban communities in which they initially settle. Outside these communities, they have followed the traditional pattern whereby English becomes the sole language in their families after one or two generations.

At the same time, in the context of an increasingly competitive international economy, government officials and business leaders have expressed growing concern over the insularity of American culture, as reflected in the U.S. population's limited international awareness and lack of foreign language skills. From this perspective, the persistence of popular pressure on immigrants to abandon their native languages and other cultural expressions might actually be counterproductive for U.S. interests at a time of growing global interdependence.

Political and Cultural Expressions

Like earlier immigrants, Latin American and Caribbean groups have gradually begun to assert their interests in the U.S. political arena, even as they maintain a strong interest in the politics of their homelands. A number of reasons exist for this seeming ambiguity of political identity.

On the one hand, countries like Cuba and Mexico feature prominently in world affairs and constitute highly visible symbols with which immigrants can continue to identify (perhaps negatively, in the case of political exiles). At the individual level, they may regard themselves as only temporarily residing in the United States and ready to return when political or economic circumstances make it possible. In any case, contemporary developments in communication and transportation make it relatively simple to maintain ties with family and friends across national boundaries and thus stay informed.

Yet as immigrants establish careers and raise families in their new country, they turn their attention to the problems in their immediate surroundings. In this sense, the ethnic politics of Latin American and Caribbean groups have followed the traditional U.S. immigrant pattern. They form neighborhood associations around issues of social welfare, religion, or business. They move to acquire U.S. citizenship. Ultimately they begin to vote, and to the extent that they are concentrated in residential neighborhoods or treated as distinct racial and ethnic minorities by the rest of the population, their votes will tend to be cast along ethnic and racial lines.

Readings 12.5 and 12.6 capture this complexity of immigrant politics. Advocating bilingual education or voting along ethnic lines does not represent political disloyalty or reluctance to integrate into American society. Rather, these are direct expressions of community efforts to overcome social and economic barriers faced by immigrants. As both interests and obstacles vary widely among different immigrant groups, so too do their political expressions, ranging from the Republican preferences of Cuban-Americans concerned with foreign policy, to the Democratic partisanship of Chicanos (Mexican-Americans) focused on labor issues.

New ethnic identities may emerge as well. Government censuses and programs count "Hispanics," based on presumed commonalities of language and culture, rather than Dominicans, Mexicans, or Colombians. Americans of other national or ethnic descent often take the same approach by identifying individuals, regardless of country of origin, as "Hispanic." In this fashion, commonalities of interest among the distinct "Hispanic" or "Latino" populations may gradually emerge to shape both political programs and individual identities (see reading 12.7). For the present, however, these tendencies are overshadowed by the resilient self-awareness of distinctive national groups.

Meanwhile, as these sorts of debates proceed, Latin American and Caribbean influences are being adopted, transformed, and re-created within the U.S. cultural mosaic. Reading 12.8 describes the multiple ways in which Latino and Caribbean music, literature, cinema, art, cuisine, and other cultural forms have found their way into the U.S. mainstream. Many of these influences are so widespread that they are as much taken for granted in small towns, where the only Spanish spoken is in the high school classroom, as they are in major cities with large immigrant communities. In a very real sense, the new neighbors have become part of the national family.

12.1 A Voice Against Massive Immigration

Immigrants have rarely encountered an enthusiastic reception after arriving on U.S. shores. In 1753, for example, Benjamin Franklin expressed his concern about the growing German population in Pennsylvania and its apparent reluctance to assimilate. "I suppose in a few years," he wrote, "[interpreters] will also be necessary in the Assembly, to tell one-half of our legislators what the other half say." In 1986, more than two centuries later, similar fears prompted Congress to pass legislation attempting to limit and control the influx of immigrants. The following selection, coauthored by former Colorado governor Richard Lamm, presents a view articulated during the debates preceding passage of the immigration reform bill. It clearly voices popular fears of more "new neighbors."

The immigration crisis has grown steadily and slowly, and therefore taken us by surprise. Today, immigration to the United States is massive, and it is out of control. The United States accepts for permanent resettlement twice as many immigrants as do all the other countries of the world combined. Legal immigration is three times as high as it was in the early 1960s; there are now well over 600,000 legal immigrants in an average year. Illegal immigration is estimated to be ten times greater; there are now well over a million apprehensions a year—without any corresponding increase in enforcement activities. Illegal aliens pour into the United States through Swiss-cheese borders. Legal and illegal immigration combined contribute nearly half of the population growth of the United States. And efforts to cope with the breakdown of immigration law or to moderate the high levels of legal immigration are stymied in Congress by an unlikely coalition of the far right and the far left, fueled by a coalition of big business and Hispanic pressure groups.

In the past, moderate levels of immigration have been good for this country and they will continue to be good for it in the future. The leavening effect of immigrants' energy, enthusiasm, effort, and different cultures have improved all of our lives. Few Americans quarrel with the value of immigration. But, at today's massive levels, immigration has major negative consequences—economic, social, and demographic—that overwhelm its advantages.

Lamm, Richard D., and Gary Imhoff. *The Immigration Time Bomb*, 1–12. New York: Truman Talley Books, 1985.

To solve the immigration crisis, we Americans have to face our limitations. We have to face the necessity of passing laws to restrict immigration and the necessity of enforcing those laws. If we fail to do so, we shall leave a legacy of strife, violence, and joblessness to our children.

Unrestricted immigration to America has been a fine dream, and dreams die hard. In one of his best-known poems, Langston Hughes asked, "What happens to a dream deferred?" He ends with the disturbing question, *"Or does it explode?"* What happens when a dream is lost can be even more disturbing.

Today, we Americans must lose the dream of unrestricted immigration and must face the reality behind the dream. We dreamed of America as a country of immigration, and we identified open immigration with freedom. We believed that someone poor, someone downtrodden, someone persecuted—from any other country in the world—could pull up stakes, come to America, and have another chance. We thought that we were the land of opportunity, not just for our own citizens but also for all the people of the world who wished to come here.

It is a beautiful dream, but it is only a dream. It is possible to dream it only when immigration to the United States is limited, controlled, and kept to moderate levels. It is not a dream we can keep today.

We were taught that the special destiny of America was to be a country of immigrants. The history we learned was that our country was built by immigration and by immigrants. In fact, this was never strictly true. The white population of the United States, as counted in our national censuses, grew from a little over three million to nearly eight million between 1790 and 1820, in the earliest decades of the Republic. This is a high rate of population growth, but it does not reflect a high rate of immigration. Immigration to the United States during this time was certainly under ten thousand people a year, and the best contemporary estimates place it at between six and seven thousand a year. For most of our history, the extraordinary population growth of the United States has actually been from natural increases—from the high rate of fertility of relatively small numbers of immigrants.

We dreamed of America as a land where immigrants could become successful by an almost magical process. In fact, immigration has always been a bittersweet transition. It has exacted a high price from immigrants, and our current recognition of the pain of immigration signals our awakening from the haze of sentimentality with which we have surrounded and obscured the family stories of the first American generation.

We dreamed of a melting pot where, without effort and without anguish, immigrants would acquire the language and culture of the United States, where they would learn the technical and social skills they would need to survive and succeed here without paying the cost of relinquishing the language and culture and mores of their native countries. In fact, assimilation has always been difficult.

We dreamed, perhaps most of all, of a land of plenty, a New Eden that would be inexhaustible, that would accept all who came here and provide them with a wilderness to conquer and the land and water and all the other resources they would need to make their lives plentiful— with just a little effort and gumption. We dreamed of a country where competition would be with nature, and not with each other; where giving to one would not mean taking from another; where materials and jobs could be made without limit and where there would be room for all. We dreamed of a country where generosity would be easy because there would be so much with which to be generous. The dream seemed to come true, for a time, but that era is over. . . .

It is not antihuman or antisocial to say that too many people can be a problem. It is simply realistic to acknowledge the fact. Human activity changes the world in many ways in addition to resource exhaustion, and not all of these ways are good even for human beings. People pollute, and too many people living in an area can degrade that area irrevocably. Immigration at high levels exacerbates our resource and environmental problems. It will leave a poorer, more crowded, more divided country for our children.

Immigration at massive levels also creates societal problems. Because the assimilation of new immigrants is difficult, for them and for the host society, too rapid a rate of immigration into an area can strain social relationships and political systems to the breaking point. In many societies less tolerant and less hospitable than our own, rapid large-scale immigration has even led to massive slaughter. Since 1951 over four million Bengalis have migrated illegally to the Indian state of Assam, and since 1979 the Assamese have been protesting the central government's inaction against this migration. Assam is now virtually under military rule; at least 5,000 people, most of them Bengalis, have been killed, and perhaps 300,000 Bengalis have been displaced by mob protests and violence.

In the United States, there has been gang warfare between Vietnamese and Hispanics in Denver; Texas shrimpers have fought immigrant Vietnamese boatmen; black neighborhoods in many cities have seen Korean and other Asian shopkeepers killed in robberies that smacked of cultural resentment; Miami has had a mayoral campaign fought primarily over whether a Hispanic mayor of Puerto Rican descent might be too close to black concerns and a rival Hispanic candidate of Cuban descent more oriented toward the Cuban community. All these rivalries, all these frictions, are primarily over the rate of change caused by massive immigration.

On a less intense level, bilingual education has caused a national debate. The question is whether non-English-speaking students should be taught in English or in their native languages and whether these bilingual programs should be aimed primarily at giving students mastery over English or at maintaining their native languages and cultures. Questions of this sort would simply never be allowed to rise in societies less open than America's—and they would never arise here if immigration were at moderate levels, if there were not concentrations of migrants large enough to sustain their native languages.

At high enough levels, immigration also creates economic problems. In many areas of the world, migrants are moving from less developed to more developed countries. They generally have fewer skills than workers in their host countries, and in those cases migrants move into unskilled jobs at the bottom of the job ladders of those countries. If their numbers are large enough, they displace native workers and—when economies are not vibrant and growing at fast enough rates—they contribute to the unemployment of natives and depress the salary levels for the jobs in which they specialize. In West Germany, for example, certain jobs became stigmatized in the late 1960s and 1970s as "Turkish jobs," performed by temporary migrant guestworkers from Turkey. When certain jobs become stigmatized in such a way, a society loses some of its cohesiveness, a large part of its social mobility, and a degree of respect for manual labor. In the United States, our own garment industry has now been stigmatized as a sector in which illegal immigrants work. Wages have fallen, sweatshops have been revived, a noble union has been corrupted by accepting the existence of "shadow locals" and tolerating the exploitation of illegal workers, and—in a self-fulfilling prophecy—employers have created a class of work that "Americans won't do." . . .

12.2 Starting Over

In the following reading, a Cuban woman recounts some of her experiences of resettlement and attempts to establish a new career in the United States. A lawyer and judge who fled Cuba in 1962 at the age of 48, Irma de León represents the early wave of Cuban refugees drawn from the better-educated, higher-income, and professional ranks of the island's population. Unable to transfer her advantages directly to this country, she found work in Miami in two of the jobs traditionally open to immigrant women: domestic service and garment factory work. Despite the fact that she ulti-

Doran, Terry, Janet Satterfield, and Chris Stade. *A Road Well Traveled: Three Generations of Cuban American Women*, 64–70. Newton, Mass.: WEEA Publishing Center, 1988.

mately failed to work again as a lawyer, her successful economic and social adaptation illustrates the experience of her refugee generation, which paved the way for the integration of later refugees into south Florida's Cuban communities.

Irma's Story: Open Mind

I was born in a small town in Cuba. My father belonged to the army, and when I was seven years old, he was transferred to the city of Cienfuegos, where I spent most of my life.

The biggest influence in my life was my mother. She always wanted to get an education herself, but her parents considered it a disgrace for their daughter to go out of the home to study, so they never let her do it. I am sure for that reason she had the firm determination her daughter would get an education. She made any kind of work and sacrifices in order to help us to accomplish it. She tried to put in our minds to be educated and to have a career because that is what counts in life. My mother is very proud of me because I did what she wanted. I am very proud, too.

We Cuban people like to improve our way of life. In Cuba, not too many people were rich, and I mean they didn't have the economic means to study. But we tried to do and to sacrifice ourselves to study. . . .

Being a woman, I had no restrictions in my choice of careers. My first choice was to be a teacher. I love children, and I was a teacher for three years at the same school where I had studied. I always had a very high sense of justice and wanted to help society in that field. I thought that my Christian background would help me do a better job, so I decided to be a judge, and for that I had to study law. As a student at the University of Havana Law School, finances were a problem, but I was determined to achieve my goal. So during my years at the university, I earned money by tutoring children and sewing clothes to pay for my needs, such as books and travel expenses. Due to my high marks, I had free tuition. I graduated with a Doctor of Law in 1945 and practiced law until I was admitted to the judiciary system. I served as a judge for six years; then the Communists fired me because I didn't fit into their system. I am very proud of the work I did during my years as a judge.

The Revolution brought an abrupt change to my life. Everything that I had been taught and stood for changed. Castro appeared on television and reported, "Last night we passed a law and everybody who doesn't agree with it will be put into prison." I knew then I would have to leave or they would kill me. In May 1962 I made a decision to leave Cuba.

"My Aching Back": From Judge to Maid

I fled to Miami with my thirteen-year-old daughter, leaving behind my husband, and abandoned career, and all our possessions. When I came I had not a penny. They don't let us bring not even a penny, nothing. I had just two dresses, but I knew very well that I had to work here so it was not a surprise for me. I was happy because I wanted to take our daughter from the system in Cuba.

The first thing I did in Miami was taking care of little children. This was something very new for me because in Cuba we have no babysitters. In Cuba, all the relatives—the grandmothers and the aunts and the older sisters—take care of the children, but here it is another business. When that was not enough, I started cleaning houses one day a week, and so later one of the ladies wanted me to be a steady maid and I decided to do that. She was paying $35 a week, which I felt was a great deal of money. I needed $400 to bring my husband from Cuba, so I said, "Oh, this is great." It was the first time that I started working with a vacuum cleaner . . . oh . . . [laughs], the first day that I cleaned all the house, my back was killing me! . . .

I was adjusting little by little to the work in that home. I cooked lunch for them and ironed, washed the clothes and everything. I was real happy with that job, very, very happy. Yes, I was a lawyer, a judge, in Cuba, but here I couldn't do that and so I was very fortunate that I could work and earn money. I have no hard feelings. No, I think that God gave me the opportunity to work and earn money, because I always said that I like to earn the money that they pay me. I don't want anything for nothing, and even if I had to work very hard as a maid, I was grateful.

Later, the lady I worked for was moving back to Washington or something, so I started working in a factory, sewing, because I loved to sew. The problem was I did not have experience with factory machines. The first day that I started working there, I pushed the pedal and the machine went backwards and the lady was asking me, "You know about this?" And I said, "Yes I have some experience." But when she saw me, oh, dear! But no, she gave me the job. That work was really something because I had to work eight hours sitting, and I couldn't even look around because I was not as fast as they ask and I couldn't make the minimum. . . .

After two years in Miami, I decided to move to Lakeland to work as a lab technician in the research laboratory of Borden Chemical Company. I had some basic knowledge of chemistry from my studies in Cuba, required to enter at the University of Havana. Borden gave me the opportunity to learn how to run analyses. I worked there for seventeen years. . . .

Trying Again to Be a Lawyer

In Cuba we have the civil law system that comes from the Roman law, and here in the United States they have the common law from England. We cannot come here and pass the bar exam, because of the different law system. For years the Cuban lawyers were trying to do something, and finally the Supreme Court of Florida ruled that the University of Florida should prepare a program on the subjects we needed to pass the bar exam.

For two years I went to Gainesville, driving 260 miles every Saturday morning. We left at six o'clock and spent all day studying. We had tests every three months and finally had a graduation. During that time I was also working at my full-time job in the lab and was by that time sixty years old. It was really something. It was hard at that age to adjust to a new study and new things.

Not only was it difficult to learn the common law system from England, but the exams were also different. In Cuba we have essay exams, but here it's multiple-choice. So the answers are very close—there were about three answers that you think were true; that's very hard to decide. The barrier of the language made it even harder, because if you don't know the real meaning of a single word, you can get mixed up in the answer. . . .We were around 200 when we started, and I think about 180 graduated from the course. Some students were old, and one died, poor man. It was hard, very hard. But then we went to take the bar exam, and only 3 passed. We were in a disadvantageous position—from 200 lawyers that started, just 3 could pass the bar exam. Of course, I failed.

There was a lot of talking after that, because many of the students said it was discrimination that we didn't pass. I don't know, really. I know especially lawyers in Miami would be in competition with other lawyers because they know the language. They told us that even American people, some they don't pass the first time. Later some students went again, and I think 10 or 15 have passed in these years.

Never Too Old

During this time of study, my husband and my family were very supportive and they encouraged my efforts. One thing I admire in this country is that no matter how old you are, you can study and do things that in our culture are not accepted well. I still hope, even at my age, someday I can take the bar exam. I am retired now, but I have been doing social work with people who don't speak English. I take them to doctors' offices, for food stamps and social security visits, et cetera. This kind of work has prevented me to devote time to prepare to take again the bar exam, but I still want to do it, and I hope someday I can do it—this is my goal. . . .

Daughter's First Date

When I first came, I was very afraid for my daughter to go out alone. But, at the same time, I couldn't isolate her. The different system here was hard for me to accept. I have an open mind, but I was very fearful. Now, after twenty years, I see going out alone as normal. My husband was still in Cuba at the time I was raising my daughter alone, so I used to think, "What would he say or think?" I was afraid for her to go to the corner. Although my daughter did not try to do all the things she saw others doing, I was especially afraid that she start dating. In Cuba the girls never date the boys alone, they always have a chaperone, and this is something that is inside us, our way of thinking. . . .

A New Community

The adjustment here in a small community like Lakeland is different than in a bigger one like Miami or another place because all your friends are Americans and you have to speak English and you have to do what they do here. For example, when I came here to Lakeland twenty years ago, they had no Cuban food, so a man started going to Tampa every week and brought Cuban food here. We did not have the food we were used to, at first, but we did have the advantage that we could learn English faster because we were surrounded by Americans. . . .

Many of the Cuban people that have spent twenty years living in Miami continue to live like in Cuba. I have seen many who will get sick or insane because they are always thinking about Cuba, what they left in Cuba, what they had in Cuba, and all the time thinking about the same thing. I said that I love Cuba, I miss Cuba, I am homesick, but if you are going to live in a place, you have to adjust. . . .

12.3   A Puerto Rican Migrant in the United States

Maplewood is the fictitious name of a real city in New England. During the nineteenth and early twentieth centuries, successive waves of immigrants from many European countries came to the region, followed by blacks from the southern United States and, more recently, Puerto Ricans. As newcomers arriving after the region's industrial base had begun to decline, the Puerto Ricans found themselves confined to relatively unskilled service and factory jobs with few opportunities for upward mobility. Culturally distinctive and economically disadvantaged, the Puerto Rican community in Maplewood has witnessed repeated efforts to form neighborhood organizations to tackle these daunting problems. One such effort was led by Cristina Estebán, who somehow found time to combine full-time employment as a garment worker, household duties as a wife and mother of three, church volunteer work, and community activism. Her account illustrates the countless difficulties many immigrants face in their new communities, as well as the ways in which they try to resolve them.

I am a Puerto Rican mother of three children. On St. Joseph's Day I will be 43 years old. I was born in a small village near the Caribbean in the southeastern part of Puerto Rico. In high school my girl friends often criticized me for taking scientific courses instead of commercial courses. With commercial courses you can work as a secretary in a sugarcane refinery, but I told them my father would never let me work as a secretary. They tried to act superior to me and asked where I would ever get the money to go to the university. I simply wanted to study, learn, become independent, and fend for myself. Nothing more.

After high school, I attended the University of Puerto Rico for two years, but my grade point was not sufficient for the Normal Diploma of an accredited teacher. I did qualify, however, as a provisional teacher, and everyone in my hometown wondered how the daughter of a poor man could become a teacher. My girl friends were left with their mouths open in admiration. My father was proud that through hard work and determination I became a professional, the first one in our family ever to be one. To this day, he will not let anyone in Puerto Rico know that I worked in a factory in Maplewood. . . .

From the moment I arrived In Maplewood, I began to learn about

Rogler, Lloyd H. *Migrant in the City: The Life of a Puerto Rican Action Group*, 104–5. Maplewood, N.J.: Waterfront Press, 1984.

the city. I got to know the majority of the Puerto Ricans living here by teaching English in the adult education program, working in church, making arrangements for weddings and baptisms, finding them jobs, taking them to see doctors and nurses, and interpreting for them. I also became aware of the many programs and services in the city which could benefit the Hispanos. But I kept to my own kind, not wanting to let myself be known to the Americans, at least not until I was more familiar with the city. To this day I have not exposed myself completely. Now, I am beginning to, and it is mostly through the confederation.

Although Americans want to help the Hispanos and try to do many things for us, it is difficult for them because of our cultural differences. Puerto Ricans are being Americanized, but we still retain much of our own way of life. Because the world is changing, we must prepare the Hispanic community and our children to cope with change. Even here in Maplewood, there is an evolution which must be understood. If we don't prepare, if we just sit and wait, then our problems will be overwhelming. I prefer the American way, and for this reason I am teaching my children to be independent. The Hispanic attitude that the husband works and the wife stays home, never going out, must change if we are to live here.

By this I don't mean that American ways are always good and our ways are always bad. Americans are so individualistic that there is little giving of personal help and, consequently, problems are more difficult to solve. Puerto Ricans value friendship and one can have implicit trust in another person in discussing a personal problem. The Puerto Rican may not know psychology or medicine, but he is always willing to be of help.

It is wrong to think Puerto Ricans come here to get help from the government. Public welfare is the last resort we use to solve our problems. When we do seek assistance however, and are required to reveal the most intimate problems of our lives, we expect immediate help. The welfare people do not understand this. When we don't get help and are just given another appointment the following week or month, anger overwhelms us. Some even commit suicide. In the grocery stores, Americans try to cheat us. In the office of the public-housing project where I live, they treat us like criminals. We have problems with American teachers, American doctors, American landlords. When Americans look down on me as a Puerto Rican, I feel bad and wish only that I could put the same coldness in my eyes to return the look. To deal with such people, you have to be strong, act with character, and have confidence in your capacity to conquer difficulties. This is what I do. . . .

Some Americans are worse than animals, but others are good-hearted. My priest is among the good ones. He helped us get the apartment in the housing project. Recently, my oldest son fell into a fit of depression and did not want to be the leader of the altar group. He told this to the priest, but the priest would not permit him to quit. The very idea that my son was disobedient to the priest made tears pour out of my eyes. Finally, my son told me that he was too big to belong to a group with only small boys. But my son is responsible and not disobedient. Apparently, the priest and the sisters had been talking to him, because a few days after this he got up early on a Saturday morning and cleaned the entire apartment without being asked. Little by little, he changed for the better.

Americans treat their children differently than we do. They leave their children at home with instructions and the children obey. Puerto Ricans fear that if they leave their children at home alone, they would fight or cry or destroy the furniture. Also, when American children play in the street, they solve their own problems and go to their parents only when it is necessary. Even then, American parents try not to interfere, but Puerto Rican parents become involved in their children's arguments. If someone gives a Puerto Rican child a dirty look he cries, and if someone throws a rock at him he runs to the arms of his parents.

I had trouble with my younger son. His teacher called me in for a special conference and started by asking me his nationality. Then she said he was lazy, did not want to work, and always turned in his written assignments with smudges on them. I admit that my son has an explosive temper, but he is not lazy. I explained to the teacher that when he gets nervous the palms of his hands sweat and dirty the paper on which he writes. Also, he feels that she hates him. She said that could not be so, but I had to explain to her that even a gesture or a glance can convey hatred. As a teacher I know this. Then she turned nasty. She said my oldest son and my daughter take after me, but this son takes after his father. She had never even met the father. What abuse! What a lack of respect!

Then last week, I took this son to a woman doctor for a physical examination. She started off by asking my son's nationality. His records were right in front of her, so she did not have to ask that. He was born in Maplewood; he is an American. But if he were not, what difference would that make to his physical condition? Then she said that my son has cavities. I told her that I always remind him to brush his teeth after each meal, but he doesn't listen. She contradicted me in front of my son and said once a day is enough. When my son complained that I gossip about him, she said I should respect him. Imagine, she was attempting to give my son power over me! I told her I demand obedience from my son, but she said she was only giving me medical advice. That was medical advice? She was so harsh that I never had the opportunity to tell her my educational level. . . .

My husband is another problem. He has a bad temper. When he gets angry he is oblivious to everything. He forgets he has a wife, children, compadres. He cares little how or to whom he speaks. Whatever comes

to his mind, he says it to the person involved. His anger is usually provoked by some problem in the community. He reads about it in the
newspaper, gets angry, and erupts. But the anger allows him to un-
drown himself. Then he feels better.

He resents my going out alone. It is only to be with other women, to
go to an organization meeting, to study American customs, but he does
not care who or why or where. He does not permit me to accept the
invitation. Once after I had accepted an invitation and paid for a ticket
to a dinner and was dressed to go out, he suddenly said I could not go.
Another time, *he* insisted on going along and I was so ashamed—there
was Mrs. Estebán with her husband, the only man among 15 women.
How humiliating!

I have had the desire to leave him and travel the world, I have considered every possibility except divorce. No, even that I cannot say.
. . . I am happier now than I was in Puerto Rico when I was single.
There I lived a narrow life because my father confined me to the house
and allowed me to go out only to church, school, or to work. The few
parties I went to were at school or at work. I never went to the movies,
or social dances, or had boyfriends. Even the relatives who came to visit
us came only to speak to my father. It was not an environment in which
to attain independence, so it was not until after marriage that I began
to have more freedom. With freedom I developed confidence in myself. . . .

The important thing about the confederation is the struggle we have
had to move the group to where it is now. Ever since we first got together we have had problems, all of which are difficult to explain. The
group started when Mr. Frank Joyce asked me why Hispanos were not
joining neighborhood groups, and I told him to invite them to a meeting and listen to what they have to say. But the Hispanos have a complex involving aggressiveness, and at the meeting this complex was apparent. They complained about bad housing, discrimination, public
welfare, and other things that only revealed their psychological problems.

At a later meeting, Rafael Zayas made the motion that I be president
and his brother Diego vice-president, but I opposed it, arguing that a
man, not a woman, should be president. The truth is that I did not
want to be president because, seeing what was going on, I felt the group
would not accomplish a thing. Also, I had a personal thing too, a complex. People look upon me as a leader, yet I feel I am not a leader.
Were I to become president, I reasoned, people would turn against me
because of envy and jealousy. I wanted to be an active member, but to
step aside and not be president. Diego was elected president by one
vote, and I was vice-president. . . .

The group's purpose was to help Hispanos have better food, housing, employment, education, and to eliminate prejudice against us.
Without voting, we decided not to be a religious or political organiza-

tion, and not to collect dues. The plan was to make the group the nucleus of all Puerto Rican organizations in the city. . . .

From the very start, Diego showed his inexperience as president. Because the American advisors insisted upon our working on our own, he once told me, "They are cheating us and treating us as if we were stupid." I told him to be patient and not to speak without facts. He began meetings with, "Well, what shall we discuss today?" When I said he should start with the reading of the minutes, he said that as president it was for him to decide what to do. You see, he was doing worse then than I am now. . . .

At the next meeting, I hardly had to speak. There was complete agreement that we should work to help the community, and each person spoke about the lack of group discipline and how poorly Diego had done as president. They repeated the same thing at the following meeting. Someone then proposed that the vice-president become president. Even though I did not want the position when the group began, this is how I became president. . . .

Many people think that because I do so much community work I have a special position or appointment in the city, but the truth is that I work voluntarily without pay. . . .

I have the same trouble explaining how I first got tied up with the antipoverty agency, but let me try. I used to work in a factory sewing ladies' bathing suits. I did this to punish my husband who, by forcing me to come to Maplewood, made me quit my position as a teacher in Puerto Rico. . . . Suddenly I decided to quit my job. I told my husband, who said, "Good, good, good. I will work to support you." He was so happy he cut down on his drinking. When I reminded him we would have to live on his salary, he agreed. He never wanted me to do factory work, because I was a professional.

When my friends heard I quit, they became curious about my plans. I thought I would see what I could get from the antipoverty agency . . . The agency did not know that in Maplewood I was in charge of the Hispanic community, not officially, but in fact. The agency was being criticized even by Americans, who said that the agency could not be of any help to Hispanos if the employees knew only two or three words of Spanish. The Hispanos in Maplewood are a people who come from the mountains of Puerto Rico and first put on shoes at the age of 12 or 14. They know little about living in a place like this. With two or three words of Spanish, an American can never understand their customs and problems. Such criticisms were correct, but for some reason the agency asked me to help without offering me a job. Maybe they wanted me to take the initiative, but I would not; that was for them to do. . . .

Before, I was only a name to the agency; they did not know me personally, nor I them. But through the confederation they have come to know me, and I have come to be involved in the broader affairs of the community. The Puerto Ricans used to live on promises, but because our group has tangible goals, we now have something substantial. The day I do not get what I want is the day I return to my own country. . . .

12.4 Caribbean Quandaries

New York, long a magnet for immigrants from around the world, now features a diverse set of Latin American and Caribbean communities. Puerto Ricans arrived first in large numbers, during the post–World War II decades, and still constitute the biggest Latino community in the city. But a more recent influx of immigrants from the Caribbean and South America is transforming the city's ethnic neighborhoods and augmenting its rich cultural mix. Half of New York's recent immigrants come from the Caribbean, with Dominicans the most numerous, but with Haiti and the English-speaking Caribbean also contributing large numbers. The following selection suggests the diversity within this Caribbean population and the difficulties that non-Hispanic Caribbean immigrants face in the "Big Apple."

The Caribbean influence on New York has been tremendous: on food (island cooking can be found in restaurants, from Vernon's Jerk Paradise in the Bronx to the yuppified Day-O and Sugar-Reef in Manhattan) and on music (*soca*, calypso music and Trinidadian steel bands can be heard in clubs all over the city and reggae has become mainstream). And since West Indian women often work in the home as nannies, baby sitters, and nurses, many New Yorkers come to know them and their culture more intimately than they might other immigrants.

It's no accident that so many Caribbean women work in these fields. Nursing is a higher-status profession in the West Indies than it is here, but because of the depressed economies in the islands, nurses are able to earn much more money here. On top of that, they are allowed special visa preference. For other undocumented Caribbean women, domestic work is one of the few available options, and New Yorkers tend

Brenner, Leslie. "The New New York," *New York Woman*, May 1991, 67–81.

to find English-speaking West Indian women particularly desirable as nannies and home attendants for the elderly.

Caribbean immigrants make up almost half of all immigrants in New York City each year, with huge influxes from the Dominican Republic, Haiti, Jamaica, other West Indian islands and Guyana.

Because the U.S. census lumps African-Americans together with Caribbean blacks (the 1990 census form asked respondents only whether they were "black or Negro"), it's difficult to document exactly who lives in which neighborhoods. In some areas that show up as "black" on census maps—such as La Saline in Brooklyn, the northeast Bronx and St. Albans, Springfield Gardens and Laurelton in Queens—there are many people of Caribbean origin. But in others, such as Brooklyn's Bedford-Stuyvesant, the population is made up mostly of African-Americans. In many cases grandparents of New York's African-Americans migrated from the south in the Fifties to areas that were Italian or Jewish. Crown Heights, for example, now a mixed area of Caribbean blacks, African-Americans and Orthodox Jews, used to be known as the Jewish Gold Coast. The original Loehmann's was in Crown Heights; it's now the New Life Tabernacle.

Up-and-coming second-generation Jews and Italians used to live in Brownsville and East New York, which served as overflow areas for the Lower East Side. African-Americans and Hispanics moved into the neighborhoods in the Sixties and Seventies, and while many of the Hispanics, following in the path of the Jews and Italians, moved out to the suburbs, the African-Americans, for economic reasons, didn't. Nonetheless, many of the attractive row houses in East New York and Bed-Stuy are owned by middle-class African Americans.

Once Grenadians, Barbadians, Trinidadians and people from the smaller islands come to New York, they tend to band together and think of themselves as West Indians. Jamaicans, however, like to maintain their own distinct identity, as do Haitians.

New York City has the largest concentration of Haitians in the U.S.; most of them live in La Saline, Flatbush, Bed-Stuy, Bushwick and East New York. Because of the language barrier, Haitians, who speak Creole and French, do not mix with the English-speaking West Indians. Most Haitians are Catholic, and many practice voodoo as well, openly or not. They have very high self-esteem as a group, perhaps partly because Haiti was the first independent black nation in the west. They refer to Dominicans (their native island mates), Puerto Ricans and Cubans somewhat condescendingly, as *pagnol,* the Creole word for Hispanic, from *espagnol.*

About a third of the Guyanese immigrants are of Indian (subcontinent) descent, but most other Caribbean immigrants are of African ancestry and tend to live in culturally mixed neighborhoods. Many Caribbean blacks say they feel racial prejudice (which is virtually unknown in the islands) less in those neighborhoods heavily populated by African-

Americans. Yet there is always tension. Caribbean immigrants often hold cultural prejudice against African-Americans and at the same time, African-Americans sometimes resent Caribbean blacks for discounting the obstacles they have always faced in getting social and economic footing. Since both groups understand the importance of political unity, their relationship, though strained, is mutually acknowledged as a pressing concern.

Drugs have also become a vital issue, particularly since the problem threatens the West Indian community despite the best efforts of the community's strong social and cultural organizations. Joyce Quamina, an immigrant from Trinidad & Tobago and business manager of the West Indian–American Day Carnival Association, has lived on the same block of President Street in Crown Heights for twenty years. She says that in the last five years, the drug problem there has worsened tremendously, "not only among kids who were born here, but West Indian kids too. It's destroying them." She goes on to explain a curious phenomenon: "A lot of American born kids have learned to talk with the Jamaican accent. It's a fad—everyone wants to be a Jamaican. It started out with the Rastas; the reggae is a very big beat. Some of them are West Indian, but not Jamaican by birth. They are doing that, and they are selling the drugs." All this is giving Jamaicans a bad name, perpetuating the negative image that many non-Caribbean New Yorkers hold of Jamaicans as drug users and dealers. But, as with so many other cultural stereotypes, one must look beyond the readily apparent to see what is really complex.

12.5 As American as Tamale Pie

Mexican-Americans have long formed a large, disadvantaged segment of the population in the U.S. Southwest. Subjected to social and economic discrimination, as well as exclusion from the political system, this group evolved distinctive subcultures in many frontier cities. When they suddenly began to be politically active in the midst of the reforms and social upheavals of the 1960s, some mainstream groups developed a variety of fears,

de la Garza, Rodolfo. "As American as Tamale Pie: Mexican-American Political Mobilization and the Loyalty Question." In *Mexican-Americans in Comparative Perspective*, edited by Walker Connor, 237–242. Washington, D.C.: Urban Institute Press, 1985.

including concerns over cultural separatism, political radicalism, and divided loyalty. In this reading, the author, a prominent Mexican-American political scientist, argues that Mexican-American political activism is not to be feared, but falls squarely within American democratic politics and is a natural outgrowth of the group's efforts to improve its social and economic standing.

Perhaps the most troublesome issues raised about the consequences of Mexican-American political mobilization concerns loyalty. This is, according to Nathan Glazer, "the most basic and final issue," one that "remains a concern for many Americans." . . . Those who raise this concern suggest that Mexican-American political mobilization will threaten national interests either because Mexican-Americans have refused to follow the path of other immigrants and assimilate into American society, or because of the ties that Mexican-Americans have or will develop with the Mexican state.

Again, a response to this issue requires an understanding of Mexican-American political history. People who raise this concern are implicitly arguing that Mexican-Americans have refused to participate in the mainstream of American life, and thus cannot be trusted to join the body politic if they mobilize in the future. Such a view ignores the historical realities within which the Mexican-American community has evolved.

. . . [S]hortly after the end of the U.S.-Mexican war in 1846–47, political systems in the southwestern states functionally disenfranchised the Mexican-origin population. Despite repeated efforts, Mexican-Americans were prevented from obtaining full access to the political process from the mid-nineteenth century until the passage of the 1975 and 1982 Voting Rights Acts. Mexican-Americans thus remained outside the political process because the political process kept them out. As the obstacles to participation have been removed, Mexican-American participation has increased. Today, when demographic factors are held constant, "Chicanos are 3 percent more likely to vote than the rest of the population." In terms of political involvement, then, there is no basis for arguing that Mexican-Americans have remained aloof from mainstream American life. Instead, the political process was closed to them for over a century.

Mexican-Americans were similarly barred from fully participating in other aspects of American society. Across the Southwest, they encountered de jure and de facto residential segregation. They were often discouraged from attending school, and those that did enroll were placed in "Mexican" schools or in segregated programs within integrated schools. The labor market was similarly segregated. Mexican-Americans were relegated to the lowest-paying, least-desirable jobs, and when they held the same type of jobs that Anglos held, they earned less than Anglos did. Because of these practices Mexican-Americans could not have become integrated into mainstream society even if they had desired. Instead of encouraging Mexican-Americans to integrate, American social, educational, and economic institutions erected barriers that contributed greatly to the maintenance and expansion of ethnically distinct Mexican-origin communities. . . .

Since Mexican-Americans were prevented from "Americanizing," it is no wonder they still speak Spanish and continue to exist as an identifiable cultural community. There is no justification for charging that they have been unwilling to integrate into mainstream society and therefore pose a threat to the country's social fabric.

Furthermore, and perhaps more important, there is no evidence that the retention of Mexican cultural practices has in itself prevented Mexican-Americans from identifying with the American political system. Prior to 1975, for example, Spanish monolinguals had difficulty participating in the electoral process because election materials were all in English. Since Spanish-language materials became available, Spanish monolinguals have registered and voted at impressively high rates.

Similarly, Mexican-American support for bilingual education does not necessarily indicate separatist inclinations. More likely, Mexican-Americans support bilingual programs largely because they think such programs will more effectively educate their children and thus aid the process of becoming integrated into the societal mainstream. One of the major objectives of these programs, after all, is to help Spanish-speaking children stay in school rather than drop out. Historically, across the Southwest, schools have punished and discriminated against them for the mere fact that they are Spanish-speaking and of Mexican origin.

Bilingual programs also have great symbolic significance to Mexican-Americans. For over a century, the Mexican-origin population has seen Mexican values and language ridiculed and suppressed. The existence of bilingual programs reverses that trend and signals an official recognition of the intrinsic worth of Mexican culture.

Mexican-Americans may be as concerned with having society acknowledge that Mexican culture is deserving of respect and recognition as they are with actively maintaining it. Except for their concern about retaining Spanish, Mexican-Americans in Los Angeles and San Antonio in the late 1960s were relatively unconcerned about retaining any specific Mexican cultural trait.

Mexican-American support for Spanish-language retention does not imply support for Spanish monolingualism. Leaders in the Mexican-American community do not advocate Spanish monolingualism. Furthermore, the number of Spanish monolinguals has decreased in recent years. Whereas about 55 percent of Mexican-Americans in Los Angeles and San Antonio were bilingual in the late 1960s, 89 percent were bilingual in 1982. Moreover, 22 percent of those over age sixty-five spoke only Spanish, compared with 6 percent of those age eighteen to twenty-five.

Finally, there is no evidence that Mexican-Americans have any political attachments to the Mexican state or to Mexican political processes. In the mid-1960s, fewer than 2 percent of Mexican-Americans in Los Angeles and San Antonio expressed a desire for retaining a sense of Mexican patriotism. In the 1980s, when asked to identify their principal concerns, Mexican-Americans almost never mention U.S.-Mexican relations or any issues related to domestic Mexican politics. Indeed, only in South Texas does immigration appear as an identifiable concern, and there only 11 percent raise it as an issue.

Mexican-Americans are unlikely to develop into an ethnic lobby supporting Mexican interests for several reasons. First, Mexican-Americans are unconcerned about the issues of greatest interest to Mexico, and the Mexican elite has no interest in the primary concerns of Mexican-Americans. Second, after briefly considering developing this kind of relationship with Mexican-Americans, Mexican officials have "discarded [this idea] from the panorama of objectives of the relations between the government of Mexico and Chicanos." Considering that Mexican-Americans have a long history of attempting to participate in U.S. sociopolitical life, manifest no political attachments to Mexico, are unconcerned about Mexican political issues, and are unlikely to become actively involved as an ethnic lobby supporting Mexican interests, one wonders why any questions about Mexican-American loyalty would even be raised. This is particularly curious since other ethnic groups such as Greek-Americans and Jewish-Americans actively engage in issues related to policy toward Greece and Israel respectively without having their loyalty questioned. . . .

Conclusion

At various times in the history of the United States, American officials and the general public have been concerned about how continued immigration will affect the country's social and political fabric. In view of the continued and expanded presence of Mexican immigrants, it is not surprising that this question is now being asked again.

The tone in which the question has been raised, however, is troublesome. Policymakers and scholars seem to assume that Mexican immigrants will have a primarily, if not exclusively, negative effect on this country. In the debate on the economic impact of Mexican immigration, charges that Mexican workers caused unemployment and were a drain on social services were given credence in the debate over national immigration reform, even though the claims could not be substantiated. Numerous studies have now shown that such assertions were either unfounded or greatly exaggerated. Nonetheless, the belief that Mexican immigrants are weakening the economy persists, although it is less pervasive than it once was.

The debate over the sociopolitical consequences of Mexican immigration seems to be following the same pattern. Opponents of this immigration argue explicitly or by implication that the presence of large numbers of Mexican immigrants poses a serious threat to the future of this country. To support their views, they claim that the Mexican-origin population has refused to "Americanize" in the way that Italians, Jews and other immigrants have. Therefore, they argue, if this minority becomes politically active, because of its size, regional concentration, and lack of commitment to American values and institutions, the Mexican-origin population has the potential to threaten the political stability and national security of the nation.

I have attempted to show that such fears are groundless . . .

12.6 Hispanics: A Common Agenda?

As Latin American and Caribbean immigrants have become naturalized U.S. citizens and registered voters, their voices have begun to be heard beyond local communities. Since the mid-1970s, they have formed an increasingly important constituency in national politics, as is reflected in the number of elected congressional representatives and executive appointments, and in the multitude of lobbying efforts. The following reading describes a formative period during the Carter administration (1976–80), when leaders of distinct Hispanic groups from diverse parts of the United States struggled to find a common agenda—while simultaneously becoming aware of their varying problems and interests.

Anglo-American society has such a perverse sense of its own ethos. Everyone knows Spanish predates English on the North American con-

Rendon, Armando B. "Latinos: Breaking the Cycle of Survival to Tackle Global Affairs." In *Latinos and the Political System,* edited by F. Chris Garcia, 447–56. Notre Dame, Ind.: University of Notre Dame Press, 1988.

tinent, yet it is labeled "foreign." Hispanic Americans, the direct descendants of the first non-natives to explore the Americas, intermarry and settle among its native peoples, but are treated as a minority group whose rights and social benefits must be doled out or hard-won.

It is no surprise then that we find that in the sphere of foreign concerns this built-in transnational people, the Hispanic, have been left out of any equations or formulas in international policy making for generations—that is, until recently. In almost direct proportion to the level of awareness of themselves as a national people, Latinos have begun to assert an increasing interest in foreign affairs. Out of an aroused nationalism has come, inevitably, a mounting interest in world politics.
. . .

The current level of Hispanic influence on U.S. foreign policy is directly linked to the increased political clout of Latinos in the Carter administration. In fact, few other events demonstrate the importance of the ethnic vote to foreign policy as does the case of Hispanic outrage when, during the transition phase between the Ford and Carter administrations, Latinos began to clamor for a variety of high-level appointments, among them key Foreign Service spots. . . .

The Todman Affair

Rather portentously, the Hispanic communities' first break with President Carter arose over inter-American affairs even before the president had learned where the Rose Garden was located at the White House. This political confrontation had its roots in the transition period from the Ford-Nixon administration.

Latino leaders had begun to pressure the White House for top-level positions including Cabinet-level appointments immediately after the November 1976 elections. President-elect Carter issued a telegram to all Cabinet designates on January 8, 1977, asking them

> to review at this time your lists of prospective appointees to policy-level decisions in your department, and to renew efforts to recruit and place Hispanics who want to serve in this Administration. I want you to draw upon the talent and resources of Hispanic citizens to extend their opportunity and involvement in this Administration.

Despite Carter's urging, appointments continued to be made with little attention to Hispanic hopefuls; no Cabinet-level and only a few sub-Cabinet positions at the assistant secretary level emerged. Hispanic factions split on the candidates; infighting over the choicest plums resulted in lost opportunities for all.

Of great significance in the aftermath of the failure of the Carter transition team to fulfill Carter's promises to Latinos has been the heightened attention by U.S. Latinos to Latin America. Everything came to a head when Terence Todman, ambassador to Costa Rica, a black career officer who had spent about two years in Latin America, was nominated as assistant secretary on inter-American affairs in the State Department. Several Latino groups and foreign affairs groups had proposed Esteban Torres, an official of the United Auto Workers International Department, to the office. . . .

The Todman experience should have convinced Latinos that even ethnicity backed up by votes is not enough. Success will come only by way of strategy and action directed at convincing, removing, or sidestepping those who feel essentially no debt to the Hispanic population nor responsibility for its status. . . .

Nationalist Concerns Among Latinos

While Latinos in general appear more thoughtful and determined in achieving the important goals of exerting greater influence at least in inter-American affairs, certain historical factors continue to distract and divide interests among the largest nationality groups: Mexican-Americans, Puerto Ricans, and Cubans.

For Cubans, the possible reestablishment of U.S. relations with Cuba is the source of virulent debate within the community, a verbal infighting that has often erupted into death-dealing violence involving Cubans and non-Cubans as its victims.

The Cuban presence has been forced upon the United States. Prior to the takeover of Cuba by Fidel Castro in 1959, the Cuban population was hardly significant in the United States. As a result of the exile immigration and more than two decades of births, Cubans virtually control Miami and other communities in Florida and, nationally, wield a political and economic influence disproportionate to their numbers. The U.S. policy toward the island remains a jarring point of contention, but more and more, many Cubans (with resignation by some older exiles and as a matter of fact by those raised in the United States) are concentrating on domestic interests, establishing viable alternatives as Americans to the unsettled nature of Cubanos interminably fighting for vindication against a regime they thoroughly revile.

In a very real sense, then, the major "foreign" concern among Cuban Americans is their homeland, their relatives and friends there, its future, and their desire to return. It is perhaps too much of a simplification to suggest that this is the overriding factor in Cuban attitudes toward international affairs, but it certainly colors all questions of U.S. involvement in Latin America. Cuban Americans, in short, are opposed to renewal of ties with Cuba. . . .

Perhaps the most complex internal issue of an international dimension is the situation of Puerto Rico as an island home for 3 million persons and motherland for perhaps as many *puertorriqueños* on the mainland. Natives of the island furiously contend among themselves as to what ultimate form of government is most practical or most desired for Puerto Rico: continued commonwealth status, statehood, or independence. Political party affiliations are intensely maintained and appear inextricably complicated to the observer. A Chicano probing islander sentiments senses that if Puerto Ricans could have their way, independence would be their heartfelt choice. . . .

Furthermore, marked differences of perception exist between island-born and mainland Puerto Ricans, although disparities have become less distinct in recent years. Capabilities in language, education, and political awareness have tended to be more pronounced among island *puertorriqueños*, many of those coming to the mainland having graduated from the island's university system with professional training and bilingual speaking skills. Island-born *puertorriqueños* boast a broader sense of world affairs since they have had to deal within the context of an ambience that is looked upon as a U.S. territory and yet falling within the sphere of Latin American interests.

Chicanos have a unique combination of factors to face that distinguishes them not only from other Hispanic groups but also from other international concerns of Cubans and Puerto Ricans. The motherland specifically is not off the mainland—it is adjacent to the United States and, as some Mexican-Americans perceive it, a part of the United States by virtue of conquest. Mexican-Americans became such as of February 2, 1848, with the signing of the Treaty of Guadalupe-Hidalgo, which brought the U.S. war against Mexico to an inglorious end. As with every other treaty the United States entered into with native peoples in North America, that treaty was breached almost before the wax seals cooled. Guarantees of land, culture, and language rights were violated from the start; Mejicanos living on their side of the new border became Americans by default—they refused to leave their homesteads and automatically became U.S. citizens at the end of the year following the signing of the treaty. . . .

In a sense, Chicanos derive their existence from an international treaty yet have never been enabled to benefit from that status either through governmental recognition of their rights or through litigation initiated by Mexican-American organizations. . . .

This historical setting serves as a backdrop for what is now the largest Hispanic nationality group in the United States . . . Perhaps the most confusing characteristic to the observer is the complexity of titles for persons of Mexican origin: Mexican-American, Mejicano, Chicano, Latin American, Raza, Hispano, and others less complimentary. Represented among these labels is an ethnicity run rampant; multiple terms to designate the same people yet with each reflecting a variance in cultural, political, and historical background and group perception. These variations among people of Mexican heritage can be the cause of friction within the overall population although goals, and needs, are generally similar.

Despite these ethnic nuances, Chicanos (my personal preference) do rally together on certain substantive issues: the predominance of U.S.-Mexican relations as a critical factor in the influence value of Chicanos in the future; the inherent fellowship felt toward the plight of undocumented Latinos; the overall effects of discrimination in jobs, schools, health care, social services, training, and politics, which ultimately touch all Hispanic peoples, documented and undocumented, in some way. . . .

The fourth segment of Hispanicity in the United States is composed of immigrants from every Spanish-speaking country in the world. Cities such as Washington, D.C., with its embassies, and San Francisco, with its cosmopolitan attractiveness, boast significant populations from Latin America. . . . Often, Latinos (the term is used with greater accuracy in Washington) in the Capital are political refugees who continue to campaign against injustice and deprivation in their home countries. Salvadorans, Chileans, Nicaraguans, Paraguayans, and others enlist the aid of the larger Hispanic and general communities, stage media events, and lobby national and local politicians. . . .

Chicanos, *puertorriqueños*, Cubanos, and Latinos, then, have distinct points of reference to concerns of hemispheric if not global dimensions. The inborn cultural and historic ties of their ethnicity naturally cause Latinos to look beyond the U.S. mainland or across fictional borders—not merely as foreign affairs specialists, but as *hermanos*, brothers under the skin, linked professionally and emotionally with the futures of our hemispheric neighbors. As a group, in turn, Latinos have begun to act jointly in achieving a great influence in foreign policy. . . .

12.7 Molina's Destiny: A Lifetime of Firsts

In 1991, Gloria Molina became the first woman ever elected to the five-member Los Angeles County Board of Supervisors. She was also the first Hispanic elected to the board in 116 years. The daughter of Mexican immigrants, Molina has won a reputation as a feisty, tenacious politician who fights hard for education, Hispanics' fair share in redistricting, social services, and jobs. The following 1988 newspaper article recounts the early years in the career of a political maverick.

It seems to be Gloria Molina's destiny to find herself described as "the first Hispanic female."

First in California's State Assembly, first on the Los Angeles City Council. Her future may include other firsts as well, Molina confided Saturday in a break from the board meeting of the Mexican-American Legal Defense and Educational Fund.

But the councilwoman, who has struggled much of her life with the sometimes conflicting agendas of feminism and Hispanic rights, said she thinks of herself simply as an elected official with 250,000 constituents.

"People are so quick to label you," she said. "When I went to the Assembly (in 1982), one man said to me: 'Oh, I'm so glad we have you, we need someone like you to work on bilingual education and child care.' I said: 'I want to work on insurance and taxation issues.' "

The male legislator's attitude was not markedly different from the attitudes Molina, who began her political career as a political activist, had discovered within the Chicano student movement.

Was it sexist? "Absolutely," she said. "Yet I could not work within NOW (the National Organization for Women) or the NAACP. They were much too strident. So we developed our own Chicana feminist organization."

The eldest of 10 children reared in a Los Angeles barrio, Molina, 39, is used to being a role model. Her parents, both born in Mexico, were ecstatic when she became a legal secretary while working her way through college.

Yet it wasn't enough for Molina. Although she never finished college, she became more and more active in community politics. She liked the

Lippman, Laura. "Molina's Destiny: A Lifetime of Firsts." *San Antonio Light,* May 1, 1988.

freedom of the activist's role and preferred being what she called "the technician behind the scenes."

When a new state legislative seat was created after the 1980 census, Molina was urged to run, even though the "male Hispanic powers" had selected their own candidate. Molina's behind-the-scenes experience proved to be invaluable in this race and she won the election for the new seat, then was re-elected twice.

Last year, Molina resigned from the Assembly to run for a recently created City Council seat, the direct result of a MALDEF lawsuit against the city. Again, she had a male Hispanic opponent. Again, she defeated him.

As a member of the 15-person city council, Molina's goal has been to ensure her constituents benefit from the city's services.

Asked if she has an agenda for her own future, Molina said: "I used to be a fatalist. Even when I was elected in 1982, I didn't think of going any farther. Now I am goal-oriented."

Her goals include seeing Hispanics elected to such positions as mayor or county supervisor. "And there's still not an Hispanic woman in Congress," she pointed out.

But whatever Molina chooses to do, it probably will be within the realm of local politics, where she enjoys the interaction possible through grass roots politics.

"You can demonstrate more clearly to people that they do have access," Molina said. And that's one context in which she doesn't mind being known as the first Hispanic female.

12.8 A Surging New Spirit

The final reading in this chapter celebrates the diverse and increasing presence of Hispanic performers, artists, styles, and tastes within the larger culture of the United States. It points not to the refusal of immigrant groups to assimilate, but rather to the popularization and acceptance of Hispanic cultural forms among a much wider audience. This process, which has occurred repeatedly throughout U.S. history as other immigrant groups

Lacayo, Richard. "A Surging New Spirit." *Time*, July 11, 1988; 46–49.

have gradually integrated into social, economic, and political institutions,
indicates the many cultural strands in our evolving national heritage.

America, the great receiver. From every culture to arrive within its borders, it embraces some new ingredient. Puritan wrath. Black cool. Irish poetics. Jewish irony. One after another, America draws them down the channels of its awareness and puts them into play in new settings. They collide and cross-pollinate and mix it up, nowhere more so than in the arts and popular culture. Sparks fly at the meeting points. The Jewish novel works variations on the keynotes of Puritan gloom. The western is reseen through John Ford's Irish eyes. Sinatra meets Duke Ellington. Every offering is admitted and set dancing with new partners. It may be better to give, but it's a lot more fun to receive.

Nowadays the mainstream is receiving a rich new current. More and more, American film, theater, music, design, dance and art are taking on a Hispanic color and spirit. Look around. You can see the special lightning, the distinctive gravity, the portable wit, the personal spin. The new marquee names have a Spanish ring: Edward James Olmos, Andy Garcia, Maria Conchita Alonso. At the movies, the summer of *La Bamba* gave way last year to the autumn of *Born in East L.A.:* now the springtime of *Stand and Deliver* blends into the summer of *Salsa.* On the record charts the story is the same: Miami Sound Machine, Los Lobos, Lisa Lisa and Cult Jam. The rhythm is gonna get you.

An equivalent Latino surge is reaching the higher cultural circles. The art world is opening its eyes to Hispanic artists whose work, sharp and full throated, owes its strength to aesthetic intelligence, not ethnic scenery. Meanwhile, Latino playwrights are supplying off-Broadway and the regional theaters with new voices. And while the great Hispanic-American Novel is still waiting to be written, the splendid figures of Latin American literature—Gabriel García Márquez, Mario Vargas Llosa, Carlos Fuentes—are being translated straight into the American literary fabric, not to mention the best-seller lists.

Then there are the developments that are harder to pin down, the Latin flavors and inflections conveyed through all the intricate paths of daily life, in the offerings at table or the bolero curve of a woman's jacket. You can't walk down the street without running into them. On the corner where the disco used to be, a Latin-beat club; kids hip hop on floors that withstood the bump. For lunch, a burrito. What's that in the salad? It's jicama. (Say *hee*-ca-ma.) Things that once seemed foreign now seem as American as . . . a burrito. With each fresh connection tastes are being rebuilt, new understandings concluded. The American mind is adding a new wing.

Yes, but is this really new? Was there ever a time without a Mexican spitfire in the movies, a hacienda-style suburb down the road, a Latin crooner singing *Cuando Cuando* to the stars? And in the past hasn't the U.S. joined the conga line, bought the Trini Lopez album, then moved on heedlessly to something else? It has and it did. But this time the prospects are different. Latin influences that were once just a pinch of spice for most Americans are bidding to become a vital part of the wider culture.

Demographics are the main reason. The number of Hispanics in the U.S. has increased 30% since 1980, to 19 million. They account now for about 7.9% of the nation's population. Most trace their roots back to Mexico (63%), Puerto Rico (12%) and Cuba (5%); the rest to the nations of Central and South America and the Caribbean. By the year 2000 their numbers are expected to reach 30 million, 15% of the whole. And roughly one-third of all U.S. Hispanics intermarry with non-Hispanics, promising the day when the two cultures will be as tightly entwined as a strand of DNA.

Another reason is more subtle. The creative work being done by Hispanics today is more than ever recognizable to Americans as the work of, well, Americans—Hispanic Americans. Paintings and music that spring from Latin sources are being filtered through a north-of-the-border sensibility. As in *La Bamba:* its story of Chicano life is told through myths of immigrant struggle and showbiz martyrdom that were born in the U.S.A. Increasingly, too, Hispanic artists and entertainers are courting the mass audience in English. Many of the nation's Latino theaters perform in English only. "I don't want to be a good Hispanic theater," says Max Ferrá, Artistic Director of Manhattan's predominantly English INTAR Hispanic American Arts Center. "I want to be a very good American theater." After writing two books in Spanish, novelist Roberto Fernández has just published his first in English, *Raining Backwards,* a comic account of Cuban life in Miami. "I did it for the same reason that Miami Sound Machine sings in English," he explains, "I wanted to reach a wider audience."

The greater visibility of Hispanics in the cultural landscape is a reminder that the roots of Spanish culture go deep into American life, especially in that spawning ground of the national self-image, the West. Much of the territory of the Western states, from Texas to California, was held first by Spain, then Mexico. The Spanish names of many Western cities—Los Angeles, San Francisco, Sante Fe—bear witness to the settlements of the early Franciscan friars. The first play on American soil was performed by Spanish colonists in New Mexico in 1598. Yet in the hills of New Mexico and the old mission towns of the Pacific Coast, the descendants of Spanish settlers who greeted the Anglo pioneers are amused (and sometimes not amused) to find themselves perennially arriving in the national consciousness. As Luis Valdez, writer and director of *La Bamba,* once put it, "We did not, in fact, come to the United States at all. The United States came to us."

Even so, for years most Americans were content to imagine the Latin world as a tropical paradise or a giant border town, a torrid zone just across the line of sexual decorum, that most heavily policed boundary in the American psyche. Though that image is being discarded, it is not going without a fight. In a Miami department store not long ago, the Cuban-born fashion designer Adolfo, a favorite of Nancy Reagan's, was pained to overhear two women express surprise that he was the creator of a collection that was elegant and simple. "Obviously," he laments, "they just assumed that anything a Cuban designed would be full of neon, sequins, and ruffles."

Which is not to say that Hispanic culture is dowdy. (Try telling yourself that after a night at a salsa club.) What it is, however, is diverse and complex, embedded with traditions inherited from baroque Spain, from the Aztecs and Mayans, from the descendants of black slaves who people the Antilles, from the mountainous country of Central America. Each winds its way differently into the American imagination, where it gets put to new uses.

There are the things that come from tropical sea-bordered places like Puerto Rico, Cuba, the Dominican Republic. African influences are the legacy of the region's old status as a center of the slave trade. They can be heard in the Afro-Caribbean rhythm that the Talking Heads deploy in their new song *Mr. Jones* to pay mock homage to a straitlaced character. No other rhythm would quite do, would say quite the same thing. Why? Because the point is not just to make a danceable cut, but to set up a dialogue between David Byrne's high-strung ironies and the irresistible counterarguments of the beat. That thrumming rhythm says forget the nerdy options of the industrial world, where the commands of the dollar sign squash the spirit. Why not a world where the brain and the hips are both engaged?

The civilization of Mexico, meanwhile, is undergirded by a powerful Indian legacy. It can be felt in the somber and ceremonial notes of Mexican Catholicism. And it can be felt in the work of a Mexican-American painter like Carlos Almaraz, whose series of car-crash paintings double as jokes about the encounter between Hispanic and Anglo in America. But the paintings are also built on a notion of duality—strangeness and beauty, violence and peace—that has roots in Aztec cosmology, which saw in pairings a sign of balance in the universe.

For all the diversity of Latin cultures, there are also some shared characteristics that bring new inflections to American life. The U.S. is a nation that puts no great premium on the past. Sometimes it seems that the prevailing notion of history is a Top 40 playlist from the 1960s. But Hispanic culture is consumed with the past, on both the personal and historical levels, and drawn to the memory play, the history painting, the musical tradition to accomplish the tasks of recollection. It was only fitting that the actor Edward James Olmos should star in *The Bal-*

lad of Gregorio Cortez, the story of a 1901 confrontation between a Mexican farmer and the Texas Rangers that has lived on ever since as a *corrido,* a story song.

Hispanic life also puts a different stress on the claims of individualism. The arts in America are absorbed by personal experience, the melodrama of the interior life, the spectacle of "me." Hispanic culture offers a counterweight in the claims of community and the shared impulse. You can see those asserting themselves in mainstream life through such means as the outdoor murals—acts of public declamation in the tradition of the great Mexican muralists—that are an essential part of the Los Angeles cityscape. Add to that sentiment the claims of family, the primal unit of Hispanic life. The Mexican poet Octavio Paz recently described it. "In the North American ethic," he wrote, "the center is the individual; in Hispanic morals the true protagonist is the family." It shows in the work of a photographer like Tony Mendoza. He sees in his extended Cuban family what it is that sometimes makes them comic, but he also knows that their fate is his, their picture is his own I.D.

So these ingredients of Hispanic feeling are absorbed, along with the Hispanic works that carry them, into the American repertory. In show business they sometimes call this process crossover, the chartmaker's term for the record or film that reaches beyond its expected audience. For many Hispanics, the whole notion is ringed all around with skepticism and mixed feelings. *(Who wants to cross over anyway? You come here.)* Not everyone is crazy about the term Hispanic, which came into vogue in the 1970s and was seized by marketers; it seems to smudge a dozen separate nationalities into an ethnic blur. And a phenomenon made up so heavily of pop charts and box-office receipts is not much help in the struggles against such things as low wages and poor education, the things that count most for Hispanics still in the barrios. There are misgivings too about the kind of treatment Hispanic life will get from big art galleries and entertainment conglomerates that can grind whole cultures into merchandise. Does anyone really need a sitcom with characters named Juan and María mouthing standard showbiz punch lines? The trick for Hispanic talents these days is to get to the market fresh, not canned.

Always chafing against clichés too narrow to contain them, Hispanics may find their greatest luxury in not being hemmed in by any preconceptions at all. Consider the Los Angeles artist known as Gronk. He has impeccable Chicano credentials: born in 1954 in mostly Chicano East Los Angeles, he was a co-founder in his younger days of an ad hoc group of Latino artists who brought their art to the streets. But all of that was the forcing ground for a talent that resists ethnic labels. His paintings carry echoes of Mexican symbolism, but they also wear the signs of European expressionism, new-wave imagery, old-fashioned camp. And he recalls low- and high-culture influences in his adolescence that are shared by half the Anglo painters in Manhattan. "Daffy Duck on TV in the morning and Camus in my back pocket," as he once described it. Someone like Gronk does not cross over at all. In him, the cultures simply converge.

Maybe convergence is the key. This is not just a box-office phenomenon, after all, but an episode in an ongoing cultural evolution, one in which Americans of all kinds learn to see a bit of Latino within themselves. In that process a Spanish term might help. The word is *corazón*, meaning heart. Let it stand for what is necessary in all relations between the Americans who are not Hispanics and the Americans who are. Their shared history, full of frictions and resentments, marked by episodes of bigotry, exploitation and even bloodshed, might yet become a comedy of reconciliation, but that would take real heart and plenty of it. Not the valentine of pop crooning, not the thumping bag inflated for election years, but the experienced heart—tread marked, willing, unconditional. The one that listens. Because, as they cross over into the American imagination, Hispanics are sending one irresistible message: we come bearing gifts.

Credits and Permissions

Chapter 2. Legacies of Empire: From Conquest to Independence

2.1 Bartolomé de las Casas, "God's Angry Man," in *Latin American Civilization: History and Society, 1492 to the Present,* ed. Benjamin Keen (Boulder, Colo.: Westview Press, 1986), pp. 66–68. Reprinted by permission of Westview Press and Benjamin Keen. Copyright © by Westview Press, 1986, Boulder, Colorado.

2.2 "Broken Spears" and "Flowers and Songs of Sorrow," in *The Broken Spears,* Miguel León-Portilla (Boston: Beacon Press, 1962), pp. 137–38, 149. Copyright © 1962 by Beacon Press. Reprinted by permission of Beacon Press.

2.3 Anthony McFarlane, "African Slave Migration," in *The Cambridge Encyclopedia of Latin America and the Caribbean,* ed. Simon Collier, Harold Blakemore, and Thomas E. Skidmore (Cambridge: Cambridge University Press, 1985), pp. 138–42. Reprinted by permission of Cambridge University Press.

2.4 Antonio Vásquez de Espinosa, "Compendium and Description of the West Indies," in *Readings in Latin American Civilization: 1492 to the Present,* 2d ed., ed. Benjamin Keen, trans. C. U. Clark (Washington, D.C.: The Smithsonian Institution, 1942), pp. 93–94. Reprinted by permission of Benjamin Keen.

2.5 Charles Gibson, *Spain in America* (New York: Harper & Row, 1966), pp. 154–56. Copyright © 1966 by Charles Gibson. Excerpts reprinted by permission of HarperCollins publishers.

2.6 James Lockhart and Stuart B. Schwartz, *Early Latin America: A History of Spanish America and Brazil* (New York: Cambridge University Press, 1983), pp. 204–7. Reprinted with permission of Cambridge University Press.

2.7 J. H. Parry, Philip Sherlock, and Anthony Maingot, *A Short History of the West Indies,* 4th ed. (New York: St. Martin's Press, 1987), pp. 140–41. Copyright © 1987. Reprinted with permission of St. Martin's Press, Inc.

2.8 Simón Bolívar, "Jamaica Letter," in *Selected Writings of Bolivar,* 2d ed., vol. 1, 1810–1822, edited by Harold Brieck, Jr. (New York: Colonial Press, 1951).

2.9 Domingo F. Sarmiento, "Facundo in Power," in *The Borzoi Reader in Latin American History,* vol. 2, edited by Helen Delpar (New York: Knopf, 1972), pp. 38–42.

Chapter 3. The Garden of Forking Paths: Dilemmas of National Development

3.1 Jonathan V. Levin, "Peru in the Guano Age," in *The Export Economies: Their Patterns of Development in Historical Perspective* (Cambridge, Mass.: Harvard University Press, 1960). Reprinted by permission of the publishers. Copyright © 1960 by the President and Fellows of Harvard College. Copyright renewed in 1988 by Jonathan V. Levin. For permission to photocopy, contact Harvard University Press.

3.2 Rodrigo Facio, "The Soto Keith Contract on Foreign Debt and the Railroad," in *The Costa Rica Reader*, ed. Marc Edelman and Joanne Kenen (New York: Grove Weidenfeld, 1989), pp. 59–62. Translated from the Spanish © 1972 by Leda Fernandez de Facio; English translation Copyright © 1989 by Marc Edelman and Joanne Kenen. Used by permission of Grove Press, Inc.

3.3 Simon Collier, *The Life, Music, and Times of Carlos Gardel* (Pittsburgh: University of Pittsburgh Press, 1986), pp. 55–59. Adaption reprinted by permission of the University of Pittsburgh Press. © 1986 by University of Pittsburgh Press.

3.4 Getulio Vargas, "Vargas and the Estado Novo," in *The Quest for Change in Latin America: Sources for a Twentieth-Century Analysis*, ed. W. Raymond Duncan and James Nelson Goodsell (New York: Oxford University Press, 1970), pp. 148–50. Copyright © 1970 by Oxford University Press, Inc. Reprinted with permission.

3.5 Lázaro Cárdenas, "The Expropriation of the Oil Industry," in *Models of Political Change in Latin America*, ed. Paul E. Sigmund (New York: Praeger, 1970), pp. 15–16. Reprinted with permission of Greenwood Publishing Group, Inc., Westport, Conn. Copyright © 1970 by Praeger Publishers.

3.6 Víctor Raúl Haya de la Torre, "The Aprista Thesis," in *Models of Political Change in Latin America*, ed. Paul E. Sigmund (New York: Praeger, 1970), pp. 185–86. Reprinted with permission of Greenwood Publishing Group, Inc., Westport, Conn. Copyright © 1970 by Praeger Publishers.

3.7 Eva Duarte Perón, *Evita by Evita: Eva Duarte Perón Tells Her Own Story* (New York: Lippincott & Crowell, 1980), pp. 53–56.

3.8 "CGT Communiqué Supports Falkland Recovery Action," in *Foreign Broadcast Information Service* (FBIS), B6, April 28, 1982.

Chapter 4. Capital Sins: Authoritarianism and Democratization

4.1 John F. Kennedy, "The Alliance for Progress," in *The Central American Crisis Reader*, ed. Robert Leiken and Barry Rubin (New York: Summit Books, 1987), pp. 119–23. Copyright © 1987 by Robert Leiken and Barry Rubin. Reprinted by permission of Summit Books, a division of Simon & Schuster, Inc.

4.2 Philip Siekman, "When Executives Turned Revolutionaries," *Fortune* 70:3 (September 1964): 147–49, 210–21. Copyright © 1964, Time Inc. All rights reserved.

4.3 Aurelio de Lyra Tavares, "The Army and the Ideological Struggle," in

Models of Political Change in Latin America, ed. Paul E. Sigmund (New York: Praeger, 1970), pp. 153–56. Reprinted with permission of Greenwood Publishing Group, Inc., Westport, Conn. Copyright © 1970 by Praeger Publishers.

4.4 Paulo Evaristo Arns, "A Testimony and an Appeal," in *Torture in Brazil,* ed. Joan Dassin (New York: Vintage Books, 1986), pp. xxv-xxviii. Reprinted by permission of Cardinal Paulo Evaristo Arns. *Torture in Brazil* was originally published in Portuguese as *Brasil: Nunca Mais,* which became Brazil's all-time nonfiction bestseller.

4.5 Luis Inacio da Silva, "Interview," in *Latin American Perspectives* 6:4 (Fall 1979): 90–100. Copyright © 1979 by Latin American Perspectives. Adaption reprinted by permission of Sage Publications, Inc.

4.6 Linda Greenbaum, "Plundering the Timber on Brazilian Indian Reservations," *Cultural Survival Quarterly* 13:1 (1989): 23–26. Reprinted with permission of Cultural Survival, Inc.

Chapter 5. Continent on the Move: Migration and Urbanization

5.1 Janice Perlman, *The Myth of Marginality: Urban Poverty and Politics in Rio de Janeiro* (Berkeley: University of California Press, 1976), pp. 68–69. Copyright © 1976 by The Regents of the University of California.

5.2 Alma Guillermoprieto, "Letter from Mexico City," *The New Yorker,* September 17, 1990, pp. 93–96. Reprinted by permission; 1990, Alma Guillermoprieto.

5.3 Marlise Simons, "Guatemalan Indians Crowd into Mexico to Escape Widening War," *Washington Post,* February 19, 1982, p. A-23. Reprinted by permission of Marlise Simons, who worked as a correspondent for the *Washington Post* and the *New York Times* in Latin America from 1971 to 1989.

5.4 Bonham D. Richardson, "Caribbean Migration, 1835–1985," in *The Modern Caribbean,* ed. Franklin W. Knight and Colin A. Palmer (Chapel Hill: University of North Carolina Press, 1989), pp. 209–12. Copyright © 1989, the University of North Carolina Press. Used by permission of the author and publisher.

5.5 Guy Gugliotta, "From Nicaragua to Texas: A Desperate Journey," *Miami Herald,* February 26–29, March 1, 1990. Reprinted with permission of the *Miami Herald.*

5.6 Mária Patricia Fernández Kelly, "Francisca: A Profile of a Maquiladora Worker," in *For We Are Sold, I and My People: Women and Industry in Mexico's Frontier* (Albany: State University of New York Press, 1983), pp. 177–83. Reprinted by permission of the State University of New York Press.

Chapter 6. Mirrors of the Heart: Color, Class, and Identity

6.1 José María Arguedas, *Yawar Fiesta,* trans. Frances Horning Barraclough (Austin: University of Texas Press, 1985), pp. 1–9. Copyright © 1985 by the University of Texas Press. Reprinted by permission of the publisher.

6.2 Mary Ann Medlin, "Doña Sara and Doña Juana: Two Bolivian Weavers," in *The Human Tradition in Latin America: The Twentieth Century*, ed. William H. Beezley and Judith Ewell (Wilmington, Del.: Scholarly Resources, 1987), pp. 219–29. Copyright © 1987 by Scholarly Resources Inc. Reprinted by permission of Scholarly Resources Inc.

6.3 *I, Rigoberta Menchú: An Indian Woman in Guatemala*, ed. Elizabeth Burgos-Debray, trans. Ann Wright (London: Verso, 1984), pp. 102–16. Reprinted with permission of Verso Press.

6.4 Mario Vargas Llosa, "Questions of Conquest," *Harper's* 281 (December 1990): 45–53. Reprinted with permission of *Harper's Magazine*.

6.5 Eric Williams, *The Negro in the Caribbean* (Westport, Conn.: Negro Universities Press, 1942), pp. 11–16, 62–66.

6.6 Aimé Césaire, *Discourse on Colonialism* (New York: Monthly Review Press, 1972), pp. 65–77. Copyright © 1972 by Monthly Review Press. Reprinted by permission of Monthly Review Foundation.

6.7 René Depestre, *A Rainbow for the Christian West* (Amherst: University of Massachusetts Press, 1977), pp. 108–13. Reprinted by permission of the University of Massachusetts Press and the Société Nouvelle Présence Africaine.

6.8 Deborah Pacini Hernández, "Race, Class, Tradition, and Identity in the Dominican Merengue," 1991. Printed with permission of Deborah Pacini Hernández, Ph.D.

Chapter 7. In Women's Hands: The Changing Roles of Women

7.1 Sor Juana Inés de la Cruz, "The Reply to Sor Philothea," in *A Sor Juana Anthology*, trans. Alan S. Trueblood (Cambridge, Mass.: Harvard University Press, 1988), pp. 210–30. Reprinted by permission of the publishers from *A Sor Juana Anthology*. Copyright © 1988 by the President and Fellows of Harvard College. For permission to photocopy, contact Harvard University Press.

7.2 Elsa M. Chaney, *Supermadre: Women in Politics in Latin America* (Austin: University of Texas Press, 1979), pp. 73–76. Reprinted with permission from Elsa M. Chaney, Ph.D., Chair, Women in International Development Program, University of Iowa, Iowa City, IA, 52242.

7.3 *I, Rigoberta Menchú: An Indian Woman in Guatemala*, ed. Elizabeth Burgos-Debray, trans. Ann Wright (London: Verso, 1984) pp. 91–101. Reprinted with permission of Verso Press.

7.4 Carolina María de Jesus, *Child of the Dark*, trans. David St. Clair (New York: Dutton, 1962), pp. 44–45, 57–58, 97–98. Translation copyright © 1962 by E. P. Dutton & Co., New York and Souvenir Press, Ltd., London. Used by permission of the publisher, Dutton, an imprint of New American Library, a division of Penguin Books USA Inc. Used in the British Commonwealth (where *Child of the Dark* is published under the title *Beyond All Pity*) by permission of Souvenir Press, Ltd., London.

7.5 Marilyn Thomson, *Women of El Salvador* (Philadelphia: Institute for the Study of Human Issues, 1986), pp. 16, 18.

7.6 Rosario León, "Bartolina Sisa: The Peasant Women's Organization in Bolivia," in *Women and Social Change in Latin America*, ed. Elizabeth Jelin (London: Zed Books, 1990), pp. 136, 138, 142, 148–49. Reprinted with permission of Zed Books Ltd., London.

7.7 Marjorie Agosin, *Scraps of Life* (Trenton, N.J.: Red Sea Press, 1987), pp. 93–99. Reprinted with permission of Red Sea Press, Inc., Trenton, NJ.

7.8 Elvia Alvarado, *Don't Be Afraid Gringo*, ed. and trans. by Medea Benjamin (New York: Harper & Row, 1987), pp. 51–56. Reprinted by permission of The Institute for Food and Development Policy and its literary agents, Raines & Raines, 71 Park Avenue, New York, NY, 10016. Copyright © 1987 by The Institute for Food and Development Policy.

7.9 Sylvia Chester, "The Women's Movement in Argentina: Balance and Strategies," in *The Latin American Women's Movement*, ed. and trans. Miranda Davies and Ana Maria Portugal (Rome and Santiago: Isis International, 1986), pp. 15–19. Reprinted by permission of Isis International, Casilla 2067, Correo Central, Santiago, Chile.

Chapter 8. Miracles Are Not Enough: Continuity and Change in Religion

8.1 "Popol Vuh," in *The Definitive Edition of the Mayan Book of the Dawn of Life and the Glories of Gods and Kings*, trans. Dennis Tedlock (New York: Simon & Schuster, 1985), pp. 21, 71–84. Copyright © 1985 by Dennis Tedlock. Reprinted by permission of Simon & Schuster, Inc.

8.2 Juan Ginés de Sepúlveda, "Tratado sobre las justas causas de la guerra contra los indios," in *Readings in Latin American Civilization: 1492 to the Present*, 4th ed., ed. Benjamin Keen (Boulder, Colo.: Westview Press, 1986), pp. 105–13. Reprinted with permission from Westview Press and Benjamin Keen.

8.3 Clarence Haring, "The Wealth of the Church," in *The Roman Catholic Church in Colonial Latin America*, ed. Richard E. Greenleaf (New York: Knopf, 1971), pp. 177–81. Copyright © 1971 by Alfred A. Knopf, Inc. Reprinted by permission of the publisher.

8.4 "The Church in the Present Day Transformation of Latin America in the Light of the Council," excerpts from *The Second Annual Conference of the Latin American Bishops* (CELAM II), vol. 2 (Bogotá: Secretariat of CELAM, 1968), pp. 58–64. Reprinted by permission of the Consejo Episcopal Latinoamericano in Bogotá, Colombia.

8.5 Gustavo Gutiérrez, *A Theology of Liberation: History, Politics and Salvation*, ed. and trans. Sister Caridad, Inda Eagleson, and John Eagleson (Maryknoll, N.Y.: Orbis Books, 1988), pp. 272–79. Reprinted with permission of Orbis Books and SCM Press Ltd., London.

8.6 John Burdick, "Gossip and Secrecy: Women's Articulation of Domestic Conflict in Three Religions of Urban Brazil," *Sociological Analysis* 51:2 (1990): 153–70. The Association for the Sociology of Religion, for permission to reprint John Burdick's essay as an abridgment of his article, which appeared in the official journal of the association.

Chapter 9. Builders of Images: Writers, Artists, and Popular Culture

9.1 Ruben Dario, "To Roosevelt," in *Selected Poems of Rubén Darío*, trans. Lysander Kemp (Austin: University of Texas Press, 1965), pp. 69–70. Copyright © 1965. Reprinted with permission of the University of Texas Press.

9.2 José Martí, "Our America," in *The America of José Martí*, trans. Juan de Onis (New York: Noonday Press, 1953), pp. 148–51. Copyright © 1954 by The Noonday Press, Inc. Excerpt reprinted by permission of Farrar, Straus & Giroux, Inc.

9.3 Graciliano Ramos, *Barren Lives*, trans. Ralph Edward Dimmick (Austin: University of Texas Press, 1973), pp. 86–92. Copyright © by the University of Texas Press. Reprinted by permission of the publisher.

9.4 Pablo Neruda, *Memoirs* (New York: Penguin, 1978), pp. 253–55. Translation copyright © 1976, 1977 by Farrar, Straus & Giroux, Inc. Excerpt reprinted by permission of Farrar, Straus & Giroux, Inc. Reprinted in the British Commonwealth by permission of Souvenir Press.

9.5 Derek Walcott, "A Sea-Chantey," in *Derek Walcott, Collected Poems, 1948–1984* (New York: Farrar, Straus & Giroux, 1986), pp. 44–46. Copyright © 1962, 1964, 1986 by Derek Walcott. Reprinted by permission of Farrar, Straus & Giroux, Inc., and Faber and Faber Ltd., London.

9.6 Gabriela Mistral, "Morning," in *Selected Poems of Gabriela Mistral*, ed. and trans. Doris Dana (Baltimore: Johns Hopkins University Press, 1971), p. 162. Reprinted with permission of the Johns Hopkins University Press.

9.7 Jorge Luis Borges, "The Shape of the Sword," in *Labyrinths: Selected Stories and Other Writings* (New York: New Directions, 1964), pp. 67–72. Copyright © 1962, 1964 by New Directions Publishing Corporation. Reprinted with permission of New Directions Publishing Corporation and Laurence Polliger Limited, London.

9.8 Gabriel García Márquez, "The Solitude of Latin America," in *Lives on the Line: The Testimony of Contemporary Latin American Authors*, trans. Marina Castañeda and ed. Doris Meyer (Berkeley: University of California Press, 1988). Reprinted with permission of the University of California Press.

9.9 Andres Oppenheimer, "Culture, Arts, Thrive in Violence: Capital Takes Refuge in a Renaissance," *Miami Herald*, April 5, 1990. Reprinted with permission of the *Miami Herald*.

Chapter 10. Get Up, Stand Up: The Problems of Sovereignty

10.1 James Monroe, "The Monroe Doctrine," in *The Evolution of Our Latin American Policy: A Documentary Record*, ed. James W. Gantenbein (New York: Columbia University Press, 1950), pp. 323–25.

10.2 Roque Saenz Peña, "A Doctrine of Intervention," in *Latin America: Yesterday and Today*, ed. John Rothchild (New York: Bantam, 1973), pp. 383–85.

10.3 Theodore Roosevelt, "The Roosevelt Corollary," in *A Compilation of the Messages and Speeches of Theodore Roosevelt*, vol. 2, ed. A. H. Lewis (Washington, D.C.: Bureau of National Literature and Art, 1906), p. 857.

10.4 Elihu Root, "The Real Monroe Doctrine," *American Journal of International Law* (1914): 427–42.

10.5 J. N. "Ding" Darling, "Guarding the Basket," *New York Herald Tribune*, 1928. Copyright © 1991, Des Moines Register and Tribune Company. Reprinted by permission.

Garnett Warren, "When the Pie Was Open'd the Birds Began to Sing," *Boston Herald*, 1906.

10.6 Michael Manley, *The Politics of Change: A Jamaican Testament* (Washington,

Chapter 11. *Fire in the Mind: Revolutions and Revolutionaries*

Chapter 12. *The Americans: Latin American and Caribbean Peoples in the United States*

12.1 Richard D. Lamm and Gary Imhoff, *The Immigration Time Bomb* (New York: Truman Talley Books, 1985), pp. 1–12. Copyright © 1985 by Richard D. Lamm and Gary Imhoff. Used by permission of the publisher, Dutton, an imprint of New American Library, a division of Penguin Books USA Inc. and the JCA Literary Agency.

12.2 Terry Doran, Janet Satterfield, and Chris Stade, *A Road Well Traveled: Three Generations of Cuban American Women* (Newton, Mass.: WEEA Publishing Center, 1988), pp. 64–70. Reprinted with permission of the WEEA Publishing Center/Education Development Center, Newton, MA, 1988.

12.3 Lloyd H. Rogler, *Migrant in the City: The Life of a Puerto Rican Action Group* (Maplewood, N.J.: Waterfront Press, 1984), pp. 104–5. This chapter was taken from a book authored by Lloyd H. Rogler, Albert Schweitzer University Professor, Fordham University, based upon participant observation in a Puerto Rican community in a city on the eastern seaboard.

12.4 Leslie Brenner, "The New New York," *New York Woman*, May 1991, pp. 67–81. Reprinted by permission of Leslie Brenner.

12.5 Rodolfo de la Garza, "As American as Tamale Pie: Mexican-American Political Mobilization and the Loyalty Question," in *Mexican-Americans in Comparative Perspective*, ed. Walker Connor (Washington, D.C.: Urban Institute Press, 1985), pp. 237–42. Reprinted by permission of the Urban Institute Press.

12.6 Armando B. Rendon, "Latinos: Breaking the Cycle of Survival to Tackle Global Affairs," in *Latinos and the Political System*, ed. F. Chris Garcia (Notre Dame, Ind.: University of Notre Dame Press, 1988), pp. 447–56. Copyright © 1988 by University of Notre Dame Press. Reprinted by permission of the publisher.

12.7 Laura Lippman, "Molina's Destiny: A Lifetime of Firsts," *San Antonio Light*, May 1, 1988. Reprinted by permission of the *San Antonio Light*.

12.8 Richard Lacayo, "A Surging New Spirit," *Time*, July 11, 1988, pp. 46–49. Copyright © 1988 Time Warner Inc. Reprinted by permission.